MODELS of MAN

MODELS of MAN

Explorations in the Western Educational Tradition

PAUL NASH

Boston University

JOHN WILEY & SONS, INC.   New York · London · Sydney

To my mother,

Who encouraged me to create my own models

Preface

This book has a single motif and a dual purpose. Its motif is the portrayal of a number of the most influential models of the educated person that have been created as part of the Western cultural tradition. This motif is not meant to be exhaustive but is presented as one way in which that tradition might be plumbed. The purposes are to engender in the reader a broad knowledge of some of the dominant and persistent ideas and problems inherent in his own intellectual tradition; and to stimulate him to go further into the original sources of this tradition in search of meanings and insights that are uniquely relevant to his own educational development.

The selection of the passages for this endeavor turned out to be much more difficult than I had anticipated. Any hope of presenting a symmetrical, quantitatively balanced body of selections was defeated by the fact that some writers are generally consistent and can be epitomized fairly in one or two passages, whereas others are more complex and various and have many hues and tones that need to be caught if an accurate picture is to be drawn. Moreover, some authors write succinctly and epigrammatically and their meaning and characteristic flavor can be captured in a short passage. Others are more discursive and expatiating and require fuller and more continuous quotation. I dealt with these problems by abandoning any attempt at symmetry and by treating each writer according to his idiosyncratic style. Thus I have tried to give some taste of each author's range and diversity as well as attempting to encircle the core of his thinking.

My task has been made more pleasant by the ready assistance I have gained from many people. Among those from whose advice I have profited, the following should be specially mentioned: Walter Ackerman, University of Judaism; Reginald D. Archambault, Brown University; Stanley E. Ballinger, Indiana University; Kenneth D. Benne, Boston University; Cyril Bibby, Kingston upon Hull Teachers' College, England; J. J. Chambliss, Rutgers State University; Jerome K. Clauser, HRB-Singer, Inc.; Geoffrey Clive, University of Massachusetts; John W. Donohue, S. J., Fordham University; Maurice Friedman, Temple University; Brian Holmes, University of London Institute of Education; Pearl Kibre, Hunter College; Paul Nyberg, University of Bridgeport; Costas M. Proussis, Holy Cross Greek Orthodox Theological School; John E. Rexine, Colgate University; Frank E. Schacht, William Hall High School, West Hartford, Conn.; B. F. Skinner, Harvard University; Isadore Twersky, Harvard University; and Robert Wellman, University of Massachusetts. None of these people, of course, is to be held responsible for the final choice of selections, which in every instance was my own. But, if I have sometimes chosen not to follow their advice, I have never failed to profit from the widening of alternatives that their suggestions presented, and from the subsequent internal dialogue as I weighed one possibility against another.

I should like to pay a particular word of appreciation to my friends, Andreas M. Kazamias and Henry J. Perkinson. It was from our previous collaboration that this present venture grew and I am grateful for their generous encouragement and continuing friendship.

At Boston University, I am indebted to Jack R. Childress and Gene D. Phillips, who have given me vital encouragement and support in the form of that most precious of academic commodities—time.

My primary debt is to my wife, who has tolerated my absences and silences with good humor, has consistently compensated for my delinquency in household tasks, and has been my perennial source for renewal of the spirit.

Paul Nash

Contents

MODELS
of MAN

Introduction

History can be looked at in at least two ways. One can study the past as a source of prescribed or actual models of human behavior. Additionally, one can search one's personal past for clues as to who one is, where one might go, what one might be good for, what one might become. A cardinal intention of this book is the attempt to stimulate both of these activities.

Books are like professors: it is easy and dangerous to take them too seriously. The reader or the student in search of autonomy—on the road toward becoming an educated person—should learn to handle all sorts of books and professors. There are many human models to which one could aspire. It is perilously limiting to focus exclusively on one, represented perhaps by an admired writer or teacher. Revered figures can give vital guidance and desirable stability at crucial moments, but we must outgrow them, for our needs are not theirs. The task of the student is to use, with personal relevance, what the teacher has to offer him, without becoming a disciple. Discipleship may be relatively harmless as a reassuring resting place on an often bewildering journey, but it always involves the hazard of complacency and stagnation. It may lead the student away from the central task of becoming himself, of finding the unique pattern that is right for him alone.

Martin Buber has told a story of Rabbi Baer of Radoshitz, who said to his teacher, "Show me one general way to the service of God." The teacher replied, "It is impossible to tell men what way they should take. For one way to serve God is through learning, another through prayer, another through fasting, and still another through eating. Everyone should carefully observe what way his heart draws him to, and then choose this way with all his strength."* In the existentialist mode, Buber wants the individual

* Martin Buber, *The Way of Man, According to the Teachings of Hasidism* (Wallingford, Pennsylvania: Pendle Hill, n.d.), 12.

1

to create an identity for himself without being suffocated by dogmas, doctrines, or ideologies. Models and examples of the past can be valuable if we know how to learn from them without being enslaved by them. A model can be used either as an authority that stultifies or as an authority that liberates. We do not grow in isolation from all authority. We come to know ourselves in relation to the authority represented by standards that transcend us. These standards become stifling not when used as examples for consideration and criticism but when regarded as dogmas to be obeyed slavishly. It is in the former spirit that the models in this book are presented.

The particular emphasis is upon the models that can be created or discovered through the process of education, considered in a sense broader than that of formal schooling. Thus the focus is on what one might become as an educated person.* Reflection on these possibilities can in turn afford insight into what potentialities lie within the children or young people for whom one has responsibility. The ideals presented here include some of the greatest that man's mind has created. Many of them grow out of great philosophical systems or modes of thought, such as idealism, materialism, realism, Thomism, existentialism, empiricism, liberalism, socialism, pragmatism, and so on. The exploration of these philosophical world-views in a personally relevant way can widen one's horizons, deepen one's knowledge, refine one's sensitivity, and enhance one's tolerance of diversity.

For it is on diversity and personal relevance that the stress should be laid. If we recognize the diverse modulations of human nature, we will be content with something less than absolute unanimity. If everyone is the same, man is reduced to nothing: he becomes something in his uniqueness. The gain to be hoped for from the knowledge of diverse models is therefore to be seen in terms of personal aspiration. From this glimpse into the rich diversity of human qualities and human ideals one can obtain material and inspiration for the perennial task of creating a model of the educated person that

---

* Original interpretive essays and bibliographical notes on most of the men whose writings are included in this volume can be found in Paul Nash, Andreas M. Kazamias, and Henry J. Perkinson, *The Educated Man: Studies in the History of Educational Thought* (New York: John Wiley and Sons, 1965).

is relevant and meaningful to oneself in his own unique situation in the world and in history.

There is a belief among some contemporary historians that a concern with current relevance is incompatible with historical accuracy, objectivity, and impartiality. I do not share this view, although I am acutely aware of the dangers to which such historians would draw our attention. It is my conviction that we can avoid the pitfalls of anachronism, parochialism, and special pleading, and still make history "useful" in the sense of being personally relevant. The ideas explored in this book often represent educational theories whose relevance to our own day may not be obvious. Theories change, but the human problems that they attempt to deal with remain with us. This volume is a record of man's courageous, endless, never wholly successful, but vital and infinitely worthwhile attempts to come to terms with those problems in the light of the wisdom he possessed at the time. It should make us modest to recognize that we still cannot neatly solve these problems and to see how daring, ingenious, profound, and searching were some of the projected theories and models of the past. And if these theories do not always bring final solutions, they often serve to refine and clarify the nature of the problem. They may also raise new aspects of old problems, even when they are not wholly adequate as theories.

Attention here is concentrated upon ideas and prescriptions rather than actions and institutions. It would be inappropriate to apologize for this, for our actions today are too often expediential and unreflective. They need to be guided by a richer store of critically analyzed ideas. As I indicate in several places, these ideas and models did not spring autonomously from minds of genius: their creators acted in response to powerful challenges. I have tried to deepen understanding of the origins of these ideas by sketching where appropriate the nature of some of those challenges. This relationship should further warn us not to take these models as unquestionable authority, for in our lives we face our own unique and unprecedented challenges. The study of these models should rather stimulate us to work out our own responses, fertilized and enriched by the knowledge of what has gone before.

1 *The Guardian: Plato*

The principal challenge against which the ideas of Plato (ca. 427 B.C.–ca. 348 B.C.) were forged was the threat of violent change. Many of the most vivid experiences of his life were the products of violence, political upset, war, social unrest, and innovation, and his abhorrence of the consequential chaos made him yearn for peace, stability, predictability, and certainty. He witnessed the Peloponnesian War and the disorder that followed it, and recognized the need for a state authority strong enough to defend itself against outside enemies and ensure civil order within. He saw the death of his beloved teacher, Socrates, at the hands of democratic Athens, and feared ever after the tyranny of the uninformed. He lived in a state where the aristocrats and democrats struggled for political power in ways that were often unsavory, and he responded by turning away from politics to philosophy and by creating a hypothetical state where power would be in the hands of those who did not seek it.

Plato's thinking expressed some of the most sublime ideals in the Western tradition and at the same time sowed the seeds of some of its most destructive dichotomies. The model of the educated person that emerges in Plato's dialogues is of a beautiful, virtuous, wise man, one who responds with love and reason to the underlying harmony of the universe. At his highest, he becomes the Guardian, the philosopher-king, the one who *knows*, in contrast to those who merely believe. Knowledge, virtue, and beauty are essentially interrelated in Plato's view. The life of the educated man will be harmonious and beautiful, for he is also the virtuous man, that is, one who has come to know the Form of the Good.

Although this Platonic ideal has never been surpassed in its profundity and sublimity, Plato's expression of it laid the basis for one of the most tragic schisms in Western thought. In his view, mankind is essentially divided into two groups: those who are potentially capable of reaching this human ideal and those who are not; those who can see and those who are blind; those whose responsibility it is to lead and those whose duty it is to follow. It is likely that this distinction was not present in Socrates' teaching but developed later in Plato's philosophy as a result of his life experiences. In an early dialogue, *the Meno*, we see Socrates taking an untutored slaveboy and by skillful questioning drawing from him the Pythagorean theorem in geometry. There are important egalitarian implications here that Plato did not emphasize in the hierarchical formulae of the *Republic*, written in middle life, and that were completely expunged from the authoritarian dicta of the *Laws*, written at the end of his life.

Plato's educational scheme contains a genuinely dynamic element, the essence of which is manifested by the study of dialectic, with its emphasis on continuing inquiry. But this study is only for the few, whose education affords them the right to make fundamental life-and-death decisions on behalf of the many. The assumptions behind such provisions match Plato's uncritical attitude toward the institution of slavery in his own society where the free citizens were both vastly outnumbered by and economically dependent upon the slave population. The educational program that Plato envisioned was designed to produce an intellectual meritocracy, although his views on heredity might in fact have impeded the development of an *élite* of merit. Such meritocratic demands mean that selection becomes a vital educational function. Today we are still wrestling with, and paying the price for, this demand. When the problems of selection dominate, other more genuinely educational concerns tend to be snuffed out.

Plato has also left us a legacy of academic separateness. There is a sense in which the Guardian's wisdom is ultimately personal and hence of limited value to the community. Plato's own school, the Academy, which he founded in 387 B.C., was situated in an isolated spot on the northern outskirts of Athens. In choosing education rather than politics, Plato sought to create a sort of cultural island of stability in a political ocean of chaos. This physical and intellectual isolation established a pattern for the academic philosopher, who in subsequent years has often maintained his intellectual and moral integrity at the cost of leaving the field of political action to those whose motives are far from pure.

It is true that Plato held the state responsible for the educational and cultural welfare of the whole community. But this responsibility was not to be discharged in an interactive way that would invite maximum participation from those whose lives were affected. It was rather a responsibility of those who knew the truth to watch over and guide those who would never attain wisdom. Plato's view of man's nature was basically pessimistic, and hence education in his hands became a process of conversion rather than one of observing, following, and nurturing spontaneous tendencies. Moreover, since there was little provision for criticism, individual creativity, and experimentation in his scheme, the Guardian's authority was unlikely to be chastened by public correction.

There can be little doubt that contemporary America would benefit from a renewed emphasis on the quest for social justice that Plato valued more highly than individual freedom. But our aspirations must be even greater than this. For we must attempt to achieve the justice, order, culture, and planning that Plato wanted and at the same time move toward wide participation in political life, individual decision-making on all levels, and a universal extension of the concept of the educated person.

The Republic

The central concern in *The Republic* is the quest for justice. In the course of the dialogue it becomes clear that, in Plato's view, justice is a kind of appropriateness or harmony. The just society will be one in which everyone is doing exactly the work for which he is fitted. Similarly, justice in the individual will be found when the various parts of his nature operate fittingly or harmoniously. For example, the just man will never allow his bodily appetites to dominate his whole behavior. When each man does his job contentedly there will be social harmony. The "born shoemaker," says Plato, should stick to his last and not aspire to become a Guardian. We might ask, however, whether there is such a thing as a "born shoemaker" or whether such concepts are not fictions convenient for those in positions of leadership and privilege. Plato's justification of his view rests on his assumption of an essential inequality among men. The model of the educated person that Plato is proffering here is not universal. It applies only to those rare men and rarer women who are capable of understanding the underlying harmony of the universe, a harmony manifested, for example, in musical rhythm, in the beauty of excellent craftsmanship, and in the grace of the human body. The education of the Guardians—those fit to rule—will be designed to enable them to come to a recognition of the essential forms (archetypical ideas that exist in the unseen world and that govern the world of the senses). The Guardian is one who possesses knowledge rather than merely belief. This idea Plato illustrates by the famous allegory of the cave. True knowledge culminates in the recognition of the Form of the Good. Since not all men are capable of achieving this wisdom, those who are so innately gifted must take responsibility for the rest: they must descend again into the cave of everyday affairs and bring the truth to others. They must do this even though the unpopularity of such action may cause them to risk their lives, as Socrates did.

It is this intrinsic inequality among men that constitutes Plato's justification for hierarchy, control, and censorship. Children should be brought up amidst beauty. But who is to say what is beautiful? In Plato's view, this is the responsibility of the Guardians, whose control over artistic, intellectual, and political activities is thereby justified. *The Republic* is one of the great statements—perhaps the greatest—in the history of education because Plato brilliantly and profoundly analyzes one of our great perennial problems: if you seek excellence in education you must make judgments of what is excellent; in order to make judgments there must be judges; and the existence of judges implies inequality. Can we have both excellence and equality?

This translation, by B. Jowett, appears in Volume 3 of *The Dialogues of Plato*, published in Oxford at the Clarendon Press in 1892.

BOOK III

[Socrates] There is no difficulty in seeing that grace or the absence of grace is an effect of good or bad rhythm.
[Glaucon] None at all.

And also that good and bad rhythm naturally assimilate to a good and bad style; and that harmony and discord in like manner follow style; for our principle is that rhythm and harmony are regulated by the words, and not the words by them.

Just so, he said, they should follow the words.

And will not the words and the character of the style depend on the temper of the soul?

Yes.

And everything else on the style?

Yes.

Then beauty of style and harmony and grace and good rhythm depend on simplicity,—I mean the true simplicity of a rightly and nobly ordered mind and character, not that other simplicity which is only an euphemism for folly?

Very true, he replied.

And if our youth are to do their work in life, must they not make these graces and harmonies their perpetual aim?

They must.

And surely the art of the painter and every other creative and constructive art are full of them,—weaving, embroidery, architecture, and every kind of manufacture; also nature, animal and vegetable,—in all of them there is grace or the absence of grace. And ugliness and discord and inharmonious motion are nearly allied to ill words and ill nature, as grace and harmony are the twin sisters of goodness and virtue and bear their likeness.

That is quite true, he said.

But shall our superintendence go no further, and are the poets only to be required by us to express the image of the good in their works, on pain, if they do anything else, of expulsion from our State? Or is the same control to be extended to other artists, and are they also to be prohibited from exhibiting the opposite forms of vice and intemperance and meanness and indecency in sculpture and building and the other creative arts; and is he who cannot conform to this rule of ours to be prevented from practising his art in our State, lest the taste of our citizens be corrupted by him? We would not have our guardians grow up amid images of moral deformity, as in some noxious pasture, and there browse and feed upon many a baneful herb and flower day by day, little by little, until they silently gather a festering mass of corruption in their own soul. Let our artists rather be those who are gifted to discern the true nature of the beautiful and graceful; then will our youth dwell in a land of health, amid fair sights and sounds, and receive the good in everything; and beauty, the effluence of fair works, shall flow into the eye and ear, like a health-giving breeze from a purer region, and insensibly draw the soul from earliest years into likeness and sympathy with the beauty of reason.

There can be no nobler training than that, he replied. . . .

Neither we nor our guardians, whom we have to educate, can ever become musical until we and they know the essential forms of temperance, courage, liberality, magnificence, and their kindred, as well as the contrary forms, in all their combinations, and can recognise them and their images wherever they are found, not slighting them either in small things or great, but believing them all to be within the sphere of one art and study.

Most assuredly.

And when a beautiful soul harmonizes with a beautiful form, and the two are cast in one mould, that will be the fairest of sights to him who has an eye to see it?

The fairest indeed.

And the fairest is also the loveliest?

That may be assumed.

And the man who has the spirit of harmony will be most in love with the loveliest but he will not love him who is of an inharmonious soul?

That is true, he replied, if the deficiency be in his soul; but if there by any merely bodily defect in another he will be patient of it, and will love all the same.

I perceive, I said, that you have or have had experiences of this sort, and I agree. But let me ask you another question: Has excess of pleasure any affinity to temperance?

How can that be? he replied; pleasure deprives a man of the use of his faculties quite as much as pain.

Or any affinity to virtue in general?

None whatever.

Any affinity to wantonness and intemperance?

Yes, the greatest.

And is there any greater or keener pleasure than that of sensual love?

No, nor a madder.

Whereas true love is a love of beauty and order—temperate and harmonious?

Quite true, he said.

Then no intemperance or madness should be allowed to approach true love?

Certainly not.

Then mad or intemperate pleasure must never be allowed to come near the lover and his beloved; neither of them can have any part in it if their love is of the right sort?

No, indeed, Socrates, it must never come near them.

Then I suppose that in the city which we are founding you would make a law to the effect that a friend should use no other familiarity to his love than a father would use to his son, and then only for a noble purpose, and he must first have the other's consent; and this rule is to limit him in all his intercourse, and he is never to be seen going further, or, if he exceeds, he is to be deemed guilty of coarseness and bad taste.

I quite agree, he said.

Thus much of music, which makes a fair ending; for what should be the end of music if not the love of beauty?

I agree, he said. . . .

BOOK IV

[*Socrates*] And so, after much tossing, we have reached land, and are fairly agreed that the same principles which exist in the State exist also in the individual, and that they are three in number.

[*Glaucon*] Exactly.

Must we not then infer that the individual is wise in the same way, and in virtue of the same quality which makes the State wise?

Certainly.

Also that the same quality which constitutes courage in the State constitutes courage in the individual, and that both the State and the individual bear the same relation to all the other virtues?

Assuredly.

And the individual will be acknowledged by us to be just in the same way in which the State is just?

That follows of course.

We cannot but remember that the justice of the State consisted in each of the three classes doing the work of its own class?

We are not very likely to have forgotten, he said.

We must recollect that the individual in whom the several qualities of his nature do their own work will be just, and will do his own work?

Yes, he said, we must remember that too.

And ought not the rational principle, which is wise, and has the care of the whole soul, to rule, and the passionate or spirited principle to be the subject and ally?

Certainly.

And, as we were saying, the united influence of music and gymnastic will bring them into accord, nerving and sustaining the reason with noble words and lessons, and moderating and soothing and civilizing the wildness of passion by harmony and rhythm?

Quite true, he said.

And these two, thus nurtured and educated, and having learned truly to know their own functions, will rule over the concupiscent, which in each of us is the largest part of the soul and by nature most insatiable of gain; over this they will keep guard, lest, waxing great and strong with the fulness of bodily pleasures, as they are termed, the concupiscent soul, no longer confined to her own sphere, should attempt to enslave and rule those who are not her natural-born subjects, and overturn the whole life of man?

Very true, he said.

Both together will they not be the best defenders of the whole soul and the whole body against attacks from without; the one counselling, and the other fighting under his leader, and courageously executing his commands and counsels?

True. . . .

And the division of labour which required the carpenter and the shoe-maker and the rest of the citizens to be doing each his own business, and not another's, was a shadow of justice, and for that reason it was of use?

Clearly.

But in reality justice was such as we were describing, being concerned however, not with the outward man, but with the inward, which is the true self and concernment of man: for the just man does not permit the several elements within him to interfere with one another, or any of them to do the work of others,—he sets in order his own inner life, and is his own master and his own law, and at peace with himself and when he has bound together the three principles within him, which may be compared to the higher, lower, and middle notes of the scale, and the intermediate intervals—when he has bound all these together, and is no longer many, but has become one entirely temperate and perfectly adjusted nature, then he proceeds to act, if he has to act, whether in a matter of property, or in the treatment of the body, or in some affair of politics or private business; always thinking and calling that which preserves and co-operates with this harmonious condition, just and good action, and the knowledge which presides over it, wisdom, and that which at any time impairs this condition, he will call unjust action, and the opinion which presides over it, ignorance. . . .

BOOK V

[Glaucon] Who then are the true philosophers?

[Socrates] Those, I said, who are lovers of the vision of truth.

That is also good, he said; but I should like to know what you mean?

To another, I replied, I might have a difficulty in explaining; but I am sure that you will admit a proposition which I am about to make.

What is the proposition?

That since beauty is the opposite of ugliness, they are two?

Certainly.

And inasmuch as they are two, each of them is one?

True again.

And of just and unjust, good and evil, and of every other class, the same remark holds: taken singly, each of them is one; but from the various combinations of them with actions and things and with one another, they are seen in all sorts of lights and appear many?

Very true.

And this is the distinction which I draw between the sight-loving, art-loving, practical class and those of whom I am speaking, and who are alone worthy of the name of philosophers.

How do you distinguish them? he said.

The lovers of sounds and sights, I replied, are, as I conceive, fond of fine tones and colours and forms and all the artificial products that are made out of them, but their mind is incapable of seeing or loving absolute beauty.

True, he replied.

Few are they who are able to attain to the sight of this.

Very true.

And he who, having a sense of beautiful things has no sense of absolute beauty, or who, if another lead him to a knowledge of that beauty is unable to follow—of such an one I ask, Is he awake or in a dream only? Reflect: is not the dreamer, sleeping or waking, one who likens dissimilar things, who puts the copy in the place of the real object?

I should certainly say that such an one was dreaming.

But take the case of the other, who recognises the existence of absolute beauty and is able to distinguish the idea from the objects which participate in the idea, neither putting the objects in the place of the idea nor the idea in the place of the objects—is he a dreamer, or is he awake?

He is wide awake.

And may we not say that the mind of the one who knows has knowledge, and that the mind of the other, who opines only, has opinion?

Certainly. . . .

BOOK VII

[Socrates] And now, I said, let me show in a figure how far our nature is enlightened or unenlightened:—Behold! human beings living in an underground den, which has a mouth open towards the light

and reaching all along the den; here they have been from their childhood, and have their legs and necks chained so that they cannot move,
and can only see before them, being prevented by the chains from
turning round their heads. Above and behind them a fire is blazing
at a distance, and between the fire and the prisoners there is a raised
way; and you will see, if you look, a low wall built along the way,
like the screen which marionette players have in front of them, over
which they show the puppets.

[*Glaucon*] I see.

And do you see, I said, men passing along the wall carrying all sorts
of vessels, and statues and figures of animals made of wood and stone
and various materials, which appear over the wall? Some of them are
talking, others silent.

You have shown me a strange image, and they are strange prisoners.

Like ourselves, I replied; and they see only their own shadows, or
the shadows of one another, which the fire throws on the opposite wall
of the cave?

True, he said; how could they see anything but the shadows if they
were never allowed to move their heads?

And of the objects which are being carried in like manner they would
only see the shadows?

Yes, he said.

And if they were able to converse with one another, would they not
suppose that they were naming what was actually before them?

Very true.

And suppose further that the prison had an echo which came from
the other side, would they not be sure to fancy when one of the passers-
by spoke that the voice which they heard came from the passing shadow?

No question, he replied.

To them, I said, the truth would be literally nothing but the shadows
of the images.

That is certain.

And now look again, and see what will naturally follow if the prisoners
are released and disabused of their error. At first, when any of them
is liberated and compelled suddenly to stand up and turn his neck
round and walk and look towards the light, he will suffer sharp pains;
the glare will distress him, and he will be unable to see the realities
of which in his former state he had seen the shadows; and then conceive
some one saying to him, that what he saw before was an illusion, but
that now, when he is approaching nearer to being and his eye is turned
towards more real existence, he has a clearer vision—what will be his
reply? And you may further imagine that his instructor is pointing to

the objects as they pass and requiring him to name them—will he
not be perplexed? Will he not fancy that the shadows which he formerly
saw are truer than the objects which are now shown to him?

Far truer.

And if he is compelled to look straight at the light, will he not have
a pain in his eyes which will make him turn away to take refuge in
the objects of vision which he can see, and which he will conceive
to be in reality clearer than the things which are now being shown
to him?

True, he said.

And suppose once more, that he is reluctantly dragged up a steep
and rugged ascent, and held fast until he is forced into the presence
of the sun himself, is he not likely to be pained and irritated? When
he approaches the light his eyes will be dazzled, and he will not be
able to see anything at all of what are now called realities.

Not all in a moment, he said.

He will require to grow accustomed to the sight of the upper world.
And first he will see the shadows best, next the reflections of men and
other objects in the water, and then the objects themselves; then he
will gaze upon the light of the moon and the stars and the spangled
heaven; and he will see the sky and the stars by night better than
the sun or the light of the sun by day?

Certainly.

Last of all he will be able to see the sun, and not mere reflections
of him in the water, but he will see him in his own proper place, and
not in another and he will contemplate him as he is.

Certainly.

He will then proceed to argue that this is he who gives the season
and the years, and is the guardian of all that is in the visible world,
and in a certain way the cause of all things which he and his fellows
have been accustomed to behold?

Clearly, he said, he would first see the sun and then reason about
him.

And when he remembered his old habitation, and the wisdom of
the den and his fellow-prisoners, do you not suppose that he would
felicitate himself on the change, and pity them?

Certainly, he would.

And if they were in the habit of conferring honours among themselves
on those who were quickest to observe the passing shadows and to
remark which of them went before, and which followed after, and which
were together; and who were therefore best able to draw conclusions
as to the future, do you think that he would care for such honours

and glories, or envy the possessors of them? Would he not say with Homer,

'Better to be the poor servant of a poor master,'

and to endure anything, rather than think as they do and live after their manner?

Yes, he said, I think that he would rather suffer anything than entertain these false notions and live in this miserable manner.

Imagine once more, I said, such an one coming suddenly out of the sun to be replaced in his old situation; would he not be certain to have his eyes full of darkness?

To be sure, he said.

And if there were a contest, and he had to compete in measuring the shadows with the prisoners who had never moved out of the den, while his sight was still weak, and before his eyes had become steady (and the time which would be needed to acquire this new habit of sight might be very considerable), would he not be ridiculous? Men would say of him that up he went and down he came without his eyes and that it was better not even to think of ascending; and if any one tried to loose another and lead him up to the light, let them only catch the offender, and they would put him to death.

No question, he said.

This entire allegory, I said, you may now append, dear Glaucon, to the previous argument; the prison-house is the world of sight, the light of the fire is the sun, and you will not misapprehend me if you interpret the journey upwards to be the ascent of the soul into the intellectual world according to my poor belief, which, at your desire, I have expressed—whether rightly or wrongly God knows. But, whether true or false, my opinion is that in the world of knowledge the idea of good appears last of all, and is seen only with an effort; and, when seen, is also inferred to be the universal author of all things beautiful and right, parent of light and of the lord of light in this visible world, and the immediate source of reason and truth in the intellectual; and that this is the power upon which he who would act rationally either in public or private life must have his eye fixed.

I agree, he said, as far as I am able to understand you. . . .

Certain professors of education must be wrong when they say that they can put a knowledge into the soul which was not there before, like sight into blind eyes.

They undoubtedly say this, he replied.

Whereas, our argument shows that the power and capacity of learning exists in the soul already; and that just as the eye was unable to turn from darkness to light without the whole body, so too the instrument of knowledge can only by the movement of the whole soul be turned from the world of becoming into that of being, and learn by degrees to endure the sight of being, and of the brightest and best of being, or in other words, of the good.

Very true.

And must there not be some art which will effect conversion in the easiest and quickest manner; not implanting the faculty of sight, for that exists already, but has been turned in the wrong direction, and is looking away from the truth?

Yes, he said, such an art may be presumed.

And whereas the other so-called virtues of the soul seem to be akin to bodily qualities, for even when they are not originally innate they can be implanted later by habit and exercise, the virtue of wisdom more than anything else contains a divine element which always remains, and by this conversion is rendered useful and profitable; or, on the other hand, hurtful and useless. Did you never observe the narrow intelligence flashing from the keen eye of a clever rogue—how eager he is, how clearly his paltry soul sees the way to his end; he is the reverse of blind, but his keen eye-sight is forced into the service of evil, and he is mischievous in proportion to his cleverness?

Very true, he said.

But what if there had been a circumcision of such natures in the days of their youth; and they had been severed from those sensual pleasures, such as eating and drinking, which, like leaden weights, were attached to them at their birth, and which drag them down and turn the vision of their souls upon the things that are below—if, I say, they had been released from these impediments and turned in the opposite direction, the very same faculty in them would have seen the truth as keenly as they see what their eyes are turned to now.

Very likely.

Yes, I said; and there is another thing which is likely, or rather a necessary inference from what has preceded, that neither the uneducated and uninformed of the truth, nor yet those who never make an end of their education, will be able ministers of State; not the former, because they have no single aim of duty which is the rule of all their actions, private as well as public; nor the latter, because they will not act at all except upon compulsion, fancying that they are already dwelling apart in the islands of the blest.

Very true, he replied.

Then, I said, the business of us who are the founders of the State will be to compel the best minds to attain that knowledge which we have already shown to be the greatest of all—they must continue to ascend until they arrive at the good; but when they have ascended and seen enough we must not allow them to do as they do now.

What do you mean?

I mean that they remain in the upper world: but this must not be allowed; they must be made to descend again among the prisoners in the den, and partake of their labours and honours, whether they are worth having or not.

But is not this unjust? he said; ought we to give them a worse life, when they might have a better?

You have again forgotten, my friend, I said, the intention of the legislator, who did not aim at making any one class in the State happy above the rest; the happiness was to be in the whole State, and he held the citizens together by persuasion and necessity, making them benefactors of the State, and therefore benefactors of one another; to this end he created them, not to please themselves, but to be his instruments in binding up the State.

True, he said, I had forgotten.

Observe, Glaucon, that there will be no injustice in compelling our philosophers to have a care and providence of others; we shall explain to them that in other States, men of their class are not obliged to share in the toils of politics: and this is reasonable, for they grow up at their own sweet will, and the government would rather not have them. Being self-taught, they cannot be expected to show any gratitude for a culture which they have never received. But we have brought you into the world to be rulers of the hive, kings of yourselves and of the other citizens, and have educated you far better and more perfectly than they have been educated, and you are better able to share in the double duty. Wherefore each of you, when his turn comes, must go down to the general underground abode, and get the habit of seeing in the dark. When you have acquired the habit, you will see ten thousand times better than the inhabitants of the den, and you will know what the several images are, and what they represent, because you have seen the beautiful and just and good in their truth. And thus our State, which is also yours, will be a reality, and not a dream only, and will be administered in a spirit unlike that of other States, in which men fight with one another about shadows only and are distracted in the struggle for power, which in their eyes is a great good. Whereas the truth is that the State in which the rulers are most reluctant to govern is always the best and most quietly governed, and the State in which they are most eager, the worst.

Quite true, he replied.

And will our pupils, when they hear this, refuse to take their turn at the toils of State, when they are allowed to spend the greater part of their time with one another in the heavenly light?

Impossible, he answered; for they are just men, and the commands which we impose upon them are just; there can be no doubt that every one of them will take office as a stern necessity, and not after the fashion of our present rulers of State.

Epistle VII

There has for some time been a question concerning the authorship of this epistle. However, recent scholarship is in overwhelming agreement that it is indeed one of Plato's authentic works. (See, for example, Glenn R. Morrow, *Plato's Epistles*, Indianapolis: Bobbs-Merrill, 1962, especially pages 3–16: "The Question of Authenticity.") The theory of knowledge presented in it is entirely compatible with Plato's epistemology as expressed in other works, especially the later dialogues. In this passage, Plato refers to a book supposedly written by Dionysius, in which the latter gives his views on that most ultimate question, the first principles of nature. These can be taken to be the basic principles underlying Plato's theory of Forms, but Plato himself never writes of them directly. He insists that these principles cannot be outlined in writing, for we are dealing here with the inadequacy of ordinary language to express ultimate ideas. Such ultimate knowledge cannot be transferred from one mind to another. It is something that the pupil must gain for himself as a result of a sudden flash of illumination, which occurs only after a lengthy period of deep, intimate contact and prolonged, dialectical discourse with a wise teacher. The moment of insight is a somewhat mystical experience and only a few are capable of attaining it. Thus we see that Plato's epistemology reinforces and justifies a selective and inegalitarian educational structure. The educated person is a member of a small *élite*. Most men are by nature incapable of acquiring true knowledge. It is only a minority who are able to gain this vision of ultimate things and achieve moral excellence.

This translation, by the Rev. R. G. Bury, is from Plato, *Epistles*, published in Cambridge, Massachusetts, in 1929 by Harvard University Press, Loeb Classical Library, with whose permission it is reprinted.

This, then, was the purport of what I said to Dionysius on that occasion. I did not, however, expound the matter fully, nor did Dionysius ask me to do so; for he claimed that he himself knew many of the most important doctrines and was sufficiently informed owing to the versions he had heard from his other teachers. And I am even told that later on he himself wrote a treatise on the subjects in which I then instructed him, composing it as though it were something of his own invention and quite different from what he had heard; but of all this I know nothing. I know indeed that certain others have written about these same subjects; but what manner of men they are not even themselves know. But thus much I can certainly declare concerning all these writers, or prospective writers, who claim to know the subjects which I seriously study, whether as hearers of mine or of other teachers, or from their own discoveries; it is impossible, in my judgement at least, that these men should understand anything about this subject. There does not exist, nor will there ever exist, any treatise of mine dealing therewith. For it does not at all admit of verbal expression like other studies, but, as a result of continued application to the subject itself and communion herewith, it is brought to birth in the soul on a sudden, as light that is kindled by a leaping spark, and thereafter it nourishes itself. Notwithstanding, of thus much I am certain, that the best statement of these doctrines in writing or in speech would be my own statement; and further, that if they should be badly stated in writing, it is I who would be the person most deeply pained. And if I had thought that these subjects ought to be fully stated in writing or in speech to the public, what nobler action could I have performed in my life than that of writing what is of great benefit to mankind and bringing forth to the light for all men the nature of reality? But were I to undertake this task it would not, as I think, prove a good thing for men, save for some few who are able to discover the truth themselves with but little instruction; for as to the rest, some it would most unseasonably fill with a mistaken contempt, and others with an overweening and empty aspiration, as though they had learnt some sublime mysteries.

But concerning these studies I am minded to speak still more at length; since the subject with which I am dealing will perhaps be clearer when I have thus spoken. For there is a certain true argument which confronts the man who ventures to write anything at all of these matters—an argument which, although I have frequently stated it in the past, seems to require statement also at the present time.

Every existing object has three things which are the necessary means by which knowledge of that object is acquired; and the knowledge itself is a fourth thing; and as a fifth one must postulate the object itself which is cognizable and true. First of these comes the name; secondly the definition; thirdly the image; fourthly the knowledge. If you wish, then, to understand what I am now saying, take a single example and learn from it what applies to all. There is an object called a circle, which has for its *name* the word we have just mentioned; and, secondly, it has a *definition*, composed of names and verbs; for "that which is everywhere equidistant from the extremities to the centre" will be the definition of that object which has for its name "round" and "spherical" and "circle." And in the third place there is that object which is in course of being portrayed and obliterated, or of being shaped with a lathe, and falling into decay; but none of these affections is suffered by the circle itself, whereto all these others are related inasmuch as it is distinct therefrom. Fourth comes *knowledge* and intelligence and true opinion regarding these objects; and these we must assume to form a single whole, which does not exist in vocal utterance or in bodily forms but in souls; whereby it is plain that it differs both from the nature of the circle itself and from the three previously mentioned. And of those four intelligence approaches most nearly in kinship and similarity to the fifth, and the rest are further removed.

The same is true alike of the straight and of the spherical form, and of colour, and of the good and the fair and the just, and of all bodies whether manufactured or naturally produced (such as fire and water and all such substances), and of all living creatures, and of all moral actions or passions in souls. For unless a man somehow or other grasps the four of these, he will never perfectly acquire knowledge of the fifth. Moreover, these four attempt to express the quality of each object no less than its real essence, owing to the weakness inherent in language; and for this reason, no man of intelligence will ever venture to commit to it the concepts of his reason, especially when it is unalterable—as is the case with what is formulated in writing.

But here again you must learn further the meaning of this last statement. Every one of the circles which are drawn in geometric exercises or are turned by the lathe is full of what is opposite to the fifth, since it is in contact with the straight everywhere; whereas the circle itself, as we affirm, contains within itself no share greater or less of the opposite nature. And none of the objects, we affirm, has any fixed name, nor is there anything to prevent forms which are now called "round" from being called "straight," and the "straight" "round"; and men will find the names no less firmly fixed when they have shifted them and apply them in an opposite sense. Moreover, the same account holds good of the Definition also, that, inasmuch as it is compounded of names and verbs, it is in no case fixed with sufficient firmness. And so with each of the Four, their inaccuracy is an endless topic; but, as we mentioned a moment ago, the main point is this, that while there are two separate things, the real essence and the quality, and the soul seeks to know not the quality but the essence, each of the Four proffers to the soul either in word or in concrete form that which is not sought; and by thus causing each object which is described or exhibited to be always easy of refutation by the senses, it fills practically all men with all manner of perplexity and uncertainty. In respect, however, of those other objects the truth of which, owing to our bad training, we usually do not so much as seek—being content with such of the images as are proffered—those of us who answer are not made to look ridiculous by those who question, we being capable of analysing and convicting the Four. But in all cases where we compel a man to give the Fifth as his answer and to explain it, anyone who is able and willing to upset the argument gains the day, and makes the person who is expounding his view by speech or writing or answers appear to most of his hearers to be wholly ignorant of the subjects about which he is attempting to write or speak; for they are ignorant sometimes of the fact that it is not the soul of the writer or speaker that is being convicted but the nature of each of the Four, which is essentially defective. But it is the methodical study of all these stages, passing in turn from one to another, up and down, which with difficulty implants knowledge, when the man himself, like his object, is of a fine nature; but if his nature is bad—and, in fact, the condition of most men's souls in respect of learning and of what are termed "morals" is either naturally bad or else corrupted—then not even Lynceus himself could make such folk see. In one word, neither receptivity nor memory will ever produce knowledge in him who has no affinity with the object, since it does not germinate to start with in alien states of mind; consequently neither those who have no natural connexion or affinity with things just, and all else that is fair, although they are both receptive and retentive in various ways of other things, nor yet those who possess such affinity but are unreceptive and unretentive—none, I say, of these will ever learn to the utmost possible extent the truth of virtue nor yet of vice. For in learning these objects it is necessary to learn at the same time both what is false and what is true of the whole of Existence, and that through the most diligent and prolonged investigation, as I said at the commencement; and it is by means of the examination of each of these objects, comparing one with another—names and definitions, visions and sense-perceptions—proving them by kindly proofs and employing questionings and answerings that are void of envy—it is by such means, and hardly so, that there bursts out the light of intelligence and reason regarding each object in the mind of him who uses every effort of which mankind is capable.

And this is the reason why every serious man in dealing with really serious subjects carefully avoids writing, lest thereby he may possibly cast them as a prey to the envy and stupidity of the public. In one word, then, our conclusion must be that whenever one sees a man's written compositions—whether they be the laws of a legislator or anything else in any other form—these are not his most serious works, if so be that the writer himself is serious: rather those works abide in the fairest region he possesses. If, however, these really are his serious efforts, and put into writing, it is not "the gods" but mortal men who "Then of a truth themselves have utterly ruined his senses."

The Laws

The last of the dialogues, *The Laws*, was probably written some thirty years after *The Republic*, when Plato was in his seventies. It is the only dialogue in which Socrates does not appear. The three participants are Cleinias, a Cretan; Megillus, a Spartan; and a visitor from Athens. The latter voices Plato's views. His concept of the educated person is one who has had a thorough choric training, that is, training in song and dancing. Such a man will be able to judge what is rhythmical and melodious in music, just as he will be able to judge what is harmonious and orderly in the universe. Not only will he perform well in music and the arts, but he will also *like* what is *good* in art. The only way to bring this about in adults is to start with them as young children: they must learn from the beginning to feel pleasure and pain about the right things (an idea that Aristotle enthusiastically endorsed). Virtue and taste must be established in the young child through the development of appropriate habits: he must learn to enjoy what he will later judge to be good and to dislike what he will later judge to be bad. Since these judgments must initially be made by others—those with maturity and wisdom—Plato's view entails both the necessity and the justification for external authority and discipline. It also necessitates the establishment of publicly agreed upon and perennially maintained standards of judgment. Plato cites Egypt as evidence that relative permanence of standards can be achieved. His model, then, is a man who seeks excellence in traditional ways and does not look for idiosyncratic forms of the good nor attempt to foster innovation.

This passage is from *The Laws of Plato*, translated by A. E. Taylor, published in London in 1934 in The Everyman's Library Series by J. M. Dent & Sons, Ltd. Reprinted by permission of J. M. Dent & Sons, Ltd., and E. P. Dutton & Company.

BOOK I

Athenian. You seem to be quite ready to listen; and I am also ready to perform as much as I can of an almost impossible task, which I will nevertheless attempt. At the outset of the discussion, let me define the nature and power of education; for this is the way by which our argument must travel onwards to the God Dionysus.

Cleinias. Let us proceed, if you please.

Ath. Well, then, if I tell you what are my notions of education, will you consider whether they satisfy you?

Cle. Let us hear.

Ath. According to my view, any one who would be good at anything must practise that thing from his youth upwards, both in sport and earnest, in its several branches: for example, he who is to be a good builder, should play at building children's houses; he who is to be a good husbandman, at tilling the ground; and those who have the care of their education should provide them when young with mimic tools. They should learn beforehand the knowledge which they will afterwards require for their art. For example, the future carpenter should learn to measure or apply the line in play; and the future warrior should learn riding, or some other exercise, for amusement, and the teacher should endeavour to direct the children's inclinations and pleasures, by the help of amusements, to their final aim in life. The most important part of education is right training in the nursery. The soul of the child in his play should be guided to the love of that sort of excellence in which when he grows up to manhood he will have to be perfected. Do you agree with me thus far?

Cle. Certainly.

Ath. Then let us not leave the meaning of education ambiguous or ill-defined. At present, when we speak in terms of praise or blame about the bringing-up of each person, we call one man educated and another uneducated, although the uneducated man may be sometimes very well educated for the calling of a retail trader, or of a captain of a ship, and the like. For we are not speaking of education in this narrower sense, but of that other education in virtue from youth upwards, which makes a man eagerly pursue the ideal perfection of citizenship, and teaches him how rightly to rule and how to obey. This is the only education which, upon our view, deserves the name; that other sort of training, which aims at the acquisition of wealth or bodily strength, or mere cleverness apart from intelligence and justice, is mean and illiberal, and is not worthy to be called education at all. But let us not quarrel with one another about a word, provided that the proposition which has just been granted hold good: to wit, that those who are rightly educated generally become good men. Neither must we cast a slight upon education, which is the first and fairest thing that the best of men can ever have, and which, though liable to take a wrong direction, is capable of reformation. And this work of reformation is the great business of every man while he lives.

Cle. Very true; and we entirely agree with you.

Ath. And we agreed before that they are good men who are able to rule themselves, and bad men who are not.

Cle. You are quite right.

Ath. Let me now proceed, if I can, to clear up the subject a little further by an illustration which I will offer you.

Cle. Proceed.

Ath. Do we not consider each of ourselves to be one?

Cle. We do.

Ath. And each one of us has in his bosom two counsellors, both foolish and also antagonistic; of which we call the one pleasure, and the other pain.

Cle. Exactly.

Ath. Also there are opinions about the future, which have the general name of expectations; and the specific name of fear, when the expectation is of pain; and of hope, when of pleasure; and further, there is reflection about the good or evil of them, and this, when embodied in a decree by the State, is called Law.

Cle. I am hardly able to follow you; proceed, however, as if I were.

Megillus. I am in the like case.

Ath. Let us look at the matter thus: May we not conceive each of us living beings to be a puppet of the Gods, either their plaything only, or created with a purpose—which of the two we cannot certainly know? But we do know, that these affections in us are like cords and strings, which pull us different and opposite ways, and to opposite actions; and herein lies the difference between virtue and vice. According to the argument there is one among these cords which every man ought to grasp and never let go, but to pull with it against all the rest; and this is the sacred and golden cord of reason, called by us the common law of the State; there are others which are hard and of iron, but this one is soft because golden; and there are several other kinds. Now we ought always to co-operate with the lead of the best, which is law. For inasmuch as reason is beautiful and gentle, and not violent, her rule must needs have ministers in order to help the golden principle in vanquishing the other principles. And thus the moral of the tale about our being puppets will not have been lost, and the meaning of the expression 'superior or inferior to a man's self' will become clearer; and the individual, attaining to right reason in this matter of pulling the strings of the puppet, should live according to its rule; while the city, receiving the same from some god or from one who has knowledge of these things, should embody it in a law, to be her guide in her dealings with herself and with other states. In this way virtue and vice will be more clearly distinguished by us. And when they have become clearer, education and other institutions will in like manner become clearer; and in particular that question of convivial entertainment, which may seem, perhaps, to have been a very trifling matter, and to have taken a great many more words than were necessary. . . .

BOOK II

Ath. Pleasure and pain I maintain to be the first perceptions of children, and I say that they are the forms under which virtue and vice are originally present to them. As to wisdom and true and fixed opinions, happy is the man who acquires them, even when declining in years; and we may say that he who possesses them, and the blessings which are contained in them, is a perfect man. Now I mean by education that training which is given by suitable habits to the first instincts of virtue in children—when pleasure, and friendship, and pain, and hatred, are rightly implanted in souls not yet capable of understanding the nature of them, and who find them, after they have attained reason, to be in harmony with her. This harmony of the soul, taken as a whole, is virtue; but the particular training in respect of pleasure and pain, which leads you always to hate what you ought to hate, and love what you ought to love from the beginning of life to the end, may be separated off; and, in my view, will be rightly called education.

Cle. I think, Stranger, that you are quite right in all that you have said and are saying about education.

Ath. I am glad to hear that you agree with me; for, indeed, the discipline of pleasure and pain which, when rightly ordered, is a principle of education, has been often relaxed and corrupted in human life. And the Gods, pitying the toils which our race is born to undergo, have appointed holy festivals, wherein men alternate rest with labour; and have given them the Muses and Apollo, the leader of the Muses, and Dionysus, to be companions in their revels, that they may improve their education by taking part in the festivals of the Gods, and with their help. I should like to know whether a common saying is in our opinion true to nature or not. For men say that the young of all creatures cannot be quiet in their bodies or in their voices; they are always wanting to move and cry out; some leaping and skipping, and overflowing with sportiveness and delight at something, others uttering all sorts of cries. But, whereas the animals have no perception of order or disorder in their movements, that is, of rhythm or harmony, as they are called, to us, the Gods, who, as we say, have been appointed to be our companions in the dance, have given the pleasurable sense of harmony and rhythm; and so they stir us into life, and we follow them, joining hands together in dances and songs; and these they call choruses, which is a term naturally expressive of cheerfulness. Shall we begin, then, with the acknowledgment that education is first given through Apollo and the Muses? What do you say?

Cle. I assent.

Ath. And the uneducated is he who has not been trained in the chorus, and the educated is he who has been well trained?

Cle. Certainly.

Ath. And the chorus is made up of two parts, dance and song?

Cle. True.

Ath. Then he who is well educated will be able to sing and dance well?

Cle. I suppose that he will.

Ath. Let us see; what are we saying?

Cle. What?

Ath. He sings well and dances well; now must we add that he sings what is good and dances what is good?

Cle. Let us make the addition.

Ath. We will suppose that he knows the good to be good, and the bad to be bad, and makes use of them accordingly: which now is the better trained in dancing and music—he who is able to move his body and to use his voice in what is understood to be the right manner but has no delight in good or hatred of evil; or he who is incorrect in gesture and voice, but is right in his sense of pleasure and pain, and welcomes what is good, and is offended at what is evil?

Cle. There is a great difference, Stranger, in the two kinds of education.

Ath. If we three know what is good in song and dance, then we truly know also who is educated and who is uneducated; but if not, then we certainly shall not know wherein lies the safeguard of education, and whether there is any or not.

Cle. True.

Ath. Let us follow the scent like hounds, and go in pursuit of beauty of figure, and melody, and song, and dance; if these escape us, there will be no use in talking about true education, whether Hellenic or barbarian. . . .

Then in a city which has good laws, or in future ages is to have them, bearing in mind the instruction and amusement which are given by music, can we suppose that the poets are to be allowed to teach in the dance anything which they themselves like, in the way of rhythm, or melody, or words, to the young children of any well-conditioned parents? Is the poet to train his choruses as he pleases, without reference to virtue or vice?

Cle. That is surely quite unreasonable, and is not to be thought of.

Ath. And yet he may do this in almost any state with the exception of Egypt.

Cle. And what are the laws about music and dancing in Egypt?

Ath. You will wonder when I tell you: Long ago they appear to have recognized the very principle of which we are now speaking—that their young citizens must be habituated to forms and strains of virtue. These they fixed, and exhibited the patterns of them in their temples; and no painter or artist is allowed to innovate upon them, or to leave the traditional forms and invent new ones. To this day, no alteration is allowed either in these arts, or in music at all. And you will find that their works of art are painted or moulded in the same forms which they had ten thousand years ago;—this is literally true and no exaggeration-their ancient paintings and sculptures are not a whit better or worse than the work of to-day, but are made with just the same skill.

Cle. How extraordinary!

Ath. I should rather say, How statemanlike, how worthy of a legislator! I know that other things in Egypt are not so well. But what I am telling you about music is true and deserving of consideration, because showing that a lawgiver may institute melodies which have a natural truth and correctness without any fear of failure. To do this, however, must be the work of God, or of a divine person; in Egypt they have a tradition that their ancient chants which have been preserved for so many ages are the composition of the Goddess Isis. And therefore, as I was saying, if a person can only find in any way the natural melodies, he may confidently embody them in a fixed and legal form. For the love of novelty which arises out of pleasure in the new and weariness of the old, has not strength enough to corrupt the consecrated song and dance, under the plea that they have become antiquated. At any rate, they are far from being corrupted in Egypt.

2 The Rational Citizen: Aristotle

The crucial turning point in Aristotle's life (384–322 B.C.) was his appointment as tutor of Alexander, the thirteen-year-old son of Philip of Macedon. Although Aristotle's term as tutor was relatively brief, his relationship with Alexander was an abiding one, with important consequences. On the death of his father, Alexander took command of the Macedonian army and began his series of conquests, which were ultimately to cover much of the known world. Under an arrangement with Aristotle, he sent back to his former tutor an enormous mass of information from the countries through which he passed. This material—everything from details of constitutions, governments, and customs to biological and botanical data—provided Aristotle with an unprecedented body of facts, with the aid of which he and his students systematized virtually the whole spectrum of human knowledge.

Although he was a pupil at Plato's Academy for almost twenty years, Aristotle differed from his master in some important respects. One of these is reflected in his passion for the collection of empirical evidence. The son of a physician, Aristotle probably caught from his father a taste for biology, which led him to a concern for the observation of nature and for exactness of methodology. Unlike Plato's predominantly dialectical and intuitive approach, Aristotle's method was based upon the belief that all the available relevant evidence should first be amassed before a solution could be anticipated. He would not allow the human mind to impose its intuitive patterns on the natural world: he preferred to use the careful observation of nature as a guide to the pattern of truth.

Armed with a body of knowledge never before available to one man, Aristotle produced a number of amazingly wide-ranging and precisely argued treatises, which have had an enormous influence upon the Western world. He was more than any other man responsible for forming the medieval European mind. His ideas formed the basis of the seven liberal arts, which dominated Western education up to the eighteenth century. He created a model of the educated man that continues to shape our thinking. In portraying his model, Aristotle showed himself to be a man who both reflected and transcended his own era and milieu. It is easy to see prevailing upper-class Greek assumptions in his recommendations: masculine superiority, a belief in fundamental human inequality that extended to the justification of slavery, the domination of politics by a traditional minority, the ultimate supremacy of the state, and so on. This conventional thinking is partly expressed in one dimension of Aristotle's model: the citizen who faithfully performs his political duties and is staunchly loyal to his friends and to his state. But Aristotle introduced another dimension by suggesting that politics is not the highest activity and that man performs at his most sublime level when he is at leisure. We might consider this to be of relevance today in the light of the increase in leisure for many people in industrialized countries. This relevance might persuade us to make another examination of Aristotle's defense of contemplation and the activity of reason as the loftiest employment of this leisure.

On the Parts of Animals

Aristotle's professed purpose in his treatise, *De Partibus Animalium,* is to examine the respective roles played by necessity and design in the structure of animal life. In the study he suggests that design is by far the more important factor. Early in the book he considers various ways in which the investigation could be conducted: whether, for example, to begin with common characteristics and then proceed to study special peculiarities or to begin immediately to examine individual species. Such debate reminds us forcibly that, for Aristotle, there were no guidelines to follow in such matters. We are here in the presence of the great pioneer of the Western intellectual tradition, whose classifications and vocabulary laid the basis of subsequent thinking in a whole range of scholastic endeavor. Even in those fields where his substantive judgments have now been displaced—such as the natural sciences—his methods are still of interest. At the beginning of this treatise, he characteristically points out that the educated person will be able to evaluate an argument—even on a subject in which he is not an expert—by the validity of the method used to expound it. In order to conform to Aristotle's model of the educated person it is not enough to be competently trained in a narrow specialty if one remains naive outside of it. To be considered educated, one must have grasped the general criteria by which the worth of arguments may be assessed.

This translation, by William Ogle, appears in volume V, *De Partibus Animalium,* of *The Works of Aristotle,* edited by J. A. Smith and W. D. Ross, published in Oxford in 1912 by the Clarendon Press, with whose permission it is reprinted.

BOOK I

Every systematic science, the humblest and the noblest alike, seems to admit of two distinct kinds of proficiency; one of which may be properly called scientific knowledge of the subject, while the other is a kind of educational acquaintance with it. For an educated man should be able to form a fair off-hand judgement as to the goodness or badness of the method used by a professor in his exposition. To be educated is in fact to be able to do this; and even the man of universal education we deem to be such in virtue of his having this ability. It will, however, of course, be understood that we only ascribe universal education to one who in his own individual person is thus critical in all or nearly all branches of knowledge, and not to one who has a like ability merely in some special subject. For it is possible for a man to have this competence in some one branch of knowledge without having it in all.

It is plain then that, as in other sciences, so in that which inquires into nature, there must be certain canons, by reference to which a hearer shall be able to criticize the method of a professed exposition, quite independently of the question whether the statements made be true or false.

Nicomachean Ethics

At the beginning of his discussion of ethics, Aristotle makes clear that we are entering a field that is an approximate science, where we should not expect exact answers. He suggests that the educated man is one who recognizes that in different areas of inquiry different degrees of precision are appropriate. Widespread disregard for this injunction has today led us to a rife misuse of the methods of science, especially through the employment of quantitative and statistical techniques in ways that give a spurious impression of exactitude. It has also caused us harm through the depreciation of those studies (particularly the humanities) where exact results are not to be found. Aristotle's central concern in the *Nicomachean Ethics* is the quest for the highest good. He maintains that this is to be found in human happiness. But this generalization will not be helpful until we know what it means to be human. What is man's uniquely human function? He is, argues Aristotle, essentially a rational creature: the good and happy man, therefore, is he who behaves in accordance with the dictates of reason. In order to conform to Aristotle's model, however, it is not enough to have good intentions. Moral excellence implies action: one must perform as well as profess. One becomes good by performing good acts. Hence the development of good habits is a crucial part of education, especially in early years. Aristotle presents here his celebrated concept of moral virtue as a mean between excess and deficiency. His model is a man who achieves through reason this mean or balance in his behavior. Education, rightly conceived, will aim toward producing a man who is virtuous and happy. Since happiness is activity in accordance with the highest virtue, and contemplation is the highest form of activity, the educated man will be one whose life is focused upon rational contemplation. Always aware of his place in society and ready to perform faithfully his duties to his community, he will be, then, a rational citizen.

This translation of the *Ethica Nicomachea,* by W. D. Ross, appears in Volume IX of *The Works of Aristotle,* edited by W. D. Ross, published in Oxford in 1925 by the Clarendon Press, with whose permission it is reprinted.

BOOK I

Our discussion will be adequate if it has as much clearness as the subject-matter admits of, for precision is not to be sought for alike in all discussions, any more than in all the products of the crafts. Now fine and just actions, which political science investigates, admit of much variety and fluctuation of opinion, so that they may be thought to exist only by convention, and not by nature. And goods also give rise to a similar fluctuation because they bring harm to many people; for before now men have been undone by reason of their wealth, and others by reason of their courage. We must be content, then, in speaking of such subjects and with such premisses to indicate the truth roughly and in outline, and in speaking about things which are only for the most part true and with premisses of the same kind to reach conclusions that are no better. In the same spirit, therefore, should each type of statement be *received;* for it is the mark of an educated man to look for precision in each class of things just so far as the nature of the subject admits; it is evidently equally foolish to accept probable reasoning from a mathematician and to demand from a rhetorician scientific proofs.

Now each man judges well the things he knows, and of these he is a good judge. And so the man who has been educated in a subject is a good judge of that subject, and the man who has received an all-round education is a good judge in general. Hence a young man is not a proper hearer of lectures on political science; for he is inexperienced in the actions that occur in life, but its discussions start from these and are about these; and, further, since he tends to follow his passions, his study will be vain and unprofitable, because the end aimed at is not knowledge but action. And it makes no difference whether he is young in years or youthful in character; the defect does not depend on time, but on his living, and pursuing each successive object, as passion directs. For to such persons, as to the incontinent, knowledge brings no profit; but to those who desire and act in accordance with a rational principle knowledge about such matters will be of great benefit. . . .

Let us again return to the good we are seeking, and ask what it can be. It seems different in different actions and arts; it is different in medicine, in strategy, and in the other arts likewise. What then is the good of each? Surely that for whose sake everything else is done. In medicine this is health, in strategy victory, in architecture a house, in any other sphere something else, and in every action and pursuit the end; for it is for the sake of this that all men do whatever else they do. Therefore, if there is an end for all that we do, this will be the good achievable by action, and if there are more than one, these will be the goods achievable by action.

So the argument has by a different course reached the same point; but we must try to state this even more clearly. Since there are evidently more than one end, and we choose some of these (e.g. wealth, flutes, and in general instruments) for the sake of something else, clearly not all ends are final ends; but the chief good is evidently something final. Therefore, if there is only one final end, this will be what we are seeking, and if there are more than one, the most final of these will be what we are seeking. Now we call that which is in itself worthy of pursuit more final than that which is worthy of pursuit for the sake of something else, and that which is never desirable for the sake of something else more final than the things that are desirable both in themselves and for the sake of that other thing, and therefore we call final without qualification that which is always desirable in itself and never for the sake of something else.

Now such a thing happiness, above all else, is held to be; for this we choose always for itself and never for the sake of something else, but honour, pleasure, reason, and every virtue we choose indeed for themselves (for if nothing resulted from them we should still choose each of them), but we choose them also for the sake of happiness, judging that by means of them we shall be happy. Happiness, on the other hand, no one chooses for the sake of these, nor, in general, for anything other than itself.

From the point of view of self-sufficiency the same result seems to follow; for the final good is thought to be self-sufficient. Now by self-sufficient we do not mean that which is sufficient for a man by himself, for one who lives a solitary life, but also for parents, children, wife, and in general for his friends and fellow citizens, since man is born for citizenship. But some limit must be set to this; for if we extend our requirement to ancestors and descendants and friends' friends we are in for an infinite series. Let us examine this question, however, on another occasion; the self-sufficient we now define as that which when isolated makes life desirable and lacking in nothing; and such we think happiness to be; and further we think it most desirable of all things, without being counted as one good thing among others—if it were so counted it would clearly be made more desirable by the addition of even the least of goods; for that which is added becomes an excess of goods, and of goods the greater is always more desirable. Happiness, then, is something final and self-sufficient, and is the end of action.

Presumably, however, to say that happiness is the chief good seems a platitude, and a clearer account of what it is is still desired. This might perhaps be given, if we could first ascertain the function of man. For just as for a flute-player, a sculptor, or any artist, and, in general, for all things that have a function or activity, the good and the 'well' is thought to reside in the function, so would it seem to be for man, if he has a function. Have the carpenter, then, and the tanner certain functions or activities, and has man none? Is he born without a function? Or as eye, hand, foot, and in general each of the parts evidently has a function, may one lay it down that man similarly has a function apart from all these? What then can this be? Life seems to be common even to plants, but we are seeking what is peculiar to man. Let us exclude, therefore, the life of nutrition and growth. Next there would be a life of perception, but *it* also seems to be common even to the horse, the ox, and every animal. There remains, then, an active life of the element that has a rational principle; of this, one part has such a principle in the sense of being obedient to one, the other in the sense of possessing one and exercising thought. And, as 'life of the rational element' also has two meanings, we must state that life in the sense of activity is what we mean; for this seems to be the more proper sense of the term. Now if the function of man is an activity of soul which follows or implies a rational principle, and if we say 'a so-and-so' and 'a good so-and-so' have a function which is the same in kind, e.g. a lyre-player and a good lyre-player, and so without qualification in all cases, eminence in respect of goodness being added to the name of the function (for the function of a lyre-player is to play the lyre, and that of a good lyre-player is to do so well):

if this is the case, [and we state the function of man to be a certain kind of life, and this to be an activity or actions of the soul implying a rational principle, and the function of a good man to be the good and noble performance of these, and if any action is well performed when it is performed in accordance with the appropriate excellence: if this is the case,] human good turns out to be activity of soul in accordance with virtue, and if there are more than one virtue, in accordance with the best and most complete. . . .

With those who identify happiness with virtue or some one virtue our account is in harmony; for to virtue belongs virtuous activity. But it makes, perhaps, no small difference whether we place the chief good in possession or in use, in state of mind or in activity. For the state of mind may exist without producing any good result, as in a man who is asleep or in some other way quite inactive, but the activity cannot; for one who has the activity will of necessity be acting, and acting well. And as in the Olympic Games it is not the most beautiful and the strongest that are crowned but those who compete (for it is some of these that are victorious), so those who act win, and rightly win, the noble and good things in life. . . .

BOOK II

Virtue, then, being of two kinds, intellectual and moral, intellectual virtue in the main owes both its birth and its growth to teaching (for which reason it requires experience and time), while moral virtue comes about as a result of habit, whence also its name (ἠθική) is one that is formed by a slight variation from the word ἔθος (habit). From this it is also plain that none of the moral virtues arises in us by nature; for nothing that exists by nature can form a habit contrary to its nature. For instance the stone which by nature moves downwards cannot be habituated to move upwards, not even if one tries to train it by throwing it up ten thousand times; nor can fire be habituated to move downward, nor can anything else that by nature behaves in one way be trained to behave in another. Neither by nature, then, nor contrary to nature do the virtues arise in us; rather we are adapted by nature to receive them, and are made perfect by habit.

Again, of all the things that come to us by nature we first acquire the potentiality and later exhibit the activity (this is plain in the case of the senses; for it was not by often seeing or often hearing that we got these senses, but on the contrary we had them before we used them, and did not come to have them by using them); but the virtues we get by first exercising them, as also happens in the case of the arts as well. For the things we have to learn before we can do them, we learn by doing them, e.g. men become builders by building and lyre-players by playing the lyre; so too we become just by doing just acts, temperate by doing temperate acts, brave by doing brave acts.

This is confirmed by what happens in states: for legislators make the citizens good by forming habits in them, and this is the wish of every legislator, and those who do not effect it miss their mark, and it is in this that a good constitution differs from a bad one.

Again, it is from the same causes and by the same means that every virtue is both produced and destroyed, and similarly every art; for it is from playing the lyre that both good and bad lyre-players are produced. And the corresponding statement is true of builders and of all the rest; men will be good or bad builders as a result of building well or badly. For if this were not so, there would have been no need of a teacher, but all men would have been born good or bad at their craft. This, then, is the case with the virtues also; by doing the acts that we do in our transactions with other men we become just or unjust, and by doing the acts that we do in the presence of danger, and being habituated to feel fear or confidence, we become brave or cowardly. The same is true of appetites and feelings of anger; some men become temperate and good-tempered, others self-indulgent and irascible, by behaving in one way or the other in the appropriate circumstances. Thus, in one word, states of character arise out of like activities. This is why the activities we exhibit must be of a certain kind; it is because the states of character correspond to the differences between these. It makes no small difference, then, whether we form habits of one kind or of another from our very youth; it makes a very great difference, or rather all the difference. . . .

It is the nature of such things to be destroyed by defect and excess, as we see in the case of strength and of health (for to gain light on things imperceptible we must use the evidence of sensible things); both excessive and defective exercise destroys the strength, and similarly drink or food which is above or below a certain amount destroys the health, while that which is proportionate both produces and increases and preserves it. So too is it, then, in the case of temperance and courage and the other virtues. For the man who flies from and fears everything and does not stand his ground against anything becomes a coward, and the man who fears nothing at all but goes to meet every danger becomes rash; and similarly the man who indulges in every pleasure and abstains from none becomes self-indulgent, while the man who shuns every pleasure, as boors do, becomes in a way insensible; temperance and courage, then, are destroyed by excess and defect, and preserved by the mean.

But not only are the sources and causes of their origination and growth the same as those of their destruction, but also the sphere of their actualization will be the same; for this is also true of the things which are more evident to sense, e.g., of strength; it is produced by taking much food and undergoing much exertion, and it is the strong man that will be most able to do these things. So too is it with the virtues; by abstaining from pleasures we become temperate, and it is when we have become so that we are most able to abstain from them; and similarly too in the case of courage; for by being habituated to despise things that are terrible and to stand our ground against them we become brave, and it is when we have become so that we shall be most able to stand our ground against them. . . .

Virtue, then, is a state of character concerned with choice, lying in a mean, i.e. the mean relative to us, this being determined by a rational principle, and by that principle by which the man of practical wisdom would determine it. Now it is a mean between two vices, that which depends on excess and that which depends on defect; and again it is a mean because the vices respectively fall short of or exceed what is right in both passions and actions, while virtue both finds and chooses that which is intermediate. Hence in respect of its substance and the definition which states its essence virtue is a mean, with regard to what is best and right an extreme.

But not every action nor every passion admits of a mean; for some have names that already imply badness, e.g. spite, shamelessness, envy, and in the case of actions adultery, theft, murder; for all of these and suchlike things imply by their names that they are themselves bad, and not the excesses or deficiencies of them. It is not possible, then, ever to be right with regard to them; one must always be wrong. Nor does goodness or badness with regard to such things depend on committing adultery with the right woman, at the right time, and in the right way, but simply to do any of them is to go wrong. It would be equally absurd, then, to expect that in unjust, cowardly, and voluptuous action there should be a mean, an excess, and a deficiency; for at that rate there would be a mean of excess and of deficiency, an excess of excess, and a deficiency of deficiency. But as there is no excess and deficiency of temperance and courage because what is intermediate is in a sense an extreme, so too of the actions we have mentioned there is no mean nor any excess and deficiency, but however they are done they are wrong; for in general there is neither a mean of excess and deficiency, nor excess and deficiency of a mean. . . .

BOOK X

If happiness is activity in accordance with virtue, it is reasonable that it should be in accordance with the highest virtue; and this will be that of the best thing in us. Whether it be reason or something else that is this element which is thought to be our natural ruler and guide and to take thought of things noble and divine, whether it be itself also divine or only the most divine element in us, the activity of this in accordance with its proper virtue will be perfect happiness. That this activity is contemplative we have already said.

Now this would seem to be in agreement both with what we said before and with the truth. For, firstly, this activity is the best (since not only is reason the best thing in us, but the objects of reason are the best of knowable objects); and, secondly, it is the most continuous, since we can contemplate truth more continuously than we can *do* anything. And we think happiness has pleasure mingled with it, but the activity of philosophic wisdom is admittedly the pleasantest of virtuous activities; at all events the pursuit of it is thought to offer pleasures marvellous for their purity and their enduringness, and it is to be expected that those who know will pass their time more pleasantly than those who inquire. And the self-sufficiency that is spoken of must belong most to the contemplative activity. For while a philosopher, as well as a just man or one possessing any other virtue, needs the necessaries of life, when they are sufficiently equipped with things of that sort the just man needs people towards whom and with whom he shall act justly, and the temperate man, the brave man, and each of the others is in the same case, but the philosopher, even when by himself, can contemplate truth, and the better the wiser he is; he can perhaps do so better if he has fellow-workers, but still he is the most self-sufficient. And this activity alone would seem to be loved for its own sake; for nothing arises from it apart from the contemplating, while from practical activities we gain more or less apart from the action. And happiness is thought to depend on leisure; for we are busy that we may have leisure, and make war that we may live in peace. Now the activity of the practical virtues is exhibited in political or military affairs, but the actions concerned with these seem to be unleisurely. Warlike actions are completely so (for no one chooses to be at war, or provokes war, for the sake of being at war; any one would seem absolutely murderous if he were to make enemies of his friends in order to bring about battle and slaughter); but the action of the statesman is also unleisurely, and—apart from the political action itself—aims at despotic power and honours, or at all events happiness, for him and his fellow citizens—a happiness different from political action, and evidently sought as being different. So if among virtuous actions political and military actions are distinguished by nobility and greatness, and these are unleisurely and aim at an end and are not desirable for their own sake, but the activity of reason, which is contemplative, seems both to be superior in serious worth and to aim at no end beyond itself, and to have its pleasure proper to itself (and this augments the activity), and the self-sufficiency, leisureliness, unweariedness (so far as this is possible for man), and all the other attributes ascribed to the supremely happy man are evidently those connected with this activity, it follows that this will be the complete happiness of man, if it be allowed a complete term of life (for none of the attributes of happiness is *in*complete).

But such a life would be too high for man; for it is not in so far as he is man that he will live so, but in so far as something divine is present in him; and by so much as this is superior to our composite nature is its activity superior to that which is the exercise of the other kind of virtue. If reason is divine, then, in comparison with man, the life according to it is divine in comparison with human life. But we must not follow those who advise us, being men, to think of human things, and, being mortal, of mortal things, but must, so far as we can, make ourselves immortal, and strain every nerve to live in accordance with the best thing in us; for even if it be small in bulk, much more does it in power and worth surpass everything. This would seem, too, to be each man himself, since it is the authoritative and better part of him. It would be strange, then, if he were to choose not the life of his self but that of something else. And what we said before will apply now; that which is proper to each thing is by nature best and most pleasant for each thing; for man, therefore, the life according to reason is best and pleasantest, since reason more than anything else *is* man. This life therefore is also the happiest. . . .

But that perfect happiness is a contemplative activity will appear from the following consideration as well. We assume the gods to be above all other beings blessed and happy; but what sort of actions must we assign to them? Acts of justice? Will not the gods seem absurd if they make contracts and return deposits, and so on? Acts of a brave

man, then, confronting dangers and running risks because it is noble
to do so? Or liberal acts? To whom will they give? It will be strange
if they are really to have money or anything of the kind. And what
would their temperate acts be? Is not such praise tasteless, since they
have no bad appetites? If we were to run through them all, the circumstances of action would be found trivial and unworthy of gods. Still,
every one supposes that they *live* and therefore that they are active;
we cannot suppose them to sleep like Endymion. Now if you take away
from a living being action, and still more production, what is left but
contemplation? Therefore the activity of God, which surpasses all others
in blessedness, must be contemplative; and of human activities, therefore,
that which is most akin to this must be most of the nature of happiness.

This is indicated, too, by the fact that the other animals have no
share in happiness, being completely deprived of such activity. For while
the whole life of the gods is blessed, and that of men too in so far
as some likeness of such activity belongs to them, none of the other
animals is happy, since they in no way share in contemplation. Happiness
extends, then, just so far as contemplation does, and those to whom
contemplation more fully belongs are more truly happy, not as a mere
concomitant but in virtue of the contemplation; for this is in itself precious. Happiness, therefore, must be some form of contemplation. . . .

Now he who exercises his reason and cultivates it seems to be both
in the best state of mind and most dear to the gods. For if the gods
have any care for human affairs, as they are thought to have, it would
be reasonable both that they should delight in that which was best
and most akin to them (i.e. reason) and that they should reward those
who love and honour this most, as caring for the things that are dear
to them and acting both rightly and nobly. And that all these attributes
belong most of all to the philosopher is manifest. He, therefore, is the
dearest to the gods. And he who is that will presumably be also the
happiest; so that in this way too the philosopher will more than any
other be happy. . . .

Now some think that we are made good by nature, others by habituation, others by teaching. Nature's part evidently does not depend on
us, but as a result of some divine causes is present in those who are
truly fortunate; while argument and teaching, we may suspect, are not
powerful with all men, but the soul of the student must first have been
cultivated by means of habits for noble joy and noble hatred, like earth
which is to nourish the seed. For he who lives as passion directs will
not hear argument that dissuades him, nor understand it if he does;
and how can we persuade one in such a state to change his ways. And
in general passion seems to yield not to argument but to force. The

character, then, must somehow be there already with a kinship to virtue, loving what is noble and hating what is base.

But it is difficult to get from youth up a right training for virtue if one has not been brought up under right laws; for to live temperately and hardily is not pleasant to most people, especially when they are young. For this reason their nurture and occupations should be fixed by law; for they will not be painful when they have become customary. But it is surely not enough that when they are young they should get the right nurture and attention; since they must, even when they are grown up, practise and be habituated to them, we shall need laws for this as well, and generally speaking to cover the whole of life; for most people obey necessity rather than argument, and punishments rather than the sense of what is noble.

This is why some think that legislators ought to stimulate men to virtue and urge them forward by the motive of the noble, on the assumption that those who have been well advanced by the formation of habits will attend to such influences; and that punishments and penalties should be imposed on those who disobey and are of inferior nature, while the incurably bad should be completely banished. . . .

Now it is best that there should be a public and proper care for such matters; but if they are neglected by the community it would seem right for each man to help his children and friends towards virtue, and that they should have the power, or at least the will, to do this.

It would seem from what has been said that he can do this better if he makes himself capable of legislating. For public control is plainly effected by laws, and good control by good laws; whether written or unwritten would seem to make no difference, nor whether they are laws providing for the education of individuals or of groups—any more than it does in the case of music or gymnastics and other such pursuits. For as in cities laws and prevailing types of character have force, so in households do the injunctions and the habits of the father, and these have even more because of the tie of blood and the benefits he confers; for the children start with a natural affection and disposition to obey. Further, private education has an advantage over public, as private medical treatment has; for while in general rest and abstinence from food are good for a man in a fever, for a particular man they may not be; and a boxer presumably does not prescribe the same style of fighting to all his pupils. It would seem, then, that the detail is worked out with more precision if the control is private; for each person is more likely to get what suits his case.

But the details can be best looked after, one by one, by a doctor or gymnastic instructor or any one else who has the general knowledge of what is good for every one or for people of a certain kind (for the sciences both are said to be, and are, concerned with what is universal); not but what some particular detail may perhaps be well looked after by an unscientific person, if he has studied accurately in the light of experience what happens in each case, just as some people seem to be their own best doctors, though they could give no help to any one else. None the less, it will perhaps be agreed that if a man does wish to become master of an art or science he must go to the universal, and come to know it as well as possible; for, as we have said, it is with this that the sciences are concerned.

And surely he who wants to make men, whether many or few, better by his care must try to become capable of legislating, if it is through laws that we can become good. For to get any one whatever—any one who is put before us—into the right condition is not for the first chance comer; if any one can do it, it is the man who knows, just as in medicine and all other matters which give scope for care and prudence.

Politics

In the *Politics* Aristotle turns to the problem of how the state can best be organized in order to achieve the good life for its citizens. His analysis is based on his comparative study of the constitutions of 158 Greek city-states. Despite the breadth of his research, his formula betrays the extent to which he, like all of us, was imprisoned by the assumptions of his own culture, for his ideal state is founded upon the institution of slavery and it excludes from power all those groups—women, manual workers, tradesmen—conventionally held in low esteem. Aristotle always sees the individual in the context of society. The citizen belongs to the state and hence the state is justified in molding him to suit the form of government that prevails. Since education is the chief means for producing the model citizen, Aristotle seeks to sketch out the type of education that will be appropriate in his ideal state. He raises a question with which men still grapple—whether education should be concerned primarily with the development of intellectual or moral qualities. The child, Aristotle maintains, should be acquainted only with that which liberalizes, not with that which vulgarizes or debases. Paid work is degrading and hence a liberal education will not prepare for it. Here we have the genesis of a persistent and pernicious split in Western thinking—the liberal/vocational dichotomy that still dominates much thought about education. We can see in Aristotle's views the inspiration for the ideal of the amateur gentleman: the liberally educated citizen does not give himself completely to professional studies, for this would be to abandon himself in unbalanced fashion to the work sector of life. Leisure is better than work: we work only in order to be free from work, just as we go to war in order to have peace. Since it is through leisure that man realizes himself most fully, the highest kind of education is that which prepares him to enjoy leisure. This is an important extension of the idea of the education of the citizen, for Aristotle's model is clearly not the citizen dominated by work but the liberal, rational citizen—one who is free in at least two senses. He is freed from the burden of degrading work through his position of social and economic privilege, and freed for the activity of intellectual contemplation through his education. Hence Aristotle's model is essentially aristocratic. Based upon class privilege and intellectual superiority, it was ideally suited to provide inspiration for upper-class education in subsequent centuries.

This translation of *Aristotle's Politics*, by Benjamin Jowett, introduction by H. W. C. Davis, was published in Oxford in 1905 by the Clarendon Press.

BOOK VIII

No one will doubt that the legislator should direct his attention above all to the education of youth, or that the neglect of education does harm to states. The citizen should be moulded to suit the form of government under which he lives. For each government has a peculiar character which originally formed and which continues to preserve it. The character of democracy creates democracy, and the character of oligarchy creates oligarchy; and always the better the character, the better the government.

Now for the exercise of any faculty or art a previous training and habituation are required; clearly therefore for the practice of virtue. And since the whole city has one end, it is manifest that education should be one and the same for all, and that it should be public, and not private—not as at present, when every one looks after his own children separately, and gives them separate instruction of the sort which he thinks best; the training in things which are of common interest should be the same for all. Neither must we suppose that any one of the citizens belongs to himself, for they all belong to the state, and are each of them a part of the state, and the care of each part is inseparable from the care of the whole. In this particular the Lacedaemonians are to be praised, for they take the greatest pains about their children, and make education the business of the state.

That education should be regulated by law and should be an affair of state is not to be denied, but what should be the character of this public education, and how young persons should be educated, are questions which remain to be considered. For mankind are by no means agreed about the things to be taught, whether we look to virtue or the best life. Neither is it clear whether education is more concerned with intellectual or with moral virtue. The existing practice is perplexing; no one knows on what principle we should proceed—should the useful in life, or should virtue, or should the higher knowledge, be the aim of our training; all three opinions have been entertained. Again, about the means there is no agreement; for different persons, starting with different ideas about the nature of virtue, naturally disagree about the practice of it. There can be no doubt that children should be taught those useful things which are really necessary, but not all things; for occupations are divided into liberal and illiberal; and to young children should be imparted only such kinds of knowledge as will be useful to them without vulgarizing them. And any occupation, art, or science, which makes the body or soul or mind of the freeman less fit for the practice or exercise of virtue, is vulgar; wherefore we call those arts vulgar which tend to deform the body, and likewise all paid employments, for they absorb and degrade the mind. There are also some liberal arts quite proper for a freeman to acquire, but only in a certain degree, and if he attend to them too closely, in order to attain perfection in them, the same evil effects will follow. The object also which a man sets before him makes a great difference; if he does or learns anything for his own sake or for the sake of his friends, or with a view to excellence, the action will not appear illiberal; but if done for the sake of others, the very same action will be thought menial and servile. The received subjects of instruction, as I have already remarked, are partly of a liberal and partly of an illiberal character.

The customary branches of education are in number four; they are— (1) reading and writing, (2) gymnastic exercises, (3) music, to which is sometimes added (4) drawing. Of these, reading and writing and drawing are regarded as useful for the purposes of life in a variety of ways, and gymnastic exercises are thought to infuse courage. Concerning music a doubt may be raised—in our own day most men cultivate it for the sake of pleasure, but originally it was included in education, because nature herself, as has been often said, requires that we should be able not only to work well, but to use leisure well; for, as I must repeat once and again, the first principle of all action is leisure. Both are required, but leisure is better than occupation; and therefore the question must be asked in good earnest, what ought we to do when at leisure? Clearly we ought not to be amusing ourselves, for then amusement would be the end of life. But if this is inconceivable, and yet amid serious occupations amusement is needed more than at other times (for he who is hard at work has need of relaxation, and amusement gives relaxation, whereas occupation is always accompanied with exertion and effort), at suitable times we should introduce amusements, and they should be our medicines, for the emotion which they create in the soul is a relaxation, and from the pleasure we obtain rest. Leisure of itself gives pleasure and happiness and enjoyment of life, which are experienced, not by the busy man, but by those who have leisure. For he who is occupied has in view some end which he has not attained; but happiness is an end which all men deem to be accompanied with pleasure and not with pain. This pleasure, however, is regarded differently by different persons, and varies according to the habit of individuals; the pleasure of the best man is the best, and springs from the noblest sources. It is clear, then, that there are branches of learning and education which we must study with a view to the enjoyment of leisure, and these are to be valued for their own sake; whereas those kinds of knowledge which are useful in business are to be deemed necessary, and exist for the sake of other things. And therefore our fathers admitted music into education, not on the ground either of its necessity or utility, for it is not necessary, nor indeed useful in the same manner as reading and writing, which are useful in money-making, in the management of a household, in the acquisition of knowledge and in political life, nor like drawing, useful for a more correct judgment of the works of artists, nor again like gymnastic, which gives health and strength; for neither of these is to be gained from music. There remains, then, the use of music for intellectual enjoyment in leisure; which appears to have been the reason of its introduction, this being one of the ways in which it is thought that a freeman should pass his leisure; as Homer says,

'How good is it to invite men to the pleasant feast,'

and afterwards he speaks of others whom he describes as inviting

'The bard who would delight them all.'

And in another place Odysseus says there is no better way of passing life than when

'Men's hearts are merry and the banqueters in the hall, sitting in order, hear the voice of the minstrel.'

It is evident, then, that there is a sort of education in which parents should train their sons, not as being useful or necessary, but because it is liberal or noble. Whether this is of one kind only, or of more than one, and if so, what they are, and how they are to be imparted, must hereafter be determined. Thus much we are now in a position to say that the ancients witness to us; for their opinion may be gathered from the act that music is one of the received and traditional branches of education. Further, it is clear that children should be instructed in some useful things—for example, in reading and writing—not only for their usefulness, but also because many other sorts of knowledge are acquired through them. With a like view they may be taught drawing, not to prevent their making mistakes in their own purchases, or in order that they may not be imposed upon in the buying or selling of articles, but rather because it makes them judges of the beauty of the human form. To be always seeking after the useful does not become free and exalted souls. Now it is clear that in education habit must go before reason, and the body before the mind; and therefore boys should be handed over to the trainer, who creates in them the proper habit of body, and to the wrestling-master, who teaches them their exercises.

Metaphysics

In the *Metaphysics,* Aristotle goes further in delineating what he means by the rational man. He suggests that the desire to know is innate in all men. But not all men are capable of attaining the same depth of knowledge. There is a distinction, Aristotle suggests, between art, which is a knowledge of universals, and experience, which is a knowledge of particulars. He who has, through art, a knowledge of theory and causes is wiser than he who has only experience. A simple test of the nature of a man's knowledge is that if he has a firm grasp of it he will be able to teach it. Some of our recent learning theory has been echoing this view of Aristotle that the rational, educated man is one whose knowledge transcends the level of isolated facts and events and reaches the level of general principles and causes.

This translation of the *Metaphysica,* by W. D. Ross, appears in Volume VIII of *The Works of Aristotle,* edited by W. D. Ross, published in Oxford in 1928 by the Clarendon Press, with whose permission it is reprinted.

BOOK A

All men by nature desire to know. An indication of this is the delight we take in our senses; for even apart from their usefulness they are loved for themselves; and above all others the sense of sight. For not only with a view to action, but even when we are not going to do anything, we prefer seeing (one might say) to everything else. The reason is that this, most of all the senses, makes us know and brings to light many differences between things.

By nature animals are born with the faculty of sensation, and from sensation memory is produced in some of them, though not in others.

And therefore the former are more intelligent and apt at learning than those which cannot remember; those which are incapable of hearing sounds are intelligent though they cannot be taught, e.g. the bee, and any other race of animals that may be like it; and those which besides memory have this sense of hearing can be taught.

The animals other than man live by appearances and memories, and have but little of connected experience; but the human race lives also by art and reasonings. Now from memory experience is produced in men; for the several memories of the same thing produce finally the capacity for a single experience. And experience seems pretty much like science and art, but really science and art come to men *through* experience; for experience made art,' as Polus says, 'but inexperience luck.' Now art arises when from many notions gained by experience one universal judgement about a class of objects is produced. For to have a judgement that when Callias was ill of this disease this did him good, and similarly in the case of Socrates and in many individual cases, is a matter of experience; but to judge that it has done good to all persons of a certain constitution, marked off in one class, when they were ill of this disease, e.g. to phlegmatic or bilious people when burning with fever—this is a matter of art.

With a view to action experience seems in no respect inferior to art, and men of experience succeed even better than those who have theory without experience. (The reason is that experience is knowledge of individuals, art of universals, and actions and productions are all concerned with the individual; for the physician does not cure *man*, except in an incidental way, but Callias or Socrates or some other called by some such individual name, who happens to be a man. If, then, a man has the theory without the experience, and recognizes the universal but does not know the individual included in this, he will often fail to cure; for it is the individual that is to be cured.) But yet we think that *knowledge* and *understanding* belong to art rather than to experience, and we suppose artists to be wiser than men of experience (which implies that Wisdom depends in all cases rather on knowledge); and this because the former know the cause, but the latter do not. For men of experience know that the thing is so, but do not know why, while the others know the 'why' and the cause. Hence we think also that the master-workers in each craft are more honourable and know in a truer sense and are wiser than the manual workers, because they know the causes of the things that are done (we think the manual workers are like certain lifeless things which act indeed, but act without knowing what they do, as fire burns—but while the lifeless things perform each of their functions by a natural tendency, the labourers perform them through habit); thus we view them as being wiser not in virtue of being able to act, but of having the theory for themselves and knowing the causes. And in general it is a sign of the man who knows and of the man who does not know, that the former can teach, and therefore we think art more truly knowledge than experience is; for artists can teach, and men of mere experience cannot.

Again, we do not regard any of the senses as Wisdom; yet surely these give the most authoritative knowledge of particulars. But they do not tell us the 'why' of anything—e.g., why fire is hot; they only say *that* it is hot.

At first he who invented any art whatever that went beyond the common perceptions of man was naturally admired by men, not only because there was something useful in the inventions, but because he was thought wise and superior to the rest. But as more arts were invented, and some were directed to the necessities of life, others to recreation, the inventors of the latter were naturally always regarded as wiser than the inventors of the former, because their branches of knowledge did not aim at utility. Hence when all such inventions were already established, the sciences which do not aim at giving pleasure or at the necessities of life were discovered, and first in the places where men first began to have leisure. This is why the mathematical arts were founded in Egypt; for there the priestly caste was allowed to be at leisure.

We have said in the *Ethics* what the difference is between art and science and the other kindred faculties; but the point of our present discussion is this, that all men suppose what is called Wisdom to deal with the first causes and the principles of things; so that, as has been said before, the man of experience is thought to be wiser than the possessors of any sense-perception whatever, the artist wiser than the men of experience, the master-worker than the mechanic, and the theoretical kinds of knowledge to be more of the nature of Wisdom than the productive. Clearly then Wisdom is knowledge about certain principles and causes.

Since we are seeking this knowledge, we must inquire of what kind are the causes and the principles, the knowledge of which is Wisdom. If one were to take the notions we have about the wise man, this might perhaps make the answer more evident. We suppose first, then, that the wise man knows all things, as far as possible, although he has not knowledge of each of them in detail; secondly, that he who can learn things that are difficult, and not easy for man to know, is wise (sense-perception is common to all, and therefore easy and no mark of Wisdom); again, that he who is more exact and more capable of teaching the causes is wiser, in every branch of knowledge; and that of the sciences, also, that which is desirable on its own account and for the sake of knowing it is more of the nature of Wisdom than that which is desirable on account of its results, and the superior science is more of the nature of Wisdom than the ancillary; for the wise man must not be ordered but must order, and he must not obey another, but the less wise must obey *him.*

3 The Orator: Isocrates

The principal challenge in the life of Isocrates (436–338 B.C.) was war, with its political and personal consequences and its illusory promise of curing ills. He was born shortly before the outbreak of the long and disastrous Peloponnesian War. On the personal level, the war presented a severe test for Isocrates, for in it he lost all that his father, a prosperous flute manufacturer, had left him. He responded to the crisis, however, by opening a school for paying pupils. As it happened, his school of oratory became his primary claim to importance: he made a considerable fortune from the fees; he attracted as his pupils some of the ablest young men of his day, many of whom subsequently became leaders in their fields; and, partly through them, he achieved a position of great influence.

War also did much to affect the way in which he attempted to use his influence. The Peloponnesian War had broken the power of the Greek states. Isocrates was deeply concerned with helping Greece to recover so that it might spread its beneficent contribution of culture into the barbarian world. He believed that the internal rivalries and wars of the Greek states jeopardized their chances of achieving greatness and prosperity. It was a problem basically the same as that presented to the world today by residual and resurgent nationalism. The Greeks declined because they failed to subordinate their local loyalties to that of a common unity: we shall suffer a similar fate if we fail to profit from their experience.

Isocrates attempted to bring about his goal of unity and prosperity for Greece through the dual means of his writing and his teaching. He saw his contribution as helping to provide Athens with able political leaders who would bring about the goals he envisaged. In pursuing this end he created, in the idea of the orator as the ideally educated man, a model that has had an abiding influence on Western education. The orator is a man of wide and deep culture—of *paideia*. And this culture is gained predominantly through language. Hence the orator is a man of language, of the Word, the *logos*. This persisting linguistic emphasis has been one of the strengths and glories of Western education, but it has also accounted for some of our blindness to other dimensions of human excellence. It is important to recognize, however, that Isocrates himself was primarily interested in the *moral* consequences of education. He believed that linguistic and intellectual study would bring about a transformation in character and conduct. He had faith in the power of knowledge to reform morals. This belief became one of the great subsequent justifications of scholarship.

There was little to be said, in Isocrates' opinion, for an education that bore no practical consequences in terms of conduct or action. He was impatient with the unworldliness of Plato and some of the other Socratics. He wanted his model to be a man who could achieve the best possible life in an imperfect world. As his interest in political questions shows, he was concerned with *this* world rather than with some hypothetical, perfect world. It was this lively awareness of the art of the possible that made his ideas so congenial to the pragmatic Romans. Isocrates' model of the orator became, in the hands of men like Quintilian, an ideal that dominated the Roman world. Thus, at the heart of the Western educational tradition there grew a tension, or even a paradox, for the model that Isocrates created was a man essentially concerned with practical action, but his educational focus was essentially linguistic. For Isocrates, there was nothing inconsistent in this. But in subsequent years the educated man of this type has often used words as a *substitute* for action, and a linguistic facility as a means to escape the hard edge of reality. Words and conduct have not always borne, for the educated man, the consonant relationship that Isocrates envisioned.

Against the Sophists

Although Isocrates considered himself a sophist, he took pains to distinguish himself from other sophists. He did this nowhere more clearly than in his tract *Against the Sophists*. This oration was published around 389 B.C., some three years after the opening of Isocrates' school in Athens, and was probably intended as an advertisement for the purposes and methods of that school. However, all that remains to us of the essay is the first part, which consists mainly of an attack on other forms of education. He criticizes the sophists of the rhetorical school for teaching oratory as if it was merely a bag of tricks that could be collected by anyone irrespective of native ability. The requisites of a good orator, in Isocrates' view, are, in descending order of importance, natural ability, practical experience, and formal training. He condemns those who regard oratory as a matter of forensic skill rather than as a quest for justice and truth. He is contemptuous of those who claim to be able to teach infallible rules for the attainment of virtue and success. Our ignorance of the future and the limited power of education combine to render such a hope nugatory. The best that we can expect from education is that it will improve our capacity to meet the unpredictable problems of life with wisdom and ingenuity.

This passage is from Volume II of Isocrates, *Orations*, translated by George Norlin, published in Cambridge, Massachusetts, in 1956 by Harvard University Press, Loeb Classical Library, with whose permission it is reprinted.

For myself, I should have preferred above great riches that philosophy had as much power as these men claim; for, possibly, I should not have been the very last in the profession nor had the least share in its profits. But since it has no such power, I could wish that this prating might cease. For I note that the bad repute which results therefrom does not affect the offenders only, but that all the rest of us who are in the same profession share in the opprobrium.

But I marvel when I observe these men setting themselves up as instructors of youth who cannot see that they are applying the analogy of an art with hard and fast rules to a creative process. For, excepting these teachers, who does not know that the art of using letters remains fixed and unchanged, so that we continually and invariably use the same letters for the same purposes, while exactly the reverse is true of the art of discourse? For what has been said by one speaker is not equally useful for the speaker who comes after him; on the contrary, he is accounted most skilled in this art who speaks in a manner worthy of his subject and yet is able to discover in it topics which are nowise the same as those used by others. But the greatest proof of the difference between these two arts is that oratory is good only if it has the qualities of fitness for the occasion, propriety of style, and originality of treatment, while in the case of letters there is no such need whatsoever. So that those who make use of such analogies ought more justly to pay out than to accept fees, since they attempt to teach others when they are themselves in great need of instruction.

However, if it is my duty not only to rebuke others, but also to set forth my own views, I think all intelligent people will agree with me that while many of those who have pursued philosophy have remained in private life, others, on the other hand, who have never taken lessons from any one of the sophists have become able orators and statesmen. For ability, whether in speech or in any other activity, is found in those who are well endowed by nature and have been schooled by practical experience. Formal training makes such men more skilful and more resourceful in discovering the possibilities of a subject; for it teaches them to take from a readier source the topics which they otherwise hit upon in haphazard fashion. But it cannot fully fashion men who are without natural aptitude into good debaters or writers, although it is capable of leading them on to self-improvement and to a greater degree of intelligence on many subjects.

But I desire, now that I have gone this far, to speak more clearly on these matters. For I hold that to obtain a knowledge of the elements out of which we make and compose all discourses is not so very difficult if anyone entrusts himself, not to those who make rash promises, but to those who have some knowledge of these things. But to choose from these elements those which should be employed for each subject, to join them together, to arrange them properly, and also, not to miss what the occasion demands but appropriately to adorn the whole speech with striking thoughts and to clothe it in flowing and melodious phrase—these things, I hold, require much study and are the task of a vigorous and imaginative mind: for this, the student must not only have the requisite aptitude but he must learn the different kinds of discourse and practise himself in their use; and the teacher, for his part, must so expound the principles of the art with the utmost possible exactness as to leave out nothing that can be taught, and, for the rest, he must in himself set such an example of oratory that the students who have taken form under his instruction and are able to pattern after him will, from the outset, show in their speaking a degree of grace and charm which is not found in others. When all of these requisites are found together, then the devotees of philosophy will achieve complete success; but according as any one of the things which I have mentioned is lacking, to this extent must their disciples of necessity fall below the mark.

Now as for the sophists who have lately sprung up and have very recently embraced these pretensions, even though they flourish at the moment, they will all, I am sure, come round to this position. But there remain to be considered those who lived before our time and did not scruple to write the so-called arts of oratory. These must not be dismissed without rebuke, since they professed to teach how to conduct law-suits, picking out the most discredited of terms, which the enemies, not the champions, of this discipline might have been expected to employ—and that too although this facility, in so far as it can be taught, is of no greater aid to forensic than to all other discourse. But they were much worse than those who dabble in disputation; for although the latter expounded such captious theories that were anyone to cleave to them in practice he would at once be in all manner of trouble, they did, at any rate, make professions of virtue and sobriety in their teaching, whereas the former, although exhorting others to study political discourse, neglected all the good things which this study affords, and became nothing more than professors of meddlesomeness and greed.

And yet those who desire to follow the true precepts of this discipline may, if they will, be helped more speedily towards honesty of character than towards facility in oratory. And let no one suppose that I claim that just living can be taught; for, in a word, I hold that there does not exist an art of the kind which can implant sobriety and justice in depraved natures. Nevertheless, I do think that the study of political discourse can help more than any other thing to stimulate and form such qualities of character.

Antidosis

This long discourse, written around 383 B.C. when Isocrates was eighty-two years old, constitutes the principal source of material on his educational ideas. It is cast in the form of a defense against a supposed charge that he had (like Socrates) corrupted his pupils through his teaching. There are frequent echoes in it of Socrates' defense in the *Apology*. In the course of defending his own methods and principles of teaching, Isocrates presents as a model for our appraisal his favorite pupil, Timotheus, who became a famous Athenian general. In 356 B.C. Timotheus was tried for alleged misconduct and heavily fined. Unable to pay, he left Athens and died shortly afterward. Isocrates describes his favorite to us in citing the qualities of a good general: honest and wise, he showed good judgment, powers of organization, and fortitude in the face of hardship; he was restrained and magnanimous in victory, always treating his enemies with gentleness and consideration. His weakness, in Isocrates' view, was that he could not bring himself to court the favor of the Athenian populace. It was this that led to his downfall. Isocrates then goes on to outline his ideas on the way in which the art of oratory should be developed in young men. He repeats his contention that, no matter how excellent the education, it can never form a good orator out of one who lacks innate talent. Today the evidence of the results of early environmental influences on the development of talent would make us much more cautious about dogmatically classifying people according to their "innate" abilities. Isocrates was no doubt impressed by the fact that he himself lacked the two qualities that he considered most essential to the achievement of excellence in oratory: a good voice and self-assurance. The power of speech Isocrates regards as nothing less than the means that has enabled man to achieve civilization. The ability to speak well is the best indication of a man's understanding. Another of Isocrates' assumptions, which the evidence would lead us to question today, is that there are people who are by nature vicious and depraved. As we gain more knowledge we find more examples of external influences (often in very early life) bearing a causal relationship to vicious human traits. However, although he does not think that education can make virtuous men out of those who are "naturally" vicious, Isocrates does suggest that a skillful education in the art of oratory can improve the character of those who engage in it and thus bring them closer to the model that he has presented to us.

These selections are from Volume II of Isocrates, *Orations*, translated by George Norlin, published in Cambridge, Massachusetts, in 1956 by Harvard University Press, Loeb Classical Library, with whose permission they are reprinted.

I think you would like to have me explain to you why in the world it is that some of the generals who have a high reputation among you and are thought to be great fighters have not been able to take even a village, while Timotheus, who lacks a robust physique and has not knocked about with itinerant armies but has shared with you the duties of a citizen, has accomplished such great things. What I have to say on this question will no doubt be offensive, but it will not be without profit for you to hear it. Timotheus was superior to all the rest in that he did not hold the same views as you with regard to the affairs of the Hellenes and of your allies and the manner in which they should be directed. For you elect as your generals men who have the most robust bodies and who have served in many campaigns with foreign armies, thinking that under their leadership you will have some success. Timotheus, on the other hand, used these men as captains and division-commanders, while he, himself, showed his ability in the very things which it is necessary for a good general to know.

What, then, are the requisites of a good general and what ability do they involve? For they cannot be summed up in a word, but must be explained clearly. First of all is the ability to know against whom and with whose help to make war; for this is the first requisite of good strategy, and if one makes any mistake about this, the result is inevitably a war which is disadvantageous, difficult, and to no purpose. Well, in this kind of sagacity there has never been anyone like him or even comparable with him, as may easily be seen from his deeds themselves. For, although he undertook most of his wars without support from the city, he brought them all to a successful issue, and convinced all the Hellenes that he won them justly. And what greater or clearer proof of his wise judgement could one adduce than this fact?

What, then, is the second requisite of a good general? It is the ability to collect an army which is adequate to the war in hand, and to organize and to employ it to good advantage. Now, that Timotheus understood how to employ his forces to good purpose, his achievements themselves have shown; that in the ability to recruit armies which were splendidly equipped and reflected honour upon Athens he excelled all other men, no one even of his enemies would dare to gainsay; and, furthermore, in the power both to bear the privations and hardships of army life, and again to find abundant resources, who of the men who were with him in the field would not pronounce him incomparable? For they know that at the beginning of his campaigns, owing to the fact that he received nothing from Athens, he found himself in great extremities, but that, even with this handicap, he was able to bring his fortunes round to the point where he not only prevailed over our enemies but paid his soldiers in full.

These are great things and compel our admiration; but the facts which I now give entitle him to even greater praise. For although he saw that you respected only the kind of generals who threatened and tried to terrify the other cities and were always for setting up some revolution or other among your allies, he did not fall in with your prejudices, nor was he willing to enhance his own reputation to the injury of Athens; on the contrary, he made it the object of his thought and of his actions to see to it that no one of the cities of Hellas should be afraid of him, but that all should feel secure excepting those which did wrong; for he realized that men who are afraid hate those who inspire this feeling in them, and that it was due to the friendship of the other cities that Athens rose to great power and prosperity, just as it was due to their hatred that she barely escaped the most disastrous fate. Bearing in mind these facts, he used the power of Athens in order to subdue her enemies, and the force of his own character in order to win the good will of the rest of the world, believing that this is a greater and nobler kind of generalship than to conquer many cities many times in battle. So concerned was he that none of the cities should in the slightest degree suspect him of sinister designs that whenever he intended to take his fleet to any of the cities which had been remiss in their contributions, he sent word to the authorities and announced his coming beforehand, lest his appearance without warning in front of their ports might plunge them into disquiet and confusion; and if he happened to harbour his fleet in any place, he would never permit his soldiers to plunder and pillage and sack the people's houses, but took as great precautions to prevent such an occurrence as the owners would take to guard their own possessions; for his mind was not upon winning for himself the good opinion of his soldiers by such licence, but upon winning for Athens the good opinion of the Hellenes. Moreover, when cities had been taken by him in battle, he would treat them with a mildness and a consideration for their rights which no one else has ever shown to allies in war; for he thought that if he showed such an attitude toward those who had made war upon him, he could give no greater guarantee that he would never bring himself to wrong the others.

Therefore it was that, because of the reputation which this conduct gave him, many of the cities which had no love for Athens used to welcome him with gates thrown wide; and he, in turn, never set up any disturbance in them, but just as he found them governed when he entered their gates, so he left them when he passed out.

And now to sum up all this: In other times many calamities were wont to be visited upon the Hellenes, but, under his leadership, no one can point to cities devastated, governments overthrown, men murdered or driven into exile, or any other of those ills that are irreparable. Nay, so complete was the respite from such misfortunes in his day that, so far back as we can remember, he is the only general under whom no complaint was raised against Athens by the other Hellenes. And surely you ought to find your ideal of a good general, not in one who by a single stroke of good fortune has attained, like Lysander, a success which it has been the lot of no other man to achieve, but one who, though loaded with many difficult responsibilities of all sorts, has always discharged them with honesty and wisdom. And just this has been the fortune of Timotheus. . . .

He has often been advised by me, among others, that while men who are in public life and desire to be in favour must adopt the principle of doing what is most serviceable and noble and of saying what is most true and just, yet they must at the same time not neglect to study and consider well how in everything they say and do they may convince the people of their graciousness and human sympathy since those who are careless of these matters are thought by their fellow-citizens to be disagreeable and offensive. "You observe," I would say to him, "the nature of the multitude, how susceptible they are to flattery that they like those who cultivate their favour better than those who seek their good; and that they prefer those who cheat them with beaming smiles and brotherly love to those who serve them with dignity and reserve. You have paid no attention to these things, but are of the opinion that if you attend honestly to your enterprises abroad, the people at home also will think well of you. But this is not the case, and the very contrary is wont to happen. For if you please the people in Athens, no matter what you do they will not judge your conduct by the facts but will construe it in a light favourable to you; and if you make mistakes, they will overlook them, while if you succeed, they will exalt your success to the high heaven. For good will has this effect upon all men.

"But you, while seeking by every means in your power to win for Athens the good will of the rest of the Hellenes, because you recognize its great advantages, nevertheless do not consider that there is any need to secure for yourself the good will of Athens; nay, you who have benefited the city in ways beyond calculation are less esteemed than those who have done nothing of note.

"And you could expect nothing else; for such men cultivate the public orators and the speakers who are effective in private gatherings and who profess to be authorities on every subject, while you not only neglect to do this, but actually make an open breach between yourself and the orators who are from time to time the most influential.

"And yet I wonder if you realize how many men have either come to grief or failed of honour because of the misrepresentations of these orators; how many in the generations that are past have left no name, although they were far better and worthier men than those who are celebrated in song and on the tragic stage. But the latter, you see, found their poets and historians, while the others secured no one to hymn their praises. Therefore, if you will only heed me and be sensible, you will not despise these men whom the multitude are wont to believe, not only with reference to each one of their fellow-citizens, but also with reference to the affairs of the whole state, but you will in some measure show attention and pay court to them in order that you may be held in honour both because of your own deeds and because of their words."

When I would speak to him in this wise, he would admit that I was right, but he could not change his nature. He was a good man and true, a credit to Athens and to Hellas, but he could not lower himself to the level of people who are intolerant of their natural superiors. So it was that the orators occupied themselves with inventing many false charges against him, and the multitude with drinking them in. . . .

In my treatment of the art of discourse, I desire, like the genealogists, to start at the beginning. It is acknowledged that the nature of man is compounded of two parts, the physical and the mental, and no one would deny that of these two the mind comes first and is of greater worth; for it is the function of the mind to decide both on personal and on public questions, and of the body to be servant to the judgements of the mind. Since this is so, certain of our ancestors, long before our time, seeing that many arts had been devised for other things, while none had been prescribed for the body and for the mind, invented and bequeathed to us two disciplines—physical training for the body of which gymnastics is a part, and, for the mind, philosophy, which I am going to explain. These are twin arts—parallel and complementary—by which their masters prepare the mind to become more intelligent and the body to become more serviceable, not separating sharply the two kinds of education, but using similar methods of instruction, excercise, and other forms of discipline.

For when they take their pupils in hand, the physical trainers instruct their followers in the postures which have been devised for bodily contests, while the teachers of philosophy impart all the forms of discourse in which the mind expresses itself. Then, when they have made them familiar and thoroughly conversant with these lessons, they set them at exercises, habituate them to work, and require them to combine in practice the particular things which they have learned, in order that they may grasp them more firmly and bring their theories into closer touch with the occasions for applying them—I say "theories," for no system of knowledge can possibly cover these occasions, since in all cases they elude our science. Yet those who most apply their minds to them and are able to discern the consequences which for the most part grow out of them, will most often meet these occasions in the right way.

Watching over them and training them in this manner, both the teachers of gymnastic and the teachers of discourse are able to advance their pupils to a point where they are better men and where they are stronger in their thinking or in the use of their bodies. However, neither class of teachers is in possession of a science by which they can make capable athletes or capable orators out of whomsoever they please. They can contribute in some degree to these results, but these powers are never found in their perfection save in those who excel by virtue both of talent and of training.

I have given you now some impression of what philosophy is. But I think that you will get a still clearer idea of its powers if I tell you what professions I make to those who want to become my pupils. I say to them that if they are to excel in oratory or in managing affairs or in any line of work, they must, first of all, have a natural aptitude for that which they have elected to do; secondly, they must submit to training and master the knowledge of their particular subject, what-

ever it may be in each case; and, finally, they must become versed
and practised in the use and application of their art; for only on these
conditions can they become fully competent and pre-eminent in any
line of endeavour. In this process, master and pupil each has his place;
no one but the pupil can furnish the necessary capacity; no one but
the master, the ability to impart knowledge; while both have a part
in the exercises of practical application: for the master must painstak-
ingly direct his pupil, and the latter must rigidly follow the master's
instructions.

Now these observations apply to any and all the arts. If anyone, ignoring the other arts, were to ask me which of these factors has the greatest
power in the education of an orator I should answer that natural ability
is paramount and comes before all else. For given a man with a mind
which is capable of finding out and learning the truth and of working
hard and remembering what it learns, and also with a voice and a
clarity of utterance which are able to captivate the audience, not only
by what he says, but by the music of his words, and, finally, with an
assurance which is not an expression of bravado, but which, tempered
by sobriety, so fortifies the spirit that he is no less at ease in addressing
all his fellow-citizens than in reflecting to himself—who does not know
that such a man might, without the advantage of an elaborate education
and with only a superficial and common training, be an orator such
as has never, perhaps, been seen among the Hellenes? Again, we know
that men who are less generously endowed by nature but excel in experience and practice, not only improve upon themselves, but surpass others
who, though highly gifted, have been too negligent of their talents.
It follows, therefore, that either one of these factors may produce an
able speaker or an able man of affairs, but both of them combined
in the same person might produce a man incomparable among his
fellows.

These, then, are my views as to the relative importance of native
ability and practice. I cannot, however, make a like claim for education;
its powers are not equal nor comparable to theirs. For if one should
take lessons in all the principles of oratory and master them with the
greatest thoroughness, he might, perhaps, become a more pleasing
speaker than most, but let him stand up before the crowd and lack
one thing only, namely, assurance, and he would not be able to utter
a word. . . .

We ought, therefore, to think of the art of discourse just as we think
of the other arts, and not to form opposite judgements about similar
things, nor show ourselves intolerant toward that power which, of all
the faculties which belong to the nature of man, is the source of most

of our blessings. For in the other powers which we possess, as I have already said on a former occasion, we are in no respect superior to other living creatures; nay, we are inferior to many in swiftness and in strength and in other resources; but, because there has been implanted in us the power to persuade each other and to make clear to each other whatever we desire, not only have we escaped the life of wild beasts, but we have come together and founded cities and made laws and invented arts; and, generally speaking, there is no institution devised by man which the power of speech has not helped us to establish. For this it is which has laid down laws concerning things just and unjust, and things honourable and base; and if it were not for these ordinances we should not be able to live with one another. It is by this also that we confute the bad and extol the good. Through this we educate the ignorant and appraise the wise; for the power to speak well is taken as the surest index of a sound understanding, and discourse which is true and lawful and just is the outward image of a good and faithful soul. With this faculty we both contend against others on matters which are open to dispute and seek light for ourselves on things which are unknown; for the same arguments which we use in persuading others when we speak in public, we employ also when we deliberate in our own thoughts and, while we call eloquent those who are able to speak before a crowd, we regard as sage those who most skillfully debate their problems in their own minds. And, if there is need to speak in brief summary of this power, we shall find that none of the things which are done with intelligence take place without the help of speech, but that in all our actions as well as in all our thoughts speech is our guide, and is most employed by those who have the most wisdom. . . .

I believe that the teachers who are skilled in disputation and those who are occupied with astronomy and geometry and studies of that sort do not injure but, on the contrary, benefit their pupils, not so much as they profess, but more than others give them credit for. Most men see in such studies nothing but empty talk and hair-splitting; for none of these disciplines has any useful application either to private or to public affairs; nay, they are not even remembered for any length of time after they are learned because they do not attend us through life nor do they lend aid in what we do, but are wholy divorced from our necessities. But I am neither of this opinion nor am I far removed from it; rather it seems to me both that those who hold that this training is of no use in practical life are right and that those who speak in praise of it have truth on their side. If there is a contradiction in this statement, it is because these disciplines are different in their nature from the other studies which make up our education; for the other branches avail us only after we have gained a knowledge of them, whereas these studies can be of no benefit to us after we have mastered them unless we have elected to make our living from this source, and only help us while we are in the process of learning. For while we are occupied with the subtlety and exactness of astronomy and geometry and are forced to apply our minds to difficult problems, and are, in addition, being habituated to speak and apply ourselves to what is said and shown to us, and not to let our wits go wool-gathering, we gain the power, after being exercised and sharpened on these disciplines, of grasping and learning more easily and more quickly those subjects which are of more importance and of greater value. I do not, however, think it proper to apply the term "philosophy" to a training which is no help to us in the present either in our speech or in our actions, but rather I would call it a gymnastic of the mind and a preparation for philosophy. It is, to be sure, a study more advanced than that which boys in school pursue, but it is for the most part the same sort of thing; for they also when they have laboured through their lessons in grammar, music, and the other branches, are not a whit advanced in their ability to speak and deliberate on affairs, but they have increased their aptitude for mastering greater and more serious studies. I would, therefore, advise young men to spend some time on these disciplines, but not to allow their minds to be dried up by these barren subtleties, nor to be stranded on the speculations of the ancient sophists, who maintain, some of them, that the sum of things is made up of infinite elements; Empedocles that it is made up of four, with strife and love operating among them; Ion, of not more than three; Alcmaeon, of only two; Parmenides and Melissus, of one; and Gorgias, of none at all. For I think that such curiosities of thought are on a par with jugglers' tricks which, though they do not profit anyone, yet attract great crowds of the empty-minded, and I hold that men who want to do some good in the world must banish utterly from their interests all vain speculations and all activities which have no bearing on our lives.

Now I have spoken and advised you enough on these studies for the present. It remains to tell you about "wisdom" and "philosophy." It is true that if one were pleading a case on any other issue it would be out of place to discuss these words (for they are foreign to all litigation), but it is appropriate for me, since I am being tried on such an issue, and since I hold that what some people call philosophy is not entitled to that name, to define and explain to you what philosophy, properly conceived, really is. My view of this question is, as it happens, very simple. For since it is not in the nature of man to attain a science by the possession of which we can know positively what we should do or what we should say, in the next resort I hold that man to be wise who is able by his powers of conjecture to arrive generally at the best course, and I hold that man to be a philosopher who occupies himself with the studies from which he will most quickly gain that kind of insight. . . .

I consider that the kind of art which can implant honesty and justice in depraved natures has never existed and does not now exist, and that people who profess that power will grow weary and cease from their vain pretensions before such an education is ever found. But I do hold that people can become better and worthier if they conceive an ambition to speak well, if they become possessed of the desire to be able to persuade their hearers, and, finally, if they set their hearts on seizing their advantage—I do not mean "advantage" in the sense given to that word by the empty-minded, but advantage in the true meaning of that term; and that this is so I think I shall presently make clear.

For, in the first place, when anyone elects to speak or write discourses which are worthy of praise and honour, it is not conceivable that he will support causes which are unjust or petty or devoted to private quarrels, and not rather those which are great and honourable, devoted to the welfare of man and our common good; for if he fails to find causes of this character, he will accomplish nothing to the purpose. In the second place, he will select from all the actions of men which bear upon his subject those examples which are the most illustrious and the most edifying; and, habituating himself to contemplate and appraise such examples, he will feel their influence not only in the preparation of a given discourse but in all the actions of his life. It follows, then, that the power to speak well and think right will reward the man who approaches the art of discourse with love of wisdom and love of honour.

Furthermore, mark you, the man who wishes to persuade people will not be negligent as to the matter of character; no, on the contrary, he will apply himself above all to establish a most honourable name among his fellow-citizens; for who does not know that works carry greater conviction when spoken by men of good repute than when spoken by men who live under a cloud, and that the argument which is made by a man's life is of more weight than that which is furnished by words? Therefore, the stronger a man's desire to persuade his hearers, the more zealously will he strive to be honourable and to have the esteem of his fellow-citizens. . . .

You must not lose sight of the fact that Athens is looked upon as having become a school for the education of all able orators and teachers of oratory. And naturally so; for people observe that she holds forth the greatest prizes for those who have this ability, that she offers the greatest number and variety of fields of exercise to those who have chosen to enter contests of this character and want to train for them, and that, furthermore, everyone obtains here that practical experience which more than any other thing imparts ability to speak; and, in addition to these advantages, they consider that the catholicity and moderation of our speech, as well as our flexibility of mind and love of letters, contribute in no small degree to the education of the orator. Therefore they suppose, and not without just reason, that all clever speakers are the disciples of Athens.

Panathenaicus

This oration was begun by Isocrates when he could look back upon virtually the whole of his career as a teacher of oratory—at the age of ninety-four. Its completion was interrupted by a long period of illness, but the essay was finally issued in 339 B.C. when Isocrates was ninety-seven. In it he gives us the most succinct description of his model of the educated person. The educated man is not a narrow specialist but, like the subsequent model of the English gentlemanly amateur, is a man of broad human culture. He may be trained in one or more of the traditional disciplines, although Isocrates damns these with faint praise by suggesting that their study may serve to keep young men out of mischief. Isocrates' model possesses good practical judgment that enables him to cope adequately with the problems of life; he is charitable in judging others and relates congenially to them; he is self-controlled in all situations, not allowing himself to be overwhelmed by either pain or pleasure; and he is not knocked off balance by success but takes it with modesty. It is clear in this discourse that Isocrates' viewpoint has a down-to-earth, practical realism about it. It is not enough to have good intentions: one must also be effective. Although he emphasizes the practical dimension, Isocrates is delineating and defending basic human values through the microcosm of everyday matters.

This passage is from Volume II of Isocrates, *Orations*, translated by George Norlin, published in Cambridge, Massachusetts, in 1956 by Harvard University Press, Loeb Classical Library, with whose permission it is reprinted.

So far from scorning the education which was handed down by our ancestors, I even commend that which has been set up in our own day—I mean geometry, astronomy, and the so-called eristic dialogues,

75

which our young men delight in more than they should, although among the older men not one would not declare them insufferable. Nevertheless, I urge those who are inclined towards these disciplines to work hard and apply themselves to all of them, saying that even if this learning can accomplish no other good, at any rate it keeps the young out of many other things which are harmful. Nay, I hold that for those who are at this age no more helpful or fitting occupation can be found than the pursuit of these studies; but for those who are older and for those who have been admitted to man's estate I assert that these disciplines are no longer suitable. For I observe that some of those who have become so thoroughly versed in these studies as to instruct others in them fail to use opportunely the knowledge which they possess, while in the other activities of life they are less cultivated than their students—I hesitate to say less cultivated than their servants. I have the same fault to find also with those who are skilled in oratory and those who are distinguished for their writings and in general with all who have superior attainments in the arts, in the sciences, and in specialized skill. For I know that the majority even of these men have not set their own house in order, that they are insupportable in their private intercourse, that they belittle the opinions of their fellow-citizens, and that they are given over to many other grave offences. So that I do not think that even these may be said to partake of the state of culture of which I am speaking.

Whom, then, do I call educated, since I exclude the arts and sciences and specialties? First, those who manage well the circumstances which they encounter day by day, and who possess a judgement which is accurate in meeting occasions as they arise and rarely misses the expedient course of action; next, those who are decent and honourable in their intercourse with all with whom they associate, tolerating easily and good-naturedly what is unpleasant or offensive in others and being themselves as agreeable and reasonable to their associates as it is possible to be; furthermore, those who hold their pleasures always under control and are not unduly overcome by their misfortunes, bearing up under them bravely and in a manner worthy of our common nature; finally, and most important of all, those who are not spoiled by successes and do not desert their true selves and become arrogant, but hold their ground steadfastly as intelligent men, not rejoicing in the good things which have come to them through chance rather than in those which through their own nature and intelligence are theirs from their birth. Those who have a character which is in accord, not with one of these things, but with all of them—these, I contend, are wise and complete men, possessed of all the virtues.

4 The Christian: Augustine

The major force in shaping the views of St. Augustine (354–430 A.D.) was the challenge of barbarism. He lived at the time of the disintegration of the Roman Empire, brought about by internal decay and military defeats. His own death, in his diocesan city of Hippo near Carthage in North Africa, occurred as the city was being besieged by the Vandals. Chaos, change, perplexity, and uncertainty characterized his era. Like Plato, who had lived in a similar period of chaos, Augustine responded to his life experiences by seeking constancy, permanence, and certainty. He found these values in Christianity, to which he was converted in 386 A.D.

Standing at the junction of the classical and Christian eras, he betrays in his thinking the unresolved tensions caused by the confluence of classical and Christian thought. Inspired by the complementary and yet contradictory ideas of Plato and St. Paul, he spent a lifetime trying to synthesize their refractory demands. Although many in the Roman Empire saw pagan thought and literature as bulwarks against barbarism, Christians of the second and third centuries A.D. were divided about the appropriate attitude to take toward these pre-Christian studies. Augustine's response to this problem was to set the predominant pattern for the whole medieval period.

The model of the educated man that he set forth in his writings was that of a scholar well grounded in pagan studies, but one who always kept this knowledge subordinate to the goal of being a more effective servant of God. By emphasizing the importance of the pagan liberal studies, Augustine opened the way for the classical dominance of education in the Middle Ages. By insisting upon the superior value of the Christian scriptures and upon the necessity for a religious dimension in education, he did much to ensure that medieval life and education would be ruled by the Church. For the educated man, knowledge of the pagan studies (which were to become the seven liberal arts) was necessary but insufficient. The criterion of value was whether his education brought him closer to a knowledge and love of the Christian God.

By making this great attempt to reconcile the irreconcilable, Augustine saddled Western education with a dilemma that plagues us still. The educated person was to be one who created a unity in his own life between the religious and intellectual dimensions, between faith and reason. But what Augustine wanted to see as a unity is in fact in our lives a continuing tension. What if these ways of ordering our universe do *not* harmonize? Which is to prevail? Which shall we abandon or what compromise shall we make? Augustine's Christian formula is that reason ultimately must be led by love: to become wise one should begin with faith rather than with reason, just as the child begins by accepting the authority of the parent before learning to decide for himself. Truth cannot be perceived until faith has brought light to the mind. There is thus an authoritative element in Augustine's thinking that has infused Western education to the present day. Since man's reason is not an infallible guide, there is a need and a justification for control, discipline, and authority. For a thousand years after Augustine's time, the source of this authority was the Christian church.

Confessions

Augustine's *Confessions* were written when he was about forty-five. In them he engages—or indulges—in the severest self-analysis. He rigorously and continually castigates himself for his early sins, although there constantly shines through his writing a faith that God was protecting and caring for him. Like many people in middle-age, he regrets the "wasted" time of his youth, not sufficiently recognizing that such "waste" may be a necessary precursor to later development. He justifies the need for Christian discipline and for forcing children to study. But he acknowledges that a "free curiosity" is more effective than a "frightful enforcement" as an aid to learning. Lamenting the irrelevant nature of his early studies, he joins those who insist that education must be related to the unique human needs of the student. The educated man, in Augustine's view, must not mistake the appearance for the substance, must not mistake knowledge of words for knowledge of reality. We are still trying today, with only moderate success, to avoid these perennial educational errors.

This translation is by the Rev. Dr. E. B. Pusey. It was published by Grant Richards in London in 1900, edited by Temple Scott.

BOOK I

In boyhood itself, however (so much less dreaded for me than youth), I loved not study, and hated to be forced to it. Yet I was forced; and this was well done towards me, but I did not well; for, unless forced, I had not learnt. But no one doth well against his will, even though what he doth, be well. Yet neither did they well who forced me, but what was well came to me from Thee, my God. For they were regardless how I should employ what they forced me to learn, except to satiate the insatiate desires of a wealthy beggary, and a shameful glory. But Thou, *by whom the very hairs of our head are numbered,* didst use for my good the error of all who urged me to learn; and my own, who would not learn, Thou didst use for my punishment a fit penalty for one, so small a boy and so great a sinner. So by those who did not well, Thou didst well for me; and by my own sin Thou didst justly punish me. For Thou hast commanded, and so it is, that every inordinate affection should be its own punishment.

But why did I so much hate the Greek, which I studied as a boy? I do not yet fully know. For the Latin I loved; not what my first masters, but what the so-called grammarians taught me. For those first lessons, reading, writing, and arithmetic, I thought as great a burden and penalty as any Greek. And yet whence was this too, but from the sin and vanity of this life, because *I was flesh, and a breath that passeth away and cometh not again?* For those first lessons were better certainly, because more certain; by them I obtained, and still retain, the power of reading what I find written, and myself writing what I will; whereas in the others, I was forced to learn the wanderings of one Æneas, forgetful of my own, and to weep for dead Dido, because she killed herself for love; the while, with dry eyes, I endured my miserable self dying among these things, far from Thee, O God my life.

For what more miserable than a miserable being who commiserates not himself weeping the death of Dido for love to Æneas, but weeping not his own death for want of love to Thee, O God. . . .

Why then did I hate the Greek classics, which have the like tales? For Homer also curiously wove the like fictions, and is most sweetly-vain, yet was he bitter to my boyish taste. And so I suppose would Virgil be to Grecian children, when forced to learn him as I was Homer. Difficulty, in truth, the difficulty of a foreign tongue, dashed, as it were, with gall all the sweetness of Grecian fable. For not one word of it did I understand, and to make me understand I was urged vehemently with cruel threats and punishments. Time was also (as an infant) I knew no Latin; but this I learned without fear or suffering, by mere observation, amid the caresses of my nursery and jests of friends, smiling and sportively encouraging me. This I learned without any pressure of punishment to urge me on, for my heart urged me to give birth to its conceptions, which I could only do by learning words not of those who taught, but of those who talked with me; in whose ears also I gave birth to the thoughts, whatever I conceived. No doubt, then, that a free curiosity has more force in our learning these things, than a frightful enforcement. Only this enforcement restrains the rovings of that freedom, through Thy laws, O my God, Thy laws, from the master's cane to the martyr's trials, being able to temper for us a wholesome bitter, recalling us to Thyself from that deadly pleasure which lures us from Thee.

Hear, Lord, my prayer; let not my soul faint under Thy discipline, nor let me faint in confessing unto Thee all Thy mercies, whereby thou has drawn me out of all my most evil ways, that Thou mightest become a delight to me above all the allurements which I once pursued; that I may most entirely love Thee, and clasp Thy hand with all my affections, and Thou mayest yet rescue me from every temptation, even unto the end. For, lo, O Lord, my King and my God, for Thy service be whatever useful thing my childhood learned; for Thy service, that I speak, write, read, reckon. For Thou didst grant me Thy discipline, while I was learning vanities; and my sin of delighting in those vanities Thou hast forgiven. In them, indeed, I learnt many a useful word, but these may as well be learned in things not vain; and that is the safe path for the steps of youth. . . .

Behold, O Lord God, yea, behold patiently as Thou art wont, how carefully the sons of men observe the covenanted rules of letters and syllables received from those who spake before them, neglecting the eternal covenant of everlasting salvation received from Thee. Insomuch, that a teacher or learner of the hereditary laws of pronunciation will more offend men by speaking without the aspirate, of a 'uman being,' in despite of the laws of grammar, than if he, a 'human being,' hate a 'human being' in despite of Thine. As if any enemy could be more hurtful than the hatred with which he is incensed against him; or could wound more deeply him whom he persecutes, than he wounds his own soul by his enmity. Assuredly no science of letters can be so innate as the record of conscience, 'that he is doing to another what from another he would be loth to suffer.' How deep are Thy ways, O God, Thou only great, *that sittest* silent *on high* and by an unwearied law dispensing penal blindness to lawless desires. In quest of the fame of eloquence, a man standing before a human judge, surrounded by a human throng, declaiming against his enemy with fiercest hatred, will take heed most watchfully, lest, by an error of the tongue, he murder the word 'human being'; but takes no heed, lest, through the fury of his spirit, he murder the real human being.

This was the world at whose gate unhappy I lay in my boyhood; this the stage where I had feared more to commit a barbarism, than having committed one, to envy those who had not. These things I speak and confess to Thee, my God; for which I had praise from them, whom I then thought it all virtue to please. For I saw not the abyss of vileness, wherein *I was cast away from Thine eyes*. Before them what more foul than I was already, displeasing even such as myself? with innumerable lies deceiving my tutor, my masters, my parents, from love of play, eagerness to see vain shows and restlessness to imitate them! Thefts also I committed, from my parents' cellar and table, enslaved by greediness, or that I might have to give to boys, who sold me their play, which all the while they liked no less than I. In this play, too, I often sought unfair conquests, conquered myself meanwhile by vain desire of pre-eminence. And what could I so ill endure, or, when I detected it, upbraided I so fiercely, as that I was doing to others? and for which if, detected, I was upbraided, I chose rather to quarrel than to yield. And is this the innocence of boyhood? Not so, Lord, not so; I cry Thy mercy, O my God. For these very sins, as riper years succeed, these very sins are transferred from tutors and masters, from nuts and balls and sparrows, to magistrates and kings, to gold and manors and slaves, just as severer punishments displace the cane. It was the low stature then of childhood which Thou our King didst commend as an emblem of lowliness, when Thou saidst, *Of such is the kingdom of heaven.*

Yet, Lord, to Thee, the Creator and Governor of the universe, most excellent and most good, thanks were due to Thee our God, even hadst Thou destined for me boyhood only. For even then I was, I lived, and felt; and had an implanted providence over my well-being—a trace of that mysterious Unity whence I was derived; I guarded by the inward sense the entireness of my sense, and in these minute pursuits, and in my thoughts on things minute, I learnt to delight in truth, I hated to be deceived, had a vigorous memory, was gifted with speech, was soothed by friendship, avoided pain, baseness, ignorance. In so small a creature, what was not wonderful, not admirable? But all are gifts of my God: it was not I who gave them me; and good these are, and these together are myself. Good, then, is He that made me, and He is my good and before Him will I exult for every good which of a boy I had. For it was my sin, that not in Him, but in His creatures—myself and others—I sought for pleasures, sublimities, truths, and so fell headlong into sorrows, confusions, errors. Thanks be to Thee, my joy and my glory and my confidence, my God, thanks be to Thee for Thy gifts; but do Thou preserve them to me. For so wilt thou preserve me, and those things shall be enlarged and perfected which Thou hast given me, and I myself shall be with Thee, since even to be Thou hast given me.

Divine Providence and the Problem of Evil

This is a translation of Augustine's *De Ordine*. In it he treats the question of whether the order of God's providence embraces all good and all evil. Although there are apparent paradoxes in the standpoint, Augustine maintains that nothing happens except within the framework of God's order. This is an orderly universe and man should reflect this order in his own life. Augustine's model of the well-educated man is one who has achieved a just and virtuous character through the harmonious reign of faith and reason. Man is both a rational animal and a child of God. We fret and worry because, in our ignorance, we perceive only a broken fragment of the total pattern. The wisely educated man will understand that, seen as a whole, God's order is inevitably beautiful and perfect.

De Ordine was written in 386 A.D. the year of Augustine's conversion to Christianity. This version, entitled *Divine Providence and the Problem of Evil*, was edited by Robert P. Russell and published by the Cosmopolitan Science and Art Company in New York in 1942. It is reprinted with the permission of Dr. Robert P. Russell, O.S.A.

CHAPTER NINETEEN

Out of several pieces of material hitherto lying around in scattered fashion and then assembled into one design, I can make a house. If indeed I am the maker and it is made, then I am the more excellent; and the more excellent precisely because I am the maker. There is no doubt but that I am on that account more excellent than a house. But not on that account am I more excellent than a swallow or a small bee; for skillfully does the one build nests, and the other construct honey-cobs. I am, however, more excellent than they, because I am a rational creature.

Now if reason is found in calculated measurements, does it follow that the work of birds is not accurately and aptly measured? Nay, it is most accurately and aptly proportioned. Therefore, it is not by making well measured things, but by grasping the nature of numbers, that I am the more excellent. What then? Have the birds been able to build carefully constructed nests without knowing it? Assuredly, they have. How is this shown? By the fact that we, too, accommodate the tongue to the teeth and palate by fixed measurements, so that letters and words rush forth from the mouth; and when we are speaking, we are not thinking of the oral movement by which we ought to do that. Moreover, what good singer, even though he be unskilled in the art of music, would not, by that same natural sense, keep in his singing both the rhythm and the melody known by memory? And what can become more subject to measure than this? The uninstructed man has no knowledge of it. Nevertheless, he does it by nature's doing. But why is man superior to brute animals, and why is he to be ranked above them? Because he understands what he does. Nothing else ranks me above the brute animal except the fact that I am a rational animal.

Then how is it that reason is immortal, and I am defined as something both rational and mortal at the same time? Perhaps reason is not immortal? But one to two, or two to four, is a ratio in the truest sense. That ratio was no truer yesterday than today, nor will it be truer tomorrow or a year hence. Even if the whole world should fall in ruins, that ratio will always necessarily be: it will always be such as it is now. Contrariwise, what the world has today, it did not have yesterday and it will not have it tomorrow. In fact, not even for the course of an hour during this very day has it had the sun in the same position. And so, since nothing in it is permanent, it does not have anything in the same way for even the shortest interval of time.

Therefore, if reason is immortal, and if I who analyze and synthesize all those things, am reason, then that by which I am called mortal is not mine. Or if the soul is not the same as reason, and I nevertheless use reason, and if through reason I am superior, then we ought to take flight from the lesser good to the greater, from the mortal to the immortal. The well instructed soul tells itself all this and more besides, and ponders over them. But I prefer to attend to them no further now, lest, while I am longing to teach you order, I myself should exceed moderation, the parent of order. Indeed, it is not by faith alone, but by trustworthy reason, that the soul leads itself little by little to most virtuous habits and the perfect life. For to the soul that diligently considers the nature and the power of numbers, it will appear manifestly unfitting and most deplorable that it should write a rhythmic line and play the harp by virtue of this knowledge, and that its life and very self—which is the soul—should nevertheless follow a crooked path and, under the domination of lust, be out of tune by the clangor of shameful vices.

But when the soul has properly adjusted and disposed itself, and has rendered itself harmonious and beautiful, then will it venture to see God, the very source of all truth and the very Father of Truth. O great God, What kind of eyes shall those be! How pure! How beautiful! How powerful! How constant! How serene! How blessed! And what is that which they can see! What is it? I ask. What should we surmise? What should we believe? What should we say? Everyday expressions present themselves, but they have been rendered sordid by things of least worth. I shall say no more, except that to us is promised a vision of beauty—the beauty of whose imitation all other things are beautiful, and by comparison with which all other things are unsightly. Whosoever will have glimpsed this beauty—and he will see it, who lives well, prays well, studies well—how will it ever trouble him why one man, desiring to have children, has them not, while another man casts out his own offspring as being unduly numerous; why one man hates children before they are born, and another man loves them after birth; or how it is not absurd that nothing will come to pass which is not with God—and therefore it is inevitable that all things come into being in accordance with order—and nevertheless God is not petitioned in vain?

Finally, how will any burdens, dangers, scorns, or smiles of fortune disturb a just man? In this world of sense, it is indeed necessary to examine carefully what time and place are, so that what delights in a portion of place or time, may be understood to be far less beautiful than the whole of which it is a portion. And furthermore, it is clear to a learned man that what displeases in a portion, displeases for no other reason than because the whole with which that portion harmonizes wonderfully, is not seen; but that in the intelligible world, every part is as beautiful and perfect as the whole.

Soliloquies

In these soliloquies, Augustine is conversing with Reason, the great clarifying instrument of the mind. The model that is presented to us is the man of virtue: it is pointed out that virtue requires reason purified by faith, hope, and charity. There are many echoes of Plato in this synthesis of Greek and Christian thought. Education must involve freeing the mind from the encumbrances of the body. This view that body and mind can be separated and that the body is essentially an evil hindrance has been a persistent assumption in the Western educational tradition. It has caused immeasurable and avoidable waste and suffering.

The *Soliloquies* were written in 387 A.D., when Augustine was thirty-three. They are among his earliest Christian work. This translation is by the Rev. Charles C. Starbuck and can be found in Volume VII of *A Select Library of the Nicene and Post-Nicene Fathers of the Christian Church*, published by the Christian Literature Company in Buffalo in 1888.

BOOK I

R. Thou art moved to good effect. For the Reason which is talking with thee promises so to demonstrate God to thy mind, as the sun demonstrates himself to the eyes. For the senses of the soul are as it were the eyes of the mind; but all the certainties of the sciences are like those things which are brought to light by the sun, that they may be seen, the earth, for instance, and the things upon it: while God is Himself the Illuminator. Now I, Reason, am that in the mind, which the act of looking is in the eyes. For to have eyes is not the same as to look; nor again to look the same as to see. Therefore the soul has need of three distinct things: to have eyes, such as it can use to good advantage, to look, and to see. Sound eyes, that means the mind pure from all stain of the body, that is, now remote and purged from the lusts of mortal things: which, in the first condition, nothing else accomplishes for her than Faith. For what cannot yet be shown forth to her stained and languishing with sins, because, unless sound, she cannot see, if she does not believe that otherwise she will not see, she gives no heed to her health. But what if she believes that the case stands as I say, and that, if she is to see at all, she can only see on these terms, but despairs of being healed; does she not utterly contemn herself and cast herself away, refusing to comply with the prescriptions of the physician? A. Beyond doubt, above all because by sickness remedies must needs be felt as severe. R. Then Hope must be added to Faith. A. So I believe. R. Moreover, if she both believes that the case stands so, and hopes that she could be healed, yet loves not, desires not the promised light itself, and thinks that she ought meanwhile to be content with her darkness, which now, by use, has become pleasant to her; does she not none the less reject the physician? A. Beyond doubt. R. Therefore Charity must needs make a third. A. Nothing so needful. R. Without these three things therefore no mind is healed, so that it can see, that is, understand its God.

When therefore the mind has come to have sound eyes, what next? A. That she look. R. The mind's act of looking is Reason; but because it does not follow that every one who looks sees, a right and perfect act of looking, that is, one followed by vision, is called Virtue; for Virtue is either right or perfect Reason. But even the power of vision, though the eyes be now healed, has not force to turn them to the light, unless these three things abide. Faith, whereby the soul believes that thing, to which she is asked to turn her gaze, is of such sort, that being seen it will give blessedness; Hope, whereby the mind judges that if she looks attentively, she will see; Charity, whereby she desires to see and to be filled with the enjoyment of the sight. The attentive view is now followed by the very vision of God, which is the end of looking; not because the power of beholding ceases, but because it has nothing further to which it can turn itself: and this is the truly perfect virtue, Virtue arriving at its end, which is followed by the life of blessedness. Now this vision itself is that apprehension which is in the soul, compounded of the apprehending subject and of that which is apprehended: as in like manner seeing with the eyes results from the conjunction of the sense and the object of sense, either of which being withdrawn, seeing becomes impossible

Therefore when the soul has obtained to see, that is, to apprehend God, let us see whether those three things are still necessary to her.

Why should Faith be necessary to the soul, when she now sees? Or Hope, when she already grasps? But from Charity not only is nothing diminished, but rather it receives large increase. For when the soul has once seen that unique and unfalsified Beauty, she will love it the more, and unless she shall with great love have fastened her gaze thereon, nor any way declined from the view, she will not be able to abide in that most blessed vision. But while the soul is in this body, even though she most fully sees, that is, apprehends God; yet, because the bodily senses still have their proper effect, if they have no prevalency to mislead, yet they are not without a certain power to call in doubt, therefore that may be called Faith whereby these dispositions are resisted, and the opposing truth affirmed. Moreover, in this life, although the soul is already blessed in the apprehension of God; yet, because she endures many irksome pains of the body, she has occasion of hope that after death all these incommodities will have ceased to be. Therefore neither does Hope, so long as she is in this life, desert the soul. But when after this life she shall have wholly collected herself in God, Charity remains whereby she is retained there. For neither can she be said to have Faith that those things are true, when she is solicited by no interruption of falsities; nor does anything remain for her to hope, whereas she securely possesses the whole. Three things therefore pertain to the soul, that she be sane, that she behold, that she see. And other three, Faith, Hope, Charity, for the first and second of those three conditions are always necessary: for the third in this life all; after this life, Charity alone.

Of the Morals of the Catholic Church

In this passage Augustine shows that he is himself aware of the tension between rational argument and religious authority. The two ought not to conflict, in his view, but in the last analysis it is authority that must prevail. In order to arrive at truth we should ensure that reason follows authority rather than precedes it. The argument suggests that the goal of education and self-development is happiness. Man finds happiness when he loves and enjoys his greatest good. Hence life and education should be concerned with the search for the greatest good—which turns out to be God. Finding and loving Him therefore constitute happiness. And since it is through Christ that we find God, the model to which Augustine would have us aspire is that of the virtuous Christian.

This translation of *De Moribus Ecclesiae Catholicae* is by the Rev. Richard Stothert and appears in Volume IV of *A Select Library of the Nicene and Post-Nicene Fathers of the Christian Church,* published by the Christian Literature Company in Buffalo in 1887.

CHAP. 2. HE BEGINS WITH ARGUMENTS, IN COMPLIANCE WITH THE MISTAKEN METHOD OF THE MANICHÆANS.

Where, then, shall I begin? With authority, or with reasoning? In the order of nature, when we learn anything, authority precedes reasoning. For a reason may seem weak, when, after it is given, it requires authority to confirm it. But because the minds of men are obscured by familiarity with darkness, which covers them in the night of sins and evil habits, and cannot perceive in a way suitable to the clearness and purity of reason, there is most wholesome provision for bringing

89

the dazzled eye into the light of truth under the congenial shade of authority. But since we have to do with people who are perverse in all their thoughts and words and actions, and who insist on nothing more than on beginning with argument, I will, as a concession to them, take what I think a wrong method in discussion. For I like to imitate, as far as I can, the gentleness of my Lord Jesus Christ, who took on Himself the evil of death itself, wishing to free us from it.

CHAP. 3. HAPPINESS IS IN THE ENJOYMENT OF MAN'S CHIEF GOOD. TWO CONDITIONS OF THE CHIEF GOOD: 1ST, NOTHING IS BETTER THAN IT; 2D, IT CANNOT BE LOST AGAINST THE WILL.

How then, according to reason, ought man to live? We all certainly desire to live happily; and there is no human being but assents to this statement almost before it is made. But the title happy cannot, in my opinion, belong either to him who has not what he loves, whatever it may be, or to him who has what he loves if it is hurtful, or to him who does not love what he has, although it is good in perfection. For one who seeks what he cannot obtain suffers torture, and one who has got what is not desirable is cheated, and one who does not seek for what is worth seeking for is diseased. Now in all these cases the mind cannot but be unhappy, and happiness and unhappiness cannot reside at the same time in one man; so in none of these cases can the man be happy. I find, then, a fourth case, where the happy life exists—when that which is man's chief good is both loved and possessed. For what do we call enjoyment but having at hand the objects of love? And no one can be happy who does not enjoy what is man's chief good, nor is there any one who enjoys this who is not happy. We must then have at hand our chief good, if we think of living happily.

We must now inquire what is man's chief good, which of course cannot be anything inferior to man himself. For whoever follows after what is inferior to himself, becomes himself inferior. But every man is bound to follow what is best. Wherefore man's chief good is not inferior to man. Is it then something similar to man himself? It must be so, if there is nothing above man which he is capable of enjoying. But if we find something which is both superior to man, and can be possessed by the man who loves it, who can doubt that in seeking for happiness man should endeavor to reach that which is more excellent than the being who makes the endeavor. For if happiness consists in the enjoyment of a good than which there is nothing better, which we call the chief good, how can a man be properly called happy who has not yet attained to his chief good? or how can that be the chief good beyond which something better remains for us to arrive at? Such, then, being the chief good, it must be something which cannot be lost against the will. For no one can feel confident regarding a good which he knows can be taken from him, although he wishes to keep and cherish it. But if a man feels no confidence regarding the good which he enjoys, how can he be happy while in such fear of losing it?

CHAP. 4. MAN—WHAT?

Let us then see what is better than man. This must necessarily be hard to find, unless we first ask and examine what man is. I am not now called upon to give a definition of man. The question here seems to me to be—since almost all agree, or at least, which is enough, those I have now to do with are of the same opinion with me, that we are made up of soul and body—What is man? Is he both of these? or is he the body only, or the soul only? For although the things are two, soul and body, and although neither without the other could be called man (for the body would not be man without the soul, nor again would the soul be man if there were not a body animated by it), still it is possible that one of these may be held to be man, and may be called so. What then do we call man? Is he soul and body, as in a double harness, or like a centaur? Or do we mean the body only, as being in the service of the soul which rules it, as the word lamp denotes not the light and the case together, but only the case, yet it is on account of the light that it is so called? Or do we mean only the mind, and that on account of the body which it rules, as horseman means not the man and the horse, but the man only, and that as employed in ruling the horse? This dispute is not easy to settle; or, if the proof is plain, the statement requires time. This is an expenditure of time and strength which we need not incur. For whether the name man belongs to both, or only to the soul, the chief good of man is not the chief good of the body; but what is the chief good either of both soul and body, or of the soul only, that is man's chief good.

CHAP. 5. MAN'S CHIEF GOOD IS NOT THE CHIEF GOOD OF THE BODY ONLY, BUT THE CHIEF GOOD OF THE SOUL.

Now if we ask what is the chief good of the body, reason obliges us to admit that it is that by means of which the body comes to be in its best state. But of all the things which invigorate the body, there is nothing better or greater than the soul. The chief good of the body, then, is not bodily pleasure, not absence of pain, not strength, not beauty, not swiftness, or whatever else is usually reckoned among the goods of the body, but simply the soul. For all the things mentioned the soul supplies to the body by its presence, and, what is above them all, life. Hence I conclude that the soul is not the chief good of man, whether we give the name of man to soul and body together, or to the soul alone. For as, according to reason, the chief good of the body is that which is better than the body, and from which the body receives vigor and life, so whether the soul itself is man, or soul and body both, we must discover whether there is anything which goes before the soul itself, in following which the soul comes to the perfection of good of which it is capable in its own kind. If such a thing can be found, all uncertainty must be at an end, and we must pronounce this to be really and truly the chief good of man.

If, again, the body is man, it must be admitted that the soul is the chief good of man. But clearly, when we treat of morals—when we inquire what manner of life must be held in order to obtain happiness— it is not the body to which the precepts are addressed, it is not bodily discipline which we discuss. In short, the observance of good *customs* belongs to that part of us which inquires and learns, which are the prerogatives of the soul; so, when we speak of attaining to virtue, the question does not regard the body. But if it follows, as it does, that the body which is ruled over by a soul possessed of virtue is ruled both better and more honorably, and is in its greatest perfection in consequence of the perfection of the soul which rightfully governs it, that which gives perfection to the soul will be man's chief good, though we call the body man. For if my coachman, in obedience to me, feeds and drives the horses he has charge of in the most satisfactory manner, himself enjoying the more of my bounty in proportion to his good con- duct, can any one deny that the good condition of the horses, as well as that of the coachman, is due to me? So the question seems to me to be not, whether soul and body is man, or the soul only, or the body only, but what gives perfection to the soul; for when this is obtained, a man cannot but be either perfect, or at least much better than in the absence of this one thing. . . .

CHAP. 11. GOD IS THE ONE OBJECT OF LOVE; THEREFORE HE
IS MAN'S CHIEF GOOD. NOTHING IS BETTER THAN GOD.
GOD CANNOT BE LOST AGAINST OUR WILL.

Following after God is the desire of happiness; to reach God is happi- ness itself. We follow after God by loving Him; we reach Him, not by becoming entirely what He is, but in nearness to Him, and in wonderful and immaterial contact with Him, and in being inwardly illuminated and occupied by His truth and holiness. He is light itself; we get enlightenment from Him. The greatest commandment, therefore, which leads to happy life, and the first, is this: "Thou shalt love the Lord thy God with all thy heart, and soul, and mind." For to those who love the Lord all things issue in good. Hence Paul adds shortly after, "I am persuaded that neither death, nor life, nor angels, nor virtue, nor things present, nor things future, nor height, nor depth, nor any other creature, shall be able to separate us from the love of God, which is in Christ Jesus our Lord." If, then, to those who love God all things issue in good, and if, as no one doubts, the chief or perfect good is not only to be loved, but to be loved so that nothing shall be loved better, as is expressed in the words, "With all thy soul, with all thy heart, and with all thy mind," who, I ask, will not at once conclude, when these things are all settled and most surely believed, that our chief good which we must hasten to arrive at in preference to all other things is nothing else than God? And then, if nothing can separate us from His love, must not this be surer as well as better than any other good? . . .

CHAP. 14. WE CLEAVE TO THE TRINITY, OUR CHIEF GOOD, BY LOVE.

We ought then to love God, the Trinity in unity, Father, Son, and Holy Spirit; for this must be said to be God Himself, for it is said of God, truly and in the most exalted sense, "Of whom are all things, by whom are all things, in whom are all things." Those are Paul's words. And what does he add? "To Him be glory." All this is exactly true. He does not say, To them; for God is one. And what is meant by, To Him be glory, but to Him be chief and perfect and wide-spread praise? For as the praise improves and extends, so the love and affection increases in fervor. And when this is the case, mankind cannot but advance with sure and firm step to a life of perfection and bliss. This, I suppose, is all we wish to find when we speak of the chief good of man, to which all must be referred in life and conduct. For the good plainly exists; and we have shown by reasoning, as far as we were able, and by the divine authority which goes beyond our reasoning, that it is nothing else but God Himself. For how can any thing be man's chief good but that in cleaving to which he is blessed? Now this is nothing but God, to whom we can cleave only by affection, desire, and love.

Concerning the Teacher

This dialogue between Augustine and his fifteen-year-old son, Adeodatus, is concerned with explicating the nature of teaching and learning. How do we learn? Not through words and teachers, affirms Augustine, for the teacher's words at best serve only to remind us of what we already know. It is Christ, the truth within us, that teaches us. This educational model of the contemplative, inward-directed man prepared the way for much of the passivity and withdrawal that have been recurrent emphases in the Christian tradition.

This passage from *De Magistro* appears in St. Augustine, *The Greatness of the Soul: The Teacher*, translated and annotated by Joseph M. Colleran, published in Westminster, Maryland, in 1950 by the Newman Press, with whose permission it is reprinted.

CHAPTER 12

Internal light, internal truth.

Augustine. Now, if regarding colors we consult light; and regarding the other sensible objects we consult the elements of this world constituting the bodies of which we have sense experience, and the senses themselves which the mind uses as interpreters to know such things; and if, moreover, regarding those things which are objects of intelligence we consult the truth within us through reasoning—then what can be advanced as proof that words teach us anything beyond the mere sound which strikes the ears? For everything we perceive, we perceive either through a sense of the body or by the mind. The former we call sensible, the latter, intelligible; or, to speak in the manner of our own authors, we call the former carnal, and the latter spiritual. When we are asked concerning the former, we answer, if the things of which we have sense knowledge are present; as when we are looking at a new moon we are asked what sort of a thing it is or where it is. In this case if the one who puts the question does not see the object, he believes words; and often he does not believe them. But learn he does not at all, unless he himself sees what is spoken about; and in that case he learns not by means of spoken words, but by means of the realities themselves and his senses. For the words have the same sound for the one who sees the object as for the one who does not see it. But when a question is asked not regarding things which we perceive while they are present, but regarding things of which we had sense knowledge in the past, then we express in speech, not the realities themselves, but the images impressed by them on the mind and committed to memory. How we can speak at all of these as true when we see they are false, I do not know—unless it be because we report on them not as things we actually see and perceive, but as things we have seen and perceived. Thus we bear these images in the depths of memory as so many attestations, so to say, of things previously perceived by the senses. Contemplating these in the mind, we have the good conscience that we are not lying when we speak. But even so, these attestations are such for us only. If one who hears me has personally perceived these things and become aware of them, he does not learn them from my words, but recognizes them from the images that are stored away within himself. If, however, he has had no sense knowledge of them, he clearly believes rather than learns by means of the words.

Now, when there is question of those things which we perceive by the mind—that is, by means of the intellect and by reason—we obviously express in speech the things which we behold immediately in that interior light of truth which effects enlightenment and happiness in the so-called inner man. And at the same time if the one who hears me likewise sees those things with an inner and undivided eye, he knows the matter of which I speak by his own contemplation, not by means of my words. Hence, I do not teach even such a one, although I speak what is true and he sees what is true. For he is taught not by my words, but by the realities themselves made manifest to him by God revealing them to his inner self. Thus, if he were asked, he could also give answers regarding these things. What could be more absurd than to think that he is taught by my speech, when even before I spoke he could explain those same things, if he were asked about them?

As for the fact that, as often happens, one denies something when he is asked about it, but is brought around by further questions to affirm it, this happens by reason of the weakness of his vision, not permitting him to consult that light regarding the matter as a whole. He is prompted to consider the problem part by part as questions are put regarding those same parts that constitute the whole, which originally he was not able to see in its entirety. If in this case he is led on by the words of the questioner, still it is not that the words teach him, but they represent questions put to him in such a way as to correspond to his capacity for learning from his own inner self.

To illustrate: if I were to ask you whether it is true that nothing can be taught by means of words—the very topic we are discussing now—you would at first think the question absurd, because you could now see the problem in its entirety. Then I should have to question you in a way adapted to your capacity for hearing that Teacher within you. So I should say: "Those things which I stated and you granted as true, and of which you are certain and which you are sure you know—where did you learn them?" You would perhaps answer that I had taught them to you. Then I would rejoin: "Let us suppose I told you that I saw a man flying. Would my words give you the same certitude as if you heard that wise men are superior to fools?" You would, of course, answer in the negative and would tell me that you do not believe the former statement, or even if you did believe it, that you did not know it; where as you knew the other statement to be absolutely certain. Certainly, the upshot of this would be that you would then realize that you had not learned anything from my words; neither in the case where you were not aware of the thing that I affirmed, nor in the case of that which you knew very well. For if you were asked about each case, you would even swear that you were unaware of the former and that you did know the latter. But then you would actually be admitting the entire proposition which you had denied, since you would now know clearly and certainly what it implies: namely, that whatever we say, the hearer either does not know whether it is true, or knows it is false, or knows that it is true. In the first of these three cases he either believes, or has a opinion, or is in doubt; in the second, he opposes and rejects the statement; in the third, he bears witness to the truth. In none of the cases, therefore, does he learn. The obvious reason is that the one who on hearing my words does not know the reality, and the one who knows that what he has heard is false, and the one who, if he were asked, could have answered precisely what was said, demonstrate that they have learned nothing from my words. . . .

CHAPTER 14

Christ teaches within the mind. Man's words are external, and serve
only to give reminders.

Teachers do not claim, do they, that their own thoughts are perceived
and grasped by the pupils, but rather the branches of learning that
they think they transmit by speaking? For who would be so absurdly
curious as to send his child to school to learn what the teacher thinks?
But when they have explained, by means of words, all those subjects
which they profess to teach, and even the science of virtue and of wisdom, then those who are called pupils consider within themselves
whether what has been said is true. This they do by gazing attentively
at that interior truth, so far as they are able. Then it is that they learn;
and when within themselves they find that what has been said is true,
they give praise, not realizing that they are praising not so much teachers
as person taught—provided that the teacher' also know what they are
saying. But people deceive themselves in calling persons "teachers" who
are not such at all, merely because generally there is no interval between
the time of speaking and the time of knowing. And because they are
quick to learn internally following the prompting of the one who speaks,
they think they have learned externally from the one who was only
a prompter.

But at some other time, God willing, we shall investigate the entire
problem of the utility of words, which, if considered properly, is not
negligible. For the present, I have reminded you that we must not attribute to words more than is proper. Thus we should no longer merely
believe, but also begin to understand how truly it has been written
on divine authority that we should not call anyone on earth a teacher,
since *there is One in heaven who is the teacher of all.* What "in heaven"
means He Himself will teach us, who has also counselled us through
the instrumentality of human beings—by means of signs, and externally—to turn to Him internally and be instructed. He will teach us,
to know and love whom is happiness of life, and this is what all proclaim
they are seeking, though there are but few who may rejoice in having
really found it.

And now I would like you to tell me what you think of this entire
disquisition of mine. Indeed, if you have come to realize that what
has been said is true, then if you had been asked about the several
propositions, you would have stated that you knew them. You see, then,

from whom you have learned these things. No, it is not from me, for you would have given me all the answers as I questioned you. But if you have not ascertained that what has been said is true, neither have I taught you, nor has He. Not I, because I am unable to teach in any case; not He, because you are still unable to learn.

Adeodatus. As for me, I have learned, thanks to being reminded by your words, that words do no more than prompt man to learn, and that what appears to be, to a considerable extent, the thought of the speaker expressing himself, really amounts to extremely little. Moreover, as to whether what is said is true, He alone teaches who when He spoke externally reminded us that He dwells within us. I shall now, with His help, love Him the more ardently the more I progress in learning.

Meanwhile, I am grateful for this disquisition delivered by you without interruption, especially for this reason, that it has anticipated and refuted every objection I was prepared to make. Not one misgiving of mine have you ignored; and there is nothing regarding which that hidden Oracle did not give me the same answer as was stated in your words.

On Christian Doctrine

The purpose of education, Augustine enjoins, is to find God. But in seeking this end we should use all sources, including profane studies. Human institutions should not be ignored when they can serve a religious purpose. Since all truth belongs to God, the range of subjects for study can be very broad, depending on the way in which they are approached. History, for example, should be studied not for its own sake but as an aid to understanding the scriptures. Again, the educated man will be an able orator, for the arts of rhetoric should be employed in defense of truth and to defeat falsehood. But oratory alone is not enough. The ideal teacher is one who seeks the truth rather than one who seeks to prevail in argument. Augustine demands both eloquence and wisdom in his model. And the wisdom he seeks will come through the intelligent study and understanding of the scriptures.

The present translation is by the Rev. Professor J. F. Shaw and appears in Volume II of *A Select Library of the Nicene and Post-Nicene Fathers of the Christian Church,* published by the Christian Literature Company in Buffalo in 1887.

BOOK II

CHAP. 18. NO HELP IS TO BE DESPISED, EVEN THOUGH IT COME FROM A PROFANE SOURCE.

But whether the fact is as Varro has related, or is not so, still we ought not to give up music because of the superstition of the heathen, if we can derive anything from it that is of use for the understanding of Holy Scripture; nor does it follow that we must busy ourselves with their theatrical trumpery because we enter upon an investigation about harps and other instruments, that may help us to lay hold upon spiritual

things. For we ought not to refuse to learn letters because they say
that Mercury discovered them; nor because they have dedicated temples
to Justice and Virtue, and prefer to worship in the form of stones things
that ought to have their place in the heart, ought we on that account
to forsake justice and virtue. Nay, but let every good and true Christian
understand that wherever truth may be found, it belongs to his Master;
and while he recognizes and acknowledges the truth, even in their religious literature, let him reject the figments of superstition, and let him
grieve over and avoid men who, "'when they knew God, glorified him
not as God, neither were thankful; but became vain in their imaginations,
and their foolish heart was darkened. Professing themselves to be wise,
they became fools, and changed the glory of the uncorruptible God
into an image made like to corruptible man, and to birds, and four-footed
beasts, and creeping things." . . .

CHAP. 39. TO WHICH OF THE ABOVE-MENTIONED STUDIES
ATTENTION SHOULD BE GIVEN, AND IN WHAT SPIRIT.

Accordingly, I think that it is well to warn studious and able young
men, who fear God and are seeking for happiness of life, not to venture
heedlessly upon the pursuit of the branches of learning that are in vogue
beyond the pale of the Church of Christ, as if these could secure for
them the happiness they seek; but soberly and carefully to discriminate
among them. And if they find any of those which have been instituted
by men varying by reason of the varying pleasure of their founders,
and unknown by reason of erroneous conjectures, especially if they involve entering into fellowship with devils by means of leagues and cove-
nants about signs, let these be utterly rejected and held in detestation.
Let the young men also withdraw their attention from such institutions
of men as are unnecessary and luxurious. But for the sake of the necessities of this life we must not neglect the arrangements of men that enable
us to carry on intercourse with those around us. I think, however, there
is nothing useful in the other branches of learning that are found among
the heathen, except information about objects, either past or present,
that relate to the bodily senses, in which are included also the experiments and conclusions of the useful mechanical arts, except also the
sciences of reasoning and of number. And in regard to all these we
must hold by the maxim, "Not too much of anything;" especially in
the case of those which, pertaining as they do to the senses, are subject
to the relations of space and time. . . .

CHAP. 42. SACRED SCRIPTURE COMPARED WITH PROFANE AUTHORS.

But just as poor as the store of gold and silver and garments which the people of Israel brought with them out of Egypt was in comparison with the riches which they afterwards attained at Jerusalem, and which reached their height in the reign of King Solomon, so poor is all the useful knowledge which is gathered from the books of the heathen when compared with the knowledge of Holy Scripture. For whatever man may have learnt from other sources, if it is hurtful, it is there condemned; if it is useful, it is therein contained. And while every man may find there all that he has learnt of useful elsewhere, he will find there in much greater abundance things that are to be found nowhere else, but can be learnt only in the wonderful sublimity and wonderful simplicity of the Scriptures. . . .

BOOK IV

CHAP. 2. IT IS LAWFUL FOR A CHRISTIAN TEACHER TO USE
THE ART OF RHETORIC.

Now, the art of rhetoric being available for the enforcing either of truth or falsehood, who will dare to say that truth in the person of its defenders is to take its stand unarmed against falsehood? For example, that those who are trying to persuade men of what is false are to know how to introduce their subject, so as to put the hearer into a friendly, or attentive, or teachable frame of mind, while the defenders of the truth shall be ignorant of that art? That the former are to tell their falsehoods briefly, clearly, and plausibly, while the latter shall tell the truth in such a way that it is tedious to listen to, hard to understand, and, in fine, not easy to believe it? That the former are to oppose the truth and defend falsehood with sophistical arguments, while the latter shall be unable either to defend what is true, or to refute what is false? That the former, while imbuing the minds of their hearers with erroneous opinions, are by their power of speech to awe, to melt, to enliven, and to rouse them, while the latter shall in defence of the truth be sluggish, and frigid, and somnolent? Who is such a fool as to think this wisdom? Since, then, the faculty of eloquence is available for both sides, and is of very great service in the enforcing either of wrong or right, why do not good men study to engage it on the side of truth, when bad men use it to obtain the triumph of wicked and worthless causes, and to further injustice and error? . . .

CHAP. 5. WISDOM OF MORE IMPORTANCE THAN ELOQUENCE TO THE CHRISTIAN TEACHER.

. . . We must beware of the man who abounds in eloquent nonsense, and so much the more if the hearer is pleased with what is not worth listening to, and thinks that because the speaker is eloquent what he says must be true. And this opinion is held even by those who think that the art of rhetoric should be taught: for they confess that "though wisdom without eloquence is of little service to states, yet eloquence without wisdom is frequently a positive injury, and is of service never." If, then, the men who teach the principles of eloquence have been forced by truth to confess this in the very books which treat of eloquence, though they were ignorant of the true, that is, the heavenly wisdom which comes down from the Father of Lights, how much more ought we to feel it who are the sons and the ministers of this higher wisdom! Now a man speaks with more or less wisdom just as he has made more or less progress in the knowledge of Scripture; I do not mean by reading them much and committing them to memory, but by understanding them aright and carefully searching into their meaning. For there are [some] who read and yet neglect them; they read to remember the words, but are careless about knowing the meaning. It is plain we must set far above these the men who are not so retentive of the words, but see with the eyes of the heart into the heart of Scripture. Better than either of these, however, is the man who, when he wishes, can repeat the words, and at the same time correctly apprehends their meaning. . . .

CHAP. 28. TRUTH IS MORE IMPORTANT THAN EXPRESSION. WHAT IS MEANT BY STRIFE ABOUT WORDS.

Such a teacher as is here described may, to secure compliance, speak not only quietly and temperately, but even vehemently, without any breach of modesty, because his life protects him against contempt. For while he pursues an upright life, he takes care to maintain a good reputation as well, providing things honest in the sight of God and men, fearing God, and caring for men. In his very speech even he prefers to please by matter rather than by words; thinks that a thing is well said in proportion as it is true in fact, and that a teacher should govern his words, not let the words govern him. This is what the apostle says: "Not with wisdom of words, lest the cross of Christ should be made of none effect." To the same effect also is what he says to Timothy: "Charging them before the Lord that they strive not about words to no profit, but to the subverting of the hearers." Now this does not mean that, when adversaries oppose the truth, we are to say nothing in defence of the truth. For where, then, would be what he says when he is describing the sort of man a bishop ought to be: "that he may be able by sound doctrine both to exhort and convince the gain-sayers?" To strive about words is not to be careful about the way to overcome error by truth, but to be anxious that your mode of expression should be preferred to that of another. The man who does not strive about words, whether he speak quietly, temperately, or vehemently, uses words with no other purpose than to make the truth plain, pleasing, and effective; for not even love itself, which is the end of the commandment and the fulfilling of the law, can be rightly exercised unless the objects of love are true and not false. For as a man with a comely body but an ill-conditioned mind is a more painful object than if his body too were deformed, so men who teach lies are the more pitiable if they happen to be eloquent in speech. To speak eloquently, then, and wisely as well, is just to express truths which it is expedient to teach in fit and proper words—words which in the subdued style are adequate, in the temperate, elegant, and in the majestic, forcible. But the man who cannot speak both eloquently and wisely should speak wisely without eloquence, rather than eloquently without wisdom.

The City of God

In this monumental work, which was the result of thirteen years of study and labor (413–426 A.D.), Augustine makes clear his two sources of authority—Greek philosophy and the Christian scriptures. He himself writes with an authority lent by these great sources of the Western tradition. Citing authors such as Plotinus and St. Paul, he draws a picture of two conflicting cities—the city of man and the city of God. We are bidden to choose between these homes. Augustine insists that the model toward which we must educate is that of the man who rises above the earthly and temporal city and seeks his home in the city of God. Education in the West has continued to struggle under the illusion that it is necessary to choose one element of this false dichotomy.

This translation is by the Rev. Marcus Dods and it appears in Volume II of *A Select Library of the Nicene and Post-Nicene Fathers of the Christian Church,* published by the Christian Literature Company in Buffalo in 1887.

BOOK X

CHAP. 14. THAT THE ONE GOD IS TO BE WORSHIPPED NOT ONLY
FOR THE SAKE OF ETERNAL BLESSINGS, BUT ALSO IN CONNECTION
WITH TEMPORAL PROSPERITY, BECAUSE ALL THINGS ARE
REGULATED BY HIS PROVIDENCE.

The education of the human race, represented by the people of God, has advanced, like that of an individual, through certain epochs, or, as it were, ages, so that it might gradually rise from earthly to heavenly things, and from the visible to the invisible. This object was kept so clearly in view, that, even in the period when temporal rewards were promised, the one God was presented as the object of worship, that men might not acknowledge any other than the true Creator and Lord of the spirit, even in connection with the earthly blessings of this transitory life. For he who denies that all things, which either angels or men can give us, are in the hand of the one Almighty, is a madman. The Platonist Plotinus discourses concerning providence, and, from the beauty of flowers and foliage, proves that from the supreme God, whose beauty is unseen and ineffable, providence reaches down even to these earthly things here below; and he argues that all these frail and perishing things could not have so exquisite and elaborate a beauty, were they not fashioned by Him whose unseen and unchangeable beauty continually pervades all things. This is proved also by the Lord Jesus, where He says, "Consider the lilies, how they grow; they toil not, neither do they spin. And yet I say unto you that Solomon in all his glory was not arrayed like one of these. But if God so clothe the grass of the field, which to-day is and to-morrow is cast into the oven, how much more shall He clothe you, O ye of little faith!" It was best, therefore, that the soul of man, which was still weakly desiring earthly things, should be accustomed to seek from God alone even these petty temporal boons, and the earthly necessaries of this transitory life, which are contemptible in comparison with eternal blessings, in order that the desire even of these things might not draw it aside from the worship of Him, to whom we come by despising and forsaking such things. . . .

BOOK XIV

CHAP. 4. WHAT IT IS TO LIVE ACCORDING TO MAN, AND WHAT TO LIVE ACCORDING TO GOD.

When, therefore, man lives according to man, not according to God, he is like the devil. Because not even an angel might live according to an angel, but only according to God, if he was to abide in the truth, and speak God's truth and not his own lie. And of man, too, the same apostle says in another place, "If the truth of God hath more abounded through my lie;"—"my lie," he said, and "God's truth." When, then, a man lives according to the truth, he lives not according to himself, but according to God; for He was God who said, "I am the truth." When, therefore, man lives according to himself—that is, according to man, not according to God—assuredly he lives according to a lie; not that man himself is a lie, for God is his author and creator, who is certainly not the author and creator of a lie, but because man was

made upright, that he might not live according to himself, but according
to Him that made him—in others words, that he might do His will
and not his own; and not to live as he was made to live, that is a
lie. For he certainly desires to be blessed even by not living so that
he may be blessed. And what is a lie if this desire be not? Wherefore
it is not without meaning said that all sin is a lie. For no sin is committed
save by that desire or will by which we desire that it be well with
us, and shrink from it being ill with us. That, therefore, is a lie which
we do in order that it may be well with us, but which makes us more
miserable than we were. And why is this, but because the source of
man's happiness lies only in God, whom he abandons when he sins,
and not in himself, by living according to whom he sins?

In enunciating this proposition of ours, then, that because some live
according to the flesh and others according to the spirit, there have
arisen two diverse and conflicting cities, we might equally well have
said, "because some live according to man, others according to God."
For Paul says very plainly to the Corinthians, "For whereas there is among
you envying and strife, are ye not carnal, and walk according to man?"
So that to walk according to man and to be carnal are the same; for
by *flesh*, that is, by a part of man, man is meant. For before he said
that those same persons were animal whom afterwards he calls carnal,
saying, "For what man knoweth the things of a man, save the spirit
of man which is in him? even so the things of God knoweth no man,
but the Spirit of God. Now we have received not the spirit of this
world, but the Spirit which is of God; that we might know the things
which are freely given to us of God. Which things also we speak, not
in the words which man's wisdom teacheth, but which the Holy Ghost
teacheth; comparing spiritual things with spiritual. But the animal man
perceiveth not the things of the Spirit of God; for they are foolishness
unto him." It is to men of this kind, then, that is, to animal men, he
shortly after says, "And I, brethren, could not speak unto you as unto
spiritual, but as unto carnal." And this is to be interpreted by the same
usage, a part being taken for the whole. For both the soul and the
flesh, the component parts of man, can be used to signify the whole
man; and so the animal man and the carnal man are not two different
things, but one and the same thing, viz., man living according to man.
In the same way it is nothing else than men that are meant either
in the words, "By the deeds of the law there shall no *flesh* be justified;"
or in the words, "Seventy-five *souls* went down into Egypt with Jacob."
In the one passage, "no flesh" signifies "no man;" and in the other,
by "seventy-five souls" seventy-five men are meant. And the expression,
"not in words which man's wisdom teacheth," might equally be "not

in words which fleshly wisdom teacheth;" and the expression, "ye walk according to man," might be "according to the flesh." And this is still more apparent in the words which followed: "For while one saith, I am of Paul, and another, I am of Apollos, are ye not men?" The same thing which he had before expressed by "ye are animal," "ye are carnal," he now expresses by "ye are men;" that is, ye live according to man, not according to God, for if you lived according to Him, you should be gods. . . .

BOOK XIX

CHAP. 25. THAT WHERE THERE IS NO TRUE RELIGION THERE ARE NO TRUE VIRTUES

For though the soul may seem to rule the body admirably, and the reason the vices, if the soul and reason do not themselves obey God, as God has commanded them to serve Him, they have no proper authority over the body and the vices. For what kind of mistress of the body and the vices can that mind be which is ignorant of the true God, and which, instead of being subject to His authority, is prostituted to the corrupting influences of the most vicious demons? It is for this reason that the virtues which it seems to itself to possess, and by which it restrains the body and the vices that it may obtain and keep what it desires, are rather vices than virtues so long as there is no reference to God in the matter. For although some suppose that virtues which have a reference only to themselves, and are desired only on their own account, are yet true and genuine virtues, the fact is that even then they are inflated with pride, and are therefore to be reckoned vices rather than virtues. For as that which gives life to the flesh is not derived from flesh, but is above it, so that which gives blessed life to man is not derived from man, but is something above him; and what I say of man is true of every celestial power and virtue whatsoever.

5 *The Jew: Maimonides*

The challenge that faced Moses ben Maimon (Maimonides) (1135–1204) can be seen in macrocosm in the growing religious and intellectual ferment that agitated twelfth-century Europe and in microcosm in the hardships and uncertainties of his own life. Born into a devout Jewish family in Cordova, Spain, he was forced as a youth to flee from that country because of religious persecution. His wanderings took him through Morocco and Palestine before he finally settled in Egypt. In Spain, Morocco, and Palestine, he saw Jews persecuted, hiding their faith and following alien religious practices, and he feared that Judaism would be abandoned or destroyed. Besides religious persecution from without and apathy within, he also saw a threat to religious fidelity and traditional assumptions in the growth of science and philosophy. His response to these threats was to spend his life in two great enterprises: the codification of Jewish law, as a guide to the faithful, and the attempted reconciliation of the Judaic religious tradition with philosophy, as a guide to the perplexed.

The principal thrust of Maimonides' life was toward the synthesis of two great world views: the Greek, with its emphasis on intellect and reason, and the rabbinical Judaic, with its emphasis on scripture, revelation, and the authority of divine law. Although he followed Aristotle in many ways, Maimonides rejected Aristotelian naturalism. He did not see human history as a drama played only between man and nature. He put God rather than man in the center of the universe. Thus God's revelation must accompany reason as a guide to conduct. Courageously unfashionable, Maimonides defended reason in an age of dogmatism and urged toleration in an age of persecution. His goal was to help the Jew to be able to use the tenets of his religious faith in order to live harmoniously and ethically amidst the growing complexity and sophistication of contemporary life.

As a result of his life-long concern with the conflict between faith and reason, Maimonides formulated a position that denies the incompatibility of the two and he created a model of the educated Jew as one who finds a harmony between them. The ideal Jew is a man of intellect: he must seek knowledge through the application of reason. Through intellectual study he comes to a knowledge of nature as the creation of God. The process thus leads to awe and love of God, which is life's highest good. Indeed, one's love of God will be in proportion to one's intellectual knowledge of His works. Hence, in Maimonides' view, intellectual study should strengthen rather than weaken religious faith.

Maimonides views man as basically physical: the good life must satisfy basic physical needs. However, intellect is the highest element in man's constitution and intellectual goals are therefore superior. It is a mark of the educated man to avoid domination by material desires and physical lusts. He uses his body as the vehicle of the intellect and cultivates it in that spirit. The body must be respected and safeguarded: health and diet should be given careful attention. There is no asceticism in Maimonides' prescription. Bodily pleasures and impulses are God-given and are to be enjoyed, although in moderation. They become evil only when indulged to excess. The Aristotelian doctrine of the mean is followed by Maimonides as an aid to the definition of justice and morality. Justice is a cardinal prerequisite for the good life. It requires, first, a body of law to ensure that citizens will perform their obligations to the community. It further requires self-restraint and moral virtue on the part of individuals, who must restrict their personal impulses for the sake of the common good.

Maimonides' picture of man is of a creature endowed with freedom. He is limited by certain hereditary factors, but within these limits he is largely free to make of himself what he will. His freedom is the basis of man's morality, for determined acts have no moral content. Detailed rules are laid down by Maimonides concerning ethically approved behavior. The model Jew will not take advantage of another person. He will always be ready to serve his fellows, both Jews and non-Jews, especially those who are disadvantaged. The Aristotelian mean is adequate as a general ethical guide, but in the service of others the Jew should give himself without moderation.

The ultimate goal for Maimonides' Jew is to find God's will and do it, to come close to God, to become God-like. Man's ideal qualities are loving-kindness, righteousness, and justice—God-like qualities that manifest themselves in the cosmos and are therefore to be imitated by man. Reason itself is not of material but of divine origin. At death it does not perish with the body but is man's link with eternity.

Mishneh Torah

Maimonides spent ten years compiling his *Mishneh Torah* (The Second Torah). Written in classical Hebrew, it was first published in 1180. It was a monumental endeavor to create a systematic and authoritative code out of the chaotic mass of talmudic literature. This great architectonic masterpiece was an attempt to find a rational basis for Jewish law. Unlike *The Guide of the Perplexed,* it had little influence outside of Judaism, but within Judaism it has become acknowledged as the major classic of the law. It is both a systematic, coherent, scholarly statement of the whole Jewish legal tradition and a practical guide to action for rabbi and judge. In the code, there are fourteen books in all. The first book contains five sections, the third of which is on laws concerning the study of the Torah. In this section are seven chapters; the first five of these are reprinted here. They contain detailed instructions on how the Torah is to be taught, including pedagogical techniques, as well as explication of the kind of behavior expected of the model Jew. It is clear that the educated Jew is primarily regarded as a man. Fathers are enjoined not to teach their daughters the Torah, since most women lack the intellectual power to master it and hence will merely trivialize it. The Jewish girl and woman today still often have to struggle to overcome the residual effects of this convenient fiction. Every Jewish man must study the Torah diligently, although he must also carry on his everyday work. Maimonides praises those who support themselves by the work of their hands. One must not devote himself entirely to study and thus have to live on the charity of others. Maimonides himself followed this injunction. He was first of all a partner of his brother, David, as a dealer in precious stones. Later, after the death of his brother at sea, Maimonides practised as a physician in Egypt.

These selections are from Maimonides, *Mishneh Torah: The Book of Knowledge,* edited and translated by Moses Hyamson, published in Jerusalem, Israel, in 1962 by Boys Town Jerusalem Publishers, with whose permission they are reprinted.

LAWS CONCERNING THE STUDY OF THE TORAH

Comprising two affirmative precepts, namely:
(1) to study the Torah; (2) to honour its teachers and those versed in it.

CHAPTER I

Women, slaves and the young (under the age of puberty) are exempt from the obligation of studying Torah. But it is a duty of the father to teach his young son Torah; as it is said, "And ye shall teach them, to your children, talking to them" (Deut. 11:19). A woman is under no obligation to teach her son, since only one whose duty it is to learn has a duty to teach.

2. Just as it is man's duty to teach his son, so it is his duty to teach his grandson, as it is said, "Make them known unto thy children and thy children's children" (Deut. 4:9). This obligation is to be fulfilled not only towards a son and grandson. A duty rests on every scholar in Israel to reach all disciples (who seek instruction from him), even if they are not his children, as it is said, "And thou shalt teach them diligently unto thy chidren" (Deut. 6:7). On traditional authority, the term "thy children" includes disciples, for disciples too are called children, as it is said "And the sons of the prophets came forth" (II Kings 2:3). This being so, why does the precept (concerning instruction) specifically mention (Deut. 4:9) a man's son and son's son? To impress upon us that the son should receive instruction in preference to a grandson, and a grandson in preference to another man's son.

3. A father (who cannot teach his son) is bound to engage a paid teacher for him. But the only obligation one owes to a neighbour's son is to teach him when it involves no expense. If a father has not had his son taught, it is the duty of the latter, as soon as he realises his deficiencies, to acquire knowledge for himself, as it is said, "That ye may learn them and observe to do them" (Deut. 5:1). And so too, you will find that study in all cases takes precedence of practice, since study leads to practice, but practice does not lead to study.

4. If a man needs to learn Torah and has a son who needs instruction, his own requirements are to be satisfied first. But if his son has better

capacity and greater ability to grasp what he learns, then the son's education takes precedence. Still, even in this case, the father must not wholly neglect the study of the Torah. For, just as it is incumbent on him to have his son taught, so is he under an obligation to obtain instruction for himself.

5. A man should always first study Torah and then marry; for if he takes a wife first, his mind will not be free for study. But if his physical desires are so overpowering as to preoccupy his mind, he should marry and then study Torah.

6. When should a father commence his son's instruction in Torah? As soon as the child begins to talk, the father should teach him the text "Moses commanded us a law" (Deut. 33:4), and the first verse of the *Shema* ("Hear O Israel, the Lord our God, the Lord is One") (Deut. 6:4). Later on, according to the child's capacity, the father should teach him a few verses at a time, till he attains the age of six or seven years, when he should take him to a teacher of young children.

7. If it is the custom of the country for a teacher of children to receive remuneration, the father is to pay the fee, and it is his duty to have his son taught, even if he has to pay for the instruction, till the child has gone through the whole of the Written Law. Where it is the custom to charge a fee for teaching the Written Law, it is permissible to take payment for such instruction. It is forbidden however to teach the Oral Law for payment, for it is said "Behold, I have taught you statutes and ordinances, even as the Lord, my God, commanded me" (Deut. 4:5). This means: "Even as I (Moses) learnt (from God) without payment, so have ye learnt from me, gratuitously. And throughout the generations, whenever you teach, do so gratuitously, even as you learnt from me." If a person cannot find any one willing to teach him without remuneration, he should engage a paid teacher, as it is said "Buy the truth" (Prov. 23:23). It should not however be assumed that it is permissible to take pay for teaching. For the verse continues "And sell it not," the inference being, that even where a man had been obliged to pay for instruction (in the Oral Law), he is nevertheless forbidden to charge, in his turn, for teaching it.

8. Every Israelite is under an obligation to study Torah, whether he is poor or rich, in sound health or ailing, in the vigour of youth or very old and feeble. Even a man so poor that he is maintained by charity or goes begging from door to door, as also a man with a wife and children to support, are under the obligation to set aside a definite period during the day and at night for the study of the Torah, as it is said "But thou shalt meditate therein day and night" (Joshua 1:8).

9. Among the great sages of Israel, some were hewers of wood, some, drawers of water, while others were blind. Nevertheless, they devoted themselves by day and by night to the study of the Torah. They are included among the transmitters of the tradition in the direct line from Moses.

10. Until what period in life ought one to study Torah? Until the day of one's death, as it is said, "And lest they (the precepts) depart from thy heart all the days of thy life" (Deut. 4:9). Whenever one ceases to study, one forgets.

11. The time allotted to study should be divided into three parts. A third should be devoted to the Written Law; a third to the Oral Law; and the last third should be spent in reflection, deducing conclusions from premises, developing implications of statements, comparing dicta, studying the hermeneutical principles by which the Torah is interpreted till one knows the essence of these principles, and how to deduce what is permitted and what is forbidden from what one has learnt traditionally. This is termed Talmud.

12. For example, if one is an artizan who works at his trade three hours daily and devotes nine hours to the study of the Torah, he should spend three of these nine hours in the study of the Written Law, three in the study of the Oral Law, and the remaining three in reflecting on how to deduce one rule from another. The words of the Prophets are comprised in the Written Law, while their exposition falls within the category of the Oral Law. The subjects styled *Pardes* (Esoteric Studies), are included in *Talmud*. This plan applies to the period when one begins learning. But after one has become proficient and no longer needs to learn the Written Law, or continually be occupied with the Oral Law, he should, at fixed times, read the Written Law and the traditional dicta, so as not to forget any of the rules of the Torah, and should devote all his days exclusively to the study of Talmud, according to his breadth of mind and maturity of intellect.

13. A woman who studies Torah will be recompensed, but not in the same measure as a man, for study was not imposed on her as a duty, and one who performs a meritorious act which is not obligatory will not receive the same reward as one upon whom it is incumbent and who fulfills it as a duty, but only a lesser reward. And notwithstanding that she is recompensed, yet the Sages have warned us that a man shall not teach his daughter Torah, as the majority of women have not a mind adequate for its study but, because of their limitations, will turn the words of the Torah into trivialities. The sages said "He who teaches his daughter Torah—it is as if he taught her wantonness"

This stricture refers only to instruction in the Oral Law. With regard to the Written Law, he ought not to teach it to her; but if he has done so, it is not regarded as teaching her wantonness.

CHAPTER II

1. Teachers of young children are to be appointed in each province, district and town. If a city has made no provision for the education of the young, its inhabitants are placed under a ban, till such teachers have been engaged. And if they persistently neglect this duty, the city is excommunicated, for the world is only maintained by the breath of school children.

2. Children are to be sent to school at the age of six or seven years, according to the strength of the individual child and its physical development. But no child is to be sent to school under six years of age. The teacher may chastise his pupils to inspire them with awe. But he must not do so in a cruel manner or in a vindictive spirit. Accordingly, he must not strike them with whips or sticks, but only use a small strap. He is to teach them the whole day and part of the night, so as to train them to study by day and by night. And there is to be no holiday except on the eve of the Sabbath or festival, towards the close of the day, and on festivals. On Sabbaths, pupils are not taught a new lesson, but they repeat what they had already learnt previously, even if only once. Pupils must not be interrupted at their studies, even for the re-building of the Temple.

3. A teacher who leaves the children and goes out (when he should be teaching them), or does other work while he is with them, or teaches lazily, falls under the ban "Cursed be he that doeth the work of the Lord with a slack hand" (Jer. 48:10). Hence, it is not proper to appoint any one as teacher unless he is God-fearing and well versed in reading and in grammar.

4. An unmarried man should not keep school for the young because the mothers come to see their children. Nor should any woman keep school, because the fathers come to see them.

5. Twenty-five children may be put in charge of one teacher. If the number in the class exceeds twenty-five but is not more than forty, he should have an assistant to help with the instruction. If there are more than forty, two teachers must be appointed.

6. A child may be transferred from one teacher to another who is more competent in reading or grammar, only however, if both the

teacher and the pupil live in the same town and are not separated by a river. But we must not take the child to school in another town nor even across a river in the same town, unless it is spanned by a firm bridge, not likely soon to collapse.

7. If one of the residents in an alley or even in a court wishes to open a school, his neighbours cannot prevent him. Nor can a teacher, already established, object to another teacher opening a school next door to him, either for new pupils or even with the intention of drawing away pupils from the existing school, for it is said, "The Lord was pleased for High righteousness' sake, to make the Torah great and Glorious" (Is. 42:21).

CHAPTER III

1. With three crowns was Israel crowned—with the crown of the Torah, with the crown of the priesthood and with the crown of sovereignty. The crown of the priesthood was bestowed upon Aaron, as it is said, "And it shall be unto him and unto his seed after him, the covenant of an everlasting priesthood" (Num. 25:13). The crown of sovereignty was conferred upon David, as it is said, "His seed shall endure forever, and his throne as the sun before Me" (Ps. 89:37). The crown of the Torah however is for all Israel, as is it said, "Moses commanded us a law, an inheritance of the congregation of Jacob" (Deut. 33:4). Whoever desires it can win it. Do not suppose that the other two crowns are greater than the crown of the Torah, for it is said, "By me, kings reign and princes decree justice. By me, princes rule" (Prov. 8:15–16). Hence the inference, that the crown of the Torah is greater than the other two crowns.

2. The sages said "A bastard who is a scholar takes precedence of an ignorant High Priest; for it is said "More precious it is than rubies" (Prov. 3:15), that is (more to be honoured is the scholar) than the High Priest who enters the Innermost sanctuary.

3. Of all precepts, none is equal in importance to the study of the Torah. Nay, study of the Torah is equal to them all, for study leads to practice. Hence, study always takes precedence of practice.

4. If the opportunity of fulfilling a specific precept would interrupt the study of the Torah and the precept can be performed by others, one should not intermit study. Otherwise, the precept should be performed and then the study be resumed.

5. At the Judgment hereafter, a man will first be called to account in regard to his fulfilment of the duty of study, and afterwards concern-

ing his other activities. Hence, the sages said, "A person should always occupy himself with the Torah, whether for its own sake or for other reasons. For study of the Torah, even when pursued from interested motives, will lead to study for its own sake."

6. He whose heart prompts him to fulfil this duty properly, and to be crowned with the crown of the Torah, must not allow his mind to be diverted to other objects. He must not aim at acquiring Torah as well as riches and honour at the same time. "This is the way for the study of the Torah. A morsel of bread with salt thou must eat, and water by measure thou must drink; thou must sleep upon the ground and live a life of hardship, the while thou toilest in the Torah" (Ethics of the Fathers 6:4). "It is not incumbent upon thee to complete the task; but neither art thou free to neglect it" (ibid 2:21). "And if thou hast studied much Torah, thou hast earned much reward. The recompense will be proportionate to the pains" (ibid 5:26).

7. Possibly you may say: When I shall have accumulated money, I shall resume my studies; when I shall have provided for my needs and have leisure from my affairs, I shall resume my studies. Should such a thought enter your mind, you will never win the crown of the Torah. "Rather make the study of the Torah your fixed occupation" (ibid 1:15) and let your secular affairs engage you casually, and do not say: "When I shall have leisure, I shall study; perhaps you may never have leisure" (ibid 2:5).

8. In the Torah it is written, "It is not in heaven. . . . neither is it beyond the sea" (Deut. 30:12–13). "It is not in heaven," this means that the Torah is not to be found with the arrogant; "nor beyond the seas," that is, it is not found among those who cross the ocean. Hence our sages said "Nor can one who is engaged overmuch in business grow wise" (Ethics of the Fathers 2:6). They have also exhorted us "Engage little in business and occupy thyself with the Torah" (Ethics of the Fathers 4:12).

9. The words of the Torah have been compared to water, as it is said, "O every one that thirsteth, come ye for water" (Is. 55:1); this teaches us that just as water does not accumulate on a slope but flows away, while in a depression it stays, so the Words of the Torah are not to be found in the arrogant or haughty but only in him who is contrite and lowly in spirit, who sits in the dust at the feet of the wise and banishes from his heart lusts and temporal delights; works a little daily, just enough to provide for his needs, if he would otherwise have nothing to eat, and devotes the rest of the day and night to the study of the Torah.

10. One however who makes up his mind to study Torah and not work but live on charity, profanes the name of God, brings the Torah into contempt, extinguishes the light of religion, brings evil upon himself and deprives himself of life hereafter, for it is forbidden to derive any temporal advantage from the words of the Torah. The sages said "Whoever derives a profit for himself from the words of the Torah is helping on his own destruction" (Ethics of the Fathers 4:17). They have further charged us "Make not of them a crown wherewith to aggrandise thyself, nor a spade wherewith to dig" (ibid 4:7). They likewise exhorted us "Love work, hate lordship" (ibid. 1:10). "All study of the Torah, not conjoined with work, must, in the end, be futile, and become a cause of sin" (ibid 2:2). The end of such a person will be that he will rob his fellow-creatures.

11. It indicates a high degree of excellence in a man to maintain himself by the labour of his hands. And this was the normal practice of the early saints. Thus, one secures all honour and happiness here and hereafter, as it is said "When thou eatest of the labour of thine hands, happy shalt thou be, and it shall be well with thee" (Ps. 128:2). Happy shalt thou be in this world, and it shall be well with thee in the world to come, which is altogether good.

12. The words of the Torah do not abide with one who studies listlessly, nor with those who learn amidst luxury, and high living, but only with one who mortifies himself for the sake of the Torah, constantly enduring physical discomfort, and not permitting sleep to his eyes nor slumber to his eyelids. "This is the law, when a man dieth in a tent" (Num. 19:14). The sages explained the text metaphorically thus: "The Torah only abides with him who mortifies himself in the tents of the wise." And so Solomon, in his wisdom, said "If thou faint in the day of adversity, thy strength is small indeed" (Prov. 24:10). He also said "Also my wisdom stood unto me" (Eccles 2:9). This is explained by our wise men thus, "The wisdom that I learnt in wrath,—this has remained with me." The sages said "There is a solemn covenant that anyone who toils at his studies in the Synagogue, will not quickly forget." He who toils privately in learning, will become wise, as it is said "With the lowly (literally, *the reserved*) is wisdom" (Prov. 11:2). If one recites aloud while studying, what he learns will remain with him. But he who reads silently soon forgets.

13. While it is a duty to study by day and by night, most of one's knowledge is acquired at night. Accordingly, when one aspires to win the crown of the Torah, he should be especially heedful of all his nights and not waste a single one of them in sleep, eating, drinking, idle talk

and so forth, but devote all of them to study of the Torah and words
of wisdom. The sages said "That sound of the Torah has worth, which
is heard by night, as it is said 'Arise, cry out in the night' (Lam. 2:19):
and whoever occupies himself with the study of the Torah at night—a
mark of spiritual grace distinguishes him by day, as it is said, 'By day
the Lord will command His loving kindness, and in the night His song
shall be with me, even a prayer unto the God of my life' (Ps. 42:9).
A house wherein the words of the Torah are not heard at night will
be consumed by fire, as it is said 'All darkness is laid up for his treasures;
a fire not blown by man shall consume him' (Job 20:26). 'Because
he hath despised the word of the Lord' (Num. 15:31)—this refers to
one who has utterly neglected (the study of) the words of the Torah."
And, so too, one who is able to occupy himself with the Torah and
does not do so, or who had read Scripture and learnt *Mishnah* and
gave them up for worldly inanities, and abandoned and completely renounced this study, is included in the condemnation, "Because he hath
despised the Word of the Lord". The sages said, "Whoever neglects
the Torah because of wealth, will, at last be forced to neglect it owing
to poverty. And whoever fulfills the Torah in poverty, will ultimately
fulfill it amidst wealth" (Ethics of the Fathers 4:11, with order of sentences reversed). And this is explicitly set forth in the Torah, as it
is said, "Because thou didst not serve the Lord thy God with joyfulness
and with gladness of heart, by reason of the abundance of all things,
therefore shalt thou serve thine enemy" (Deut. 28:47–48). It is also
said "That He might afflict thee. . . . to do thee good at thy latter
end. . . ." (Deut. 8:16).

CHAPTER IV

1. Torah should only be taught to a worthy pupil whose conduct
is exemplary or whose disposition is simple. One however who walks
in a way that is not good should first be reclaimed, trained in the right
way and tested (as to his sincerity); then he is admitted into the *Beth
Hamidrash* (College) and given instruction. The sages say: "To teach
a pupil who is unworthy is like casting a stone to Mercury (the idol),
as it is said, "As one puts a stone in a sling, so is he that giveth honour
to a fool" (Prov. 26:8). There is no honour but the Torah, as it is
said, "The wise shall inherit honour" (Prov. 3:35). So too, if a teacher
does not walk in the right way—even if he is a great scholar and all
the people are in need of him—instruction is not to be received from
him till he reforms; as it is said, "For the priest's lips shall keep knowledge, and they shall seek the law from his mouth, for he is the messenger

of the Lord of Hosts" (Mal. 2:7). Our sages applied this text thus:
"If the teacher is like an angel of the Lord of Hosts, they may seek
the Law from his mouth. But if he is not, then they shall not seek
the Law from his mouth."

2. How is instruction to be imparted? The teacher is seated in the
schoolroom facing the class, with the pupils around him like a crown,
so that they can all see him and hear his words. The teacher is not
to sit on a stool while his pupils are seated on the floor. Either all
sit on the floor, or all on stools. Formerly the teacher used to be seated,
while the pupils stood. But before the destruction of the Second Temple,
it already had become the universal custom that pupils, while being
taught, should be seated.

3. If it was his custom to teach the pupils personally, he may do
so. If however, he taught through a *Meturgeman* (an interpreter), the
latter stands between him and his pupils. The teacher addresses the
interpreter, who declaims what he has just heard to all the pupils. And
when they put questions to the interpreter, he asks the teacher.   The
teacher replies to the interpreter who addresses the answer to the one
who put the question. The teacher should not raise his voice above
the interpreter's voice. Nor should the latter raise his voice above that
of the teacher, when he addresses a question to him. The interpreter
may not detract aught from the teacher's words, nor add to them nor
vary them—unless he is the teacher's father or instructor. In addressing
the interpreter, the teacher uses the introductory formula: "Thus my
revered preceptor said to me" or "Thus my revered father said to me."
But when the interpreter repeats the words to the listener, he recites
them in the name of the sage quoted, and mentions the name if he
were the teacher's father or teacher, and says "Thus said our Master
so-and-so" (naming him). He does so, even if the teacher abstained
from naming the sage on the ground that it is forbidden to mention
one's teacher or father by name.

4. If the teacher taught and his pupils did not understand, he should
not be angry with them or fall into a rage, but should repeat the lesson
again and again till they have grasped the full meaning of the Halacha
(rule) he is expounding. So also, the pupil should not say "I understand"
when he has not understood, but should ask again and again. And if
the master is angry with him and storms at him, he should say "Master,
it is Torah. I need to learn, and my intellectual capacities are deficient."

5. A disciple should not feel ashamed before his fellow-students who
grasp the lesson after hearing it once or twice, while he needs to hear
it several times before he knows it. For if this makes him feel ashamed,

he will go through college without having learnt anything. The ancient sages accordingly said, "A bashful man cannot learn, nor a passionate man teach" (Ethics of the Fathers 2:6). These observations only apply when the students' lack of understanding is due to the difficulty of the subject or to their mental deficiency. But if the teacher clearly sees that they are negligent and indolent in their study of the Torah and that this is the cause of their failure to understand, it is his duty to scold them and shame them with words of reproach, and so stimulate them to be keen. And in this regard, the sages said "Arouse awe in the pupils." It is thus improper for a teacher to indulge in frivolity before his pupils, or to jest in their presence, or eat and drink with them—so that the fear of him be upon them, and they will thus learn from him quickly.

6. Questions are not to be put to the teacher immediately on his entering the school, but only after his mind is composed. Nor should a pupil put a question as soon as he has come in, but only after he himself is composed and rested. Two pupils are not to put questions at one time. The teacher is not to be questioned on a topic not pertaining to the lesson, but only on the subject that is being treated, so as not to embarrass him. The teacher however should set "pitfalls" before his pupils, both in his questions and in what he does in their presence, in order to sharpen their wits, and ascertain whether they remember what he had taught them or do not remember it. Needless to add, that he has the right to question them on a subject other than that on which they are at the moment engaged, in order to stimulate them to be diligent in study.

7. No questions should be asked standing, nor answers given standing; nor should they be addressed by any one from an elevation, or from a distance, or when one is behind the elders. The teacher may only be questioned on the topic that is being studied. The questions are to be put in a respectful manner. One should not ask concerning more than three Halachoth (rules) in the topic.

8. Two individuals put questions. One of these questions is germane to the subject under discussion, while the other is not. Heed is given to the question that is germane. One question refers to a legal rule, the other to exegesis; the former receives attention. One question is exegetical; the other homiletical; the former is taken up. One question is homiletical; the other appertains to an inference *a fortiori;* the latter is answered. One question refers to an *a fortiori* inference, the other to an inference from similarity of phrases; the former is dealt with. Questions are put by two persons, one of whom is a graduated scholar,

the other a disciple; attention is paid to the scholar. One of them is a disciple, the other is unlettered; heed is given to the disciple. Where both are graduated scholars, disciples or unlettered, and the questions of both concern two legal rules, or two responses, or two practical issues, the interpreter may in these cases give the preference to either.

9. No one should sleep in the Beth Hamidrash (House of Study). If a student dozes there, his knowledge becomes a thing of shreds. Thus Solomon, in his wisdom, said, "And drowsiness shall clothe one in rags" (Prov. 23:21). No conversation may be held in the House of Study, except in reference to the words of the Torah. Even if one sneezes there, the others do not wish him 'good health.' Needless to add, other topics must not be discussed. The sanctity of a Beth Hamidrash is greater than that of synagogues.

CHAPTER V

1. Just as a person is commanded to honour and revere his father, so is he under an obligation to honour and revere his teacher, even to a greater extent than his father; for his father gave him life in this world, while his teacher who instructs him in wisdom, secures for him life in the world to come. If he sees an article that his father had lost and another article that his teacher had lost, the teacher's property should be recovered first, and then the father's. If his father and his teacher are loaded with burdens, he should first relieve his teacher and then his father. If his father and teacher are in captivity, he should first ransom his father. But, if his father is a scholar, even though not of the same rank as his teacher, he should first recover his father's lost property and then his teacher's. There is no honour higher than that which is due to the teacher; no reverence profounder than that which should be paid him. The sages said "Reverence for thy teacher shall be like the fear of Heaven" (Ethics of the Fathers 4:15). They further said, "Whoever distrusts the authority of his teacher—it is as if he disputes with the *Shechinah!;* as it is said, "When they strove against the Lord" (Num. 26:9). Whoever starts a quarrel with his teacher, it is as if he started a quarrel with the *Shechinah;* as it is said, "Where the children of Israel strove with the Lord, and He was sanctified in them" (Num. 20:13). And whoever cherishes resentment against his teacher—it is as if he cherishes resentment against the Lord, as it is said, "Your murmurings are not against us, but against the Lord" (Ex. 16:8). Whoever harbours doubts about his teacher—it is as if he harbours doubts about the *Shechinah;* as it is said, "And the people spoke against God and against Moses" (Num. 21:3).

2. Who is to be regarded as disputing his teacher's authority? One who sets up a college, holds sessions, discourses and instructs without his teacher's permission, during the latter's lifetime, and even if he be a resident in another country. To give decisions in his teacher's presence is forbidden at all times. Whoever gives a decision in his teacher's presence is deserving of death.

3. If there was a distance of twelve *mils* between him and his teacher and a question was put to him concerning a rule of practice, he may give the answer; and, to save a man from doing what is forbidden, he may give a decision even in his teacher's presence. For instance, if he sees one committing a violation of the Law, because that person did not know that it is prohibited, or out of sheer wickedness, it is his duty to check the wrongdoer and say to him "This is forbidden.' He should do so, even in the presence of his master, and even if the latter has not given him permission. For to save God's name from being profaned, we forego the honour due to the teacher. This however is only permitted casually. But to assume the function of a decisionist and give decisions regularly to all enquirers, even if he and his teacher live at opposite ends of the earth, is forbidden to a disciple, during his teacher's lifetime, unless he has his teacher's permission. Nor even after his teacher's death, may any disciple regularly give decisions, unless he has attained a standard of knowledge qualifying him to do so.

4. A disciple who is not thus qualified and nevertheless gives decisions is "wicked, foolish and of an arrogant spirit" (Ethics of the Fathers 4:9). And of him it is said, "For she hath cast down many wounded" (Prov. 7:26). On the other hand, a sage, who is qualified and refrains from rendering decisions, withholds knowledge of the Torah and puts stumbling blocks before the blind. Of him it is said "Even the mighty are all her slain" (Prov. 7:26). The students of small minds who have acquired an insufficient knowledge of the Torah, and yet seek to aggrandise themselves before the ignorant and among their townsmen by impertinently putting themselves forward and presuming to judge and render decisions in Israel—these are the ones who multiply strife, devastate the world, quench the light of the Torah and spoil the vineyard of the Lord of hosts. Of such, Solomon, in his wisdom, said "Seize for us the foxes, the little foxes that spoil the vineyard" (Song of Songs 2:15).

5. A disciple is forbidden to call his teacher by his name, even when the latter is not present. This rule only applies if the name is unusual, so that any one hearing it knows who is meant. In his presence, the pupil must never mention his teacher's name, even if he desires to call

another person who bears the same name; the same is the rule with his father's name. In referring to them even after their death, he should use a descriptive title, ("my honoured father," or "my honoured teacher"). A disciple may not greet his teacher or return his greeting in the same manner as people are wont to greet their companions and return their greetings. But he should bow to his teacher and address him with reverence and deference "Peace be unto thee, my teacher." If the teacher greeted him first, he should respond "Peace to thee, my teacher and master."

6. So too, he should not remove his phylacteries in his teacher's presence, nor recline in his presence, but should sit respectfully, as one sits before a king. He should not recite his prayers, while standing in front of his teacher, or behind him, or at his side; needless to add, that he must not step (backward or forward) side by side with the teacher, but should stand at a distance in the rear, not however, exactly behind his teacher, and then he can offer up his devotions. He must not go with his teacher into the same bath room. He must not sit in his teacher's seat. When his teacher and a colleague dispute with one another, he must not, in his teacher's presence, interpose his opinion as to who is right. He must not contradict his teacher's statements. He may not sit down in his teacher's presence, till he is told "be seated," nor stand up, till he is told to stand up, or till he obtains permission to stand up. And when he quits, he must not turn his back, but should retire with his face to his teacher.

7. It is his duty to rise before his teacher, from the moment he sees him at a distance, (and keep standing) till he disappears from view and is no longer visible; then the disciple may resume his seat. It is a person's duty to visit his teacher on the festivals.

8. Courtesy must not be shown to a pupil in the teacher's presence, unless the teacher himself is wont to show courtesy to that pupil. The various offices that a slave performs for his master, a pupil performs for his teacher. If however he is in a place where he is unknown, and has no phylacteries with him, and fears that people will say that he is a slave, he does not help his teacher to put on or remove his shoes. Whoever refuses his pupil's services, withholds kindness from him and removes from him the fear of Heaven. A pupil who neglects any of the courtesies due to his master causes the *Schechinah* to depart from Israel.

9. If a pupil saw his teacher violating the ordinances of the Torah, he should say to him, "Our master, thus and thus, has thou taught us." Whenever a pupil recites a dictum in his teacher's presence, he

should say "Thus, our master, hast thou taught us." He should never quote a dictum that he has not heard from his teacher, without giving the authority for it. When his teacher dies, he rends all the garments he wears till he bares his breast. These rents he never sews up. These rules only apply to the chief teacher from whom one has learnt most of what he knows. But his relation to one from whom he did not acquire most of his knowledge is that of a junior to a senior fellow-student. Towards such a senior student (who was at the same time his teacher), the disciple is not required to observe all the above-mentioned points of courtesy. But the junior has to stand up before him, and, on his demise, has to rend his garments, just as he does for a deceased relative for whom he mourns. Even if one learnt from a person one thing only, be it great or small, one has to stand up before that person and rend one's garments at his demise.

10. No scholar who possesses good manners will speak before his superior in knowledge, even if he has learnt nothing from him.

11. If one's chief teacher desires to excuse all his pupils or any one of them from all or any of these observances, he may do so. But even then, the disciple must show courtesy to him, even at the moment when he explicitly dispenses with it.

12. As pupils are bound to honour their teacher, so a teacher ought to show courtesy and friendliness to his pupils. The sages said "Let the honour of thy disciples be as dear to thee as thine own" (Ethics of the Fathers 4:15). A man should take an interest in his pupils and love them, for they are his spiritual children who will bring him happiness in this world and in the world hereafter.

13. Disciples increase the teacher's wisdom and broaden his mind. The sages said, "Much wisdom I learnt from my teachers, more from my colleagues; from my pupils, most of all." Even as a small piece of wood kindles a large log, so a pupil of small attainments sharpens the mind of his teacher, so that by his questions, he elicits glorious wisdom.

The Guide of the Perplexed

In 1190 appeared Maimonides' greatest philosophical work, *The Guide of the Perplexed*. It was written in Arabic but translated immediately into Hebrew and Latin. Widely considered to be the greatest philosophical treatise of Judaism, it had enormous subsequent influence on Jewish, Islamic, and Christian thought. St. Thomas Aquinas and Spinoza were two major thinkers deeply affected by the *Guide*. It was Maimonides' major attempt to respond to the challenge of Greek, especially Aristotelian, thought. The "perplexed" to whom Maimonides addressed himself were those men who did not wish to abandon their traditional religious beliefs but who were bewildered by the contradictory evidence of science and philosophy. His two-fold approach was to use philosophy to justify prophetic religion and to use religion to deepen philosophy. God is the embodiment of law in the universe; man's duty is to study the law in order to gain the knowledge that will bring him closer to God. The model Jew does not avoid knowledge but seeks it in all possible ways. Since the Torah commands man to love God, and since one must acquire knowledge of God in order to love Him, the acquisition of knowledge is thereby laid upon the Jew as a religious ordinance. In his simile of the palace in the following selection, Maimonides affirms that knowledge of science and philosophy enables man to approach nearer to God (that is, to enter the palace). The path of the wise man is three-fold: to learn the truths of traditional religion; to learn to prove them philosophically; and to derive from them rules for one's conduct. The best of men will thus aspire toward the greatest possible knowledge of God and will attempt to serve God through the practice of loving-kindness, righteousness, and justice. Those who never forget God become most like God, that is, wise. Maimonides makes clear that it is the task of the thinker to interpret the authority of scripture. In other words, reason becomes one of the authorities or standards by which truth is judged. But the ideal Jew is not merely a rational philosopher. The philosopher studies what reason makes accessible and suspends judgment on the rest. The Jew (like Maimonides himself) accepts the truth of the Torah. He uses philosophy to amplify and sustain revelation, but he does not hold back from giving his assent to that which reason cannot substantiate.

This passage is taken from Maimonides, *The Guide of the Perplexed*, translated by M. Friedlander, published in New York in 1881 by the Hebrew Publishing Company.

PART III

CHAPTER 51

The present chapter does not contain any additional matter that has not been treated in the [previous] chapters of this treatise. It is a kind of conclusion, and at the same time it will explain in what manner those worship God who have obtained a true knowledge concerning God; it will direct them how to come to that worship, which is the highest aim man can attain, and show how God protects them in this world till they are removed to eternal life.

I will begin the subject of this chapter with a simile. A king is in his palace, and all his subjects are partly in the country, and partly abroad. Of the former, some have their backs turned towards the king's palace, and their faces in another direction; and some are desirous and zealous to go to the palace, seeking "to inquire in his temple," and to minister before him, but have not yet seen even the face of the wall of the house. Of those that desire to go to the palace, some reach it, and go round about in search of the entrance gate; others have passed through the gate, and walk about in the ante-chamber; and others have succeeded in entering into the inner part of the palace, and being in the same room with the king in the royal palace. But even the latter do not immediately on entering the palace see the king, or speak to him; for, after having entered the inner part of the palace, another effort is required before they can stand before the king—at a distance, or close by—hear his words, or speak to him. I will now explain the simile which I have made. The people who are abroad are all those that have no religion, neither one based on speculation nor one received

by tradition. Such are the extreme Turks that wander about in the north,
the Kushites who live in the south, and those in our country who are
like these. I consider these as irrational beings, and not as human beings;
they are below mankind, but above monkeys, since they have the form
and shape of man, and a mental faculty above that of the monkey.

Those who are in the country, but have their backs turned towards
the king's palace, are those who possess religion, belief, and thought,
but happen to hold false doctrines, which they either adopted in consequence of great mistakes made in their own speculations, or received
from others who misled them. Because of these doctrines they recede
more and more from the royal palace the more they seem to proceed.
These are worse than the first class, and under certain circumstances
it may become necessary to slay them, and to extirpate their doctrines,
in order that others should not be misled.

Those who desire to arrive at the palace, and to enter it, but have
never yet seen it, are the mass of religious people; the multitude that
observe the divine commandments, but are ignorant. Those who arrive
at the palace, but go round about it, are those who devote themselves
exclusively to the study of the practical law; they believe traditionally
in true principles of faith, and learn the practical worship of God, but
are not trained in philosophical treatment of the principles of the Law,
and do not endeavour to establish the truth of their faith by proof.
Those who undertake to investigate the principles of religion, have come
into the ante-chamber; and there is no doubt that these can also be
divided into different grades. But those who have succeeded in finding
a proof for everything that can be proved, who have a true knowledge
of God, so far as a true knowledge can be attained, and are near the
truth, wherever an approach to the truth is possible, they have reached
the goal, and are in the palace in which the king lives.

My son, so long as you are engaged in studying the Mathematical
Sciences and Logic, you belong to those who go round about the palace
in search of the gate. Thus our Sages figuratively use the phrase: "Ben-
zoma is still outside." When you understand Physics, you have entered
the hall; and when, after completing the study of Natural Philosophy,
you master Metaphysics, you have entered the innermost court, and
are with the king in the same palace. You have attained the degree
of the wise men, who include men of different grades of perfection.
There are some who direct all their mind toward the attainment of
perfection in Metaphysics, devote themselves entirely to God, exclude
from their thought every other thing, and employ all their intellectual
faculties in the study of the Universe, in order to derive therefrom
a proof for the existence of God, and to learn in every possible way

how God rules all things; they form the class of those who have entered
the palace, namely, the class of prophets. One of these has attained
so much knowledge, and has concentrated his thoughts to such an extent
in the idea of God, that it could be said of him, "And he was with
the Lord forty days," & c. (Exod. xxxiv. 28); during that holy communion
he could ask Him, answer Him, speak to Him, and be addressed by
Him, enjoying beatitude in that which he had obtained to such a degree
that "he did neither eat bread nor drink water" (ibid.); his intellectual
energy was so predominant that all coarser functions of the body, especially those connected with the sense of touch, were in abeyance. Some
prophets are only able to see, and of these some approach near and
see, whilst others see from a distance: comp. "The Lord hath appeared
from far unto me" (Jer. xxxi. 3). We have already spoken of the various
degrees of prophets; we will therefore return to the subject of this chapter, and exhort those who have attained a knowledge of God, to concen-
trate all their thoughts in God. This is the worship peculiar to those
who have acquired a knowledge of the highest truths; and the more
they reflect on Him, and think of Him, the more are they engaged
in His worship. Those, however, who think of God, and frequently mention His name, without any correct notion of Him, but merely following
some imagination, or some creed received from another person, are,
in my opinion, like those who remain outside the palace and distant
from it. They do not mention the name of God in truth, nor do they
reflect on it. That which they imagine and mention does not correspond
to any being in existence; it is a thing invented by their imagination,
as has been shown by us in our discussion on the Divine Attributes
(Part I. ch. 1). The true worship of God is only possible when correct
notions of Him have previously been conceived. When you have arrived
by way of intellectual research at a knowledge of God and His works,
then commence to devote yourselves to Him, try to approach Him and
strengthen the intellect, which is the link that joins you to Him. Thus
Scripture says, "Unto thee it was showed, that thou mightest know that
the Lord He is God" (Deut. iv. 35); "Know therefore this day, and
consider it in thine heart, that the Lord He is God" (ibid. 36); "Know
ye that the Lord is God" (Ps. c. 3). Thus the Law distinctly states
that the highest kind of worship, to which we refer in this chapter,
is only possible after the acquisition of the knowledge of God. For
it is said, "To love the Lord your God, and to serve Him with all your
heart and with all your soul," (Deut. xi. 13), and, as we have shown
several times, man's love of God is identical with his knowledge of
Him. The Divine Service enjoined in these words must, accordingly,
be preceded by the love of God. Our Sages have pointed out to us

that it is a service in the heart, which explanation I understand to mean
this: man concentrates all his thoughts on the First Intellect, and is
absorbed in these thoughts as much as possible. David therefore commands his son Solomon these two things, and exhorts him earnestly
to do them: to acquire a true knowledge of God, and to be earnest
in His service after that knowledge has been acquired. For He says,
"And thou, Solomon my son, know thou the God of thy father, and
serve Him with a perfect heart . . . if thou seek Him, He will be found
of thee; but if thou forsake Him, He will cast thee off for ever" (1
Chron. xxviii. 9). The exhortation refers to the intellectual conceptions,
not to the imaginations; for the latter are not called "knowledge," but
"that which cometh into your mind" (Ez. xx. 32). It has thus been
shown that it must be man's aim, after having acquired the knowledge
of God, to deliver himself up to Him, and to have his heart constantly
filled with longing after Him. He accomplishes this generally by seclusion and retirement. Every pious man should therefore seek retirement
and seclusion, and should only in case of necessity associate with others.

Note. —I have shown you that the intellect which emanates from God
unto us is the link that joins us to God. You have it in your power
to strengthen that bond, if you choose to do so, or to weaken it gradually
till it breaks, if you prefer this. It will only become strong when you
employ it in the love of God, and seek that love; it will be weakened
when you direct your thoughts to other things. You must know that
even if you were the wisest man in respect to the true knowledge of
God, you break the bond between you and God whenever you turn
entirely your thoughts to the necessary food or any necessary business;
you are then not with God, and He is not with you; for that relation
between you and Him is actually interrupted in those moments. The
pious were therefore particular to restrict the time in which they could
not meditate upon the name of God, and cautioned others about it,
saying, "Let not your minds be vacant from reflections upon God." In
the same sense did David say, "I have set the Lord always before me;
because He is at my right hand, I shall not be moved" (Ps. xvi. 8);
i.e., I do not turn my thoughts away from God; He is like my right
hand, which I do not forget even for a moment on account of the
ease of its motions, and therefore I shall not be moved, I shall not
fall.

We must bear in mind that all such religious acts as reading the
Law, praying, and the performance of other precepts, serve exclusively
as the means of causing us to occupy and fill our mind with the precepts
of God, and free it from worldly business for we are thus, as it were,
in communication with God, and undisturbed by any other thing. If

we, however, pray with the motion of our lips, and our face toward the wall, but at the same time think of our business; if we read the Law with our tongue, whilst our heart is occupied with the building of our house, and we do not think of what we are reading; if we perform the commandments only with our limbs, we are like those who are engaged in digging in the ground, or hewing wood in the forest, without reflecting on the nature of those acts, or by whom they are commanded, or what is their object. We must not imagine that [in this way] we attain the highest perfection; on the contrary, we are then like those in reference to whom Scripture says, "Thou art near in their mouth, and far from their reins" (Jer. xii. 2).

I will now commence to show you the way how to educate and train yourselves in order to attain that great perfection.

The first thing you must do is this: Turn your thoughts away from everything while you read *Shema* or during the *Tefillah*, and do not content yourself with being devout when you read the first verse of Shema, or the first paragraph of the prayer. When you have successfully practised this for many years, try in reading the Law or listening to it, to have all your heart and all your thought occupied with understanding what you read or hear. After some time when you have mastered this, accustom yourself to have your mind free from all other thoughts when you read any portion of the other books of the prophets, or when you say any blessing; and to have your attention directed exclusively to the perception and the understanding of what you utter. When you have succeeded in properly performing these acts of divine service, and you have your thought, during their performance, entirely abstracted from worldly affairs, take then care that your thought be not disturbed by cares for your wants or for superfluous food. In short, think of worldly matters when you eat, drink, bathe, talk with your wife and little children, or when you converse with other people. These times, which are frequent and long, I think, must suffice to you for reflecting on everything that is necessary as regards business, household, and health. But when you are engaged in the performance of religious duties, have your mind exclusively directed to what you are doing.

When you are alone by yourself, when you are awake on your couch, be careful to meditate in such precious moments on nothing but the intellectual worship of God, viz., to approach Him and to minister before Him in the true manner which I have described to you—not in hollow emotions. This I consider as the highest perfection wise men can attain by the above training.

When we have acquired a true knowledge of God, and rejoice in that knowledge in such a manner, that whilst speaking with others,

or attending to our bodily wants, our mind is all that time with God;
when we are with our heart constantly near God, even whilst our body
is in the society of men; when we are in that state which the Song
on the relation between God and man poetically describes in the following words: "I sleep, but my heart waketh; it is the voice of my beloved
that knocketh" (Song v. 2):—then we have attained not only the height
of ordinary prophets, but of Moses, our Teacher, of whom Scripture
relates: "And Moses alone shall come near before the Lord" (ibid. xxxiv.
28); "But as for thee, stand thou here by Me" (Deut. v. 28). The meaning of these verses has been explained by us.

The Patriarchs likewise attained this degree of perfection; they approached God in such a manner that with them the name of God became
known in the world. Thus we read in Scripture: "The God of Abraham,
the God of Isaac, and the God of Jacob. . . . This is My name for
ever" (Ex. iii. 15). Their mind was so identified with the knowledge
of God, that He made a lasting covenant with each of them: "Then
will I remember my covenant with Jacob," & c. (Lev. xxvi. 42). For
it is known from statements made in Scripture that these four, viz.,
the Patriarchs and Moses, had their minds exclusively filled with the
name of God, that is, with His knowledge and love; and that in the
same measure was Divine Providence attached to them and their descendants. When we therefore find them also, engaged in ruling others,
in increasing their property, and endeavouring to obtain possession of
wealth and honour, we see in this fact a proof that when they were
occupied in these things, only their bodily limbs were at work, whilst
their heart and mind never moved away from the name of God. I think
these four reached that high degree of perfection in their relation to
God, and enjoyed the continual presence of Divine Providence, even
in their endeavours to increase their property, feeding the flock, toiling
in the field, or managing the house, only because in all these things
their end and aim was to approach God as much as possible. It was
the chief aim of their whole life to create a people that should know
and worship God. Comp. "For I know him, that he will command his
children and his household after him" (Gen. xviii. 19). The object of
all their labours was to publish the Unity of God in the world, and to
induce people to love Him; and it was on this account that they succeeded in reaching that high degree; for even those [worldly] affairs
were for them a perfect worship of God. But a person like myself must
not imagine that he is able to lead men up to this degree of perfection.
It is only the next degree to it that can be attained by means of the
above-mentioned training. And let us pray to God and beseech Him
that He clear and remove from our way everything that forms an ob-

struction and a partition between us and Him, although most of these obstacles are our own creation, as has several times been shown in this treatise. Comp. "Your iniquities have separated between you and your God" (Is. lix. 2).

An excellent idea presents itself here to me, which may serve to remove many doubts, and may help to solve many difficult problems in metaphysics. We have already stated in the chapters which treat of Divine Providence, that Providence watches over every rational being according to the amount of intellect which that being possesses. Those who are perfect in their perception of God, whose mind is never separated from Him, enjoy always the influence of Providence. But those who, perfect in their knowledge of God, turn their mind sometimes away from God, enjoy the presence of Divine Providence only when they meditate on God; when their thoughts are engaged in other matters divine Providence departs from them. The absence of Providence in this case is not like its absence in the case of those who do not reflect on God at all; it is in this case less intense, because when a person perfect in his knowledge [of God] is busy with worldly matters, he has not knowledge in actuality, but only knowledge in potentiality [though ready to become actual]. This person is then like a trained scribe when he is not writing. Those who have no knowledge of God are like those who are in constant darkness and have never seen light. We have explained in this sense the words: "The wicked shall be silent in darkness" (1 Sam. ii. 9), whilst those who possess the knowledge of God, and have their thoughts entirely directed to that knowledge, are, as it were, always in bright sunshine; and those who have the knowledge, but are at times engaged in other themes, have then as it were a cloudy day: the sun does not shine for them on account of the cloud that intervenes between them and God.

Hence, it appears to me that it is only in times of such neglect that some of the ordinary evils befall a prophet or a perfect and pious man; and the intensity of the evil is proportional to the duration of those moments, or to the character of the things that thus occupy their mind. Such being the case, the great difficulty is removed that led philosophers to assert that Providence does not extend to every individual, and that man is like any other living being in this respect, viz., the argument based on the fact that good and pious men are afflicted with great evils. We have thus explained this difficult question even in accordance with the philosophers' own principles. Divine Providence is constantly watching over those who have obtained that blessing which is prepared for those who endeavor to obtain it. If man frees his thoughts from worldly matters, obtains a knowledge of God in the right way, and rejoices in that knowledge, it is impossible that any kind of evil should befall him while he is with God, and God with him. When he does not meditate on God, when he is separated from God, then God is also separated from him; then he is exposed to any evil that might befall him; for it is only that intellectual link with God that secures the presence of Providence and protection from evil accidents. Hence it may occur that the perfect man is at times not happy, whilst no evil befalls those who are imperfect; in these cases what happens to them is due to chance. This principle I find also expressed in the Law. Comp. "And I will hide my face from them, and they shall be devoured, and many evils and troubles shall befall them; so that they will say in that day, Are not these evils come upon us, because our God is not among us?" (Deut. xxxi. 17). It is clear that we ourselves are the cause of this hiding of the face, and that the screen that separates us from God is of our own creation. This is the meaning of the words: "And I will surely hide My face in that day, for all the evils which they shall have wrought" (ibid. ver. 18). There is undoubtedly no difference in this regard between one single person and a whole community. It is now clearly established that the cause of our being exposed to chance, and abandoned to destruction like cattle, is to be found in our separation from God. Those who have their God dwelling in their hearts, are not touched by any evil whatever. For God says: "Fear thou not, for I am with thee; be not dismayed, for I am thy God" (Isa. xli. 10). "When thou passest through the waters, I will be with thee; and through the rivers, they shall not overflow thee" (ibid. xliii. 2). For if we prepare ourselves, and attain the influence of the Divine Intellect, Providence is joined to us, and we are guarded against all evils. Comp. "The Lord is on my side; I will not fear; what can man do unto me?" (Ps. cxviii. 6). "Acquaint now thyself with Him, and be at peace" (Job xxii. 21); i.e., turn unto Him, and you will be safe from all evil.

Consider the Psalm on mishaps, and see how the author describes that great Providence, the protection and defence from all mishaps that concern the body, both from those that are common to all people, and those that concern only one certain individual; from those that are due to the laws of Nature, and those that are caused by our fellow-men. The Psalmist says: "Surely He will deliver thee from the snare of the fowler, and from the noisome pestilence. He shall cover thee with His feathers, and under His wings shalt thou trust: His truth shall be thy shield and buckler. Thou shalt not be afraid for the terror by night; nor for the arrow that flieth by day" (Ps. xic. 3-5). The author then relates how God protects us from the troubles caused by men, saying, If you happen to meet on your way with an army fighting with drawn swords, killing thousands at your left hand and myriads at your right hand, you will not suffer any harm; you will behold and see how God judges and punishes the wicked that are being slain, whilst you remain unhurt. "A thousand shall fall at thy side, and ten thousand at thy right hand; but it shall not come nigh thee. Only with thine eyes shalt thou behold and see the reward of the wicked" (ibid. vers. 7, 8). The author then continues his description of the divine defence and shelter, and shows the cause of this great protection, saying that such a man is well guarded, "Because he hath set his love upon Me, therefore will I deliver him: I will set him on high, because he hath known My name" (ibid. ver. 14). We have shown in previous chapters that by the "knowledge of God's name," the knowledge of God is meant. The above passage may therefore be paraphrased as follows: "This man is well guarded, because he hath known Me, and then (*bi chashak*) loved Me." You know the difference between the two Hebrew terms that signify "to love," *ahab* and *chashak*. When a man's love is so intense that his thought is exclusively engaged with the object of his love, it is expressed in Hebrew by the term *chashak*.

The philosophers have already explained how the bodily forces of man in his youth prevent the development of moral principles. In a greater measure this is the case as regards the purity of thought which man attains through the perfection of those ideas that lead him to an intense love of God. Man can by no means attain this so long as his bodily humours are hot. The more the forces of his body are weakened, and the fire of passion quenched, in the same measure does man's intellect increase in strength and light; his knowledge becomes purer, and he is happy with his knowledge. When this perfect man is stricken in age and is near death, his knowledge mightily increases, his joy in that knowledge grows greater, and his love for the object of his knowledge more intense, and it is in this great delight that the soul separates from the body. To this state our Sages referred, when in reference to the death of Moses, Aaron, and Miriam, they said that death was in these three cases nothing but a kiss. They say thus: We learn from the words, "And Moses the servant of the Lord died there in the land of Moab by the mouth of the Lord" (Deut. xxxiv. 5), that his death was a kiss. The same expression is used of Aaron: "And Aaron the priest went up into Mount Hor . . . by the mouth of the Lord, and died there" (Num. xxxiii. 38). Our Sages said that the same was the case with Miriam; but the phrase "by the mouth of the Lord" is not employed, because it was not considered appropriate to use these words in the description of her death as she was a female. The meaning of this saying is that these three died in the midst of the pleasure derived from the knowledge of God and their great love for Him. When our Sages figuratively call the knowledge of God united with intense love for Him a kiss they follow the well-known poetical diction, "Let Him kiss me with the kisses of His mouth" (Song i. 2). This kind of death, which in truth is deliverance from death, has been ascribed by our Sages to none but to Moses, Aaron, and Miriam. The other prophets and pious men are beneath that degree; but their knowledge of God is strengthened when death approaches. Of them Scripture says, "Thy righteousness shall go before thee; the glory of the Lord shall be thy reward" (Is. lviii. 8). The intellect of these men remains then constantly in the same condition, since the obstacle is removed that at times has intervened between the intellect and the object of its action; it continues for ever in that great delight, which is not like bodily pleasure. We have explained this in our work, and others have explained it before us.

Try to understand this chapter, endeavour with all your might to spend more and more time in communion with God, or in the attempt to approach Him; and to reduce the hours which you spend in other occupations, and during which you are not striving to come nearer unto Him. This instruction suffices for the object of this treatise.

6 *The Scholastic: Aquinas*

The transition from the twelfth to the thirteenth century witnessed one of the critical turning points in Western history. Around this time there was a rapid increase in the infusion into the West of the ideas of the great Greek, Jewish, and Arab philosophers. In particular, the introduction of a wave of Aristotelian and Neo-Platonic literature into Christendom created a serious conflict between Hellenic and Christian thinking. Twelfth-century Christianity revered the cloistered life of the monastery, looked to theology for intellectual authority, and put its emphasis on faith, God, meditation, and mysticism. In the thirteenth century, men were increasingly compelled to face the challenges represented by the worldly life of the university, the authority of philosophy, and the evidence of reason, experience, and the natural world.

St. Thomas Aquinas (1225–1274) responded to this crisis by a monumental attempt to reconcile these two great streams in the Western tradition. In his teaching at the University of Paris and in his writings—particularly the great *Summa Theologiae* (his codification of Christian doctrine) and the *Summa Contra Gentiles* (his defense of the Christian faith against Averroism)—Aquinas tried to bring together in harmony reason and revelation, philosophy and theology, university and monastery, activity and contemplation. Whether he succeeded or not is still an open question, but his massive attempt played a vital part in the creation of what we still recognize today as Western civilization. His theological-philosophical doctrine, known as Thomism, has been a potent intellectual force throughout the West and has been the official basis of Catholic theology since 1879. As a theology, Thomism looks for authority to God and scripture. As a philosophy, it looks for authority to human reason and experience. This double loyalty leads to difficulties, of course, and it has prompted critics like Bertrand Russell to claim that Aquinas does not engage in philosophy at all but in special pleading. To philosophize, Russell argues, is to follow the argument wherever it may lead, whereas Aquinas knows the conclusion in advance and tries to find arguments to support it.

It is true that theology emerges as primary in Aquinas' treatises. He starts with fundamental assumptions based upon divine revelation and goes on to a philosophical examination and explication of man and nature. The model of the educated man that emerges from this process is that of the scholastic, a man whose rational intelligence has been rigorously disciplined for the pursuit of moral excellence and whose highest happiness is found in the contemplation of the Christian God. This model of Aquinas—himself the greatest of the scholastics—has had a tremendous subsequent influence on Western education, especially in fostering the notion of intellectual discipline. St. Thomas wrote little specifically on education and the outlines for his model have to be gathered through a broad gleaning of his writings, particularly in the *Summa Theologiae*, the *Summa Contra Gentiles*, and *De Veritate* (On Truth), which contains a section of the teacher (*De Magistro*).

It is well known that Aquinas followed closely the philosophy of Aristotle, whom he called the Philosopher. Thus he concurred with Aristotle in maintaining that happiness should be man's principal goal and that the attainment of moral virtue should be the cardinal aim of education. But he differed from Aristotle in important respects, such as his high regard for the vocational and practical dimensions of life. Later Thomists were often more exclusively intellectual than Aquinas, who made an important place in his hierarchy of values for the practical uses of reason. The educated man, in Aquinas' view, is one who is capable of effective action based on the truth gained through contemplation. The contemplative life is more highly regarded by Aquinas than the active life. But a life that combines the active with the contemplative is even better than the merely contemplative. Teaching represents for St. Thomas an ideal combination of the two.

Although the teacher is thus an ideal figure in Aquinas' world-view, he is regarded as only a secondary agent in the educational process. The primary agent of education is the learner. Hence the model that Aquinas outlines is a man capable of self-education. He is intellectually autonomous, able to conduct his own process of research and discovery. The Church, however, has usually not been big enough or confident enough to endorse Aquinas' message: it has put the learner clearly under the authoritative superordination of the teacher.

The continuing importance of Thomism in the modern world has meant that this scholastic model has presented an abiding educational ideal. However, it has encountered increasing difficulty in overcoming challenges to some of its cardinal tenets. It has not adequately come to terms with modern science, reconciled itself to the significance of evolution, or recognized the validity of experimental testing of accepted truths. It is extremely difficult to harmonize the egalitarian and participatory demands of democracy with the hierarchical and often authoritarian propensities of the Thomist-scholastic.

Christian Theology

According to St. Thomas, man must seek truth through both faith and reason, theology and philosophy, revelation and research. Both kinds of route should lead to the same truths because all truth is ultimately God's. However, the route of faith must ultimately be considered higher than that of reason, for it gives access to truths that are not available through rational inquiry.

This selection is from St. Thomas Aquinas, *Summa Theologiae,* Volume I, "Christian Theology," translated by Thomas Gilby, O.P. Copyright 1964 Blackfriars in conjunction with McGraw-Hill, New York, and Eyre and Spottiswoode, London. Used by permission of McGraw-Hill Book Company.

SUMMA THEOLOGIAE, FIRST PART

QUESTION 1, FIRST ARTICLE

It should be urged that human well-being called for schooling in what God has revealed, in addition to the philosophical researches pursued by human reasoning.

Above all because God destines us for an end beyond the grasp of reason; according to Isaiah, Eye hath not seen, O God, without thee what thou hast prepared for them that love thee. Now we have to recognize an end before we can stretch out and exert ourselves for it. Hence the necessity for our welfare that divine truths surpassing reason should be signified to us through divine revelation.

We also stood in need of being instructed by divine revelation even in religious matters the human reason is able to investigate. For the rational truth about God would have appeared only to few, and even so after a long time and mixed with many mistakes; whereas on knowing this depends our whole welfare, which is in God. In these circumstances,

143

then, it was to prosper the salvation of human beings, and the more widely and less anxiously, that they were provided for by divine revelation about divine things.

These then are the grounds of holding a holy teaching which has come to us through revelation beyond the discoveries of the rational sciences.

Hence: 1. Admittedly the reason should not pry into things too high for human knowledge, nevertheless when they are revealed by God they should be welcomed by faith: indeed the passage in *Ecclesiasticus* goes on, *Many things are shown thee above the understanding of men*. And on them Christian teaching rests.

2. The diversification of the sciences is brought about by the diversity of aspects under which things can be known. Both an astronomer and a physical scientist may demonstrate the same conclusion, for instance that the earth is spherical; the first, however, works in a mathematical medium prescinding from material qualities, while for the second his medium is the observation of material bodies through the senses. Accordingly there is nothing to stop the same things from being treated by the philosophical sciences when they can be looked at in the light of natural reason and by another science when they are looked at in the light of divine revelation. Consequently the theology of holy teaching differs in kind from that theology which is ranked as a part of philosophy.

Knowing and Naming God

The following argument demonstrates Aquinas' theological-philosophical approach. It might be considered, according to rational evidence, that no created mind could see the essence of God. But this view is rejected by Aquinas, primarily because it does not accord with faith. It is also rejected on philosophical grounds, although these are more questionable and rest on certain unproven assumptions.

The selection is taken from St. Thomas Aquinas, *Summa Theologiae*, Volume III, "Knowing and Naming God," translated by Herbert McCabe, O.P. Copyright 1964 Blackfriars in conjunction with McGraw-Hill, New York, and Eyre and Spottiswoode, London. Used by permission of McGraw-Hill Book Company.

SUMMA THEOLOGIAE, FIRST PART

QUESTION 12, FIRST ARTICLE

In so far as a thing is realized it is knowable; but God is wholly realized—there is nothing about him which might be but is not—and so in himself he is supremely knowable. What is in itself supremely knowable may, however, so far exceed the power of a particular mind as to be beyond its understanding, rather as the sun is invisible to the bat because it is too bright for it. With this in mind some have said that no created mind can see the essence of God.

This view, however, is not admissible in the first place on theological grounds as being inconsistent with faith. The ultimate happiness of man consists in his highest activity, which is the exercise of his mind. If therefore the created mind were never able to see the essence of God, either it would never attain happiness or its happiness would consist in something other than God. This is contrary to faith, for the ultimate

145

perfection of the rational creature lies in that which is the source of its beginning—each thing achieves its perfection by rising as high as its source.

The view is also philosophically untenable, for it belongs to human nature to look for the causes of things—that is how intellectual problems arise. If therefore the mind of the rational creature were incapable of arriving at the first cause of things, this natural tendency could not be fulfilled. So we must grant that the blessed do see the essence of God.

Union of Body and Soul

Aquinas shows here, as elsewhere, his reliance on the authority of Aristotle. He follows Aristotle in asserting that the proper function of man is to use his intellect to achieve understanding. The intellectual principle is thus the appropriate "form" of man. Intellect is man's highest power and so far transcends corporeal matter that it is no longer subject to material demands.

These passages are from Volume I of *Basic Writings of Saint Thomas Aquinas,* edited by Anton C. Pegis, published in New York, copyright 1945 by Random House, Inc., with whose permission they are reprinted.

SUMMA THEOLOGIAE, FIRST PART

QUESTION 76, FIRST ARTICLE

We must assert that the intellect which is the principle of intellectual operation is the form of the human body. For that whereby primarily anything acts is a form of the thing to which the act is attributed. For instance, that whereby a body is primarily healed is health, and that whereby the soul knows primarily is knowledge; hence health is a form of the body, and knowledge is a form of the soul. The reason for this is that nothing acts except so far as it is in act; and so, a thing acts by that whereby it is in act. Now it is clear that the first thing by which the body lives is the soul. And as life appears through various operations in different degrees of living things, that whereby we primarily perform each of all these vital actions in the soul. For the soul is the primary principle of our nourishment, sensation, and local movement; and likewise of our understanding. Therefore this principle by which primarily we understand, whether it be called the intellect or the intellectual soul, is the form of the body. This is the demonstration used by Aristotle. . . .

Now the proper operation of man as man is to understand, for it is in this that he surpasses all animals. Whence Aristotle concludes that the ultimate happiness of man must consist in this operation as properly belonging to him. Man must therefore derive his species from that which is the principle of this operation. But the species of each thing is derived from its form. It follows therefore that the intellectual principle is the proper form of man.

But we must observe that the nobler a form is, the more it rises above corporeal matter, the less it is subject to matter, and the more it excels matter by its power and its operation. Hence we find that the form of a mixed body has an operation not caused by its elemental qualities. And the higher we advance in the nobility of forms, the more we find that the power of the form excels the elementary matter; as the vegetative soul excels the form of the metal, and the sensitive soul excels the vegetative soul. Now the human soul is the highest and noblest of forms. Therefore, in its power it excels corporeal matter by the fact that it has an operation and a power in which corporeal matter has no share whatever. This power is called the intellect.

Intellect of the First Man

Since the goal of life is a supernatural one, we cannot direct our lives properly without the truths of faith. Nor can we instruct others without both natural and supernatural knowledge.

This passage is taken from Volume I of *Basic Writings of Saint Thomas Aquinas,* edited by Anton C. Pegis, published in New York, copyright 1945 by Random House, Inc., with whose permission it is reprinted.

SUMMA THEOLOGIAE, FIRST PART

QUESTION 94, THIRD ARTICLE

It is natural for the perfect to come before the imperfect, as act comes before potentiality; for whatever is in potentiality is made actual only by something actual. And since God first created things not only for their own existence, but also that they might be principles of other things, so creatures were produced in their perfect state to be the principles as regards others. Now man can be the principle of another man, not only by corporeal generation, but also by instruction and government. Hence, just as the first man was produced in his perfect bodily state for the work of generation, so also was his soul established in a perfect state to instruct and govern others.

Now no one can instruct others unless he has knowledge; and so the first man was established by God in such a manner as to have the knowledge of all those things for which man has a natural aptitude. And such are whatever are virtually contained in the first self-evident principles, that is, whatever truths man is naturally able to know. Moreover, in order to direct his own life and that of others, man needs to know not only those things which can be naturally known, but also things surpassing natural knowledge, because the life of man is directed to a supernatural end; just as it is necessary for us to know the truths of faith in order to direct our own lives. Therefore the first man was endowed with such a knowledge of these supernatural truths as was necessary for the direction of human life in that state. But those things which cannot be known by merely human effort, and which are not necessary for the direction of human life, were not known by the first man: e.g., the thoughts of men, future contingent events, and some individual facts, as for instance the number of pebbles in a stream, and the like.

The Intellectual Virtues

The educated man possesses the intellectual virtues of wisdom, understanding, and science, which Aquinas puts in a descending hierarchy of value. Science depends upon understanding, which is therefore a higher virtue, and both depend upon wisdom, which is therefore a more perfect virtue than either. Wisdom is superior because it is the means whereby we judge the first principles and conclusions of the sciences. Art has the nature of a virtue, but it falls short of being a perfect virtue because it can be done badly.

These selections are from Volume II of *Basic Writings of Saint Thomas Aquinas*, edited by Anton C. Pegis, published in New York, copyright 1945 by Random House, Inc., with whose permission they are reprinted.

SUMMA THEOLOGIAE, SECOND PART

QUESTION 57, SECOND ARTICLE

As has already been stated, the virtues of the speculative intellect are those which perfect the speculative intellect for the consideration of truth; for this is its good work. Now truth is subject to a twofold consideration, namely, as known in itself, and as known through another. What is known in itself is as a *principle* and is at once understood by the intellect; and that is why the habit that perfects the the intellect for the consideration of such truth is called *understanding*, which is the *habit of principles*.

On the other hand, a truth which is known through another is understood by the intellect, not at once, but by means of the reason's inquiry, and is as a *term*. This may happen in two ways: first, so that it is the last in some particular genus; secondly, so that it is the ultimate term of all human knowledge. And, since *things that are later knowable*

in relation to us are knowable first and chiefly in their nature, hence
it is that that which is last with respect to all human knowledge is
that which is knowable first and chiefly in its nature. And about these
truths is *wisdom,* which considers the highest causes, as is stated in
Metaph. i. Therefore it rightly judges and orders all truths, because there
can be no perfect and universal judgment except by resolution to first
causes.—But in regard to that which is last in this or that genus of
knowable truths, it is *science* that perfects the intellect. Therefore, according to the diverse genera of knowable truths, there are diverse habits
of the sciences; whereas there is but one wisdom.

QUESTION 57, THIRD ARTICLE

Art is nothing else but *the right reason about certain works to be
made.* And yet the good of these things depends, not on the disposition
of man's appetite, but on the goodness of the work done. For a craftsman
as such is commendable, not for the will with which he does a work,
but for the quality of the work. Art, therefore, properly speaking, is
an operative habit. And yet it has something in common with the speculative habits, since the disposition of the things considered by them
is a matter of concern to the speculative habits also, although they
are not concerned with the disposition of the appetite towards their
objects. For as long as the geometrician demonstrates the truth, it matters
not how his appetite is disposed, whether he be joyful or angry; even
as neither does this matter in a craftsman, as we have observed. And
so art has the nature of a virtue in the same way as the speculative
habits, in so far, namely, as neither art nor a speculative habit makes
a good work as regards the use of the habit, which is distinctive of
a virtue that perfects the appetite, but only as regards the ability to
work well.

The Office of a Wise Man

The appropriate occupation of the wise man is the contemplation of truth, especially the truth concerning the first principle of being. It is also his responsibility to disseminate the truth he has found and to refute falsehood. These are essentially intellectual tasks.

The selection is taken from Saint Thomas Aquinas, *Summa Contra Gentiles,* First Book, translated by the English Dominican Fathers, published in London in 1924 by Burns Oates and Washbourne, Ltd. Reprinted by permission of Burns and Oates, Ltd.

CHAPTER 1

My mouth shall meditate truth, and my lips shall hate wickedness.—PROV. viii. 7.

The general use which, in the Philosopher's opinion, should be followed in naming things, has resulted in those men being called *wise* who direct things themselves and govern them well. Wherefore among other things which men conceive of the wise man, the Philosopher reckons that *it belongs to the wise man to direct things.* Now the rule of all things directed to the end of government and order must needs be taken from their end: for then is a thing best disposed when it is fittingly directed to its end, since the end of everything is its good. Wherefore in the arts we observe that the art which governs and rules another is the one to which the latter's end belongs: thus the medical art rules and directs the art of the druggist, because health which is the object of medicine is the end of all drugs which are made up by the druggist's art. The same may be observed in the art of sailing in relation to the art of ship-building, and in the military art in relation to the equestrian art and all warlike appliances. These arts which govern others are called *master-arts* (*architectonicæ*), that is *principal arts,* for which reason their craftsmen, who are called *master-craftsmen* (*archi-*

tectores), are awarded the name of wise men. Since, however, these same craftsmen, through being occupied with the ends of certain singular things, do not attain to the universal end of all things, they are called wise about this or that, in which sense it is said (1 Cor. iii. 10): *As a wise architect, I have laid the foundation;* whereas the name of being wise simply is reserved to him alone whose consideration is about the end of the universe, which end is also the beginning of the universe: wherefore, according to the Philosopher, it belongs to the wise man to consider the *highest causes.*

Now the last end of each thing is that which is intended by the first author or mover of that thing: and the first author and mover of the universe is an intellect, as we shall prove further on. Consequently the last end of the universe must be the good of the intellect: and this is truth. Therefore truth must be the last end of the whole universe; and the consideration thereof must be the chief occupation of wisdom. And for this reason divine Wisdom, clothed in flesh, declares that He came into the world to make known the truth, saying (Jo. xviii. 37): *For this was I born, and for this cause came I into the world, that I should give testimony to the truth.* Moreover the Philosopher defines the First Philosophy as being the *knowledge of truth,* not of any truth, but of that truth which is the source of all truth, of that, namely, which relates to the first principle of being of all things; wherefore its truth is the principle of all truth, since the disposition of things is the same in truth as in being.

Now it belongs to the same thing to pursue one contrary and to remove the other: thus medicine which effects health, removes sickness. Hence, just as it belongs to a wise man to meditate and disseminate truth, especially about the first principle, so does it belong to him to refute contrary falsehood.

Wherefore the twofold office of the wise man is fittingly declared from the mouth of Wisdom, in the words above quoted; namely, to meditate and publish the divine truth, which antonomastically is *the* truth, as signified by the words, *My mouth shall meditate truth;* and to refute the error contrary to truth, as signified by the words, *and my lips shall hate wickedness,* by which is denoted falsehood opposed to divine truth, which falsehood is contrary to religion that is also called *godliness,* wherefore the falsehood that is contrary thereto receives the name of *ungodliness.*

Free Choice

Animals do not have free choice: they act from instinct and possess no alternatives. Man has free choice through his powers of reason. He makes rational judgments and so selects freely from among alternatives.

The excerpt is taken from Volume I of *Basic Writings of Saint Thomas Aquinas,* edited by Anton C. Pegis, published in New York, copyright 1945 by Random House, Inc., with whose permission it is reprinted.

SUMMA THEOLOGIAE, FIRST PART

QUESTION 83, FIRST ARTICLE

Man has free choice, or otherwise counsels, exhortations, commands, prohibitions, rewards and punishments would be in vain. In order to make this evident, we must observe that some things act without judgment, as a stone moves downwards; and in like manner all things which lack knowledge. And some act from judgment, but not a free judgment; as brute animals. For the sheep, seeing the wolf, judges it a thing to be shunned, from a natural and not a free judgment; because it judges, not from deliberation, but from natural instinct. And the same thing is to be said of any judgment in brute animals. But man acts from judgment, because by his apprehensive power he judges that something should be avoided or sought. But because this judgment, in the case of some particular act, is not from a natural instinct, but from some act of comparison in the reason, therefore he acts from free judgment and retains the power of being inclined to various things. For reason in contingent matters may follow opposite courses, as we see in dialectical syllogisms and rhetorical arguments. Now particular operations are contingent, and therefore in such matters the judgment of reason may follow opposite courses, and is not determinate to one. And in that man is rational, it is necessary that he have free choice.

155

Human Law

Law is necessary because of the evil propensities of man. Good men are better led by admonition than coercion, but evil men must be compelled to virtue. We need laws because it is easier to judge what is right universally and in advance than to take each case as it arises. The latter approach permits subjective factors to pervert our judgment.

The passage is taken from Volume II of *Basic Writings of Saint Thomas Aquinas*, edited by Anton C. Pegis, published in New York, copyright 1945 by Random House, Inc., with whose permission it is reprinted.

SUMMA THEOLOGIAE, SECOND PART

QUESTION 95, FIRST ARTICLE

As we have stated above, man has a natural aptitude for virtue; but the perfection of virtue must be acquired by man by means of some kind of training. Thus we observe that a man is helped by diligence in his necessities, for instance, in food and clothing. Certain beginnings of these he has from nature, viz., his reason and his hands; but he has not the full complement, as other animals have, to whom nature has given sufficiently of clothing and food. Now it is difficult to see how man could suffice for himself in the matter of this training, since the perfection of virtue consists chiefly in withdrawing man from undue pleasures, to which above all man is inclined, and especially the young, who are more capable of being trained. Consequently a man needs to receive this training from another, whereby to arrive at the perfection of virtue. And as to those young people who are inclined to acts of virtue by their good natural disposition, or by custom, or rather by the gift of God, paternal training suffices, which is by admonitions. But since some are found to be dissolute and prone to vice, and not

156

easily amenable to words, it was necessary for such to be restrained from evil by force and fear, in order that, at least, they might desist from evil-doing, and leave others in peace, and that they themselves, by being habituated in this way, might be brought to do willingly what hitherto they did from fear, and thus become virtuous. Now this kind of training, which compels through fear of punishment, is the discipline of laws. Therefore, in order that man might have peace and virtue, it was necessary for laws to be framed; for, as the Philosopher says, *as man is the most noble of animals if he be perfect in virtue, so he is the lowest of all, if he be severed from law and justice.* For man can use his reason to devise means of satisfying his lusts and evil passions, which other animals are unable to do.

What Is Required for Happiness

In his inquiry into what is required for human happiness, Aquinas makes a distinction between happiness in this earthly life and perfect happiness. Thus he concludes that man's body, external goods, and friends are all instrumental to earthly happiness but that none of these is necessary for perfect happiness, which consists in man's vision of God and hence does not depend upon mundane instruments.

These selections are from St. Thomas Aquinas, *Summa Theologica,* Part II (First Part), translated by Fathers of the English Dominican Province, published in London in 1927 (2nd edition) by Burns Oates and Washbourne, Ltd. Reprinted by permission of Burns and Oates, Ltd., and Benziger Brothers, Inc.

QUESTION 4, FIFTH ARTICLE

Happiness is twofold; the one is imperfect and is had in this life; the other is perfect, consisting in the vision of God. Now it is evident that the body is necessary for the happiness of this life. For the happiness of this life consists in an operation of the intellect, either speculative or practical. And the operation of the intellect in this life cannot be without a phantasm, which is only in a bodily organ. . . . Consequently that happiness which can be had in this life, depends, in a way, on the body.

But as to perfect Happiness, which consists in the vision of God, some have maintained that it is not possible to the soul separated from the body; and have said that the souls of saints, when separated from their bodies, do not attain to that Happiness until the Day of Judgment, when they will receive their bodies back again. And this is shown to be false, both by authority and by reason. By authority, since the Apostle says (2 Cor. v. 6): *While we are in the body, we are absent from the Lord;* and he points out the reason of this absence, saying: *For we walk by faith and not by sight.* Now from this it is clear that so long as we walk by faith and not by sight, bereft of the vision of the Divine Essence, we are not present to the Lord. But the souls of the saints, separated from their bodies, are in God's presence; wherefore the text continues: *But we are confident and have a good will to be absent . . . from the body, and to be present with the Lord.* Whence it is evident that the souls of the saints, separated from their bodies, *walk by sight,* seeing the Essence of God, wherein is true Happiness.

Again this is made clear by reason. For the intellect needs not the body, for its operation, save on account of the phantasms, wherein it looks on the intelligible truth. . . . Now it is evident that the Divine Essence cannot be seen by means of phantasms. . . . Wherefore, since mans' perfect Happiness consists in the vision of the Divine Essence, it does not depend on the body. Consequently, without the body the soul can be happy.

We must, however, notice that something may belong to a thing's perfection in two ways. First, as constituting the essence thereof; thus the soul is necessary for man's perfection. Secondly, as necessary for its well-being: thus, beauty of body and keenness of perception belong to man's perfection. Wherefore though the body does not belong in the first way to the perfection of human Happiness, yet it does in the second way. For since operation depends on a thing's nature, the more perfect is the soul in its nature, the more perfectly it has its proper operation, wherein its happiness consists. Hence Augustine, after inquiring . . . *whether that perfect Happiness can be ascribed to the souls of the dead separated from their bodies,* answers *that they cannot see the Unchangeable Substance, as the blessed angels see It; either for some other more hidden reason, or because they have a natural desire to rule the body.*

QUESTION 4, SEVENTH ARTICLE

For imperfect happiness, such as can be had in this life, external goods are necessary, not as belonging to the essence of happiness, but by serving as instruments to happiness, which consists in an operation of virtue, as stated in *Ethic.* i. 13. For man needs, in this life, the necessaries of the body, both for the operation of contemplative virtue, and for the operation of active virtue, for which latter he needs also many other things by means of which to perform its operations.

On the other hand, such goods as these are nowise necessary for perfect Happiness, which consists in seeing God. The reason of this is that all suchlike external goods are requisite either for the support of the animal body or for certain operations which belong to human life, which we perform by means of the animal body: whereas that perfect Happiness which consists in seeing God, will be either in the soul separated from the body, or in the soul united to the body then no longer animal but spiritual. Consequently these external goods are nowise necessary for that Happiness, since they are ordained to the animal life. And since, in this life, the felicity of contemplation, as being more God-like, approaches nearer than that of action to the likeness of that perfect Happiness, therefore it stands in less need of these goods of the body, as stated in *Ethic.* x. 8.

QUESTION 4, EIGHTH ARTICLE

If we speak of the happiness of this life, the happy man needs friends, as the Philosopher says (*Ethic.* ix. 9), not, indeed, to make use of them, since he suffices himself; nor to delight in them, since he possess perfect delight in the operation of virtue; but for the purpose of a good operation, viz., that he may do good to them; that he may delight in seeing them do good; and again that he may be helped by them in his good work. For in order that man may do well, whether in the works of the active life, or in those of the contemplative life, he needs the fellowship of friends.

But if we speak of perfect Happiness which will be in our heavenly Fatherland, the fellowship of friends is not essential to Happiness; since man has the entire fulness of his perfection in God. But the fellowship of friends conduces to the well-being of Happiness. Hence Augustine says . . . that *the spiritual creatures receive no other interior aid to happiness than the eternity, truth, and charity of the Creator. But if they can be said to be helped from without, perhaps it is only by this that they see one another and rejoice in God, at their fellowship.*

Man's Ultimate Happiness

The appropriately human task of man is the contemplation of truth—for its own sake rather than in an instrumental sense. Man's ultimate happiness is to be found in the contemplation of the highest truth, that is, in the contemplation of God.

This passage is from Saint Thomas Aquinas, *Summa Contra Gentiles*, Third Book, translated by the English Dominican Fathers, published in London in 1928 by Burns Oates and Washbourne, Ltd. Reprinted by permission of Burns and Oates, Ltd.

CHAPTER 37

Accordingly if man's ultimate happiness consists not in external things, which are called goods of chance; nor in goods of the body; nor in goods of the soul, as regards the sensitive faculty; nor as regards the intellective faculty, in the practice of moral virtue; nor as regards intellectual virtue in those which are concerned about action, namely art and prudence; it remains for us to conclude that man's ultimate happiness consists in the contemplation of the truth.

For this operation alone is proper to man, and none of the other animals communicates with him therein.

Again. This is not directed to anything further as its end: since the contemplation of the truth is sought for its own sake.

Again. By this operation man is united to things above him, by becoming like them: because of all human actions this alone is both in God and in separate substances. Also, by this operation man comes into contact with those higher beings, through knowing them in any way whatever.

Besides, man is more self-sufficing for this operation, seeing that he stands in little need of the help of external things in order to perform it.

Further. All other human operations seem to be directed to this as their end. Because perfect contemplation requires that the body should be disencumbered, and to this effect are directed all the products of art that are necessary for life. Moreover, it requires freedom from the disturbance caused by the passions, which is achieved by means of the moral virtues and prudence; and freedom from external disturbance, to which all the regulations of the civil life are direct. So that, if we consider the matter rightly, we shall see that all human occupations are brought into the service of those who contemplate the truth. Now, it is not possible that man's ultimate happiness consist in contemplation based on the understanding of first principles: for this is most imperfect, as being universal and containing potential knowledge of things. Moreover, it is the beginning and not the end of human study, and comes to us from nature, and not through the study of the truth. Nor does it consist in contemplation based on the sciences that have the lowest things for their object: since happiness must consist in an operation of the intellect in relation to the highest objects of intelligence. It follows then that man's ultimate happiness consists in wisdom, based on the consideration of divine things. It is therefore evident by way of induction that man's ultimate happiness consists solely in the contemplation of God, which conclusion was proved above by arguments.

Whether One Man Can Teach Another

The interior light of the intellect is the principal agency of learning. The student must therefore be active in his own education. The teacher does not directly bring about knowledge in the student, but he can help the student to acquire knowledge by suggesting and demonstrating effective methods of learning. Aquinas draws an analogy with medicine, suggesting that the doctor does not directly cure but merely assists the interior principle of nature, which brings about the cure.

This selection is taken from Volume I of *Basic Writings of Saint Thomas Aquinas,* edited by Anton C. Pegis, published in New York, copyright 1945 by Random House, Inc., with whose permission it is reprinted.

SUMMA THEOLOGIAE, FIRST PART

QUESTION 117, FIRST ARTICLE

On this question there have been various opinions. For Averroes, commenting on *De anima* iii., maintains that all men have one possible intellect in common, as was stated above. From this it followed that the same intelligible species belong to all men. Consequently, he held that one man does not cause another to have a knowledge distinct from that which he has himself; but that he communicates the identical knowledge which he has himself, by moving him to order rightly the phantasms in his soul, so that they be rightly disposed for intelligible apprehension. This opinion is true so far as knowledge is the same in the disciple and the teacher, if we consider the identity of the thing known;

for the same objective truth is known by both of them. But so far as he maintains that all men have but one possible intellect, and the same intelligible species, differing only according to the diversity of phantasms, his opinion is false, as was stated above.

Besides this, there is the opinion of the Platonists, who held that our souls are possessed of knowledge from the very beginning, through the participation of separate Forms, as was stated above; but that the soul is hindered, through its union with the body, from the free consideration of those things which it knows. According to this, the disciple does not acquire fresh knowledge from his teacher, but is roused by him to consider what he knows; so that to learn would be nothing else than to remember. In the same way they held that natural agents act only dispositively towards the reception of forms, which matter acquires by a participation in separate species. But against this we have proved above that the possible intellect of the human soul is in pure potentiality to intelligibles, as Aristotle says.

We must therefore decide the question differently, by saying that the teacher causes knowledge in the learner by reducing him from potentiality to act, as the Philosopher says. In order to make this clear, we must observe that of effects proceeding from an exterior principle, some proceed from the exterior principle alone, as the form of a house is caused to be in matter by art alone. But other effects proceed sometimes from an exterior principle, sometimes from an interior principle; and thus health is caused in a sick man sometimes by an exterior principle (namely, by the medical art), sometimes by an interior principle (as when a man is healed by the power of nature). In these latter effects two things must be noticed. First, that art in its work imitates nature, for just as nature heals a man by alteration, digestion and rejection of the matter that caused the sickness, so does art. Secondly, we must remark that the exterior principle, art, acts, not as principal agent, but as helping the principal agent, which is the interior principle, by strengthening it, and by furnishing it with instruments and assistance, of which the interior principle makes use in producing the effect. Thus the physician strengthens nature, and administers food and medicine which nature is to use for the intended end.

Now knowledge is acquired in man, both from an interior principle, as is clear in one who procures knowledge by discovery; and from an exterior principle, as is clear in one who learns by instruction. For in every man there is a certain principle of knowledge, namely the light of the agent intellect, through which certain universal principles of all the sciences are naturally understood as soon as proposed to the intellect. Now when anyone applies these universal principles to certain particular things, the memory or experience of which he acquires through the senses, then, advancing by discovery from the known to the unknown, he obtains knowledge of what he knew not before. Therefore anyone who teaches leads the disciple from things known by the disciple to the knowledge of things previously unknown to him; for, as the Philosopher says: *All teaching and all learning proceed from previous knowledge.*

Now the teacher leads the disciple in two ways from the preknown to knowledge of the unknown. First, by proposing to him certain helps or means of instruction, which his intellect can use for the acquisition of science. For instance, he may put before him certain less universal propositions, of which nevertheless the disciple is able to judge from previous knowledge; or he may propose to him some sensible examples, either by way of likeness or of opposition, or something of the sort, from which the intellect of the learner is led to the knowledge of a truth previously unknown. Secondly, by strengthening the intellect of the learner; not, indeed, by some active power as though of a higher nature (as was explained above of the angelic illuminations), because all human intellects are of one grade in the natural order; but inasmuch as he proposes to the disciple the order from principles to conclusions, for the disciple may not have sufficient power of reasoning to be able to draw the conclusions from the principles. Hence the Philosopher says that *a demonstration is a syllogism that causes science.* In this way a demonstrator causes his hearers to know.

The Teacher

Knowledge can be gained with certainty only through the application of general, self-evident principles to specific matters. We discover these self-evident principles through the application of reason, which is implanted in us by God. Thus God alone is the interior
and principal Teacher. Man can be only an exterior, facilitating
teacher. Knowledge pre-exists potentially in the pupil. The human
teacher can help the pupil to apply his own reason and thus bring
his potential knowledge to actuality.

These selections are taken from St. Thomas Aquinas, *The
Teacher: The Mind*, translated by James V. McGlynn, S. J., published in Chicago in 1953 by Henry Regnery Company, with whose
permission they are reprinted.

ARTICLE I

Certain seeds of knowledge pre-exist in us, namely, the first concepts
of understanding, which by the light of the agent intellect are immediately known through the species abstracted from sensible things. These
are either complex, as axioms, or simple, as the notions of being, of
the one, and so on, which the understanding grasps immediately. In
these general principles, however, all the consequences are included
as in certain seminal principles. When, therefore, the mind is led from
these general notions to actual knowledge of the particular things, which
it knew previously in general and, as it were, potentially, then one is
said to acquire knowledge. . . .

As there are two ways of being cured, that is, either through the
activity of unaided nature or by nature with the aid of medicine, so
also there are two ways of acquiring knowledge. In one way, natural
reason by itself reaches knowledge of unknown things, and this way

166

is called *discovery*; in the other way, when someone else aids the learner's natural reason, and this is called *learning by instruction*. . . .

Now, in discovery, the procedure of anyone who arrives at the knowledge of something unknown is to apply general self-evident principles to certain definite matters, from these to proceed to particular conclusions, and from these to others. Consequently, one person is said to teach another inasmuch as, by signs, he manifests to that other the reasoning process which he himself goes through by his own natural reason. And thus, through the instrumentality, as it were, of what is told him, the natural reason of the pupil arrives at a knowledge of the things which he did not know. Therefore, just as the doctor is said to heal a patient through the activity of nature, so a man is said to cause knowledge in another through the activity of the learner's own natural reason, and this is teaching. So, one is said to teach another and be his teacher. This is what the Philosopher means when he says: "Demonstration is a syllogism which makes someone know."

But, if someone proposes to another things which are not included in self-evident principles, or does not make it clear that they are included, he will not cause knowledge in the other but, perhaps, opinion or faith, although even this is in some way caused by inborn first principles, for from these self-evident principles he realizes that what necessarily follows from them is to be held with certitude, and that what is contrary to them is to be rejected completely, and that assent may be given to or withheld from whatever neither follows necessarily from nor is contrary to self-evident principles. Now, the light of reason by which such principles are evident to us is implanted in us by God as a kind of reflected likeness in us of the uncreated truth. So, since all human teaching can be effective only in virtue of that light, it is obvious that God alone teaches interiorly and principally, just as nature alone heals interiorly and principally. Nevertheless, both to heal and to teach can still be used in a proper sense in the way we have explained.

ANSWERS TO DIFFICULTIES

1. Since our Lord had ordered the disciples not to be called teachers, the *Gloss* explains how this prohibition is to be understood, lest it be taken absolutely. For we are forbidden to call man a teacher in this sense, that we attribute to him the pre-eminence of teaching, which belongs to God. It would be as if we put our hope in the wisdom of men, and did not rather consult divine truth about those things which we hear from man. And this divine truth speaks in us through the impression of its likeness, by means of which we can judge of all things. . . .

6. We do not say that a teacher communicates knowledge to the pupil, as though the knowledge which is in the teacher is numerically the same as that which arises in the pupil. It is rather that the knowledge which arises in the pupil through teaching is similar to that which is in the teacher, and this was raised from potency into art, as has been said.

7. As the doctor is said to cause healing, although he works exteriorly, while nature alone works interiorly, so man is said to teach the truth, although he declares it exteriorly, while God teaches interiorly. . . .

11. In the pupil, the intelligible forms of which knowledge received through teaching is constituted are caused directly by the agent intellect and mediately by the one who teaches. For the teacher sets before the pupil signs of intelligible things, and from these the agent intellect derives the intelligible likenesses and causes them to exist in the possible intellect. Hence, the words of the teacher, heard or seen in writing, have the same efficacy in causing knowledge as things which are outside the soul. For from both the agent intellect receives intelligible likenesses, although the words of the teacher are more proximately posed to cause knowledge than things outside the soul, in so far as they are signs of intelligible forms. . . .

13. The whole certainty of scientific knowledge arises from the certainty of principles. For conclusions are known with certainty when they are reduced to the principles. Therefore, that something is known with certainty is due to the light of reason divinely implanted within us, by which God speaks within us. It comes from man, teaching from without, only in so far as, teaching us, he reduces conclusions to the principles. Nevertheless, we would not attain the certainty of scientific knowledge from this unless there were within us the certainty of the principles to which the conclusions are reduced.

7   *The Classical Humanist: Erasmus*

At the end of the fifteenth century in Europe the great changes that challenged men's abilities to make sense and order out of their lives were the breakup of medieval feudalism and the increasingly obvious abuses and corruptions within the Church. There was an anxiety and an uncertainty abroad that led easily into the intensity and fanaticism of a Martin Luther and to the consequent counter-vailing violence. But Desiderius Erasmus (1466–1536) chose another way. Born in the north European city of Rotterdam, where a spirit of cool temperance and stoical control was common, and deeply steeped in the classical learning of Greece, Erasmus responded in a spirit of Aristotelian moderation.

Faced with the disintegration of medieval Europe into disputatious national and religious factions, Erasmus sought peace, reconciliation, and unity. He sought to unify faith and reason by a feat of piety and scholarship that would synthesize Christianity and antiquity. Although he was sharply critical of the corruptions of the Church and the absurdities of the scholastics, he was more rational and liberal than Luther and wanted to avoid repudiating the best of the past in a blaze of splenetic passion. Rather than contribute to the fragmenting of the unity of Christendom, he sought to cleanse, purify, and strengthen Christianity through the study of its classical sources. However, his attempt to reform the Church through the application of gentle reason and toleration was swept aside by the fanaticism of the Reformation and Counter-Reformation.

Nevertheless, he has left us a model of the educated man that still is worthy of our attention. His model was a man of humane tolerance, wide and cosmopolitan interests, moral excellence, and sound learning—a learning based on the Latin and Greek languages. The re-evaluation of classical studies at the time of the Renaissance was nowhere better exemplified than by Erasmus. He escaped and condemned the debasement of humanism that occurred through the grammatical trivializing and rule-memorizing of the grammarians. He emphasized the literary beauty and moral content of the classics, and he saw Latin as a common, uniting language that would counteract the divisiveness of the vernacular tongues—a problem that still remains unsolved. But he, too, had his blindness—to empirical science—and the prestige he lent to a one-sided concept of the "humanities" contributed in subsequent centuries to that unfortunate and false dichotomy between the supposed "two cultures" from which we are still not emancipated today.

The Praise of Folly

Before examining Erasmus' model of the educated man, we might join him as he clears the ground, as it were. This he does by using the technique of satire to outline what the educated man is *not*. We can gain from this a fair impression of the kind of model that Erasmus would recommend, since it will be in many cases the opposite of what he condemns. *The Praise of Folly* was probably written in 1509 and first published in 1511. In it, Erasmus attacks with merciless wit the abuses, superstitions, vulgarity, and foolishness of his day. Among those who receive a slash from his pen are the grammarians, lawyers, logicians, sophists, scientists, theologians, and religious. Erasmus' intention is to encourage us not to take ourselves too seriously, to add a lightness and a grace to life, an exhortation critically needed today by many professional educators, whose besetting sin is pomposity. He is urging upon us a self-critical attitude: we should be sceptical and even ironical toward our own work and convictions, as toward the world. Erasmus treads the difficult knife edge between complacency and irresponsibility: his irony does not descend to cynicism; his wit does not degenerate into superciliousness.

This passage is from Erasmus, *The Praise of Folly*, translated by Hoyt Hopewell Hudson, published in Princeton, New Jersey, in 1941, copyright by Princeton University Press, with whose permission it is reprinted.

But I should be most foolish myself and worthy of the manifold laughter of Democritus, if I should go on counting forms of folly and madness among the folk. Let me turn to those who maintain among mortals an appearance of wisdom and, as the saying is, seek for the golden bough. Among these the grammarians hold first place. Nothing could

171

be more calamity-stricken, nothing more afflicted, than this generation of men, nothing so hated of God, if I were not at hand to mitigate the pains of their wretched profession by a certain sweet infusion of madness. For they are not only liable to the five curses which the Greek epigram calls attention to in Homer, but indeed to six hundred curses; as being hunger-starved and dirty in their schools—I said "their schools," but it were better said "their knowledge-factories" or "their mills"—or even "their shambles"—among herds of boys. There they grow old with their labors, they are deafened by the noise, they sicken by reason of the stench and nastiness. Yet thanks to me, they see themselves as first among men; so greatly do they please themselves when they terrify the timorous band by a menacing look and tone; when they beat the little wretches with ferules, rods, or straps; and when, imitating the ass in Aesop, they storm fiercely in all directions, as whim may dictate. And do you know, all the dirtiness seems sheer elegance, the stench is perfume of sweet marjoram, and the miserable servitude considered to be a kingdom, such a one that they would not trade their tyranny for the empire of Phalaris or Dionysius. . . .

Among men of learned professions, the lawyers may claim first place for themselves, nor is there any other class quite so self-satisfied; for while they industriously roll up the stone of Sisyphus by dint of weaving together six hundred laws in the same breath, no matter how little to the purpose, and by dint of piling glosses upon glosses and opinions upon opinions, they contrive to make their profession seem the most difficult of all. What is really tedious commends itself to them as brilliant. Let us put in with them the logicians and sophists, a breed of men more loquacious than the famed brass kettles at Dodona; any one of them can out-chat twenty picked women. They would be happier, however, if they were merely talkative, and not quarrelsome as well, to such a degree that they will stubbornly cut and thrust over a lock of goat's wool, quite losing track of the truth in question while they go on disputing. Their self-love makes them happy, and equipped with three syllogisms they will unhesitatingly dare to join battle upon any subject with any man. Mere frowardness brings them back unbeaten, though you match Stentor against them.

Near these march the scientists, reverenced for their beards and the fur on their gowns, who teach that they alone are wise while the rest of mortal men flit about as shadows. How pleasantly they dote, indeed, while they construct their numberless worlds, and measure the sun, moon, stars, and spheres as with thumb and line. They assign causes for lightning, winds, eclipses, and other inexplicable things, never hesitating a whit, as if they were privy to the secrets of nature, artificer of things, or as if they visited us fresh from the council of the gods. Yet all the while nature is laughing grandly at them and their conjectures. For to prove that they have good intelligence of nothing, this is a sufficient argument: they can never explain why they disagree with each other on every subject. Thus knowing nothing in general, they profess to know all things in particular; though they are ignorant even of themselves, and on occasion do not see the ditch or the stone lying across their path, because many of them are blear-eyed or absent-minded; yet they proclaim that they perceive ideas, universals, forms without matter, primary substances, quiddities, and ecceities—things so tenuous, I fear, that Lynceus himself could not see them. When they especially disdain the vulgar crowd is when they bring out their triangles, quadrangles, circles, and mathematical pictures of the sort, lay one upon the other, intertwine them into a maze, then deploy some letters as if in line of battle, and presently do it over in reverse order—and all to involve the uninitiated in darkness. Their fraternity does not lack those who predict future events by consulting the stars, and promise wonders even more magical; and these lucky scientists find people to believe them.

Perhaps it were better to pass over the theologians in silence, and not to move such a Lake Camarina, or to handle such an herb *Anagyris foetida,* as that marvellously supercilious and irascible race. For they may attack me with six hundred arguments, in squadrons, and drive me to make a recantation; which if I refuse, they will straightway proclaim me an heretic. By this thunderbolt they are wont to terrify any toward whom they are ill-disposed. No other people are so loth to acknowledge my favors to them; yet the divines are bound to me by no ordinary obligations. They are happy in their self-love, and as if they already inhabited the third heaven they look down from a height on all other mortal men as on creatures that crawl on the ground, and they come near to pitying them. They are protected by a wall of scholastic definitions, arguments, corollaries, implicit and explicit propositions; they have so many hideaways that they could not be caught even by the net of Vulcan; for they slip out on their distinctions, by which also they cut through all knots as easily as with a double-bitted axe from Tenedos; and they abound with newly-invented terms and prodigious vocables. Furthermore, they explain as pleases them the most arcane matters, such as by what method the world was founded and set in order, through what conduits original sin has been passed down along the generations, by what means, in what measure, and how long the perfect Christ was in the Virgin's womb, and how accidents subsist in the Eucharist without their subject. . . .

Coming nearest to these in felicity are the men who generally call themselves "the religious" and "monks"—utterly false names both, since most of them keep as far away as they can from religion and no people are more in evidence in every sort of place. But I do not see how anything could be more dismal than these monks if I did not succor them in many ways. For though people as a whole so detest this race of men that meeting one by accident is supposed to be bad luck, yet they flatter themselves to the queen's taste. For one thing, they reckon it the highest degree of piety to have no contact with literature, and hence they see to it that they do not know how to read. For another, when with asinine voices they bray out in church those psalms they have learned, by rote rather than by heart, they are convinced that they are anointing God's ears with the blandest of oil. Some of them make a good profit from their dirtiness and mendicancy, collecting their food from door to door with importunate bellowing; nay, there is not an inn, public conveyance, or ship where they do not intrude, to the great disadvantage of the other common beggars. Yet according to their account, by their very dirtiness, ignorance, want of manners, and insolence, these delightful fellows are representing to us the lives of the apostles.

Erasmus to Ulrich von Hutten

The following letter, written around 1517, was Erasmus' response
to a request from his friend and fellow humanist, Ulrich von Hutten, for a written portrait of their common friend, Sir Thomas More,
whom Erasmus had known since about 1499. Here is a statement
to balance *The Praise of Folly,* for in place of the mordant satire
of that stricture Erasmus allows himself the most glowing panegyric
as he describes his ideally educated man. Thomas More is all that
can be hoped for from the best kind of education. The model that
Erasmus describes is of a man who is somewhat simple and even
austere in his personal habits; he is little interested in ritual, for-
mality, or pomp. A perfect friend, he is always considerate, selfless,
thoughtful, and generous. He does not slavishly conform to conventional thinking but is full of sound common sense. Humble and
quite free from conceit, he lacks any assumption of superiority or
aloofness. Sincere and genuine in religion, he is faithful without
superstition, pious without pomposity.

The letter is taken from Volume III of *The Epistles of Erasmus,*
translated by Francis Morgan Nichols, published in three volumes
[1918] in New York in 1962 by Russell and Russell, Inc., with
whose permission it is reprinted.

Most illustrious Hutten, your love, I had almost said your passion
for the genius of Thomas More,—kindled as it is by his writings, which,
as you truly say, are as learned and witty as anything can possibly
be,—is I assure you, shared by many others; and moreover the feeling
in this case is mutual; since More is so delighted with what you have
written, that I am myself almost jealous of you. . . .

As to your asking me to paint you a full-length portrait of More,
I only wish my power of satisfying your request were equal to your

earnestness in pressing it. For to me too, it will be no unpleasant task to linger awhile in the contemplation of a friend who is the most delightful character in the world. But, in the first place, it is not given to every man to be aware of all More's accomplishments; and in the next place, I know not whether he will himself like to have his portrait painted by any artist that chooses to do so. For indeed I do not think it more easy to make a likeness of More than of Alexander the Great, or of Achilles; neither were those heroes more worthy of immortality. . . .

I have never seen any person less fastidious in his choice of food. As a young man, he was by preference a water-drinker, a practice he derived from his father. But, not to give annoyance to others, he used at table to conceal this habit from his guests by drinking, out of a pewter vessel, either small beer almost as weak as water, or plain water. As to wine, it being the custom, where he was, for the company to invite each other to drink in turn out of the same cup, he used sometimes to sip a little of it, to avoid appearing to shrink from it altogether, and to habituate himself to the common practice. . . .

He likes to be dressed simply, and does not wear silk, or purple, or gold chains, except when it is not allowable to dispense with them. He cares marvellously little for those formalities, which with ordinary people are the test of politeness; and as he does not exact these ceremonies from others, so he is not scrupulous in observing them himself, either on occasions of meeting or at entertainments, though he understands how to use them, if he thinks proper to do so; but he holds it to be effeminate and unworthy of a man to waste much of his time on such trifles. . . .

He seems to be born and made for friendship, of which he is the sincerest and most persistent devotee. Neither is he afraid of that multiplicity of friends, of which Hesiod disapproves. Accessible to every tender of intimacy, he is by no means fastidious in choosing his acquaintance, while he is most accommodating in keeping it on foot, and constant in retaining it. If he has fallen in with anyone whose faults he cannot cure, he finds some opportunity of parting with him, untying the knot of intimacy without tearing it; but when he has found any sincere friends, whose characters are suited to his own, he is so delighted with their society and conversation, that he seems to find in these the chief pleasure of life, having an absolute distaste for tennis and dice and cards, and the other games with which the mass of gentlemen beguile the tediousness of Time. It should be added that, while he is somewhat neglectful of his own interest, no one takes more pains in attending to the concerns of his friends. What more need I say? If anyone requires a perfect example of true friendship, it is in More that he will best find it. . . .

There is nothing that occurs in human life, from which he does not seek to extract some pleasure, although the matter may be serious in itself. If he has to do with the learned and intelligent, he is delighted with their cleverness, if with unlearned or stupid people, he finds amusement in their folly. He is not offended even by professed clowns, as he adapts himself with marvellous dexterity to the tastes of all; while with ladies generally, and even with his wife, his conversation is made up of humour and playfulness. You would say it was a second Democritus, or rather that Pythagorean philosopher, who strolls in leisurely mood through the market-place, contemplating the turmoil of those who buy and sell. There is no one less guided by the opinion of the multitude, but on the other hand no one sticks more closely to common sense. . . .

His character is entirely free from any touch of avarice. He has set aside out of his property what he thinks sufficient for his children, and spends the rest in a liberal fashion. When he was still dependent on his profession, he gave every client true and friendly counsel with an eye to their advantage rather than his own, generally advising them, that the cheapest thing they could do was to come to terms with their opponents. If he could not persuade them to do this, he pointed out how they might go to law at least expense; for there are some people whose character leads them to delight in litigation. . . .

Meantime there is no assumption of superiority. In the midst of so great a pressure of business he remembers his humble friends; and from time to time he returns to his beloved studies. Whatever authority he derives from his rank, and whatever influence he enjoys by the favour of a powerful sovereign, are employed in the service of the public, or in that of his friends. It has always been part of his character to be most obliging to every body, and marvellously ready with his sympathy; and this disposition is more conspicuous than ever, now that his power of doing good is greater. Some he relieves with money, some he protects by his authority, some he promotes by his recommendation, while those whom he cannot otherwise assist are benefited by his advice. No one is sent away in distress, and you might call him the general patron of all poor people. He counts it a great gain to himself, if he has relieved some oppressed person, made the path clear for one that was in difficulties, or brought back into favour one that was in disgrace. No man more readily confers a benefit, no man expects less in return. And successful as he is in so many ways,—while success in generally accompanied by self-conceit,—I have never seen any mortal being more free from this failing. . . .

However a verse he may be from all superstition, he is a steady adherent of true piety; having regular hours for his prayers, which are not uttered by rote, but from the heart. He talks with his friends about a future life in such a way as to make you feel that he believes what he says, and does not speak without the best hope. Such is More, even at Court; and there are still people who think that Christians are only to be found in monasteries!

The School-Master's
Admonitions

In any time of rapid change men tend to become increasingly concerned with manners. When all around is changing one becomes anxious as to whether he is doing the right thing. The courtesy literature of the Renaissance reflects this concern about correct behavior in an age that had lost many of the predictabilities and certainties of the Middle Ages. The following admonition was first published in 1522. Incorporated into Erasmus' *De civilitate* (1530), it was reprinted many times in the next two hundred years and translated into several languages. In it, the school-master instructs a boy how to behave with good manners, with his superiors, in school, and when eating.

The passage is taken from Volume I of *The Colloquies of Desiderius Erasmus,* translated by N. Bailey, edited by the Rev. E. Johnson, published by Gibbings and Company in London in 1900.

THE SCHOOLMASTER AND BOY

Sch. You seem not to have been bred at Court, but in a Cow-stall; you behave yourself so clownishly. A Gentleman ought to behave himself like a Gentleman. As often or whenever any one that is your Superior speaks to you, stand straight, pull off your Hat, and look neither doggedly, surlily, saucily, malapertly, nor unsettledly, but with a staid, modest, pleasant Air in your Countenance, and a bashful Look fix'd upon the Person who speaks to you; your Feet set close one by t'other; your Hands without Action: Don't stand, titter, totter, first standing upon one Foot, and then upon another, nor playing with your Fingers, biting your Lip, scratching your Head, or picking your Ears: Let your Cloaths be put on tight and neat, that your whole Dress, Air, Motion and Habit, may bespeak a modest and bashful Temper.

Bo. What if I shall try, Sir?

Ma. Do so.

Bo. Is this right?

Ma. Not quite.

Bo. Must I do so?

Ma. That's pretty well.

Bo. Must I stand so?

Ma. Ay, that's very well, remember that Posture; don't be a Prittle prattle nor Prate apace nor be a minding any Thing but what is said to you. If you are to make an Answer, do it in few Words, and to the Purpose, every now and then prefacing with some Title of Respect, and sometimes use a Title of Honour, and now and then make a Bow, especially when you have done speaking: Nor do you go away without asking Leave, or being bid to go: Now come let me see how you can practise this. How long have you been from Home?

Bo. Almost six Months.

Ma. You should have said Sir.

Bo. Almost six Months, Sir.

Ma. Don't you long to see your Mother?

Bo. Yes, sometimes.

Ma. Have you a Mind to go to see her?

Bo. Yes, with your Leave, Sir.

Ma. Now you should have made a Bow; that's very well, remember to do so; when you speak, don't speak fast, stammer, or speak in your Throat, but use yourself to pronounce your Words distinctly and clearly. If you pass by any ancient Person, a Magistrate, a Minister, or Doctor, or any Person of Figure, be sure to pull off your Hat, and make your Reverence: Do the same when you pass by any sacred Place, or the Image of the Cross. When you are at a Feast, behave yourself chearfully, but always so as to remember what becomes your Age: Serve yourself last; and if any nice Bit be offer'd you, refuse it modestly; but if they press it upon you, take, it, and thank the Person, and cutting off a bit of it, offer the rest either to him that gave it to you, or to him that sits next to you. If any Body drinks to you merrily, thank him, and drink moderately. If you don't care to drink, however, kiss the Cup. Look pleasantly upon him that speaks to you; and be sure not to speak till you are spoken to. If any Thing that is obscene be said, don't laugh at it, but keep your Countenance, as though you did not understand it; don't reflect on any Body, nor take place of any Body, nor boast of any Thing of your own, nor undervalue any Thing of another Bodies. Be courteous to your Companions that are your Inferiors; traduce no Body; don't be a Blab with your Tongue, and by this Means you'll get a good Character, and gain Friends without Envy. If the Entertainment shall be long, desire to be excus'd, bid much good may it do the Guests, and withdraw from Table: See that you remember these Things.

Bo. I'll do my Endeavour, Sir. Is there any Thing else you'd have me do?

Ma. Now go to your Books.

Bo. Yes, Sir.

The Liberal Education
of Children

In 1529 Erasmus published what has been considered his most mature treatise on education, *De Pueris Statim ac Liberaliter Instituendis*, which has been translated as, *That Children Should Straightway From Their Earliest Years Be Trained in Virtue and Sound Learning*. Erasmus insists that we must start the process of education as early as possible. But children should not be regarded as miniature adults: the teacher should put himself in their position and recognize how much they lack experience and knowledge. They should be gently and humanely raised and educated. Central to Erasmus' argument is his assertion that, in contrast to the animals, man lacks strong instinctive powers: his strength lies in his educability. Man's unique gift is his malleable, educable mind. A boy does not really become a man until he is an *educated* man. If his reason remains untutored he is still an animal.

The selection is from *Desiderius Erasmus Concerning the Aim and Method of Education*, by William Harrison Woodward, published by Cambridge University Press in 1904.

§ 4. THE SUPREME IMPORTANCE OF EDUCATION
TO HUMAN WELL-BEING.

To dumb creatures Mother Nature has given an innate power or instinct whereby they may in great part attain to their right capacities. But Providence in granting to man alone the privilege of reason has thrown the burden of development of the human being upon training. Well, therefore, has it been said that the first means, the second, and the third means to happiness is right training or education. Sound education is the condition of real wisdom. And if an education which is soundly planned and carefully carried out is the very fount of all human excellence, so, on the other hand, careless and unworthy training is the true source of folly and vice. This *capacity for training* is, indeed, the chief aptitude which has been bestowed upon humanity. Unto the animals nature has given swiftness of foot or of wing, keenness of sight, strength or size of frame, and various weapons of defence. To Man, instead of physical powers, is given a mind apt for training; in this single gift all others are comprised, for him, at least, who turns it to due profit. We see that where native instinct is strong—as in squirrels or bees—capacity for being taught is wanting. Man, lacking instinct, can do little or nothing of innate power; scarce can he eat, or walk, or speak, unless he be guided thereto. How then can we expect that he should become competent to the duties of life unless straightway and with much diligence he be brought under the discipline of a worthy education? Let me enforce this by the well-known story of Lycurgus, who, to convince the Spartans, brought out two hounds, one of good mettle, but untrained and therefore useless in the field, and the other poorly bred and well-drilled at his work; "Nature," he said, "may be strong, yet Education is more powerful still." . . .

§ 7.   REASON THE TRUE MARK OF MAN.

Now it is the possession of Reason which constitutes a Man. If trees or wild beasts grow, men, believe me, are fashioned. Men in olden time who led their life in forests, driven by the mere needs and desires of their natures, guided by no laws, with no ordering in communities, are to be judged rather as savage beasts than as men. For Reason, the mark of humanity, has no place where all is determined by appetite. It is beyond dispute that a man not instructed through reason in philosophy and sound learning is a creature lower than a brute, seeing that there is no beast more wild or more harmful than a man who is driven hither and thither by ambition, or desire, anger or envy, or lawless temper. Therefore do I conclude that he that provides not that his own son may presently be instructed in the best learning is neither a man nor the son of a man. Would it not be a horror to look upon a human soul clad in the form of a beast, as Circe is fabled to have done by her spells? But is it not worse that a father should see his own image slowly but surely becoming the dwelling-place of a brute's nature? It is said a bear's cub is at birth but an ill-formed lump which by a long process of licking is brought into shape. Nature, in giving you a son, presents you, let me say, a rude, unformed creature, which it is your part to fashion so that it may become indeed a man. If this fashioning be neglected you have but an animal still: if it be contrived earnestly and wisely, you have, I had almost said, what may prove a being not far from a God. . . .

§ 28. THE NEED OF SYMPATHY IN ONE WHO SHALL TEACH YOUNG CHILDREN.

It is the mark of a good teacher to stand towards his charge somewhat in the relation of a parent: both learning and teaching are made easier thereby. He will also in a sense become a boy again that he may draw his pupil to himself. Though this by no means justifies the choice of the old and infirm as teachers of youth: these indeed have no need to stimulate a childish temper, they are only too truly once more in their second infancy. Rather should the master be in the full vigour of early manhood, able to sympathise naturally with youth, ready to adapt himself to its demands. He will follow in his first instruction the methods of the mother in the earliest training of her nursling. As she prattles baby language, stirs and softens baby food, stoops and guides the tottering steps—so will the master act in things of the mind. Slowly is the transition made to walking alone or to eating solid food; the tender frame is thus carefully hardened. In exactly the same manner instruction is at first simple, taught by way of play, taught by degrees. The sense of effort is lost in the pleasure of such natural exercise: insensibly the mind becomes equal to harder tasks. Wholly wrong are those masters who expect their little pupils to act as though they were but diminutive adults, who forget the meaning of *youth*, who have no standard of what can be done or be understood except that of their own minds. Such a master will upbraid, exact, punish, as though he were dealing with students as old as himself, and forgets that he was ever himself a child. Pliny warned such a one when he spoke thus to a master: "Remember that your pupil is but a youth still, and that you were once one yourself." But how often does the schoolmaster of to-day prove by his harsh discipline that he wholly forgets this simple truth!

The Art of Learning

This dialogue is between Erasmus ("Desiderius") and John Erasmius Froben ("Erasmius"), who was Erasmus' godson and the son of his publisher. The boy was thirteen years old when the colloquy was first published in 1529. Apparently he was a mediocre student. As indifferent students do today, he was looking for a sort of "instant education." He placed his hopes on the *Ars notoria* (the Latin title of the colloquy), the medieval name for a mysterious art that enabled a man to gain knowledge with incredible facility. It promised a command of the arts and sciences in fourteen days. Erasmus quickly disabuses the boy of these delusions. Then, as now, there is no short cut to education. In order to become an educated man, one needs diligence and a love of learning. It is education, Erasmus maintains, that distinguishes man from the animals. The educated person possesses self-control, which he uses to discipline his mind. He is not misled by words: he realizes that words escape unless weighed down with meaning, and hence he seeks a genuine understanding of his humanistic studies rather than merely a verbal facility. And all of this takes patience and time. There is no "instant education."

The passage appears, under the title, "The Notable Art," in Volume III of *The Colloquies of Erasmus*, translated by N. Bailey, edited by the Rev. E. Johnson, published in London by Gibbings and Company in 1900.

DESIDERIUS, ERASMIUS

De. How do you succeed in your Studies, Erasmius?

Er. But very slowly; but I should make a better Proficiency, if I could obtain one Thing of you.

De. You may obtain any Thing of me, provided it be for your Good; do but tell me what it is.

185

Er. I believe there is nothing of the most hidden Arts, but what you are acquainted with.

De. I wish I were.

Er. I am told there is a certain compendious Art, that will help a Man to accomplish himself with all the liberal Sciences by a very little Labour.

De. What is that you talk of? Did you ever see the Book?

Er. I did see it, and that was all, having no Body to instruct me in the Use of it.

De. What was the Subject of the Book?

Er. It treated of various Forms of Dragons, Lions, Leopards; more and various Circles, and Words written in them, some in Greek, some in Latin, and some in Hebrew, and other barbarous Languages.

De. Pray, in how many Days Time did the Title-Page promise you the Knowledge of the Arts and Sciences?

Er. In fourteen.

De. In Truth a very noble Promise. But did you ever know any Body that has become learned by that notable Art?

Er. No.

De. No, nor no Body ever did, or ever will, till we can see an Alchymist grow rich.

Er. Why, is there no such Art·then? I wish with all my Heart there was.

De. Perhaps you do, because you would not be at the Pains which is requir'd to become learned.

Er. You are right.

De. It seem'd meet to the divine Being, that the common Riches, Gold, Jewels, Silver, Palaces, and Kingdoms, should be bestow'd on the slothful and undeserving; but the true Riches, and such as are properly our own, must be gotten by Labour. Nor ought we to think that Labour troublesome, by which so valuable a Thing is procured; when we see a great many Men run thro' dreadful Dangers, and work their Way thro' unimaginable Labours, to get temporary Things, and such as are really vile too, if compar'd to Learning; and do not always attain what they strive for neither. But indeed the Pains that Studies cost, are mingled with a great Deal of Sweetness, if you make but a little Proficiency in 'em. And again, it is for the most Part in your own Power to cut off the greatest Part of the Tiresomness of attaining them.

Er. How is that to be done?

De. In the first Place, by bringing your Mind to the Love of Studies. And secondly to admire 'em.

Er. How must that be done?

De. Consider how many Learning has enrich'd, how many it has promoted to the highest Honours: Then again, consider with yourself, how great the Difference is between a Man and a Beast.

Er. You give very good Advice.

De. Then you ought to tame, and bring your Mind to be consistent with itself; and to take Pleasure in those Things that bring Profit rather than Pleasure. For those Things that are honourable in themselves, altho' they are something troublesome in the Beginning, yet they grow pleasant by Use; and by that Means you will give the Master less Trouble, and you will more easily make a Progress; according to the Saying of Isocrates, which deserves to be written in Gold Letters on the Cover of your Book; . . . 'If thou be desirous to learn, thou shalt learn many Things well.'

Er. I am quick enough at Apprehension, but I presently forget what I have learned.

De. Then you tell me your Vessel is leaky.

Er. You're much about the Matter; but what Remedy is there for it?

De. Why, you must stop the Chinks that it don't run out.

Er. What must I stop 'em with?

De. Not with Moss, nor Mortar, but with Diligence. He that learns Words, and does not understand the Meaning of 'em, soon forgets 'em: For Words, as Homer says, have Wings, and easily fly away, unless they be kept down by the Weight of the Meaning. Therefore let it be your first Care thoroughly to understand the Meaning of them, and then frequently revolve them in your Mind, and repeat them; and then, as I have said, you ought to break your Mind, that it may be able to use Application as often as is necessary; for that Mind that is so wild, that it can't be brought to this, is not fit for Learning.

Er. I know too well how hard a Matter that is.

De. Whosoever has so voluble a Mind, that it cannot fix itself upon any Thought, he neither can attend long on the Person teaching, nor fix what he has learn'd in the Memory. An Impression may be made even upon Lead, because it is fixed; but no Impression can be set upon Water or Quicksilver, because they are fluid. But if you can but bring your Mind to this, if you converse constantly with Men of Learning, whose Discourses do daily produce so many things worthy Notice, you may learn a great Deal with but little Pains.

Er. That is very right.

De. For besides the Table-Talk, their daily Conversation after Dinner, you hear eight fine Sentences, collected out of the most approv'd Authors; and after Supper as many. Now do but reckon up what a Sum this will amount to in a Month, and how many more in a Year.

Er. A very large Sum, if I could but remember them all.

De. And then, again, when you hear nothing but true Latin spoken, what hinders you, but that you may learn Latin in a very few Months, when Lads, who have no Learning, do learn the French or Spanish Tongue in a very little Time?

Er. I will take your Course, and try whether I can bring this Mind of mine to submit to the Yoke of the Muses.

De. I know no other notable Art, but Industry, Delight, and Assiduity.

Erasmus to Christian
of Lubeck

Erasmus knew Christian Northoff as a student in Paris in 1496–1497. This letter was probably written in 1497 and first published in Paris around 1514. It contains revealing advice on the best method of study, based upon Erasmus' own experience and reflection. The friendly and humane attitude toward students that Erasmus shows no doubt reflected his treatment of his own students. The insistence that lasting learning must be accompanied by pleasure and interspersed with games, the emphasis on the association between the right method and ease of performance, and the gentle humaneness of tone, all became characteristic notes of the best of sixteenth-century humanism.

This letter appears in Volume III of *The Colloquies of Desiderius Erasmus*, translated by N. Bailey, edited by the Rev. E. Johnson, published by Gibbings and Company in London in 1900.

My special Friend Christian,

Making no doubt but that you have an ardent Desire of Literature, I thought you stood in no Need of Exhortation; but only a Guide to direct you in the Journey you have already enter'd upon: And that I look'd upon as my Duty to be, to you, the most nearly ally'd to me, and engaging; that is to say, to acquaint you with the Steps that I myself took, even from a Child: Which if you shall accept as heartily as I communicate, I trust I shall neither repent me of giving Directions, nor you of observing them. Let it be your first Care to chuse you a Master, who is a Man of Learning; for it cannot be, that one that is unlearned himself can render another learned. As soon as you have gotten such an one, endeavour all you can to engage him to treat you

189

with the Affection of a Father, and yourself to act towards him with
the Affection of a Son. And indeed, Reason ought to induce us to consider, that we own more to those, from whom we receive the Way
of living well, than to those to whom we owe our first Living in the
World; and that a mutual Affection is of so great Moment to Learning,
that it will be to no Purpose to have a Teacher, if he be not your
Friend too. In the next Place, hear him attentively and assiduously.
The genius of Learners is often spoil'd by too much Contention. Assiduity holds out the longer, being moderate, and by daily Augmentations
grows to a Heap larger than can be thought. There is nothing more
pernicious than to be glutted with any Thing; and so likewise with
Learning. And therefore an immoderate pressing on to Learning is sometimes to be relax'd; and Divertisements are to be intermix'd: But then
they should be such as are becoming a Gentleman, and Student, and
not much different from the Studies themselves. Nay, there ought to
be a continual Pleasure in the very midst of Studies, that it may appear
to us rather a Pastime than a Labour; for nothing will be of long Duration, that does not affect the Mind of the Doer with some Sort of Pleasure. It is the utmost Madness to learn that which must be unlearned
again. Think that you ought to do the same by your Genius, that Physi-
cians are wont to do in preserving the Stomach. Take Care that you
don't oppress your Genius by Food, that is either noxious, or too much
of it; both of them are equally offensive. Let alone Ebrardus, Catholicon,
Brachylogus, and the rest of these Sort of Authors, all whose Names
I neither can mention, nor is it worth while so to do, to others who
take a Pleasure to learn Barbarism with an immense Labour. At the
first it is no great Matter how much you Learn; but how well you
learn it. And now take a Direction how you may not only learn well,
but easily too; for the right Method of Art qualifies the Artist to perform
his Work not only well and expeditiously, but easily too. Divide the
Day into Tasks, as we read Pliny the Second, and Pope Pius the Great
did, Men worthy to be remember'd by all Men. In the first Part of
it, which is the chief Thing of all, hear the Master interpret, not only
attentively, but with a Sort of Greediness, not being content to follow
him in his Dissertations with a slow Pace, but striving to out-strip him
a little. Fix all his Sayings in your Memory, and commit the most material of them to Writing, the faithful Keeper of Words. And be sure
to take Care not to rely on them, as that ridiculous rich Man that Seneca
speaks of did, who had form'd a Notion, that whatsoever of Literature
any of his Servants had, was his own. By no Means have your Study
furnish'd with learned Books, and be unlearned yourself. Don't suffer
what you hear to slip out of your Memory, but recite it either with

yourself, or to other Persons. Nor let this suffice you, but set apart some certain Time for Meditation; which one Thing as St. Aurelius writes does most notably conduce to assist both Wit and Memory. An Engagement and combating of Wits does in an extraordinary Manner both shew the Strength of Genius's, rouzes them, and augments them. If you are in Doubt of any Thing, don't be asham'd to ask; or if you have committed an Error, to be corrected. Avoid late and unseasonable Studies, for they murder Wit, and are very prejudicial to Health. The Muses love the Morning, and that is a fit Time for Study. After you have din'd, either divert yourself at some Exercise, or take a Walk, and discourse merrily, and Study between-whiles. As for Diet, eat only as much as shall be sufficient to preserve Health, and not as much or more than the Appetite may crave. Before Supper, take a little Walk, and do the same after Supper. A little before you go to sleep read something that is exquisite, and worth remembering; and contemplate upon it till you fall asleep; and when you awake in the Morning, call yourself to an Account for it. Always keep this Sentence of Pliny's in your Mind, 'All that Time is lost that you don't bestow on Study.' Think upon this, that there is nothing more fleeting than Youth, which, when once it is past, can never be recall'd. But now I begin to be an Exhorter, when I promis'd to be a Director. My sweet Christian, follow this Method, or a better, if you can; and so farewell.

On the Right Method
of Instruction

This is a translation of Erasmus' *De Ratione Studii,* which was probably written around 1506 and first published in 1511. In it, the foremost humanist of the sixteenth century presents his recommended program of liberal studies. Erasmus lists the best classical writers to study and describes the best methods of mastering grammar, learning to write, and analyzing a text. It is noteworthy that, in language instruction, he places emphasis upon constant use of the language through reading, writing, speaking, and listening, rather than upon the memorization of grammatical rules. It has taken our schools four centuries to absorb this lesson. Erasmus' educational model will be a man with a thorough knowledge of words and their meanings. He will be a master of language. Those who have a contempt for this form of education are exactly those most in need of it, Erasmus claims, for they are easily misled by others' skillful use of words. The languages to be learned by the humanist are the classical languages, Latin and Greek. In supposing that their literature contains all of mankind's vital knowledge, Erasmus betrays a parochialism that has impoverished Western education ever since. Today we are paying dearly, for example, for our long-sustained ignorance of Asia and Africa.

This passage is from *Desiderius Erasmus Concerning the Aim and Method of Education* by William Harrison Woodward, published by Cambridge University Press in 1904.

§. 1. THOUGHT AND EXPRESSION FORM THE TWO-FOLD MATERIAL OF INSTRUCTION.

All knowledge falls into one of two divisions: the knowledge of "truths" and the knowledge of "words": and if the former is first in importance the latter is acquired first in order of time. They are not to be commended who, in their anxiety to increase their store of truths, neglect the necessary art of expressing them. For ideas are only intelligible to us by means of the words which describe them; wherefore defective knowledge of language reacts upon our apprehension of the truths expressed. We often find that no one is so apt to lose himself in verbal arguments as the man who boasts that facts, not words, are the only things that interest him. This goes to prove that true education includes what is *best* in both kinds of knowledge, taught, I must add, under the *best* guidance. For, remembering how difficult it is to eradicate early impressions, we should aim from the first at learning what need never be unlearnt, and that only.

§ 2.   EXPRESSION CLAIMS THE FIRST PLACE IN POINT OF TIME. BOTH THE GREEK AND LATIN LANGUAGES NEEDFUL TO THE EDUCATED MAN.

Language thus claims the first place in the order of studies and from the outset should include both Greek and Latin. The argument for this is two-fold. First, that within these two literatures are contained all the knowledge which we recognise as of vital importance to mankind. Secondly, that the natural affinity of the two tongues renders it more profitable to study them side by side than apart. Latin particularly gains by this method. Quintilian advised that a beginning should be made with Greek before systematic work in Latin is taken in hand. Of course he regarded proficiency in both as essential. The elements, therefore, of Greek and Latin should be acquired early, and should a thoroughly skilled master not be available, then—but only then—let the learner fall back upon self-teaching by means of the study of classical masterpieces.

§ 3.   THE RIGHT METHOD OF ACQUIRING GRAMMAR RESTS UPON READING AND NOT UPON DEFINITIONS AND RULES.

. . . Whilst a knowledge of the rules of accidence and syntax is most necessary to every student, still they should be as few, as simple, and as carefully framed as possible. I have no patience with the stupidity of the average teacher of grammar who wastes precious years in hammering rules into children's heads. For it is not by learning rules that we acquire the power of speaking a language, but by daily intercourse with those accustomed to express themselves with exactness and refinement, and by the copious reading of the best authors. . . .

Some proficiency in expression being . . . attained the student devotes his attention to the *content* of the ancient literatures. It is true, of course, that in reading an author for purposes of vocabulary and style the student cannot fail to gather something besides. But I have in my mind much more than this when I speak of studying "contents." For I affirm that with slight qualification the whole of attainable knowledge lies enclosed within the literary monuments of ancient Greece. This great inheritance I will compare to a limpid spring of whose undefiled waters it behoves all who truly thirst to drink and be restored.

The Education of a
Christian Prince

The *Institutio Principis Christiani* was probably published in 1516
when Erasmus was about fifty and the intellectual leader of Europe.
He had recently been appointed councillor at the court of Prince
Charles, the future Emperor Charles V, who was then about sixteen
years old. The treatise had the young prince in mind as the recipient
of the advice. It is interesting to compare it with two other contemporary books that treated problems of power and leadership—
Thomas More's *Utopia* (1516) and Machiavelli's *The Prince*
(1513). For Erasmus, the model of the educated prince is above
all a man of Christian virtue. The specific qualities he should possess are wisdom magnanimity, temperance, and integrity, all securely based on a foundation of Christian piety and morality. Erasmus repeatedly points out that it is not by appearances but by
underlying virtue and good actions that the prince must ultimately
be judged. He must be a selfless man, putting the safety and welfare
of his people above even his own life. But he is an aristocratic
leader sharing much in common with Plato's philosopher-king.
Erasmus makes clear that his prince is not like the common people:
he should be different from them in opinions and desires. And yet
he should be raised among those he will lead. Erasmus shows an
awareness of the importance of mutual understanding for harmoniz-
ing relations between leader and led. Failure to learn this lesson
brought about the subsequent downfall of many European aristoc-
racies. The prince should not court a cheap popularity with the
people but should stick to his convictions even when it is costly
to do so. The people must be firmly governed: if they do not do
what is good for them they must be won over, by subterfuge if
necessary. Finally, the prince must not be a warmonger: the edu-

cated man is a man of peace. Not even against the Turks (for which one can today read "communists") should one go to war. We should rather ensure that our own actions are in accord with our professed values. For through war we easily degenerate into doing the very things we claim to be fighting against. The truth of Erasmus' warning has subsequently been demonstrated time and time again.

These selections are from Desiderius Erasmus, *The Education of a Christian Prince,* translated by Lester K. Born, published in New York in 1965 by Octagon Books, Inc., pages 148–151, 154–155, 162–163, 206–207, 212–213, 256. Copyright 1936 by Columbia University Press. Reprinted with permission.

Before all else the story of Christ must be firmly rooted in the mind of the prince. He should drink deeply of His teachings, gathered in handy texts, and then later from those very fountains themselves, whence he may drink more purely and more effectively. He should be taught that the teachings of Christ apply to no one more than to the prince.

The great mass of people are swayed by false opinions and are no different from those in Plato's cave, who took the empty shadows as the real things. It is the part of a good prince to admire none of the things that the common people consider of great consequence, but to judge all things on their own merits as "good" or "bad." But nothing is truly "bad" unless joined with base infamy. Nothing is really "good" unless associated with moral integrity.

Therefore, the tutor should first see that his pupil loves and honors virtue as the finest quality of all, the most felicitous, the most fitting a prince; and that he loathes and shuns moral turpitude as the foulest and most terrible of things. Lest the young prince be accustomed to regard riches as an indispensable necessity, to be gained by right or wrong, he should learn that those are not true honors which are commonly acclaimed as such. True honor is that which follows on virtue and right action of its own will. The less affected it is, the more it redounds to fame. The low pleasures of the people are so far beneath a prince, especially a Christian prince, that they hardly become any man. There is another kind of pleasure which will endure, genuine and true, all through life. Teach the young prince that nobility, statues, wax masks, family-trees, all the pomp of heralds, over which the great mass of people stupidly swell with pride, are only empty terms unless supported by deeds worth while. The prestige of a prince, his greatness, his majesty, must not be developed and preserved by fortune's wild display, but by wisdom, solidarity, and good deeds.

Death is not to be feared, nor should we wail when it comes to others, unless it was a foul death. The happiest man is not the one who has lived the longest, but the one who has made the most of his life. The span of life should be measured not by years but by our deeds well performed. Length of life has no bearing on a man's happiness. It is how well he lived that counts. Surely virtue is its own reward. It is the duty of a good prince to consider the welfare of his people even at the cost of his own life if need be. But that prince does not really die who loses his life in such a cause. All those things which the common people cherish as delightful, or revere as excellent, or adopt as useful, are to be measured by just one standard—worth. On the other hand, whatever things the common people object to as disagreeable, or despise as lowly, or shun as pernicious, should not be avoided unless they are bound up with dishonor. . . .

You cannot be a prince, if you are not a philosopher; you will be a tyrant. There is nothing better than a good prince. A tyrant is such a monstrous beast that his like does not exist. Nothing is equally baneful, nothing more hateful to all. Do not think that Plato rashly advanced the idea, which was lauded by the most praiseworthy men, that the blessed state will be that in which the princes are philosophers, or in which the philosophers seize the principate. I do not mean by philosopher, one who is learned in the ways of dialectic or physics, but one who casts aside the false pseudo-realities and with open mind seeks and follows the truth. To be a philosopher and to be a Christian is synonymous in fact. The only difference is in the nomenclature.

What is more stupid than to judge a prince on the following accomplishments: his ability to dance gracefully, dice expertly, drink with a gusto, swell with pride, plunder the people with kingly grandeur, and do all the other things which I am ashamed even to mention, although there are plenty who are not ashamed to do them? The common run of princes zealously avoid the dress and manner of living of the lower classes. Just so should the true prince be removed from the sullied opinions and desires of the common folk. The one thing which he should consider base, vile, and unbecoming to him is to share the opinions of the common people who never are interested in anything worth while. How ridiculous it is for one adorned with gems, gold, the royal purple, attended by courtiers, possessing all the other marks of honor, wax

images and statues, wealth that clearly is not his, to be so far superior
to all because of them, and yet in the light of real goodness of spirit
to be found inferior to many born from the very dregs of society. . . .

If you want to show yourself an excellent prince, see that no one
outshines you in the qualities befitting your position—I mean wisdom,
magnanimity, temperance, integrity. If you want to make trial of yourself
with other princes, do not consider yourself superior to them if you
take away part of their power or scatter their forces; but only if you
have been less corrupt than they, less greedy, less arrogant, less wrathful,
less headstrong.

No one will gainsay that nobility in its purest form becomes a prince.
There are three kinds of nobility: the first is derived from virtue and
good actions; the second comes from acquaintance with the best of
training; and the third from an array of family portraits and the geneal-
ogy or wealth. It by no means becomes a prince to swell with pride
over this lowest degree of nobility, for it is so low that it is nothing
at all, unless it has itself sprung from virtue. Neither must he neglect
the first, which is so far the first that it alone can be considered in
the strictest judgment. . . .

You, too, must take up your cross, or else Christ will have none of
you. "What," you ask, "is my cross?" I will tell you: Follow the right,
do violence to no one, plunder no one, sell no public office, be corrupted
by no bribes. To be sure, your treasury will have far less in it then otherwise, but take no thought for that loss, if only you have acquired the interest from justice. While you are using every means and interest to benefit
the state, your life is fraught with care; you rob your youth and genius
of their pleasures; you wear yourself down with long hours of toil.
Forget that and enjoy yourself in the consciousness of right. As you
would rather stand for an injury than avenge it at great loss to the
state, perchance you will lose a little something of your empire. Bear
that; consider that you have gained a great deal because you have
brought hurt to fewer than you would otherwise have done. Do your
private emotions as a man—reproachful anger, love for your wife, hatred
of an enemy, shame—urge you to do what is not right and what is
not to the welfare of the state? Let the thought of honor win. Let
the concern for the state completely cover your personal ambitions. If
you cannot defend your realm without violating justice, without wanton
loss of human life, without great loss to religion, give up and yield
to the importunities of the age! If you cannot look out for the possessions
of your subjects without danger to your own life, set the safety of the
people before your very life! But while you are conducting yourself
in this fashion, which befits a true Christian prince, there will be plenty

to call you a dolt, and no prince at all! Hold fast to your cause. It is far better to be a just man than an unjust prince. It is clear now, I think, that even the greatest kings are not without their crosses, if they want to follow the course of right at all times, as they should. . . .

The prince's tutor shall see that a hatred of the very words "tyranny" and "dominion" are implanted in the prince. . . . If he finds any examples of good princes who are as different as possible from the tyrant he should zealously bring them forth with frequent praise and commendation. Then let him create the picture of each, and impress upon mind and eye, to the extent of his capabilities, the king and the tyrant, so that the prince may burn to emulate the one and detest the latter even more [than before].

Let the teacher paint a sort of celestial creature, more like to a divine being than a mortal: complete in all the virtues; born for the common good; yea, sent by the God above to help the affairs of mortals by looking out and caring for everyone and everything; to whom no concern is of longer standing or more dear than the state; who has more than a paternal spirit toward everyone who holds the life of each individual dearer than his own; who works and strives night and day for just one end—to be the best he can for everyone; with whom rewards are ready for all good men and pardon for the wicked, if only they will reform—for so much does he want to be of real help to his people, without thought of recompense, that if necessary he would not hesitate to look out for their welfare at great risk to himself; who considers his wealth to lie in the advantages of his country; who is ever on the watch so that everyone else may sleep deeply; who grants no leisure to himself so that he may spend his life in the peace of his country; who worries himself with continual cares so that his subjects may have peace and quiet. Upon the moral qualities of this one man alone depends the felicity of the state. Let the tutor point this out as the picture of a true prince! . . .

The prince will see to it that he is loved by his subjects in return, but in such a way that his authority is no less strong among them. There are some who are so stupid as to strive to win good will for themselves by incantations and magic rings, when there is no charm more efficacious than good character itself; nothing can be more lovable than that, for, as this is a real and immortal good, so it brings a man true and undying good will. The best formula is this: let him love, who would be loved, so that he may attach his subjects to him as God has won the peoples of the world to Himself by His goodness.

They are also wrong who win the hearts of the masses by largesses, feasts, and gross indulgence. It is true that some popular favor, instead of affection, is gained by these means, but it is neither genuine nor permanent. In the meanwhile the greed of the populace is developed, which, as happens, after it has reached large proportions thinks nothing is enough. Then there is an uprising, unless complete satisfaction is made to their demands. By this means your people are not won, but corrupted. . . .

For my part, I should like to see the prince born and raised among those people whom he is destined to rule, because friendship is created and confirmed most when the source of good will is in nature itself. The common people shun and hate even good qualities when they are unknown to them, while evils which are familiar are sometimes loved. This matter at hand has a twofold advantage to offer, for the prince will be more kindly disposed toward his subjects and certainly more ready to regard them as his own. The people on their part will feel more kindness in their hearts and be more willing to recognize his position as prince. For this reason I am especially opposed to the accepted [idea of] alliances of the princes with foreign, particularly with distant, nations. . . .

A prince who is about to assume control of the state must be advised at once that the main hope of a state lies in the proper education of its youth. This Xenophon wisely taught in his *Cyropaedia*. Pliable youth is amenable to any system of training. Therefore the greatest care should be exercised over public and private schools and over the education of the girls, so that the children may be placed under the best and most trustworthy instructors and may learn the teachings of Christ and that good literature which is beneficial to the state. As a result of this scheme of things, there will be no need for many laws or punishments, for the people will of their own free will follow the course of right.

Education exerts such a powerful influence, as Plato says, that a man who has been trained in the right develops into a sort of divine creature, while on the other hand, a person who has received a perverted training degenerates into a monstrous sort of savage beast. Nothing is of more importance to a prince than to have the best possible subjects.

The first effort, then, is to get them accustomed to the best influences, because any music has a soothing effect to the accustomed ear, and there is nothing harder than to rid people of those traits which have become second nature to them through habit. None of those tasks will be too difficult if the prince himself adheres to the best manners. . . . However, if the people prove intractable and rebel against what is good for them, then you must bide your time and gradually lead them over to your end, either by some subterfuge or by some helpful pretence. This works just as wine does, for when that is first taken it has no effect, but when it has gradually flowed through every vein it captivates the whole man and holds him in its power. . . .

Not even against the Turks do I believe we should rashly go to war, first reflecting in my own mind that the kingdom of Christ was created, spread out, and firmly established by far different means. Perchance then it is not right that it should be maintained by means differing from those by which it was created and extended. We see how many times under pretexts of wars of this kind the Christian people have been plundered and nothing else has been accomplished. Now, if the matter has to do with faith, that has been increased and made famous by the suffering of martyrs and not by forces of soldiery; but if it is for ruling power, wealth, and possessions, we must continuously be on guard lest the cause have too little of Christianity in it. But on the contrary, to judge from some who are conducting wars of this kind, it may more readily happen that we degenerate into Turks than that they become Christians through our efforts. First let us see that we ourselves are genuine Christians, and then, if it seems best, let us attack the Turks.

8   The Pansophist: Comenius

The Movarian Brethren were a group of Protestant pietists inspired by the Bohemian martyr, Jan Hus. John Amos Comenius (1592–1670) was a member, and eventually Bishop, of the Brethren. His membership in this group was a determining influence in his life, for after the outset of the Thirty Years' War, which began when he was twenty-six, he became part of a persecuted and hounded minority. In the face of political and religious persecution, he was forced to become a refugee across Europe. But, to this challenge to his life and ideals, Comenius responded with energy and resourcefulness.

His wanderings brought him into contact with some of the intellectual leaders of Europe, especially in Germany, Poland, Sweden, England, and Holland. From his wide friendships he obtained stimulation and support. From his experience of persecution, hardship, and divisiveness he forged a philosophy that emphasized political unity, religious reconciliation, educational cooperation, and intellectual harmony. He created a model of the educated person as a pansophist, one who seeks knowledge from all sources in order to become more like the God in whose image he is made—omniscient and universally compassionate.

All of Comenius' life and writings were marked by this striving for unity and brotherhood. Although a passionate lover of his own language, people, and religion, he transcended his parochial loyalties and gained a breadth of perspective that is still an inspiration to us as we face this perennial problem. He was the precursor of modern attempts at educational, scientific, and cultural cooperation, best epitomized today in UNESCO. It was all of humanity, rather than a part of it, that educed his concern: he sought educational opportunities for people of all classes, sexes, and levels of intelligence.

Nature was a constant guide and touchstone for Comenius. Per-

ceiving all nature as imbued with God's spirit, he was drawn to
the inductive method of Francis Bacon as a means of discovering
God's eternal laws in man and the universe. However, like Bacon
he advocated rather than applied the method of induction. His
feeling for nature also predisposed him toward the note of sense
realism that infuses much of his pedagogical writing. Sharply critical of the excessively verbal emphasis of contemporary education
he wanted his educated person to be enlightened through a first-
hand knowledge of things as well as through words. Despite his
realism, however, he provided little place for individual creativity;
he favored imitation, obedience, and following the teacher.

The pietistic Protestantism of Comenius stirred some democratic
leaven into his writings that often served subsequently to inspire
those who wished to broaden the base of educational opportunity
The Protestant Dissenters of the Commonwealth period in England
in particular, profited from his ideas. Comenius' philosophy was
really a theology and sometimes even special pleading: he often
did violence to the truth in order to make the evidence serve a
previously formulated conclusion. Nevertheless, his religious belief
led him to envision a model of the educated man that was potentially everyman—and everywoman. It is this enormously difficult
but exalted ideal that many educators are working (not without
opposition) to implement today.

School of Infancy

In characteristically orderly fashion, Comenius divided the first twenty-four years of life into four periods of six years each—infancy, childhood, boyhood, and youth—and assigned to each a special school: the home ("the school of the mother's knee"), the vernacular school, the Latin school or *Gymnasium,* and the university, respectively. For the guidance of parents during the crucial first six years of the child's life, Comenius wrote the *School of Infancy.* It was written around 1628–1630 while Comenius was pastor of the Moravian Church and a teacher in the Brethren's school at Leszno in Poland. Originally written in Bohemian, it was translated into German and first published in 1633 at Leszno. These early years are vitally important in Comenius' view, for "it is impossible to make the tree straight that has grown crooked." Already in these years the processes should be begun that will result in the properly educated adult—one who has gained faith and piety, moral virtue, and knowledge of languages and arts, in that order of importance. Comenius shows here his belief in the broad-ranging importance of education. There is a long list of moral qualities that should be developed in the young child: he should be truthful, obedient, temperate, clean, just, generous, industrious, patient, courteous, and modest.

This selection appears in Johann Amos Comenius, *School of Infancy: An Essay on the Education of Youth During the First Six Years,* edited by Will S. Monroe, published by D. C. Heath and Company in Boston, in 1896.

CHAPTER 2   OBLIGATIONS OF PARENTS

Parents, . . . will not fully perform their duty, if they merely teach their offspring to eat, to drink, to walk about, to talk, and to be adorned

with clothing; for these things are merely subservient to the body, which
is not the man, but his tabernacle only; the guest (the rational soul)
dwells within, and rightly claims greater care than its outward tenement
Plutarch has rightly derided such parents as desire beauty, riches, and
honors for their children, and endeavor to promote them in these re
spects, regarding very little the adornment of the soul with piety and
virtue, saying: "That those persons valued the shoe more than the foot."
And Crates the Theban, a Gentile philosopher, vehemently complaining
of the madness of such parents, declared, as the poet relates:—

"Were I permitted to proclaim aloud everywhere,
I should denounce all those infatuated and shamefully wicked,
Whom destructive money agitates with excessive zeal.
Ye gather riches for your children, and neither nourish them with
doctrine,
Nor cherish within them intellectual capability."

The first care, therefore, ought to be of the soul, which is the principal
part of the man, so that it may become, in the highest degree possible
beautifully adorned. The next care is for the body, that it may be made
a habitation fit and worthy of an immortal soul. Regard the mind as
rightly instructed which is truly illuminated from the effulgence of the
wisdom of God, so that man, contemplating the presence of the Divine
Image in himself, may diligently observe and guard that excellence

Now there are two departments of true celestial wisdom which man
ought to seek, and into which he ought to be instructed. The one, a
clear and true knowledge of God and all of his wonderful works; the
other, prudence,—carefully and wisely to regulate self and all external
and internal actions appertaining to the present and future life.

Primarily as to the future life, because properly speaking that is life,
from which both death and mortality pass into exile, since the present
is not so much life as the way to life; consequently, whosoever has
attained so much in this life as to prepare himself by faith and piety
for a future life, must be judged to have fully performed his duty here.

Yet, notwithstanding this, inasmuch as God, by bestowing longevity
upon many, assigns them certain duties, places in the course of their
life various occurrences, supplying occasions for acting prudently. Parents must by all means provide for the training of their children in
the duties of faith and piety; so must they also provide for the more
polite culture in the moral sciences, in the liberal arts, and in other
necessary things; to the end that when grown up they may become
truly men, prudently managing their own affairs, and be admitted to

the various functions of life, which, whether ecclesiastical or political, civil or social, God has willed them to fulfill, and thus, having righteously and prudently passed through the present life, they may, with the greater joy, migrate to the heavens.

In a word, the purpose for which youth ought to be educated is threefold: (1) Faith and Piety; (2) Uprightness in respect of morals; (3) Knowledge of languages and arts. These, however, in the precise order in which they are here propounded, and not inversely. In the first place, youth must be exercised in piety, then in the morals or virtues, finally in the more advanced literature. The greater the proficiency the youth makes in the latter, the better.

Whosoever has within his house youth exercising themselves in these three departments, possesses a garden in which celestial plantlets are sown, watered, bloom, and flourish; a studio, as it were, of the Holy Spirit, in which He elaborates and polishes those vessels of mercy, those instruments of glory, so that in them, as lively images of God, the rays of His eternal and infinite power, wisdom, and bounty, may shine more and more. How inexpressibly blessed are parents in such a paradise! . . .

CHAPTER 4 CHARACTER OF EARLY INSTRUCTION

. . . Children ought to be instructed in morals and virtue, especially in the following: 1. In temperance, that they may learn to eat and drink according to the wants of nature; not too greedily, or cram themselves with food and drink beyond what is sufficient. 2. In cleanliness and decorum, so that, as concerns food, dress, and care of the body, they may be accustomed to observe decency. 3. In respect towards superiors, whose actions, conversations, and instructions they should learn to revere. 4. In complaisance, so that they may be prompt to execute all things immediately at the nod and voice of their superiors. 5. It is especially necessary that they be accustomed to speak truth, so that all their words may be in accordance with the teaching of Christ, "that which is, is; that which is not, is not." They should on no account be accustomed to utter falsehood, or to speak of anything otherwise than it really is, either seriously or in mirth. 6. They must likewise be trained to justice, so as not to touch, move stealthily, withdraw, or hide anything belonging to another, or to wrong another in any respect. 7. Benignity ought also to be instilled into them, and a love of pleasing others, so that they may be generous, and neither niggardly nor envious. 8. It is especially profitable for them to be accustomed to labor, as to acquire an aversion for indolence. 9. They should be taught not only to speak, but also to be silent when needful; for instance, during prayers, or while others are speaking. 10. They ought to be exercised in patience, so that they may not expect that all things should be done at their nod; from their earliest age they should gradually be taught to restrain their desires. 11. They should serve their elders with civility and readiness. This being an essential ornament of youth, they should be trained to it from their infancy. 12. From what has been said, courteousness will arise, by which they may learn to show good behavior to every one, to salute, to join hands, to bend the knee, to give thanks for little gifts, etc. 13. To avoid the appearance of rudeness or levity, let them at the same time learn gravity of deportment, so as to do all things modestly and gracefully. A child initiated in such virtues will easily, as occurred in the case of Christ, obtain for itself the favor of God and man.

The Great Didactic

It is in this major work that the educational implications of Comenius' philosophy of pansophism are most fully outlined. There is a breathtaking grandeur about Comenius' model of the educated person. Made in the image of God, man is potentially omniscient and capable of learning all things. Whatever may be said about the *naïveté* of Comenius' expectations, it is difficult to withhold a certain admiration for his faith in the limitless powers of the human mind. Educability is of the very essence of man, who can be defined as a teachable animal. Indeed, only the educated man can be considered properly a man. Youth presents precious opportunities for education that should not be wasted. The human brain is like wax: when young it is easy to make impressions on it, but as it grows older it becomes harder and difficult to alter. Comenius' model has a universal quality about it. Because all human beings are rational creatures of God, education should be not only for the bright sons of the rich but also for girls, for the poor, and for the dull and backward. Comenius' plea was unusual in the seventeenth century, but it presaged the gradual extension of educational opportunities to disadvantaged groups—a campaign that has to be waged in every generation, including our own. The educated man described by Comenius is not one who has merely read what others have said but one who has penetrated "to the root of things" and whose genuine understanding enables him to use what he has learned. This characteristic note of realism sounded by Comenius is another reminder of which educators perennially stand in need. Since teachers tend to have more than average facility with language, they often lose themselves and their pupils in words. They sometimes come to regard words as ends in themselves and forget how dangerous they can be when not freighted with meaning.

This selection is taken from Volume II of John Amos Comenius, *The Great Didactic*, translated and edited by M. W. Keatinge, published in London by Adam and Charles Black in 1907.

CHAPTER IV

THERE ARE THREE STAGES IN THE PREPARATION FOR
ETERNITY: TO KNOW ONESELF (AND WITH ONESELF
ALL THINGS); TO RULE ONESELF; AND TO DIRECT
ONESELF TO GOD.

6. . . . Man is naturally required to be: (1) acquainted with all
things, (2) endowed with power over all things and over himself; (3)
to refer himself and all things to God, the source of all.

Now, if we wish to express these three things by three well-known
words, these will be:

(i.)   Erudition.
(ii)   Virtue of seemly morals.
(iii.) Religion or piety.

Under Erudition we comprehend the knowledge of all things, arts, and
tongues; under Virtue, not only external decorum, but the whole disposition of our movements, internal and external; while by Religion we
understand that inner veneration by which the mind of man attaches
and binds itself to the supreme Godhead.

7. In these three things is situated the whole excellence of man, for
they alone are the foundation of the present and of the future life.
All other things (health, strength, beauty, riches, honour, friendship,
good-fortune, long life) are as nothing, if God grant them to any, but
extrinsic ornaments of life, and if a man greedily gape after them, en-
gross himself in their pursuit, occupy and overwhelm himself with them
to the neglect of those more important matters, then they become superfluous vanities and harmful obstructions. . . .

CHAPTER V

THE SEEDS OF THESE THREE (LEARNING, VIRTUE, AND
PIETY) ARE NATURALLY IMPLANTED IN US

. . . 4. It is evident that man is naturally capable of acquiring a
knowledge of all things, since, in the first place, he is the image of
God. For an image, if it be accurate, necessarily reproduces the outlines
of its archetype, as otherwise it will not be an image. Now omniscience

is chief among the properties of God, and it follows that the image of this must be reflected in man. And why not? Man, in truth, stands in the centre of the works of God and possesses a lucid mind, which, like a spherical mirror suspended in a room, reflects images of all things that are around it. All things that are around it, we say; for our mind not only seizes on things that are close at hand, but also on things that are far off, whether in space or in time; it masters difficulties, hunts out what is concealed, uncovers what is veiled, and wears itself out in examining what is inscrutable; so infinite and so unbounded is its power. If a thousand years were granted to man, in which, by grasping one thing after another, he might continually learn something fresh, he would still find some spot from which the understanding might gain fresh objects of knowledge.

So unlimited is the capacity of the mind that in the process of perception it resembles an abyss. The body is enclosed by small boundaries; the voice roams within wider limits; the sight is bounded only by the vault of heaven; but for the mind, neither in heaven nor anywhere outside heaven, can a boundary be fixed. It ascends as far over the heavens above as below the depths beneath, and would do so if they were even a thousand times more vast than they are; for it penetrates through space with incredible speed. Shall we then deny that it can fathom and grasp all things? . . .

CHAPTER VI

IF A MAN IS TO BE PRODUCED, IT IS NECESSARY THAT HE BE FORMED BY EDUCATION

1. The seeds of knowledge, of virtue and of piety are, as we have seen, naturally implanted in us; but the actual knowledge, virtue, and piety are not so given. These must be acquired by prayer, by education, and by action. He gave no bad definition who said that man was a "teachable animal." And indeed it is only by a proper education that he can become a man. . . .

9. For those who are in any position of authority, for kings, princes, magistrates, pastors of churches, and doctors, it is as necessary to be imbued with wisdom as it is for a guide to have eyes, an interpreter to have speech, a trumpet to be filled with sound, or a sword to have an edge. Similarly, those in subordinate positions should be educated that they may know how to obey their superiors wisely and prudently,

not under compulsion, with the obedience of an ass, but of their own free will and from love of order. For a rational creature should be led, not by shouts, imprisonment, and blows, but by reason. Any other method is an insult to God, in whose image all men are made, and fills human affairs with violence and unrest. . . .

CHAPTER VII

A MAN CAN MOST EASILY BE FORMED IN EARLY YOUTH, AND CANNOT BE FORMED PROPERLY EXCEPT AT THIS AGE

. . . 4. It is the nature of everything that comes into being, that while tender it is easily bent and formed, but that, when it has grown hard, it is not easy to alter. Wax, when soft, can be easily fashioned and shaped; when hard it cracks readily. A young plant can be planted, transplanted, pruned, and bent this way or that. When it has become a tree these processes are impossible. New-laid eggs, when placed under a hen, grow warm quickly and produce chickens; when they are old they will not do so. If a rider wish to train a horse, a ploughman an ox, a huntsman a dog or a hawk, a bear-leader a bear for dancing, or an old woman a magpie, a raven, or a crow, to imitate the human voice, they must choose them for the purpose when quite young; otherwise their labour is wasted.

5. It is evident that this holds good with man himself. His brain, which we have already compared to wax, because it receives the images of external objects that present themselves to its organs of sense, is, in the years of childhood, quite wet and soft, and fit for receiving all images that come to it. Later on, as we find by experience, it grows hard and dry by degrees, so that things are less readily impressed or engraved upon it. Hence Cicero's remark, "Boys pick up countless things with rapidity." In the same way it is only in the years of boyhood, when the muscles are still capable of being trained, that the hands and the other members can be trained to produce skilled work. If a man is to become a good writer, painter, tailor, smith, cabinet-maker, or musician, he must apply himself to the art from his early youth, when the imagination is active and the fingers flexible: otherwise he will never produce anything. If piety is to take root in any man's heart, it must be engrafted while he is still young; if we wish any one to be virtuous, we must train him in early youth; if we wish him to make great progress in the pursuit of wisdom, we must direct his faculties

towards it in infancy, when desire burns, when thought is swift, and when memory is tenacious. "An old man who has still to learn his lessons is a shameful and ridiculous object; training and preparation are for the young, action for the old" (Seneca, *Epist*. 36). . . .

CHAPTER IX

ALL THE YOUNG OF BOTH SEXES SHOULD BE SENT TO SCHOOL

1. The following reasons will establish that not the children of the rich or of the powerful only, but of all alike, boys and girls, both noble and ignoble, rich and poor, in all cities and towns, villages and hamlets, should be sent to school.

2. In the first place, all who have been born to man's estate have been born with the same end in view, namely, that they may be men, that is to say, rational creatures, the lords of other creatures, and the images of their Creator. All, therefore, must be brought on to a point at which, being properly imbued with wisdom, virtue, and piety, they may usefully employ the present life and be worthily prepared for that to come. God Himself has frequently asserted that with Him there is no respect of persons, so that, if, while we admit some to the culture of the intellect, we exclude others, we commit an injury not only against those who share the same nature as ourselves, but against God Himself, who wishes to be acknowledged, to be loved, and to be praised by all upon whom He has impressed His image. In this respect the fervour of all men will increase in proportion to the flame of knowledge that has been kindled. For our love is in direct ratio to our knowledge.

3. Now we do not know to what uses divine providence has destined this or that man; but this is certain, that out of the poorest, the most abject, and the most obscure, He has produced instruments for His glory. Let us, therefore, imitate the sun in the heavens, which lights, warms, and vivifies the whole earth, so that whatever is able to live, to flourish, and to blossom, may do so.

4. Nor is it any obstacle that some seem to be naturally dull and stupid, for this renders more imperative the universal culture of such intellects. The slower and the weaker the disposition of any man, the more he needs assistance, that he may throw off his brutish dulness and stupidity as much as possible. Nor can any man be found whose intellect is so weak that it cannot be improved by culture. A sieve, if you continually pour water through it, grows cleaner and cleaner,

although it cannot retain the liquid; and, in the same way, the dull
and the weak-minded, though they may make no advance in letters,
become softer in disposition and learn to obey the civil magistrates
and the ministers of the Church. There have, besides, been many instances in which those who are naturally stupid have gained such a
grasp of the sciences as to excel those who were more gifted. As the
poet truly says: "Industry overcomes all obstacles." Again, just as some
men are strong as children, but afterwards grow sick and ailing, while
others, whose bodies are sickly and undersized in youth, develope into
robust and tall men; so it is with intellects. Some develope early, but
soon wear out and grow dull, while others, originally stupid, become
sharp and penetrating. In our orchards we like to have not only trees
that bring forth early fruit but also those that are late-bearing; for
each thing, as says the son of Sirach, finds praise in its season, and
at length, though late, shows that it has not existed in vain. Why, therefore, should we wish that in the garden of letters only one class of
intellects, the forward and active, should be tolerated? Let none be
excluded unless God has denied him sense and intelligence.

5. Nor can any sufficient reason be given why the weaker sex (to
give a word of advice on this point in particular) should be altogether
excluded from the pursuit of knowledge (whether in Latin or in their
mother-tongue). They also are formed in the image of God, and share
in His grace and in the kingdom of the world to come. They are endowed
with equal sharpness of mind and capacity for knowledge (often with
more than the opposite sex), and they are able to attain the highest
positions, since they have often been called by God Himself to rule
over nations, to give sound advice to kings and princes, to the study
of medicine and of other things which benefit the human race, even
to the office of prophesying and of inveighing against priests and bishops.
Why, therefore, should we admit them to the alphabet, and afterwards
drive them away from books? Do we fear their folly? The more we
occupy their thoughts, so much the less will the folly that arises from
emptiness of mind find a place. . . .

7. . . . We are not advising that women be educated in such a way
that their tendency to curiosity shall be developed, but so that their
sincerity and contentedness may be increased, and this chiefly in those
things which it becomes a woman to know and to do; that is to say,
all that enables her to look after her household and to promote the
welfare of her husband and her family. . . .

CHAPTER XII

IT IS POSSIBLE TO REFORM SCHOOLS

1. To cure deep-seated maladies is difficult and often well-nigh impossible. But if any one offer an efficacious remedy, does the sick man reject his services? Does he not rather wish to obtain aid as quickly as possible, and especially if he think that the physician is guided not by mere opinion but by solid reason? We, at any rate, in this our undertaking, have reached the point at which we must make plain (1) what we actually promise, and (2) on what principles we intend to proceed.

2. We promise, then, such a system of education that

(i.) All the young shall be educated (except those to whom God has denied understanding).

(ii.) And in all those subjects which are able to make a man wise, virtuous, and pious.

(iii.) That the process of education, being a preparation for life, shall be completed before maturity is reached.

(iv.) That this education shall be conducted without blows, rigour, or compulsion, as gently and pleasantly as possible, and in the most natural manner (just as a living body increases in size without any straining or forcible extension of the limbs; since if food, care, and exercise are properly supplied, the body grows and becomes strong, gradually, imperceptibly, and of its own accord. In the same way I maintain that nutriment, care, and exercise, prudently supplied to the mind, lead it naturally to wisdom, virtue, and piety).

(v.) That the education given shall be not false but real, not superficial but thorough; that is to say, that the rational animal, man, shall be guided, not by the intellects of other men, but by his own; shall not merely read the opinions of others and grasp their meaning or commit them to memory and repeat them, but shall himself penetrate to the root of things and acquire the habit of genuinely understanding and making use of what he learns.

(vi.) That this education shall not be laborious but very easy. The class instruction shall last only four hours each day, and shall be conducted in such a manner that one master may teach hundreds of pupils at the same time, with ten times as little trouble as is now expended on the teaching of one. . . .

CHAPTER XIV

THE EXACT ORDER OF INSTRUCTION MUST BE BORROWED
FROM NATURE, AND MUST BE OF SUCH A KIND THAT
NO OBSTACLE CAN HINDER IT.

1. Let us then commence to seek out, in God's name, the principles on which, as on an immovable rock, the method of teaching and of learning can be grounded. If we wish to find a remedy for the defects of nature, it is in nature herself that we must look for it, since it is certain that art can do nothing unless it imitate nature.

2. A few examples will make this clear. We see a fish swimming in the water; it is its natural mode of progression. If a man wish to imitate it, it is necessary for him to use in a similar manner the limbs that are at his disposal; instead of fins he must employ his arms, and instead of a tail, his feet, moving them as a fish moves its fins. Even ships are constructed on this plan; in the place of fins they must employ oars or sails, and in the place of a tail, the rudder. We see a bird flying through the air; it is its natural mode of progression. When Daedalus wished to imitate it, he had to take wings (large enough to carry such a heavy body) and set them in motion. . . .

7. It is now quite clear that that order, which is the dominating principle in the art of teaching all things to all men, should be, and can be, borrowed from no other source but the operations of nature. As soon as this principle is thoroughly secured, the processes of art will proceed as easily and as spontaneously as those of nature.

The Analytical Didactic

Modern scholars have come to distinguish three didactics that Comenius wrote. The first, the *Didaktica*, was written in Czech between 1628 and 1638; it was discovered in Leszno in 1841 and published in 1849. It is similar in ideas and treatment to the *Didactica Magna*, written in Latin between 1633 and 1638 and first published in 1657. The third, the *Analytical Didactic*, was composed between 1644 and 1647 and first published as the tenth chapter of Comenius' *Linguarum Methodus Novissima* in 1649. This third didactic is different from the other two in that it is more rigorously systematic and analytical, with statements carefully deduced from supposed axioms. The following excerpt gives an example of its style in treating the centrally important concept of discipline. Comenius regards discipline as essential for learning. But not any discipline will suffice. In order to determine what manner of discipline to exercise, we must study human nature. Since man is Godlike and desires freedom, we should design a discipline that is creative rather than destructive. Hence it must be related to the needs and goals of the individual, it must be consistent, and it must be humane.

The selection is taken from *The Analytical Didactic of Comenius*, translated by Vladimir Jelinek, published in Chicago, copyright 1953 by the University of Chicago. Reprinted by permission of The University of Chicago Press.

36. In Latin the word *discipline* has several meanings. Sometimes it signifies that which is taught and learned (hence the arts and sciences are called *liberal disciplines*); sometimes it denotes the act of teaching and learning (as when we are said to be brought up under someone's discipline); but the word is used most properly, as here, to denote a means of enforcing instruction. This sort of discipline is always and

everywhere necessary if the diffusion of knowledge is to be of any value. Hammer and anvil do not give the right shape to iron if there are no tongs to hold the iron and allow the hammer to strike sure blows; in the same way teacher and teaching fail to give the right stamp to the mind of a pupil if there is no awe or respect to hold his mind in the grip of careful attention.

LI. *Without discipline one learns nothing or at least nothing correctly*

37. It is desirable, however, to provide a discipline that is adjusted (1) to the end in view; that is, discipline should be efficient in compelling a student to accomplish the task at hand; (2) to human nature; that is, discipline should develop human nature, not destroy it (but since the desire to be free and unconstrained is inseparable from human nature, which is like an image of God, every forcible discipline seems to be a destroyer of human nature); and (3) to levels of need; that is, just as there are various kinds of talent, so there are various sources and levels of error and the correction of error.

LII. *Discipline should be constant, never slackening; it should always be treated seriously, never in jest*

LIII. *Discipline should never be harsh.*

LIV. *Discipline should be of various levels.*

38. There are about ten levels of discipline:

(1) A teacher whose learning merits esteem should possess such authority and command such respect that a pupil would think it sinful to offend him.

(2) A teacher should watch his pupils intently, so that they will realize that they are being watched.

(3) A teacher should always lead the way, so that his pupils may see that they have someone to follow.

(4) A teacher should always look about him to see whether he is being followed and how well.

(5) A teacher should constantly lead a pupil by the hand, to make sure that the pupil follows him properly and does not deviate into error.

(6) A teacher should incite his pupils to rivalry (based on friendly competition), so that they may sharpen one another's wits. (Strife enhances virtue.)

(7) A teacher should give frequent tests (sometimes at set intervals, sometimes unexpectedly, especially to the least trustworthy pupils, in order to make sure that they are not missing any part of the instruction).

(8) To make sure that no error becomes a habit a teacher should always admonish a pupil as soon as the pupil commits a fault (in Axiom XLVII we indicated the force of such immediate correction during the very act).

(9) A teacher should rebuke those who are guilty of wilful error or conspicuous negligence; he should reprimand them and hold them up as a warning example to others, lest impunity become license.

(10) If, however, any pupil should refuse to follow such guidance (although this does not seem possible except in one extremely evil), let him be expelled, lest he prove a hindrance and a stumbling block to others.

Corollaries: 1. We do not want beatings and anger to be part of so sacred a matter as the cultivation of the spirit.

2. If, however, a boy must be whipped, employ the rod rather than the hand and avoid all bitter words, enraged looks, and cruel blows. In that way your pupils will see that you are not indulging in anger and hate but that you are acting advisedly and for their welfare.

The Orbis Pictus

Comenius' most widely read and immediately influential book was the *Orbis Sensualium Pictus* (*The Visible World Illustrated*), first published in 1657. Commonly thought to have been the first children's picture book, it was for a century the most popular textbook in Europe and was still being reprinted in the nineteenth century. It represents Comenius' closest realization of his own didactic principles. The educated man is one whose senses are attuned to the learning possibilities of the world. All learning comes through the senses. Therefore, if we would create understanding, we must educate the senses through studying things and words together. Comenius attempts this by the use of pictures with numbers, to which words in the text refer. Latin and the vernacular language (in this case English) are placed side by side. There is a constant concern to saturate words with meaning. In its pedagogical dimension, however, this attempt at sense realism had to wait for Pestalozzi and the other nineteenth-century reformers of elementary educational practice.

These selections are from the English and Latin edition of 1727, translated by Charles Hoole. They appear in John Amos Comenius, *The Orbis Pictus*, edited by C. W. Bardeen, published in Syracuse, New York, by C. W. Bardeen in 1887.

THE AUTHOR'S PREFACE TO THE READER

Instruction is the means to expel Rudeness, with which young wits ought to be well furnished in Schools: But so, as that the teaching be 1. *True*, 2. *Full*, 3. *Clear*, and 4. *Solid*.

1. It will be *true*, if nothing be taught but such as is beneficial to

one's life; lest there be a cause of complaining afterwards. We know not necessary things, because we have not learned things necessary.

2. It will be *full,* if the mind be polished for wisdom, the tongue for eloquence, and the hands for a neat way of living. This will be that *grace* of one's life, *to be wise, to act, to speak.*

3, 4. It will be *clear,* and by that, firm and *solid,* if whatever is taught and learned, be not obscure, or confused, but apparent, distinct, and articulate, as the fingers on the hands.

The ground of this business, is, that sensual objects may be rightly presented to the senses, for fear they may not be received. I say, and say it again aloud, that this last is the foundation of all the rest: because we can neither act nor speak wisely, unless we first rightly understand all the things which are to be done, and whereof we are to speak. Now there is nothing in the understanding, which was not before in the sense. And therefore to exercise the senses well about the right perceiving the differences of things, will be to lay the grounds for all wisdom, and all wise discourse, and all discreet actions in one's course of life. Which, because it is commonly neglected in schools, and the things which are to be learned are offered to scholars, without being understood or being rightly presented to the senses, it cometh to pass, that the work of teaching and learning goeth heavily onward, and affordeth little benefit. . . .

ORBIS SENSUALIUM PICTUS,

A WORLD OF THINGS OBVIOUS TO THE SENSES DRAWN IN PICTURES.

Invitation.   I.   Invitatio.

The Master and the Boy.	*Magister & Puer.*

M. Come, Boy, learn to be wise.

M. Veni, Puer, disce sapere.

P. What doth this mean, *to be wise?*

P. Quid hoc est, *Sapere?*

M. To understand rightly,

M. Intelligere recte,

to do rightly, and to speak out rightly all that are necessary.

agere recte, et eloqui **recte** omnia necessaria.

P. Who will teach me this?

P. Quis docebit me hoc?

M. I, by God's help.

M. Ego, cum DEO.

P. How?

P. Quomodo?

M. I will guide thee thorow all.

M. Ducam te per omnia.

I will shew thee all.

Ostendam tibi omnia.

I will name thee all.

Nominabo tibi omnia.

P. See, here I am; lead me in the name of God.

P. En, adsum; duc me in nomine DEI.

M. Before all things, thou oughtest to learn the plain *sounds*, of which man's *speech* consisteth; which *living creatures* know how *to make*, and thy *Tongue* knoweth how *to imitate*, and thy *hand* can *picture out.*

M. Ante omnia, debes discere simplices *Sonos* **ex** quibus *Sermo* humanus constat; quos *Animalia* sciunt *formare*, & tua *Lingua* scit *imitari*, & tua *Manus* potest *pingere.*

Afterwards we will go into the *World*, and we will view all things.

Postea ibimus *Mundum*, & spectabimus omnia.

Here thou hast a lively and Vocal Alphabet.

Hic habes vivum et **vo**cale Alphabetum.

Cornix cornicatur, à à The *Crow* crieth.	A a
Agnus balat, b è è è The *Lamb* blaiteth.	B b
Cicàda stridet, cì cì The *Grasshopper* chirpeth.	C c
Upupa dicit,. du du The *Whooppoo* saith.	D d
Infans ejulat, è è è The *Infant* crieth.	E e
Ventus flat, fi fi The *Wind* bloweth.	F f
Anser gingrit, ga ga The *Goose* gagleth.	G g
Os halat, hà'h hà'h The *Mouth* breatheth out.	H h
Mus mintrit, ì ì ì The *Mouse* chirpeth.	I i
Anas tetrinnit, kha, kha The *Duck* quaketh.	K k
Lupus ululat, lu ulu The *Wolf* howleth.	L
[mum *Ursus* murmurat, mum- The *Bear* grumbleth.	M m

Felis clamat,	nau nau	N n
The *Cat* crieth.		
Auriga clamat,	ò ò ò	O o
The *Carter* crieth.		
Pullus pipit,	pi pi	P p
The *Chicken* peepeth.		
Cúculus cuculat,	kuk ku	Q q
The *cuckow* singeth.		
Canis ringitur,	err	R r
The *dog* grinneth.		
Serpens sibilat,	si	S s
The *Serpent* hisseth.		
Graculus clamat,	tac tac	T t
The *Jay* crieth.		
Bubo ululat,	ù ù	U u
The *Owl* hooteth.		
Lepus vagit,	va	W w
The *Hare* squeaketh.		
Rana coaxat,	coax	X x
The *Frog* croaketh.		
Asinus rudit,	y y y	Y y
The *Asse* ̯brayeth.		
Tabanus dicit,	ds ds	Z z
The *Breeze* or *Horse-flie* saith.		

Humanity. CXV. Humanitas.

Men are made	Homines facti sunt
for one another's *good ;*	ad mutua *commoda ;*
therefore let them be *kind.*	ergo sint *humani.*
Be thou sweet and lovely	Sis suavis & amabilis
in thy *Countenance,* 1.	*Vultu,* 1.
gentle and civil	comis & urbanus
in thy *Behaviour* and *Manners,* 2.	*Gestu* ac *Moribus,* 2.
affable and true spoken	affabilis & verax,
with thy *Mouth,* 3.	*Ore,* 3.
affectionate and *candid*	candens & *candidus*
in thy *Heart,* 4.	*Corde,* 4.
So love,	Sic ama,
and so shalt thou be loved;	sic amaberis ;
and there will be	& fiat
a mutual *Friendship,* 5.	mutua *Amicitia,* 5.
as that of *Turtle-doves,* 6.	ceu *Turturum,* 6.
hearty, gentle, and	concors, mansueta,
wishing well on both parts.	& benevola utrinque.
Froward Men are	Morosi homines, sunt
hateful, teasty, unpleasant.	odiosi, torvi, illepidi.
contentious, *angry,* 7.	contentiosi, *iracundi,* 7.
cruel, 8.	*crudeles,* 8.
and implacable,	ac implacabiles,
(rather Wolves and Lions,	(magis Lupi & Leones,
than Men)	quàm homines)
and such as fall out among	& inter se discordes,
themselves, hereupon	hinc
they fight in a *Duel,* 9.	confligunt *Duelle,* 9.
Envy, 10.	*Invidia,* 10.
wishing ill to others,	malè cupiendo aliis,
pineth away her self.	conficit seipsam.

The Pampaedia

At the end of the terrible Thirty Years' War, Comenius began work on an ambitious project (which was still uncompleted at his death) to create a plan for the universal reform of human society. The means of achieving this goal were to be three-fold: the international unification and supervision of education; international peace-making through political coordination; religious harmony through the reconciliation of the Christian churches. The uncompleted work was entitled *General Consultation on the Reform of Human Affairs.* It was seven parts, of which *The Pampaedia* was the fourth. Most of the *Consultation* was thought to have been lost until rediscovered in manuscript in 1934. *The Pampaedia* was published in Czech in 1948. It outlines an educational scheme even more broad-ranging than that of *The Great Didactic*, for it describes a plan of universal education covering the whole of human life, from womb to grave. Education should be universally available for all mankind. Although a patriotic bishop, Comenius is never narrowly nationalistic or sectarian in his appeal. All men and women are to be educated to become pansophists: they are to be educated in all things that contribute to their human perfection; and they are to be educated in all ways—intellectual, physical, moral, and spiritual.

This selection, translated from the Czech by Iris Urwin, is taken from *John Amos Comenius, 1592–1670: Selections,* Introduction by Jean Piaget, published in Paris in 1957 by UNESCO, with whose permission it is reprinted.

CHAPTER I

What universal education is and why
it is to be desired, 1-10; in what sense we want learning for all men,
about all things and in all ways, 11-15.

Pampaedia is universal education for the whole of the human race; for among the Greeks παιδεία means both teaching itself and the disci-

226

pline by which men acquire education, while πᾶν means universal. Therefore our goal is to be: learning πάντες, πάντα, πάντως (for all men, about all things, in all ways).

2. Let this desire for universal education remind us of what is to be considered under the prime classification, which we have seen in the realm of ideas: *Nothing, Something, Everything,* in order better to clarify our desire and the measure of our desire.

3. *Nothing* is here *no education at all,* such as we see with pity and horror among the most barbarous peoples, where unhappy mortals are born, live and die after the manner of beasts.

4. *Something* is here *some degree of education,* to this or that end, such as can be seen among more cultivated peoples who share among themselves the sciences, the arts, languages and other knowledge.

5. *Everything* will here be *universal education, by* which we seek to give man, the image of God, whatever is possible for the greatest glory he can attain beneath Heaven.

6. This desire resolves into three parts. Our first wish is that all men should be educated fully to full humanity; not any one individual, nor a few nor even many, but all men together and singly, young and old, rich and poor, or high and of lowly birth, men and women—in a word, all whose fate it is to be born human beings: so that at last the whole of the human race may become educated, men of all ages, all conditions, both sexes and all nations.

7. Our second wish is that every man should be wholly educated, rightly formed not only in one single matter or in a few or even in many, but in all things which perfect human nature; that he should be able to know the truth and not be deluded by what is false; to love god and not be seduced by evil; to do what should be done and not permit what should be avoided; to talk wisely about everything with everybody when there is need, and not to be dumb in any matter; and finally to deal with things, with men and with God in all matters reasonably and not hastily, thereby never wandering from the goal of happiness.

8. And educated in all ways. Not to pomp and show, but to truth; that is to say, in order to make men as like as possible to the image of God, in which they were created: truly rational and wise, truly active and spirited, truly moral and honourable, truly pious and holy and thereby truly happy and blessed, both here and in eternity.

9. Briefly: in order to enlighten all men with true wisdom; to order their lives by true government; to unite them with God by true religion so that none may mistake his mission in this world. This can be achieved if all learn:

(i) To be ignorant of nothing that is necessary, looking at all things with open eyes;

(ii) Choosing what is best and acting calmly in all situations, to delight in all things but need little;

(iii) Finding the highest good and uniting indissolubly with that alone, to achieve blessedness.

In a word: to be wise for eternity, but not to be unwise here.

10. Therefore we propose to recommend three unusual things, repeating ourselves in order to be clearly understood: that we should set out to lead towards universal education (1) all men (2) in all things, so that they become educated (3) in all ways.

11. All men: that is to say, all peoples, conditions, families, persons, never omitting anybody; for all are human beings with the same future life before them and the same road leading to it, pointed out by God but beset with snares and divers obstacles. It will therefore be necessary to warn and instruct all men prudently about these things, in order to drive foolishness from out our midst, if that be possible, so that the lament of wise men that 'the world is full of fools' will be no longer called for.

12. In all things: that is to say, in all things that can make man wise and happy. But what are these things? They are the four wise things which Solomon commends in the four exceeding wise little creatures:

(i) Provision for the future, which he praises in the ants (Proverbs, xxx. 25);

(ii) Prudence in the present, to do nothing except by safe ways, which he observes in the conies (v. 26);

(iii) Inclination to concord, without coercive force, which he praises in the locusts (v. 27);

(iv) Finally, that whatever is done, however slight, should be harmonious, regular and systematic; as is the work of the spider, even if otherwise it is useless (v. 28).

This then is what we seek by the universal education of the mind: that all men (1) should be equipped with knowledge for their future life and filled with longing for it, and led along the right paths to it; (2) should be taught so to enclose the business of this life in the bounds of prudence that all things here are secure to the best possible degree; (3) should learn so to walk in the paths of concord that none may go dangerously astray on the road of time and eternity and that they may restore dissidents to unity; and finally (4) should be filled with such ardour in their thoughts, words and deeds that all three may be as much in harmony as is possible. Achieving these four things, unhappy mortals would have an antidote for their unhappiness; most of them take no thought for the future, hazard the present, each disagreeing with all the rest and with himself (in thoughts, words and deeds), struggling and wasting themselves in discord and perishing.

13. In all ways: that is to say, towards truth, so that rightly formed by her each man will stand beyond the precipices of error and hazard, and walk in the paths of righteousness. For now few mortals rely on their own foundation or that of things; most of them follow blind instinct, or the opinions of others. These disagreeing diversely with each other and with things themselves, there is no end to hesitation, stumbling, lapsing and finally ruin. If an equal remedy is to be sought for this evil, it cannot be other than to follow not the guidance of blind habit or persuasion, but the adamantine rule of God and of things themselves, and for every man through all this to learn, to know and to be able to stand firmly everywhere and to walk everywhere in safety.

14. May I repeat our desire for the third time? Allow this, I beg, so that what we would strive for may be clear in all ways. We want all men to become pansophists, i.e.:

(i) Understanding the articulation of things, thoughts and words;

(ii) Understanding the aims, means and manner of carrying out all actions (their own and those of other people);

(iii) Able to distinguish the essential from the accidental, the indifferent from the dangerous, in actions diverging from and converging on the goal (and similarly in thoughts and words). And hence able to observe digression of thoughts, words and deeds, both their own and others, and at all times and in all places to know how to turn them back to the right path—

For if all men were to learn all things in all ways, all men would be wise and the world would be full of order, light and peace.

15. Bearing this in mind, we can already define universal education differently, and more precisely: it is a levelled road for spreading the light of pansophy over the minds, words and deeds of men. Or a means by which wisdom can be transplanted in the minds, tongues, hearts and hands of all men. For this reason we have placed on the frontispiece of this treatise a symbol taken from the gardener's craft: there gardeners are taking shoots from the tree of all knowledge and grafting them on to young trees, anxious to fill the whole of God's garden, our human race, with young trees of a like nature.

The Way of Light

Central to Comenius' philosophy was the belief that God has created an order in the universe that is observable in the forms of
nature. Although his hypothesis of the unified plan of the universe
was thus religiously based, Comenius wanted to make this natural
order intellectually intelligible, to give the world rational coherence
and meaning. All men should be helped to understand this unity
by being drawn into wisdom, into the way of light. The *Via Lucis*
was published in Amsterdam in 1668. In it, Comenius maintains
that it is man's nature to inquire and learn unceasingly. The appeal
to nature will also govern the method of inquiry: it will be through
a first-hand study of things rather than through the authority and
opinions of others. The educated man is one who comes to know
for himself. He is freed from a subordination to the authority of
previous opinions: knowledge then flows into his freed mind. He
recognizes that he can gain knowledge only through his own reasoning, not through another's.

These selections are from John Amos Comenius, *The Way of
Light,* translated by E. T. Campagnac, published in 1938 by Liverpool University Press, with whose permission they are reprinted.

CHAPTER 1

. . . 6. There is a saying about Solon that he used to boast that he
grew old learning something new every day. We should be wrong if
we attributed this quality to Solon alone, for that impulse towards knowledge was not peculiar to him; it is common to human nature, although
it may not reveal itself in so lively a fashion in all men, or direct itself
only to the better things, as it ought. It is the nature of man without
ceasing to discover the infinity of his own desires and of his capacity;

this is the mark of divinity set upon him; he finds no resting-place for himself in the finite world, but has within his own heart inducements, and indeed relentless spurs, which make him climb and struggle panting onwards to the very abyss of infinity, i.e., to God. In truth, it is with that end that he is sent into the world, that he may learn to seek God and to recognise the Creator by his works, until the time comes when God shall deign to reveal himself to man without veil and face to face. . . .

CHAPTER 14

19. . . . Augustine numbers among the fools men who would rather learn than know, and would prefer feeding to being satisfied; that is to say, men who embrace means not for the sake of ends, and are busy for the sake of being busy merely. In order, then, that we, and with us the whole world, may get wisdom, let us teach men (in this School of God's wisdom which must immediately be reformed) to learn not for the sake of learning, but for the sake of knowing; and yet to know not for the sake of knowing but for the sake of exercising themselves in action, and finally to exercise themselves not only for the sake of exercise, but in order to attain the goal of all activities, which is rest and happiness.

20. And this result will be attained if they are taught first things first, and the better things in preference to others, and all things by direct sight and by personal experience, constant and practical. First things first—that is, step by step, by raising themselves from the first and lowest through the intermediary to the final and highest things. For so at last all things will become clear, as they proceed fluently and spontaneously from each other; and all things will become strongly established as they rest one upon another. And they must be taught the better things in preference: by not allowing those that are less necessary to cause delay or to steal the place of those which are more necessary, but arranging that the lighter matters be dealt with in a lighter fashion, and the more serious in a more serious fashion, with an unwavering regard for the more important ends. And when we say that men must learn by their own direct vision, we mean that we must impose the necessary things upon men by knowledge and not by authority (for knowledge is a liberal thing and loves to flow into liberal minds): and we must not only provide them in words however precise and carefully chosen, but present the facts themselves to the senses directly as far

as that is possible, so that all men will see by exercising their own eyes, and feel with their own senses and know of their own knowledge everything as it really is. For knowledge in effect is to know a thing as it is in itself and not as it is reputed to be. To know a thing through the reasoning of another person is not knowledge, but belief: just as masticating with another person's mouth is not masticating, but witnessing the process of mastication. I do not taste the cake which you eat or the wine which you drink; a blind man does not see the picture which a man with sight tells him that he himself can see; and similarly if another man tells me that he knows, has seen, read or experienced, that affords me no ground for claiming to know, but only for believing that he has seen, read or experienced. And it was in knowledge very much of this sort (knowledge which consists in loyal acceptance of the authority of the teachers and in an intellectual process not its own but of other people) that the world hitherto used to acquiesce, though unwillingly, and with occasional revolts and with longing to break through the barriers of its servitude. For, indeed, most things which have been transmitted to us from those earlier ages have been of this character, dark and confused. But the time is come for us to rise from the rudiments to completeness of knowledge, no longer to be like children tossed hither and thither by the waves, or permit ourselves to be blown about by every wind of doctrine, but to have such knowledge as befits grown men, so that no one can justly charge our knowledge with emptiness or obscurity or any other harmful defect.

9 The Gentleman: Locke

The dominant factors among the changing conditions of English seventeenth-century life to which John Locke (1632–1704) responded were the rise of the new bourgeoisie and the rise of the new science. His answer to both of these challenges involved a questioning of traditional, social-political patterns and customary modes of intellectual inquiry. On the latter score, Locke's response took its characteristic tone from the scientific and methodological innovations of Bacon, Descartes, Galileo, and Newton. Bringing the thinking of these men to a focus in his readiness to apply science and reason to the study of human affairs, Locke combined a predilection for the new method of science with an openness to the teachings of experience. This gave him toward many traditional institutions a fresh and questioning attitude, which fitted him well to act as spokesman for a rising class of men who were increasingly importunate in their demands for power and predominantly skeptical and practical in their intellectual temper.

Hitherto, English society had been governed by the monarchy, the Church, and the hereditary aristocracy. But now this new class was feeling its strength—a strength based not upon claims of birth but upon wealth derived from industry and commerce. This bourgeois class pressed for an increasing share of the power and privileges of English life. However, it has been an inexorable rule of English society that a new group can gain power only through winning admission to the circle of gentlemen. It was the achievement of Locke to contribute substantially to a modification of the criteria of gentlemanliness, which permitted members of the bourgeoisie to pass into the accepted circle. Originally an aristocratic model, the gentleman ideal became increasingly democratized. In keeping with the moral demands of the Puritan revolution, behavior became a more important criterion than birth. As this process continued, an education that could produce such behavior became highly valued. John Locke was a key figure in the creation of a new educational ideal of the bourgeois gentleman.

Not only was this ideal influential in shaping the subsequent course of English educational history. Locke's Puritan individualism also had considerable effect on the development of American educational ideals. This individualism manifests itself repeatedly in Locke's work. The gentleman is to have a private tutor rather than be submitted to the communal perils of public schooling. There is a strong emphasis upon the pedagogical importance of seeking to discover the individual pupil's special aptitudes. The educated man is one who is able to make autonomous decisions, who is not swayed by group thinking. Locke became the chief spokesman for classical liberalism through his eloquent defense of individual freedom from religious and state authority. But he did not recognize the possibilities of the use of institutional power for interventions that would enhance the freedom of the individual. In this blindness, too, he has a great deal in common with much contemporary American opinion.

Locke's concern for freedom, moreover, was severely limited by national and sectarian considerations. For example, he espoused the doctrine of natural rights in terms of general theory. But, in terms of specific recommendation, these rights were to be limited by considerations of social class, religious affiliation, and national loyalty. He had no sympathy with the radical and visionary suggestions of the Levellers and the Diggers for the creation of a classless society.

In this, as in all matters, Locke fled from passion, enthusiasm, and irrationality, and sought control, balance, and rational thought. He saw science, reason, and experience as safeguards against both the stagnation of unreflective tradition and the perils of enthusiastic radicalism. The religion appropriate for a gentleman is thus one that engenders dignity, virtue, and order. No gentleman would allow religious fervor or fanaticism to cloud his judgment or loosen his self-control. Similarly, scholarly learning is always to be a subordinate goal of a gentleman's education. Here is a manifestation of the amateur spirit, which, together with Locke's low regard for the arts, have remained characteristics of the gentlemanly tradition.

Some Thoughts Concerning Education

Locke's fullest expression of his educational ideas can be found in *Some Thoughts Concerning Education*, first published in 1693. The class limitations of his educational model are soon revealed, for he admits at the outset that he is concerned only with the class of gentlemen, who, once their education is properly arranged, will "quickly bring all the rest into Order." It is understandable, therefore, that Locke should be concerned about the dangers of spoiling this privileged child through soft and luxurious living. He recommends for the young gentleman a regimen of physical toughening: it is merely a question of inuring the body to hardship. Similarly, the mind should be exercised and toughened by mental rigor. We see here the germ of the doctrine of mental discipline, which exerted such a strong and sometimes absurd influence on subsequent educational practices. It should be noted, however, that Locke's view on this matter was more ambiguous than that of many of his followers. Locke's Puritan background is repeatedly in evidence in his injunctions that the gentleman should learn to control his natural appetites and desires through his reason. The early development of good habits is crucial; hence children should from the beginning be denied the gratification of their whims. Locke shows little recognition of the fact that, unless our basic needs are satisfied, we cannot gain the primary security that enables us to go out into a challenging world. Not until the gentleman reaches the age of reason, suggests Locke, should he be permitted to govern himself: before that time he must be governed by others. Locke does recognize, however (as some of his followers have not), that if discipline is too severe the spirit of the child will be broken. Control and surveillance of the gentleman must be strict in order to guard him against the dangers of society. Servants are particularly to be watched, for they are apt to lead the young gentleman into evil ways. The company of school-fellows is also dangerous (as Locke himself found during his unhappy sojourn as a pupil at Westminister). Fathers are foolish who risk their sons' virtue and innocence "for a little Greek and Latin": the wise ones will hire a tutor to teach their sons at home. Locke was largely blind to the possible benefits to be gained from company. He saw society principally as a threat. The qualities of the gentlemanly model that Locke commends to us can be summed up in four cardinal aims of his education: virtue, wisdom, breeding, and learning. The order is important and has remained so to the present day. Virtue as reflected in conduct—with honesty as a crucial quality—is still a primary criterion of English gentlemanliness. A gentleman's word is as good as his bond, in popular belief. Learning must always be subordinate, never ostentatious, always worn lightly. Those who followed Locke often distorted his ideas in ways that violated the spirit of his writings. He considered Latin as necessary for a gentleman, for example, but he would have deplored its employment as a prestigious talisman of a useless and expensive education. He objected to Latin's monopoly of the curriculum and became a spokesman for the rising bourgeoisie's demand for a *useful* education—one that would help their sons to operate in the real world of business and commerce. Even more radically, he suggested that the gentleman should learn a trade, such as carpentry. However, he brought his recommendation within the mode of gentlemanly thinking by suggesting that the carpentry should be pursued not in a serious spirit but as a diversion.

The following excerpts are from John Locke, *Some Thoughts Concerning Education,* edited by R. H. Quick, published in Cambridge in 1927 by Cambridge University Press, with whose permission they are reprinted.

THE EPISTLE DEDICATORY

My Business is not to recommend this Treatise to You, whose Opinion of it I know already; nor it to the World, either by your Opinion or

Patronage. The well Educating of their Children is so much the Duty and Concern of Parents, and the Welfare and Prosperity of the Nation so much depends on it, that I would have every one lay it seriously to Heart; and after having well examin'd and distinguish'd what Fancy, Custom, or Reason advises in the Case, set his helping Hand to promote every where that Way of training up Youth, with Regard to their several Conditions, which is the easiest, shortest, and likeliest to produce virtuous, useful, and able Men in their distinct Callings; tho' that most to be taken Care of is the Gentleman's Calling. For if those of that Rank are by their Education once set right, they will quickly bring all the rest into Order. . . .

§ 4. The Consideration I shall here have of *Health*, shall be, not what a Physician ought to do with a sick and crazy Child; but what the Parents, without the Help of Physick, should do for the *Preservation and Improvement of an healthy*, or at least *not sickly Constitution* in their Children. And this perhaps might be all dispatch'd in this one short Rule, *viz*. That Gentlemen should use their Children, as the honest Farmers and substantial Yeomen do theirs. But because the Mothers possibly may think this a little too hard, and the Fathers too short, I shall explain my self more particularly; only laying down this as a general and certain Observation for the Women to consider, *viz*. That most Children's Constitutions are either spoil'd, or at least harm'd, by *Cockering* and *Tenderness*.

§ 5. The first Thing to be taken care of, is, that Children be not too *warmly clad or cover'd*, Winter or Summer. The Face when we are born, is no less tender than any other Part of the Body. 'Tis Use alone hardens it, and makes it more able to endure the Cold. And therefore the *Scythian* Philosopher gave a very significant Answer to the *Athenian*, who wonder'd how he could go naked in Frost and Snow. *How*, said the *Scythian, can you endure your Face expos'd to the sharp Winter Air? My Face is us'd to it*, said the *Athenian. Think me all Face*, reply'd the *Scythian*. Our Bodies will endure any Thing, that from the Beginning they are accustom'd to. . . .

§ 30. And thus I have done with what concerns the Body and Health, which reduces itself to these few and easy observable Rules: Plenty of *open Air, Exercise*, and *Sleep*, plain *Diet*, no *Wine* or *strong Drink*, and very little or no *Physick*, not too warm and strait *Clothing*, especially the *Head* and *Feet* kept cold, and the *Feet* often us'd to cold Water, and expos'd to wet.

§ 31. Due Care being had to keep the Body in Strength and Vigour, so that it may be able to obey and execute the Orders of the *Mind*;

the next and principal Business is, to set the *Mind* right, that on all Occasions it may be dispos'd to consent to nothing but what may be suitable to the Dignity and Excellency of a rational Creature.

§ 32. If what I have said in the beginning of this Discourse be true, as I do not doubt but it is, *viz.* That the Difference to be found in the Manners and Abilities of Men is owing more to their *Education* than to any Thing else, we have reason to conclude that great Care is to be had of the forming Children's *Minds,* and giving them that Seasoning early, which shall influence their Lives always after: For when they do well or ill, the Praise and Blame will be laid there; and when any Thing is done awkwardly, the common saying will pass upon them, that it's suitable to their *Breeding.*

§ 33. As the Strength of the Body lies chiefly in being able to endure Hardships, so also does that of the Mind. And the great Principle and Foundation of all Virtue and Worth is plac'd in this: That a Man is able to *deny himself* his own Desires, cross his own Inclinations, and purely follow what Reason directs as best, tho' the Appetite lean the other Way. . . .

§ 38. It seems plain to me, that the Principle of all Virtue and Excellency lies in a Power of denying our selves the Satisfaction of our own Desires, where Reason does not authorize them. This power is to be got and improv'd by Custom, made easy and familiar by an *early* Practice. If therefore I might be heard, I would advise, that, contrary to the ordinary Way, Children should be us'd to submit their Desires, and go without their Longings, even *from their very Cradles.* The first Thing they should learn to know, should be, that they were not to have any Thing because it pleas'd them, but because it was thought fit for them. If Things suitable to their Wants were supply'd to them, so that they were never suffer'd to have what they once cry'd for, they would learn to be content without it, would never, with Bawling and Peevishness, contend for Mastery, nor be half so uneasy to themselves and others as they are, because *from the first* Beginning they are not thus handled. If they were never suffer'd to obtain their Desire by the Impatience they express'd for it, they would no more cry for another Thing, than they do for the Moon. . . .

§ 40. Those therefore that intend ever to govern their Children, should begin it whilst they are *very little* and look that they pefectly comply with the Will of their Parents. Would you have your Son obedient to you when past a Child be sure then to establish the Authority of a Father *as soon* as he is capable of Submission, and can understand in whose Power he is. If you would have him stand in awe of you, imprint it in his *Infancy;* and as he approaches more to a Man, admit him nearer to your Familiarity; so shall you have him your obedient Subject (as is fit) whilst he is a Child, and your affectionate Friend when he is a Man. For methinks they mightily misplace the Treatment due to their Children, who are indulgent and familiar when they are little, but severe to them, and keep them at a distance, when they are grown up: For Liberty and Indulgence can do no good to *Children*; their Want of Judgment makes them stand in need of Restraint and Discipline; and on the contrary, Imperiousness and Severity is but an ill Way of Treating Men, who have Reason of their own to guide them; unless you have a mind to make your children, when grown up, weary of you, and secretly to say within themselves, *When will you die, Father?* . . .

§ 45. 1. He that has not a Mastery over his Inclinations, he that knows not how to *resist* the Importunity of *present Pleasure or Pain,* for the sake of what Reason tells him is fit to be done, wants the true Principle of Virtue and Industry, and is in danger never to be good for any Thing. This Temper therefore, so contrary to unguided Nature, is to be got betimes; and this Habit, as the true Foundation of future Ability and Happiness, is to be wrought into the Mind as early as may be, even from the first Dawnings of Knowledge or Apprehension in Children, and so to be confirm'd in them, by all the Care and Ways imaginable, by those who have the Oversight of their Education.

§ 46. 2. On the other Side, if the *Mind* be curb'd, and *humbled too* much in Children; if their *Spirits* be abas'd and *broken* much, by too strict an Hand over them, they lose all their Vigour and Industry, and are in a worse State than the former. For extravagant young Fellows, that have Liveliness and Spirit, come sometimes to be set right, and so make able and great Men; but *dejected Minds,* timorous and tame, and *low Spirits,* are hardly ever to be rais'd, and very seldom attain to any Thing. To avoid the Danger that is on either Hand, is the great Art; and he that has found a Way how to keep up a Child's Spirit easy, active, and free, and yet at the same time to restrain him from many Things he has a Mind to, and to draw him to Things that are uneasy to him; he, I say, that knows how to reconcile these seeming Contradictions, has, in my Opinion, got the true Secret of Education. . . .

§ 68. I mention'd above one great Mischief that came by Servants to Children, when by their Flatteries they take off the Edge and Force of the Parents' Rebukes, and so lessen their Authority: And here is another great Inconvenience which Children receive from the ill Examples which they meet with amongst the meaner Servants.

They are wholly, if possible, to be kept from such Conversation; for the Contagion of these ill Precedents, both in Civility and Virtue, horribly infects Children, as often as they come within reach of it. They frequently learn from unbred or debauch'd Servants such Language, untowardly Tricks and Vices, as otherwise they possibly would be ignorant of all their Lives.

§ 69. 'Tis a hard Matter wholly to prevent this Mischief. You will have very good luck, if you never have a clownish or vicious Servant, and if from them your Children never get any Infection: But yet as much must be done towards it as can be, and the Children kept as much as may be *in the Company of their Parents*, and those to whose Care they are committed. To this Purpose, their being in their Presence should be made easy to them; they should be allow'd the Liberties and Freedoms suitable to their Ages, and not be held under unnecessary Restraints, when in their Parents' or Governor's Sight. If it be a Prison to them, 'tis no Wonder they should not like it. They must not be hinder'd from being Children, or from playing, or doing as Children, but from doing ill; all other Liberty is to be allow'd them. Next, to make them in love with the *Company of their Parents*, they should receive all their good Things there, and from their Hands. The Servants should be hinder'd from making court to them by giving them strong Drink, Wine, Fruit, Play-Things, and other such Matters, which may make them in love with their Conversation.

§ 70. Having nam'd *Company*, I am almost ready to throw away my Pen, and trouble you no farther on this Subject: For since that does more than all Precepts, Rules and Instructions, methinks 'tis almost wholly in vain to make a long Discourse of other Things, and to talk of that almost to no Purpose. For you will be ready to say, What shall I do with my Son? If I keep him always at home, he will be in danger to be my young Master; and if I send him abroad, how is it possible to keep him from the Contagion of Rudeness and Vice, which is every where so in Fashion? In my House he will perhaps be more innocent, but more ignorant too of the World; wanting there Change of Company, and being us'd constantly to the same Faces, he will, when he comes abroad, be a sheepish or conceited Creature.

I confess, both Sides have their inconveniences. Being abroad, 'tis true, will make him bolder, and better able to bustle and shift among Boys of his own Age; and the Emulation of School-Fellows often puts Life and Industry into young Lads. But till you can find a School wherein it is possible for the Master to look after the Manners of his Scholars, and can shew as great Effects of his Care of forming their Minds to Virtue, and their Carriage to good Breeding, as of forming their Tongues to the learned Languages, you must confess, that you have a strange Value for Words, when preferring the Languages of the ancient *Greeks* and *Romans* to that which made 'em such brave Men, you think it worth while to hazard your Son's Innocence and Virtue for a little *Greek* and *Latin*. For, as for that Boldness and Spirit which Lads get amongst their Play-Fellows at School, it has ordinarily such a Mixture of Rudeness and ill-turn'd Confidence, that those misbecoming and disingenuous Ways of shifting in the World must be unlearnt, and all the Tincture wash'd out again, to make Way for better Principles and such Manners as make a truly worthy Man. He that considers how diametrically opposite the Skill of living well, and managing, as a Man should do, his Affairs in the World, is to that Mal-pertness, Tricking, or Violence learnt amongst School-Boys, will think the Faults of a privater Education infinitely to be preferr'd to such Improvements, and will take Care to preserve his Child's Innocence and Modesty at Home, as being nearer of Kin, and more in the Way of those Qualities which make an useful and able Man. Nor does any one find, or so much as suspect, that that Retirement and Bashfulness which their Daughters are brought up in, makes them less knowing, or less able Women. Conversation, when they come into the World, soon gives them a becoming Assurance; and whatsoever, beyond that, there is of rough and boisterous, may in Men be very well spar'd too; for Courage and Steadiness, as I take it, lie not in Roughness and ill Breeding.

Virtue is harder to be got, than a Knowledge of the World; and if lost in a young Man, is seldom recover'd. Sheepishness and Ignorance of the World, the Faults imputed to a private Education, are neither the necessary Consequences of being bred at Home, nor if they were, are they incurable Evils. Vice is the more stubborn, as well as the more dangerous Evil of the two; and therefore in the first Place to be fenced against. If that sheepish Softness which often enervates those who are bred like Fondlings at Home, be carefully to be avoided, it is principally so for Virtue's sake; for fear lest such a yielding Temper should be too susceptible of vicious Impressions, and expose the Novice too easily to be corrupted. A young Man before he leaves the Shelter of his Father's House, and the Guard of a Tutor, should be fortify'd with Resolution, and made acquainted with Men, to secure his Virtues, lest he should be led into some ruinous Course, or fatal Precipice, before he is sufficiently acquainted with the Dangers of Conversation, and has Steadiness enough not to yield to every Temptation. Were it not for this, a young Man's Bashfulness and Ignorance in the World, would not so much need an early Care. Conversation would cure it in a great Measure; or if that will not do it early enough, it is only a stronger Reason for a good Tutor at Home. For if Pains be to be taken to give him a manly Air and Assurance betimes, it is chiefly as a Fence to his Virtue when he goes into the World under his own Conduct. . . .

'Tis *Virtue* then, direct *Virtue,* which is the hard and valuable Part to be aim'd at in Education, and not a forward Pertness, or any little Arts of Shifting. All other Considerations and Accomplishments should give way and be postpon'd to this. This is the solid and substantial Good which Tutors should not only read Lectures, and talk of, but the Labour and Art of Education should furnish the Mind with, and fasten there, and never cease till the young Man had a true Relish of it, and plac'd his Strength, his Glory, and his Pleasure in it. . . .

This I am sure, a Father that breeds his Son at home, has the Oppor-tunity to have him more in his own Company, and there give him what Encouragement he thinks fit, and can keep him better from the Taint of Servants and the meaner Sort of People than is possible to be done abroad. . . .

§ 134. That which every Gentleman (that takes any care of his Educa-tion) desires for his Son, besides the Estate he leaves him, is contain'd (I suppose) in these four Things, *Virtue, Wisdom, Breeding,* and *Learn-ing.* I will not trouble my self whether these Names do not some of them sometimes stand for the same Thing, or really include one another. It serves my Turn here to follow the popular Use of these Words, which, I presume, is clear enough to make me be understood, and I hope there will be no difficulty to comprehend my Meaning.

§ 135. I place *Virtue* as the first and most necessary of those Endow-ments that belong to a Man or a Gentleman; as absolutely requisite to make him valued and beloved by others, acceptable or tolerable to himself. Without that, I think, he will be happy neither in this nor the other World. . . .

§ 139. Having laid the Foundations of Virtue in a true Notion of a God, such as the Creed wisely teaches, as far as his Age is capable, and by accustoming him to pray to Him; the next thing to be taken care of, is to keep him exactly to speaking of *Truth,* and by all the ways imaginable inclining him to be good-natur'd. Let him know that twenty Faults are sooner to be forgiven than the *straining of Truth* to cover any one *by an Excuse.* And to teach him betimes to love and be *good-natur'd* to others, is to lay early the true Foundation of an honest Man; all Injustice generally springing from too great Love of our selves and too little of others. . . .

§ 140. *Wisdom* I take in the popular Acceptation, for a Man's managing his Business ably and with foresight in this World. This is the Product of a good natural Temper, Application of Mind, and Experience together, and so above the reach of Children. The greatest thing that in them can be done towards it, is to hinder them, as much as may be, from being *cunning*; which, being the Ape of *Wisdom*, is the most distant from it that can be: And as an Ape for the Likeness it has to a Man, wanting what really should make him so, is by so much the uglier; *Cunning* is only the want of Understanding, which because it cannot compass its Ends by direct Ways, would do it by a Trick and Circumvention; and the Mischief of it is, a *cunning* Trick helps but once, but hinders ever after. No Cover was ever made either so big or so fine as to hide it self: No body was ever so *cunning* as to conceal their being so: And when they are once discovered, every Body is shy, every Body distrustful of *crafty* Men; and all the World forwardly join to oppose and defeat them; whilst the open, fair, *wise* Man has every body to make way for him, and goes directly to his Business. To accustom a Child to have true Notions of things, and not to be satisfied till he has them; to raise his Mind to great and worthy Thoughts, and to keep him at a Distance from Falshood and Cunning, which has always a broad Mixture of Falshood in it; is the fittest Preparation of a Child for *Wisdom*. The rest, which is to be learn'd from Time, Experience, and Observation, and an Acquaintance with Men, their Tempers and Designs, is not to be expected in the Ignorance and Inadvertency of Childhood, or the inconsiderate Heat and Unwariness of Youth: All that can be done towards it, during this unripe Age, is, as I have said, to accustom them to Truth and Sincerity; to a submission to Reason; and as much as may be, to Reflection on their own Actions.

§ 141. The next good Quality belonging to a Gentleman, is *good Breeding*. There are two sorts of *ill Breeding*: the one a *sheepish Bashfulness*, and the other a *mis-becoming Negligence and Disrespect in* our Carriage; both which are avoided by duly observing this one Rule, *Not to think meanly of ourselves, and not to think meanly of others.* . . .

§ 147. You will wonder, perhaps, that I put *Learning* last, especially if I tell you I think it the least Part. This may seem strange in the Mouth of a bookish Man and this making usually the chief, if not only bustle and stir about Children, this being almost that alone which is thought on, when People talk of Education, makes it the greater Paradox. When I consider, what ado is made about a little *Latin* and *Greek*, how many Years are spent in it, and what a Noise and Business it makes to no Purpose, I can hardly forbear thinking that the Parents of Children still live in fear of the School-master's Rod, which they look on as the only Instrument of Education; as a Language or two to be its whole Business. How else is it possible that a Child should be chain'd to the Oar seven, eight, or ten of the best Years of his Life, to get a Language or two, which, I think, might be had at a great deal cheaper rate of Pains and Time, and be learn'd almost in playing? . . .

Reading and Writing and *Learning* I allow to be necessary, but yet not the chief Business. I imagine you would think him a very foolish Fellow, that should not value a virtuous or a wise Man infinitely before a great Scholar. Not but that I think *Learning* a great Help to both in well-dispos'd Minds; but yet it must be confess'd also, that in others not so dispos'd, it helps them only to be the more foolish, or worse Men. I say this, that when you consider of the Breeding of your Son, and are looking out for a School-Master or a Tutor, you would not have (as is usual) *Latin* and *Logick* only in your Thoughts. *Learning* must be had, but in the second Place, as subservient only to greater Qualities. Seek out somebody that may know how discreetly to frame his Manners: Place him in Hands where you may, as much as possible, secure his Innocence, cherish and nurse up the good, and gently correct and weed out any bad Inclinations, and settle in him good Habits. This is the main Point, and this being provided for, *Learning* may be had into the Bargain, and that, as I think, at a very easy rate, by Methods that may be thought on. . . .

§ 164. *Latin* I look upon as absolutely necessary to a Gentleman; and indeed Custom, which prevails over every thing, has made it so much a Part of Education, that even those Children are whipp'd to it, and made spend many Hours of their precious Time uneasily in *Latin,* who, after they are once gone from the School, are never to have more to do with it as long as they live. Can there be any thing more ridiculous, than that a Father should waste his own Money and his Son's Time in setting him to learn the *Roman Language* when at the same Time he designs him for a Trade, wherein he having no use of *Latin,* fails not to forget that little which he brought from School, and which 'tis ten to one he abhors for the ill Usage it procured him? Could it be believed, unless we had every where amongst us Examples of it, that a Child should be forced to learn the Rudiments of a Language which he is never to use in the Course of Life that he is designed to, and neglect all the while the writing a good Hand and casting Accounts, which are of great Advantage in all Conditions of Life, and to most trades indispensably necessary? . . .

§ 201. I have one thing more to add, which as soon as I mention I shall run the danger of being suspected to have forgot what I am about, and what I have above written concerning Education all tending towards a Gentleman's Calling, with which a Trade seems wholly inconsistent. And yet I cannot forbear to say, I would have him *learn a*

Trade, a manual Trade; nay, two or three, but one more particularly.

§ 202. The busy Inclination of Children being always to be directed to something that may be useful to them, the Advantages proposed from what they are set about may be considered of two Kinds: 1. Where the Skill itself that is got by Exercise is worth the having. Thus Skill not only in Languages and learned Sciences, but in Painting, Turning, Gardening, tempering and working in Iron, and all other useful Arts is worth the having. 2. Where the Exercise itself, without any Consideration, is necessary or useful for Health. . . .

§ 204. . . . For a Country Gentleman I should propose one, or rather both these, *viz. Gardening* or *Husbandry* in general, and working in Wood, as a *Carpenter, Joiner,* or *Turner,* these being fit and healthy Recreations for a man of Study or Business. For since the Mind endures not to be constantly employed in the same Thing or Way, and sedentary or studious Men should have some Exercise, that at the same Time might divert their Minds and employ their Bodies, I know none that could do it better for a Country Gentleman than these two; the one of them affording him Exercise when the Weather or Season keeps him from the other. Besides that, by being skill'd in the one of them, he will be able to govern and teach his Gardener; by the other, contrive and make a great many things both of Delight and Use: Though these I propose not as the chief End of his Labour, but as Temptations to it; diversion from his other more serious Thoughts and Employments by useful and healthy manual Exercise being what I chiefly aim at in it.

Working Schools

Locke's imprisonment by the assumptions of his own social class is nowhere more clearly demonstrated than in his proposal for the establishment of working-class schools, which he drew up while he was King's Commissioner of Trade and Plantations. His suggestion is that a school for poor children be set up in each parish. Attendance should be compulsory for all children between three and fourteen whose parents seek relief from the parish. Gathering the children together in this school will obviate the need to provide any relief to their parents, who will have to fend for themselves and for all their children under three. In any case, Locke suggests, the father often spends his relief money on beer rather than on his children. We can find many echoes of Locke's attitude in contemporary complaints by the affluent in America about the abuse of welfare services by the poor and the unemployed. The children in the working schools will not be a financial drain upon the parish, Locke assures us, for they will be fed on bread and water. If the weather is bitter enough, perhaps a little warm water-gruel could be added to their diet. Lest any should think this a wasteful extravagance, Locke is quick to point out that he does not envisage the need for any extra fuel to warm the gruel. The fire that warms the room will suffice for both purposes. One can perhaps be forgiven for doubting whether, in fact, there would be any heat left to warm the room after the fire had warmed the backside of the overseer. The final triumph of capitalist free enterprise is anticipated in Locke's confident expectation that, since the children will be put to work at activities like spinning and knitting, the school will actually make a profit for the parish.

This passage appears as Appendix A of John Locke, *Some Thoughts Concerning Education*, edited by R. H. Quick, published in Cambridge in 1927 by Cambridge University Press, with whose permission it is reprinted.

The children of labouring people are an ordinary burden to the parish, and are usually maintained in idleness, so that their labour also is generally lost to the public till they are twelve or fourteen years old.

The most effectual remedy for this that we are able to conceive, and which we therefore humbly propose, is, that, in the fore-mentioned new law to be enacted, it be further provided that working schools be set up in every parish, to which the children of all such as demand relief of the parish, above three and under fourteen years of age, whilst they live at home with their parents, and are not otherwise employed for their livelihood by the allowance of the overseers of the poor, shall be obliged to come.

By this means the mother will be eased of a great part of her trouble in looking after and providing for them at home, and so be at the more liberty to work; the children will be kept in much better order, be better provided for, and from infancy be inured to work, which is of no small consequence to the making of them sober and industrious all their lives after; and the parish will be either eased of this burden or at least of the misuse in the present management of it. For, a great number of children giving a poor man a title to an allowance from the parish, this allowance is given once a week or once a month to the father in money, which he not seldom spends on himself at the alehouse, whilst his children, for whose sake he had it, are left to suffer, or perish under the want of necessaries, unless the charity of neighbours relieve them.

We humbly conceive that a man and his wife in health may be able by their ordinary labour to maintain themselves and two children. More than two children at one time under the age of three years will seldom happen in one family. If therefore all the children above three years old be taken off from their hands those who have never so many, whilst they remain themselves in health, will not need any allowance for them.

We do not suppose that children of three years old will be able at that age to get their livelihoods at the working school, but we are sure that what is necessary for their relief will more effectually have that use if it be distributed to them in bread at that school than if it be given to their fathers in money. What they have at home from their parents is seldom more than bread and water, and that, many of them, very scantily too. If therefore care be taken that they have each of them their belly-full of bread daily at school, they will be in no danger of famishing, but, on the contrary, they will be healthier and stronger than those who are bred otherwise. Nor will this practice cost the overseers any trouble; for a baker may be agreed with to furnish and bring into the school-house every day the allowance of bread necessary for all the scholars that are there. And to this may be also added, without any trouble, in cold weather, if it be thought needful, a little warm water-gruel; for the same fire that warms the room may be made use of to boil a pot of it.

From this method the children will not only reap the fore-mentioned advantages with far less charge to the parish than what is now done for them, but they will be also thereby the more obliged to come to school and apply themselves to work, because otherwise they will have no victuals, and also the benefit thereby both to themselves and the parish will daily increase; for, the earnings of their labour at school every day increasing, it may reasonably be concluded that, computing all the earnings of a child from three to fourteen years of age, the nourishment and teaching of such a child during that whole time will cost the parish nothing; whereas there is no child now which from its birth is maintained by the parish but, before the age of fourteen, costs the parish £50 or £60.

Another advantage also of bringing children thus to a working school is that by this means they may be obliged to come constantly to church every Sunday, along with their schoolmasters or dames, whereby they may be brought into some sense of religion; whereas ordinarily now, in their idle and loose way of breeding up, they are as utter strangers both to religion and morality as they are to industry.

In order therefore to the more effectual carrying on of this work to the advantage of this kingdom, we further humbly propose that these schools be generally for spinning or knitting, or some other part of the woolen manufacture, unless in countries [that is, districts] where the place shall furnish some other materials fitter for the employment of such poor children; in which places the choice of those materials for their employment may be left to the prudence and direction of the guardians of the poor of that hundred. And that the teachers in these schools be paid out of the poor's rate, as can be agreed.

This, though at first setting up it may cost the parish a little, yet we humbly conceive (the earnings of the children abating the charge of their maintenance, and as much work being required of each of them as they are reasonably able to perform) it will quickly pay its own charges with an overplus.

That, where the number of the poor children of any parish is greater than for them all to be employed in one school they be there divided into two, and the boys and girls, if thought convenient, taught and kept to work separately.

That the handicraftsmen in each hundred be bound to take every other of their respective apprentices from amongst the boys in some one of the schools in the said hundred without any money; which boys they may so take at what age they please, to be bound to them till the age of twenty-three years, that so the length of time may more than make amends for the usual sums that are given to handicraftsmen with such apprentices.

That those also in the hundred who keep in their hands land of their own to the value of £25 per annum, or upwards, or who rent £50 per annum or upwards, may choose out of the schools of the said hundred what boy each of them pleases, to be his apprentice in husbandry on the same condition.

That whatever boys are not by this means bound out apprentices before they are full fourteen shall, at the Easter meeting of the guardians of each hundred every year, be bound to such gentlemen, yeomen, or farmers within the said hundred as have the greatest number of acres of land in their hands, who shall be obliged to take them for their apprentices till the age of twenty-three, or bind them out at their own cost to some handicraftsmen provided always that no such gentleman, yeoman, or farmer shall be bound to have two such apprentices at a time.

That grown people also (to take away their pretence of want of work) may come to the said working schools to learn, where work shall accordingly be provided for them.

That the materials to be employed in these schools and among other the poor people of the parish be provided by a common stock in each hundred, to be raised out of a certain portion of the poor's rate of each parish as requisite; which stock, we humbly conceive, need be raised but once; for, if rightly managed, it will increase.

Conduct of the Understanding

In 1690 Locke's masterpiece, on which he had worked for some twenty years, was published. This was his *Essay Concerning the Human Understanding,* which contains the most comprehensive statement of his theory of knowledge. At his death, he left unfinished and unpublished a manuscript on the *Conduct of the Understanding,* which was intended to be a revision of the *Essay.* Subsequently published separately, this treatise is a valuable complement to *Some Thoughts Concerning Education,* for it gives additional information on the intellectual education of the gentleman that causes us to modify somewhat the model drawn in the earlier work. Locke here adds to the picture of the rather complacent, socially secure gentleman, the dimension of the enlightened, rational gentleman. As an educated man, the gentleman will think for himself: he will not supinely take his opinions from authority—whether of his family, his church, or the conventional thinking of his society. The educated gentleman will not be a prisoner of parochial prejudices. He will not be afraid to venture beyond the confines of popular assumption. Such a man will not suffer from the disability of being able to see only one side of a question or one part of a problem. Nor will he make the mistake of seeking truth only through books. He will adopt an empirical approach to problems—tentative, experimental, open. Always ready to receive new evidence, he will not condemn others' views before he has carefully examined them. His characteristic habit will be his application of reason rather than passion to human affairs. Reason is the criterion by which we can distinguish the gold from the dross in life. All men are potentially capable of rational thinking and behavior. But only he becomes rational who habitually and vigorously exercises his powers of reason. Practice is crucial. The best means for developing this reasoning power is the study of mathematics. There is a clear assumption of transfer in Locke's thinking: rational thinking about mathematics will generate rational thinking in general. Much was subsequently made of this argument. It became used, in analogue, as a justification for the domination of the curriculum by the classics (something Locke had explicitly condemned) through the nineteenth century. But when supporters of the doctrine of formal mental discipline and the theory of faculty psychology subsequently used Locke as support for their views they were going beyond, and sometimes directly contrary to, his explicit recommendations. It is important to recognize that the emphasis on reason that characterizes the *Conduct* adds a potentially universal dimension to the socially limited concept of the gentleman depicted in the *Thoughts*.

These excerpts are taken from John Locke, *Conduct of the Understanding*, edited by Thomas Fowler, published by the Clarendon Press in Oxford in 1890.

SECTION I

INTRODUCTION

The last resort a man has recourse to in the conduct of himself is his understanding; for though we distinguish the faculties of the mind, and give the supreme command to the will as to an agent, yet the truth is, the man which is the agent determines himself to this or that voluntary action upon some precedent knowledge, or appearance of knowledge, in the understanding. No man ever sets himself about any thing but upon some view or other which serves him for a reason for what he does: and whatsoever faculties he employs, the understanding, with such light as it has, well or ill informed, constantly leads; and by that light, true or false, all his operative powers are directed. The will itself, how absolute and uncontrollable soever it may be thought, never fails in its obedience to the dictates of the understanding. Temples have their sacred images, and we see what influence they have always had over a great part of mankind. But in truth the ideas and images in men's minds are the invisible powers that constantly govern them, and to these they all universally pay a ready submission. It is therefore of the highest concernment that great care should be taken of the understanding, to conduct it right in the search of knowledge and in the judgments it makes. . . .

SECTION III

REASONING

Besides the want of determined ideas, and of sagacity and exercise in finding out and laying in order intermediate ideas, there are three miscarriages that men are guilty of in reference to their reason, whereby this faculty is hindered in them from that service it might do and was designed for. And he that reflects upon the actions and discourses of mankind, will find their defects in this kind very frequent and very observable.

1. The first is of those who seldom reason at all, but do and think according to the examples of others, whether parents, neighbours, ministers, or who else they are pleased to make choice of to have an implicit faith in, for the saving of themselves the pains and trouble of thinking and examining for themselves.

2. The second is of those who put passion in the place of reason, and, being resolved that shall govern their actions and arguments, neither use their own nor hearken to other people's reason, any farther than it suits their humour, interest, or party and these one may observe commonly content themselves with words which have no distinct ideas to them, though, in other matters, that they come with an unbiassed indifferency to, they want not abilities to take and hear reason, where they have no secret inclination that hinders them from being tractable to it.

3. The third sort is of those who readily and sincerely follow reason, but, for want of having that which one may call *large, sound round-about sense,* have not a full view of all that relates to the question and may be of moment to decide it. We are all short sighted, and very often see but one side of a matter; our views are not extended to all that has a connection with it. From this defect I think no man is free. We see but in part, and we know but in part, and therefore it is no wonder we conclude not right from our partial views. This might instruct the proudest esteemer of his own parts, how useful it is to talk and consult with others, even such as come short of him in capacity, quickness and penetration: for since no one sees all, and we generally have different prospects of the same thing, according to our different, as I may

say, positions to it, it is not incongruous to think nor beneath any man to try, whether another may not have notions of things which have escaped him, and which his reason would make use of it they came into his mind. The faculty of reasoning seldom or never deceives those who trust to it; its consequences from what it builds on are evident and certain, but that which it oftenest, if not only, misleads us in is that the principles from which we conclude, the grounds upon which we bottom our reasoning, are but a part, something is left out which should go into the reckoning to make it just and exact. Here we may imagine a vast and almost infinite advantage that angels and separate spirits may have over us; who, in their several degrees of elevation above us, may be endowed with more comprehensive faculties, and some of them perhaps have perfect and exact views of all finite beings that come under their consideration, can, as it were, in the twinkling of an eye, collect together all their scattered and almost boundless relations. A mind so furnished, what reason has it to acquiesce in the certainty of its conclusions!

In this we may see the reason why some men of study and thought, that reason right and are lovers of truth, do make no great advances in their discoveries of it. Error and truth are uncertainly blended in their minds; their decisions are lame and defective, and they are very often mistaken in their judgments: the reason whereof is, they converse but with one sort of men, they read but one sort of books, they will not come in the hearing but of one sort of notions; the truth is, they canton out to themselves a little Goshen in the intellectual world, where light shines, and, as they conclude, day blesses them; but the rest of the vast *Expansum* they give up to night and darkness, and so avoid coming near it. They have a pretty traffick with known correspondents in some little creek; within that they confine themselves, and are dexterous managers enough of the wares and products of that corner with which they content themselves, but will not venture out into the great ocean of knowledge, to survey the riches that nature hath stored other parts with, no less genuine, no less solid, no less useful, than what has fallen to their lot in the admired plenty and sufficiency of their own little spot, which to them contains whatsoever is good in the universe. Those who live thus mued up within their own contracted territories, and will not look abroad beyond the boundaries that chance, conceit, or laziness has set to their enquiries, but live separate from the notions, discourses and attainments of the rest of mankind, may not amiss be represented by the inhabitants of the Marian islands; who, being separated by a large tract of sea from all communion with the habitable parts of the earth, thought themselves the only people of the

world. And though the straitness of the conveniences of life amongst
them had never reached so far as to the use of fire, till the Spaniards,
not many years since, in their voyages from Acapulco to Manilia brought
it amongst them; yet in the want and ignorance of almost all things,
they looked upon themselves, even after that the Spaniards had brought
amongst them the notice of variety of nations abounding in sciences,
arts and conveniences of life, of which they knew nothing, they looked
upon themselves, I say, as the happiest and wisest people of the universe.
But for all that, no body, I think, will imagine them deep naturalists,
or solid metaphysicians; no body will deem the quickest sighted amongst
them to have very enlarged views in ethics or politics, nor can any
one allow the most capable amongst them to be advanced so far in
his understanding as to have any other knowledge but of the few little
things of his and the neighbouring islands within his commerce, but
far enough from that comprehensive enlargement of mind which adorns
a soul devoted to truth, assisted with letters, and a free consideration
of the several views and sentiments of thinking men of all sides. Let
not men therefore that would have a sight of, what every one pretends
to be desirous to have a sight of, truth in its full extent, narrow and
blind their own prospect. Let not men think there is no truth but in
the sciences that they study, or the books that they read. To prejudge
other men's notions before we have looked into them is not to shew
their darkness, but to put out our own eyes. *Try all things, hold fast
that which is good*, is a divine rule coming from the Father of light
and truth; and it is hard to know what other way men can come at
truth, to lay hold of it, if they do not dig and search for it as for
gold and hid treasure; but he that does so must have much earth and
rubbish before he gets the pure metal; sand, and pebbles, and dross
usually lie blended with it, but the gold is nevertheless gold, and will
enrich the man that employs his pains to seek and separate it. Neither
is there any danger he should be deceived by the mixture. Every man
carries about him a touchstone, if he will make use of it, to distinguish
substantial gold from superficial glitterings, truth from appearances. And
indeed the use and benefit of this touchstone, which is natural reason,
is spoiled and lost only by assumed prejudices, overweening presump-
tion, and narrowing our minds. The want of exercising it in the full
extent of things intelligible, is that which weakens and extinguishes
this noble faculty in us. Trace it, and see whether it be not so. The
day labourer in a country village has commonly but a small pittance
of knowledge, because his ideas and notions have been confined to the
narrow bounds of a poor conversation and employment; the low mechanic of a country town does somewhat outdo him; porters and cobblers

of great cities surpass them. A country gentleman, who, leaving Latin and Learning in the university, removes thence to his mansion house, and associates with neighbours of the same strain, who relish nothing but hunting and a bottle; with those alone he spends his time, with those alone he converses, and can away with no company whose discourse goes beyond what claret and dissoluteness inspire. Such a patriot formed in this happy way of improvement, cannot fail, as we see, to give notable decisions upon the bench at quarter sessions, and eminent proofs of his skill in politics, when the strength of his purse and party have advanced him to a more conspicuous station. To such a one truly an ordinary coffee-house gleaner of the city is an errant stateman, and as much superior to, as a man convesant about Whitehall and the court is to an ordinary shopkeeper. To carry this a little farther. Here is one muffled up in the zeal and infallibility of his own sect, and will not touch a book or enter into debate with a person that will question any of those things which to him are sacred. Another surveys our differences in religion with an equitable and fair indifference, and so finds probably that none of them are in every thing unexceptionable. These divisions and systems were made by men, and carry the mark of fallible on them; and in those whom he differs from, and, till he opened his eyes, had a general prejudice against, he meets with more to be said for a great many things than before he was aware of, or could have imagined. Which of these two now is most likely to judge right in our religious controversies, and to be most stored with truth, the mark all pretend to aim at? All these men that I have instanced in, thus unequally furnished with truth and advanced in knowledge, I suppose of equal natural parts; all the odds between them has been the different scope that has been given to their understandings to range in, for the gathering up of information, and furnishing their heads with ideas, notions and observations, whereon to employ their minds and form their understandings.

It will possibly be objected, who is sufficient for all this? I answer, more than can be imagined. Every one knows what his proper business is, and what, according to the character he makes of himself, the world may justly expect of him; and to answer that, he will find he will have time and opportunity enough to furnish himself, if he will not deprive himself by a narrowness of spirit of those helps that are at hand. I do not say to be a good geographer that a man should visit every mountain, river promontory and creek upon the face of the earth, view the buildings, and survey the land every where, as if he were going to make a purchase. But yet every one must allow that he shall know a country better that makes often sallies into it, and traverses it up and down, than he that like a mill horse goes still round in the same track, or keeps within the narrow bounds of a field or two that delight him. He that will enquire out the best books in every science, and inform himself of the most material authors of the several sects of philosophy and religion, will not find it an infinite work to acquaint himself with the sentiments of mankind concerning the most weighty and comprehensive subjects. Let him exercise the freedom of his reason and understanding in such a latitude as this, and his mind will be strengthened, his capacity enlarged, his faculties improved; and the light, which the remote and scattered parts of truth will give to one another, will so assist his judgment, that he will seldom be widely out, or miss giving proof of a clear head and a comprehensive knowledge. At least, this is the only way I know to give the understanding its due improvement to the full extent of its capacity, and to distinguish the two most different things I know in the world, a logical chicaner from a man of reason. Only, he that would thus give the mind its flight, and send abroad his enquiries into all parts after truth, must be sure to settle in his head determined ideas of all that he employs his thoughts about, and never fail to judge himself, and judge unbiassedly of all that he receives from others, either in their writings or discourses. Reverence or prejudice must not be suffered to give beauty or deformity to any of their opinions. . . .

SECTION VI

PRINCIPLES

. . . The faculties of our souls are improved and made useful to us just after the same manner as our bodies are. Would you have a man write or paint, dance or fence well, or perform any other manual operation dexterously and with ease, let him have ever so much vigour and activity, suppleness and address naturally, yet no body expects this from him unless he has been used to it, and has employed time and pains in fashioning and forming his hand or outward parts to these motions. Just so it is in the mind; would you have a man reason well, you must use him to it betimes, exercise his mind in observing the connection of ideas and following them in train. Nothing does this better than mathematics, which therefore I think should be taught all those who have the time and opportunity, not so much to make them mathemati-

cians as to make them reasonable creatures; for though we all call ourselves so, because we are born to it if we please, yet we may truly
say nature gives us but the seeds of it; we are born to be, if we please,
rational creatures, but it is use and exercise only that makes us so,
and we are indeed so no farther than industry and application has carried us. . . .

SECTION VII

MATHEMATICS

I have mentioned mathematics as a way to settle in the mind a habit
of reasoning closely and in train; not that I think it necessary that all
men should be deep mathematicians, but that having got the way of
reasoning, which that study necessarily brings the mind to, they might
be able to transfer it to other parts of knowledge as they shall have
occasion. For, in all sorts of reasoning, every single argument should
be managed as a mathematical demonstration, the connection and dependence of ideas should be followed till the mind is brought to the
source on which it bottoms and observes the coherence all along, though,
in proofs of probability, one such train is not enough to settle the judgment as in demonstrative knowledge.

10 *The Natural Man: Rousseau*

Although Jean Jacques Rousseau (1712–1778) found at first much in common with the *philosophes* of the Enlightenment (especially in their impatience with the encrustations of tired traditions), many of his most important social and educational formulations were reactions against predominant features of Enlightenment thinking. In particular, he reacted negatively against the excessive formalism and rationalism of eighteenth-century France. Many people were apparently ready to respond sympathetically to Rousseau's unique brand of reaction, for he became the most influential of all modern writers on education. Out of his reaction he forged a model of the educated person as the natural man—a figure that he presented in contrast to the pathetic product of contemporary civilization.

Nature and civilization became the great polarities between which Rousseau stretched the creative tension of his ideas. It is, of course, an abiding tension, for civilization as an educational goal represents a valid concern to raise standards of taste and discrimination, whereas nature epitomizes the equally valid concern to respect and nurture the unique and spontaneous inner impulses of the child. But civilization, in Rousseau's view, represented values like rationalism, conscious reflection, control, complexity, and objectivity, against which he offered values like romanticism, intuitive spontaneity, freedom, simplicity, and subjectivity.

One of the great puzzles of Rousseau's work is the contrast between the romantic individualism of *Emile* and the *Confessions*, on the one hand, and the severe social (some would say totalitarian) demands of *The Social Contract* and *Considerations on the Government of Poland,* on the other. To some extent this can be explained by the intuitive prophet's contempt for a petty consistency. But it is possible to see a consistent thread running through Rousseau's writings, if we are willing to recognize that he used the concept of "nature" in several different ways. In *Emile,* he was postulating a corrupt society, from which the child should be protected. Especially up to the time of adolescence, the natural, spontaneous development of the child should be our touchstone. In *The Social Contract*, Rousseau was hypothesizing an ideal society, whose influence holds promise for the highest development of the individual. The natural man in the ideal society will be able to profit from his natural education by recognizing the innate principles that govern nature, man, and society, and by operating in harmony with them.

Confessions

Rousseau began writing his *Confessions* in England, where he had sought refuge from persecution. He completed the work between the time of his return to France in 1770 and his death in 1778. The book created a considerable stir because of the unprecedentedly intimate way in which the author recounted his feelings and because of the passion with which he defended a life lived in accordance with the promptings of nature. Rousseau's mother died at his birth, and for the first ten years of his life he was brought up and educated by his warm, affectionate, emotional, and intemperate father. To the rather strange and intense diet of novels that he and his father shared, Rousseau attributes his own romantic nature and attitudes. He is glad that his early experiences permitted him to develop strong feelings unrelated to intellectual conceptions. The idea that feeling should precede thinking is a recurrent note in his writings. Rousseau claims that, because he avoided premature intellectualization of emotion, his intellectual powers were allowed to grow without distortion. For his hypothetical pupil, Emile, he recommended the same focus in the early years upon emotional development and the avoidance of forced intellectual precocity. Although this is a valuable correction still needed (or perhaps needed more than ever) today, the corresponding danger is the depreciation of the young child's genuine intellectual and moral powers, which Rousseau chose to ignore rather than explore creatively. It is ironical—and yet not unfamiliar—that he should have condemned the use of books with young children when he himself was such a glutton for literature as a child. It is another example of the common habit of judging from a position of privilege. Once we possess an object or undergo an experience, we may turn—sometimes in a spirit of partial disillusionment—and judge that object or experience to be useless or even dangerous for others.

The passage is from Jean Jacques Rousseau, *Confessions,* published by Random House, Inc., in New York.

I was brought into the world in an almost dying condition; little hope was entertained of saving my life. I carried within me the germs of a complaint which the course of time has strengthened, and which at times allows me a respite only to make me suffer more cruelly in another manner. One of my father's sisters, an amiable and virtuous young woman, took such care of me that she saved my life. At this moment, while I am writing, she is still alive, at the age of eighty, nursing a husband younger than herself, but exhausted by excessive drinking. Dear aunt, I forgive you for having preserved my life; and I deeply regret that, at the end of your days, I am unable to repay the tender care which you lavished upon me at the beginning of my own. My dear old nurse Jacqueline is also still alive, healthy and robust. The hands which opened my eyes at my birth will be able to close them for me at my death.

I felt before I thought: this is the common lot of humanity. I experienced it more than others. I do not know what I did until I was five or six years old. I do not know how I learned to read; I only remember my earliest reading, and the effect it had upon me; from that time I date my uninterrupted self-consciousness. My mother had left some romances behind her, which my father and I began to read after supper. At first it was only a question of practising me in reading by the aid of amusing books; but soon the interest became so lively, that we used to read in turns without stopping, and spent whole nights in this occupation. We were unable to leave off until the volume was finished. Sometimes, my father, hearing the swallows begin to twitter in the early morning, would say, quite ashamed, "Let us go to bed; I am more of a child than yourself."

In a short time I acquired, by this dangerous method, not only extreme facility in reading and understanding what I read, but a knowledge of the passions that was unique in a child of my age. I had no idea of things in themselves, although all the feelings of actual life were already known to me. I had conceived nothing, but felt everything. These confused emotions which I felt one after the other, certainly did not warp the reasoning powers which I did not as yet possess; but they shaped them in me of a peculiar stamp, and gave me odd and romantic notions of human life, of which experience and reflection have never been able wholly to cure me.

Emile

Rousseau's *Emile* was one of the most influential books ever written. In it, the author outlined a program for the education of his imaginary pupil, Emile, in terms that were eloquent and radical enough to change the course of educational history. In sharp opposition to the formalistic, rationalistic values of eighteenth-century Europe, Rousseau presents as his educational model the natural man. Several features of this model should be noted. The natural man has often been regarded as the antisocial man. This is an error of interpretation that can be corrected by setting Rousseau's views in the larger context of *The Social Contract* and other writings and even by a careful reading of *Emile* itself. However, the natural man is an individual who is capable of acting contrary to the conventional judgments of a corrupt society. It was the abuses and corruptions of contemporary European (and particularly French) society that Rousseau was condemning, rather than the concept of society as an ideal. In debased societies the individual and social goals of education inevitably conflict: we cannot educate for both manhood and citizenship. Rousseau's choice is the goal of individual manhood. The natural man is a man who is, above all, educated for freedom—the supreme good. Do what you want to do, and want only what you have the power to obtain: this is the formula for freedom, happiness, and a good education. Emile will develop his freedom through being made dependent only on things, never on people. Do not obey the child nor have him obey you; do not try to control him overtly; never let your will clash with the child's. Instead, arrange the physical environment so that the child will learn what you want him to learn without your commanding him. Clearly, this is a long way from the adult's abdicating his authority and it raises difficult and profound questions about the nature of freedom. There is no doubt that Rousseau's plea presaged the widespread substitution of a gentle, manipulative authority for a more

violent, coercive authority, but whether there was a consequential
gain in freedom is a question that requires more extensive examination than we can give here.* However, Rousseau is confident that
the natural man will be free to adapt himself to any circumstances
or challenges because his education has not been narrowly vocational or prematurely intellectual. It is important not to try to develop precocious intellectual prowess, especially in the first twelve
years of life. The mind should be inactive until the reason is fully
developed. We should not try to teach children to mouth platitudes
or to repeat concepts that they are incapable of understanding.
For this reason, Emile will have no catechistical religious education
but will be left open to appreciate natural religion—the faith
prompted by an awareness of the goodness of nature. This goodness
manifests itself in the original nature of man. Breaking sharply
with the doctrine of original sin, Rousseau urges us to trust the
child's spontaneous impulses, which are always healthy. Man's innate
goodness shows itself in self-love, which is a natural and beneficent emotion, and from which develops love for others. Psycho-
analysts like Erich Fromm have more recently given clinical sub-
stantiation to Rousseau's intuitive insight by demonstrating that
a basic measure of self-love, self-acceptance, self-regard, is necessary before we can find the security, confidence, and strength to
care for another person; and that hatred of others is often the unconscious projection of an unexamined and unacknowledged self-
hatred. There is also, in Rousseau's view, an essential relationship
between nature and equality. The natural man is not concerned
with superiority and inferiority. The most harmful inequalities arise
not from nature but out of society. It is only as we conform to
the classifications and competitions engendered by society that we
begin to feel the unpleasant emotions of pride, envy, and selfish
ambition. It is interesting, in the light of Rousseau's egalitarian
commitment, to observe his recommendations for the education
of underprivileged groups, such as the poor and the female sex.
Emile will be rich, for only the rich need a natural education:
it would be superfluous to supply for the poor the kind of education
that Rousseau prescribes, for the circumstances of their lives al-

* Those who wish to pursue the question further may refer to my *Authority and
Freedom in Education* (New York: John Wiley and Sons, 1966), especially
Chapters 3–4.

ready provide it. The most dramatic change in Rousseau's attitude is seen when he comes to the education of Sophie, Emile's female counterpart. The radical view of man is replaced by a most conventional view of woman. The daring innovations disappear and Rousseau tamely accepts all the clichés of his day.

The following excerpts are taken from *The Emile of Jean Jacques Rousseau*, edited by William Boyd, published in New York in 1962 by Teachers College Press, with whose permission they are reprinted.

Consistency is plainly impossible when we seek to educate a man for others, instead of for himself. If we have to combat either nature or society, we must choose between making a man or making a citizen. We cannot make both. There is an inevitable conflict of aims, from which come two opposing forms of education: the one communal and public, the other individual and domestic.

To get a good idea of communal education, read Plato's *Republic*. It is not a political treatise, as those who merely judge books by their titles think. It is the finest treatise on education ever written. Communal education in this sense, however, does not and can not now exist. There are no longer any real fatherlands and therefore no real citizens. The words 'fatherland' and 'citizen' should be expunged from modern languages. . . .

There remains then domestic education, the education of nature. But how will a man who has been educated entirely for himself get on with other people? If there were any way of combining in a single person the twofold aim, and removing the contradictions of life, a great obstacle to happiness would be removed. But before passing judgment on this kind of man it would be necessary to follow his development and see him fully formed. It would be necessary, in a word, to make the acquaintance of the natural man. This is the subject of our quest in this book. . . .

In the natural order where all men are equal, manhood is the common vocation. One who is well educated for that will not do badly in the duties that pertain to it. The fact that my pupil is intended for the army, the church or the bar, does not greatly concern me. Before the vocation determined by his parents comes the call of nature to the life of human kind. Life is the business I would have him learn. When he leaves my hands, I admit he will not be a magistrate, or a soldier,

or a priest. First and foremost, he will be a man. All that a man must
be he will be when the need arises, as well as anyone else. Whatever
the changes of fortune he will always be able to find a place for himself. . . .

Instead of the difficult task of educating a child, I now undertake
the easier task of writing about it. To provide details and examples
in illustration of my views and to avoid wandering off into airy speculations, I propose to set forth the education of Emile, an imaginary pupil,
from birth to manhood. I take for granted that I am the right man
for the duties in respect of age, health, knowledge and talents.

A tutor is not bound to his charge by the ties of nature as the father
is, and so is entitled to choose his pupil, especially when as in this
case he is providing a model for the education of other children. I
assume that Emile is no genius, but a boy of ordinary ability: that
he is the inhabitant of some temperate climate, since it is only in temperate climates that human beings develop completely; that he is rich,
since it is only the rich who have need of the natural education that
would fit them to live under all conditions; that he is to all intents
and purposes an orphan, whose tutor having undertaken the parents'
duties will also have their right to control all the circumstances of his
upbringing; and, finally, that he is a vigorous, healthy, well-built
child. . . .

True happiness comes with equality of power and will. The only
man who gets his own way is the one who does not need another's
help to get it: from which it follows that the supreme good is not authority, but freedom. The true freeman wants only what he can get, and
does only what pleases him. This is my fundamental maxim. Apply
it to childhood and all the rules of education follow.

There are two kinds of dependence: dependence on things, which
is natural, and dependence on men, which is social. Dependence on
things being non-moral is not prejudicial to freedom and engenders
no vices: dependence on men being capricious engenders them all. The
only cure for this evil in society would be to put the law in place
of the individual, and to arm the general will with a real power that
made it superior to every individual will.

Keep the child in sole dependence on things and you will follow
the natural order in the course of his education. Put only physical obstacles in the way of indiscreet wishes and let his punishments spring from
his own actions. Without forbidding wrong-doing, be content to prevent
it. Experience or impotence apart from anything else should take the
place of law for him. Satisfy his desires, not because of his demands
but because of his needs. He should have no consciousness of obedience

when he acts, nor of mastery when someone acts for him. Let him experience liberty equally in his actions and in yours. . . .

Let us lay it down as an incontestable principle that the first impulses of nature are always right. There is no original perversity in the human heart. Of every vice we can say how it entered and whence it came. The only passion natural to man is self-love, or self-esteem in a broad sense. This self-esteem has no necessary reference to other people. In so far as it relates to ourselves it is good and useful. It only becomes good or bad in the social application we make of it. Until reason, which is the guide of self-esteem, makes its appearance, the child should not do anything because he is seen or heard by other people, but only do what nature demands of him. Then he will do nothing but what is right. . . .

May I set forth at this point the most important and the most useful rule in all education? It is not to save time but to waste it. The most dangerous period in human life is that between birth and the age of twelve. This is the age when errors and vices sprout, before there is any instrument for their destruction. When the instrument is available the roots have gone too deep to be extracted. The mind should remain inactive till it has all its faculties.

It follows from this that the first education should be purely negative. It consists not in teaching virtue and truth, but in preserving the heart from vice and the mind from error. If you could do nothing and let nothing be done, so that your pupil came to the age of twelve strong and healthy but unable to distinguish his right hand from his left, the eyes of this understanding would be open to reason from your very first lessons. In the absence of both prejudices and habits there would be nothing in him to oppose the effects of your teaching and care. . . .

Assuming that my method is that of nature and that I have not made any mistakes in putting it into practice, I have now brought my pupil through the land of the sensations right up to the bounds of childish reason. The first step beyond this should take him towards manhood. But before entering on this new stage let us cast our eyes backward for a moment on the one we have traversed. Each age and state of life has its own proper perfection, its own distinctive maturity. People sometimes speak about a complete man. Let us think rather of a complete child. This vision will be new for us and perhaps not less agreeable.

When I picture to myself a boy of ten or twelve, healthy, strong and well built for his age, only pleasant thoughts arise in me, whether for his present or for his future. I see him bright, eager, vigorous, care-free, completely absorbed in the present, rejoicing in abounding vitality. I see him in the years ahead using senses, mind and power as they develop from day to day. I view him as a child and he pleases me. I think of him as a man and he pleases me still more. His warm blood seems to heat my own. I feel as if I were living in his life and am rejuvenated by his vivacity.

The clock strikes and all is changed. In an instant his eye grows dull and his merriment disappears. No more mirth, no more games! A severe, hard-faced man takes him by the hand, says gravely, 'Come away, sir,' and leads him off. In the room they enter I get a glimpse of books. Books! What a cheerless equipment for his age. As he is dragged away in silence, he casts a regretful look around him. His eyes are swollen with tears he dare not shed, his heart heavy with sighs he dare not utter.

Come, my happy pupil, and console us for the departure of the wretched boy. Here comes Emile, and at his approach I have a thrill of joy in which I see he shares. It is his friend and comrade, the companion of his games to whom he comes. His person, his bearing, his countenance reveal assurance and contentment. Health glows in his face. His firm step gives him an air of vigour. His complexion is refined without being effeminate; sun and wind have put on it the honourable imprint of his sex. His eyes are still unlighted by the fires of sentiment and have all their native serenity. His manner is open and free without the least insolence or vanity.

His ideas are limited but precise. If he knows nothing by heart, he knows a great deal by experience. If he is not as good a reader in books as other children, he reads better in the book of nature. His mind is not in his tongue but in his head. He has less memory but more judgment. He only knows one language, but he understands what he says and if he does not talk as well as other children he can do things better than they can.

Habit, routine and custom mean nothing to him. What he did yesterday has no effect on what he does today. He never follows a fixed rule and never accepts authority or example. He only does or says what seems good to himself. For this reason you must not expect stock speeches or studied manners from him but just the faithful expression of his ideas and the conduct that comes from his inclinations.

You will find in him a few moral notions relating to his own situation, but not being an active member of society he has none relating to manhood. Talk to him about liberty, property and even convention, and he may understand you thus far. But speak to him about duty and obedience, and he will not know what you mean. Command him to do something, and he will pay no heed. But say to him: 'If you will do me this favour, I will do the same for you another time;' and immediately he will hasten to oblige. For his part, if he needs any help he will ask the first person he meets as a matter of course. If you grant his request he will not thank you, but will feel that he has contracted a debt. If you refuse, he will neither complain nor insist. He will only say: 'It could not be done.' He does not rebel against necessity once he recognises it.

Work and play are all the same to him. His games are his occupations: he is not aware of any difference. He goes into everything he does with a pleasing interest and freedom. It is indeed a charming spectacle to see a nice boy of this age with open smiling countenance, doing the most serious things in his play or profoundly occupied with the most frivolous amusements.

Emile has lived a child's life and has arrived at the maturity of childhood, without any sacrifice of happiness in the achievement of his own perfection. He has acquired all the reason possible for his age, and in doing so has been as free and as happy as his nature allowed him to be. If by chance the fatal scythe were to cut down the flower of our hopes we would not have to bewail at the same time his life and his death, nor add to our griefs the memory of those we caused him. We would say that at any rate he had enjoyed his childhood and that nothing we had done had deprived him of what nature gave. . . .

The passions are the chief instruments for our preservation. The child's first sentiment is self-love, the only passion that is born with man. The second, which is derived from it, is the love he has for the people he sees ready to help him, and from this develops a kindly feeling for mankind. But with fresh needs and growing dependence on others comes the consciousness of social relations and with it the sense of duties and preference. It is at this point that the child may become domineering, jealous, deceitful, vindictive. Self-love being concerned only with ourselves is content when our real needs are satisfied, but self-esteem which involves comparisons with other people never is and never can be content because it makes the impossible demand that others should prefer us to themselves. That is how it comes that the gentle kindly passions issue from self-love, while hate and anger spring from self-esteem. Great care and skill are required to prevent the human heart being depraved by the new needs of social life. . . .

My readers, I foresee, will be surprised to see me take my pupil through the whole of the early years without mentioning religion. At fifteen he was not aware that he had a soul, and perhaps at eighteen it is not yet time for him to learn. For if he learns sooner than is necessary he runs the risk of never knowing.

My picture of hopeless stupidity is a pedant teaching the catechism to children. If I wanted to make a child dull I would compel him to explain what he says when he repeats his catechism. It may be objected that since most of the Christian doctrines are mysteries it would be necessary for the proper understanding of them to wait, not merely till the child becomes a man but till the man is no more. To that I reply, in the first place, that there are mysteries man can neither conceive nor believe and that I see no purpose in teaching them to children unless it be to teach them to lie. I say, further, that to admit there are mysteries one must understand that they are incomprehensible, and that this is an idea which is quite beyond children. For an age when all is mystery, there can be no mysteries, properly so-called.

Let us be on guard against presenting the truth to those unable to comprehend it. The effect of that is to substitute error for truth. It would be better to have no idea of the Divine Being than to have ideas that are mean, fantastic and unworthy. . . .

Sophie should be as typically woman as Emile is man. She must possess all the characteristics of humanity and of womanhood which she needs for playing her part in the physical and the moral order. Let us begin by considering in what respects her sex and ours agree and differ.

In the mating of the sexes each contributes in equal measure to the common end but not in the same way. From the diversity comes the *first* difference which has to be noted in their personal relations. It is the part of the one to be active and strong, and of the other to be passive and weak. Accept this principle and it follows in the *second* place that woman is intended to please man. If the man requires to please the woman in turn the necessity is less direct. Masterfulness is his special attribute. He pleases by the very fact that he is strong. This is not the law of love, I admit. But it is the law of nature, which is more ancient than love.

The faculties common to the sexes are not equally shared between them; but take them all in all, they are well balanced. The more womanly a woman is, the better. Whenever she exercises her own proper powers she gains by it: when she tries to usurp ours she becomes our inferior. Believe me, wise mother, it is a mistake to bring up your daughter to be like a good man. Make her a good woman, and you can be sure that she will be worth more for herself and for us. This does not mean that she should be brought up in utter ignorance and confined to domestic tasks. A man does not want to make his companion a servant and deprive himself of the peculiar charms of her company. That is quite against the teaching of nature, which has endowed women with quick pleasing minds. Nature means them to think, to judge, to love, to know and to cultivate the mind as well as the countenance. This is the equipment nature has given them to compensate for their lack of strength and enable them to direct the strength of men.

As I see it, the special functions of women, their inclinations and their duties, combine to suggest the kind of education they require. Men and women are made for each other but they differ in the measure of their dependence on each other. We could get on better without women than women could get on without us. To play their part in life they must have our willing help, and for that they must earn our esteem. By the very law of nature women are at the mercy of men's judgments both for themselves and for their children. It is not enough that they should be estimable: they must be esteemed. It is not enough that they should be beautiful: they must be pleasing. It is not enough that they should be wise: their wisdom must be recognised. Their honour does not rest on their conduct but on their reputation. Hence the kind of education they get should be the very opposite of men's in this respect. Public opinion is the tomb of a man's virtue but the throne of a woman's.

On the good constitution of the mothers depends that of the children and the early education of men is in their hands. On women too depend the morals, the passions, the tastes, the pleasures, aye and the happiness of men. For this reason their education must be wholly directed to their relations with men. To give them pleasure, to be useful to them, to win their love and esteem, to train them in their childhood, to care for them when they grow up, to give them counsel and consolation, to make life sweet and agreeable for them: these are the tasks of women in all times for which they should be trained from childhood.

The Social Contract

The commonest way to misinterpret Rousseau is to ignore *The Social Contract*. Written concurrently, *Emile* and *The Social Contract* were published in the same year, 1762. In the latter, however, we see the natural man in his ideal social setting, a modification that brings some important changes—some would say contradictions—to the picture drawn in *Emile*. The focus of *The Social Contract* is the search for individual freedom within the matrix of legitimate social authority. This is not the suffocating authority of the corrupt societies with which Rousseau was familiar and which he condemned so forcefully, but the ideal State's liberating authority, which is necessary for the highest reaches of individual freedom. That this book was written by the apostle of nature is sometimes hard to remember, for now we find that the state of untrammeled nature is not the highest condition of man: the civil state is higher because it alone makes possible justice and morality. Freedom is now identified as obedience to self-prescribed law. The model that Rousseau holds up is the man who achieves morality by voluntarily identifying with the common good, who subsumes his individual will under the general will. Rousseau acknowledges that the social contract involves the loss of natural liberty, but he judges this loss to be more than compensated by the gain of civil liberty. Alongside Rousseau's condemnation of the social inequalities engendered by a corrupt society, which he outlined in *Emile*, we must place his present argument that the social contract makes possible moral and legal equality among men, thus compensating for natural inequalities. How far Rousseau has ventured from the predominant tone of *Emile* can be seen in his discussion of civil religion. Not only is this religion to be merely a matter of professing a creed, to which all must adhere nominally whatever their actual beliefs, but the punishment for those who refuse to make public profession is banishment, and the punishment for those who agree to the creed

272

but subsequently depart from it is death. Such mandates exert a strong tension when placed in opposition to *Emile's* focus on the natural man's individual rights.

These excerpts are taken from Jean Jacques Rousseau, *The Social Contract*, edited by Charles Frankel, published in New York, copyright 1947 by the Hafner Publishing Company, with whose permission they are reprinted.

BOOK I

CHAPTER I

SUBJECT OF THE FIRST BOOK

Man is born free, and yet we see him everywhere in chains. Those who believe themselves the masters of others cease not to be even greater slaves than the people they govern. How this happens I am ignorant; but, if I am asked what renders it justifiable, I believe it may be in my power to resolve the question. . . .

CHAPTER VI

OF THE SOCIAL COMPACT

I will suppose that men in the state of nature are arrived at that crisis when the strength of each individual is insufficient to overcome the resistance of the obstacles to his preservation. This primitive state can therefore subsist no longer; and the human race would perish unless it changed its manner of life.

As men cannot create for themselves new forces, but merely unite and direct those which already exist, the only means they can employ for their preservation is to form by aggregation an assemblage of forces that may be able to overcome the resistance, to be put in motion as one body, and to act in concert.

This assemblage of forces must be produced by the concurrence of many; but as the force and the liberty of each man are the chief instruments of his preservation, how can he engage them elsewhere without danger to himself, and without neglecting the care which is due himself?

This difficulty, which leads directly to my subject, may be expressed in these words:

"Where shall we find a form of association which will defend and protect with the whole common force the person and the property of each associate, and by which every person, while uniting himself with all, shall obey only himself and remain as free as before?" Such is the fundamental problem of which the Social Contract gives the solution.

The articles of this contract are so unalterably fixed by the nature of the act that the least modification renders them vain and of no effect; so that they are the same everywhere, and are everywhere tacitly understood and admitted, even though they may never have been formally announced; until, the social compact being violated, each individual is restored to his original rights, and resumes his native liberty, while losing the conventional liberty for which he renounced it.

The articles of the social contract will, when clearly understood, be found reducible to this single point: the total alienation of each associate, and all his rights, to the whole community; for, in the first place, as every individual gives himself up entirely, the condition of every person is alike; and being so, it would not be to the interest of any one to render that condition offensive to others.

Nay, more than this, the alienation being made without any reserve, the union is as complete as it can be, and no associate has any further claim to anything: for if any individual retained rights not enjoyed in general by all, as there would be no common superior to decide between him and the public, each person being in some points his own judge, would soon pretend to be so in everything; and thus would the state of nature be continued and the association necessarily become tyrannical or be annihilated.

Finally, each person gives himself to all, and so not to any one individual; and as there is no one associate over whom the same right is not acquired which is ceded to him by others, each gains an equivalent for what he loses, and finds his force increased for preserving that which he possesses.

If, therefore, we exclude from the social compact all that is not essential, we shall find it reduced to the following terms:

Each of us places in common his person and all his power under the supreme direction of the general will; and as one body we all receive each member as an indivisible part of the whole.

From that moment, instead of as many separate persons as there are contracting parties, this act of association produces a moral and collective body, composed of as many members as there are votes in the assembly, which from this act receives its unity, its common self, its life, and its will. This public person, which is thus formed by the union of all other persons, took formerly the name of "city," and now takes that of "republic" or "body politic." It is called by its members "State" when it is passive, "Sovereign" when in activity, and, whenever it is compared with other bodies of a similar kind, it is denominated "power." The associates take collectively the name of "people," and separately, that of "citizens," as participating in the sovereign authority, and of "subjects," because they are subjected to the laws of the State. But these terms are frequently confounded and used one for the other; and it is enough that man understands how to distinguish them when they are employed in all their precision. . . .

CHAPTER VIII

OF THE CIVIL STATE

The passing from the state of nature to the civil state produces in man a very remarkable change, by substituting justice for instinct in his conduct, and giving to his actions a moral character which they lacked before. It is then only that the voice of duty succeeds to physical impulse, and a sense of what is right, to the incitements of appetite. Man, who had till then regarded none but himself, perceives that he must act on other principles, and learns to consult his reason before he listens to his inclinations. Although he is deprived in this new state of many advantages which he enjoyed from nature, he gains in return others so great, his faculties so unfold themselves by being exercised, his ideas are so extended, his sentiments so exalted, and his whole mind so enlarged and refined, that if, by abusing his new condition, he did not sometimes degrade it even below that from which he emerged, he ought to bless continually the happy moment that snatched him forever from it, and transformed him from a circumscribed and stupid animal to an intelligent being and a man.

In order to draw a balance between the advantages and disadvantages attending his new situation, let us state them in such a manner that they may be easily compared. Man loses by the social contract his *natural* liberty, and an unlimited right to all which tempts him, and which he can obtain; in return he acquires *civil* liberty, and proprietorship of all he possesses. That we may not be deceived in the value of these compensations, we must distinguish natural liberty, which knows no bounds but the power of the individual, from civil liberty, which is limited by the general will; and between possession, which is only the effect of force or of the right of the first occupant, from property, which must be founded on a positive title. In addition we might add to the other acquisitions of the civil state that of moral liberty, which alone renders a man master of himself; for it is *slavery* to be under the impulse of mere appetite, and *freedom* to obey a law which we prescribe for ourselves. But I have already said too much on this head, and the philosophical sense of the word "liberty" is not at present my subject. . . .

CHAPTER IX

OF REAL PROPERTY

. . . I shall conclude this chapter and book with a remark which must serve for the basis of the whole social system: it is that, instead of destroying the natural equality of mankind, the fundamental compact substitutes, on the contrary, a moral and legal equality for that physical inequality which nature placed among men, and that, let men be ever so unequal in strength or in genius, they are all equalized by convention and legal right. . . .

BOOK II

CHAPTER III

WHETHER THE GENERAL WILL CAN ERR

It follows from what has been said that the general will is always right and tends always to the public advantage but it does not follow that the deliberations of the people have always the same rectitude. Our will always seeks our own good, but we do not always perceive what it is. The people are never corrupted, but they are often deceived, and only then do they seem to will what is bad.

There is frequently much difference between the *will of all* and the *general will*. The latter regards only the common interest; the former regards private interest, and is indeed but a sum of private wills: but remove from these same wills the pluses and minuses that cancel each other, and then the general will remains as the sum of the differences.

If, when the people, sufficiently informed, deliberated, there was to be no communication among them, from the grand total of trifling differences the general will would always result, and their resolutions be always good. But when cabals and partial associations are formed at the expense of the great association, the will of each such association, though *general* with regard to its members, is *private* with regard to the State: it can then be said no longer that there are as many voters as men, but only as many as there are associations. By this means the differences being less numerous, they produce a result less general. Finally, when one of these associations becomes so large that it prevails over all the rest, you have no longer the sum of many opinions dissenting in a small degree from each other, but one great dictating dissentient; from that moment there is no longer a general will, and the predominating opinion is only an individual one. . . .

BOOK IV

CHAPTER VIII

OF CIVIL RELIGION

The right which the social compact gives the Sovereign over the subjects extends no further than is necessary for the public good. No Sovereign can therefore have a right to control the opinions of the subjects any further than as these opinions may effect the community. It is of consequence to the State that each of its citizens should have a religion which will dispose him to love his duties; but the dogmas of that religion interest neither the State nor its members except as far as they affect morality and those duties which he who professes them is required to discharge towards others. For the rest, every individual may entertain what opinions he pleases, without it pertaining to the Sovereign to take cognizance of them; for, having no jurisdiction in the other world, whatever the fate of its subjects in the life to come, it is not the Sovereign's business, provided they are good citizens in the present one.

There is therefore a purely civil profession of faith, the articles of which it is the business of the Sovereign to arrange, not precisely as dogmas of religion, but as sentiments of sociability without which it is impossible to be either a good citizen or a faithful subject. The Sovereign has no power by which it can oblige men to believe them, but it can banish from the State whoever does not believe them; not as an impious person, but as an unsociable one, who is incapable of sincerely loving the laws and justice, and of sacrificing, if occasion should require it, his life to his duty as a citizen. But if any one, after he has publicly subscribed to these dogmas, shall conduct himself as if he did not believe them, he is to be punished by death. He has committed the greatest of all crimes: he has lied in the face of the law.

The dogmas of civil religion ought to be simple, few in number, precisely fixed, and without explanation or comment. The existence of a powerful, wise, and benevolent Divinity, who foresees and provides the life to come, the happiness of the just, the punishment of the wicked, the sanctity of the social contract and the laws: these are its positive dogmas. Its negative dogmas I would confine to one—intolerance, which is only congenial to the cults we have excluded.

Those who make a distinction between civil and theological intolerance are, in my opinion, mistaken. The two are inseparable. It is impossible to live in peace with those whom we believe dammed; to love them would be to hate God who punishes them: we positively must either reclaim them or torment them. Wherever theological intolerance is admitted, it is impossible for it not to produce some civil effect: as soon as it has produced it, the Sovereign ceases to be such, even in temporal concerns: the priests are from that time so absolutely masters that kings themselves are nothing more than their officers.

Now that there neither is, nor can be any more, an exclusive national religion, all religions that tolerate others ought to be tolerated, so long as their dogmas discover nothing contradictory to the duties of a citizen. But those who dare to say: "Ouside the Church there is no salvation," should be driven from the State, unless that State is the Church, and the prince the pontiff. Such a dogma is only suited to a theocratic government; in all others it is exceedingly pernicious. The very reason which it is said made Henry IV embrace the Roman religion is the one which should make any honest man renounce it, and particularly any prince who is capable of reason.

Considerations on the Government of Poland

Written in 1772 and published posthumously, *Considerations on the Government of Poland* was Rousseau's response to a Polish nobleman who sought advice concerning the reform of Polish government, in the light of his country's disunity. Rousseau's formula was to use the instrument of education in order to create a nationalistic spirit among the Polish people. This would appear to be a thorough *volte-face* from the urgings of *Emile*. Now Rousseau is advocating the use of social institutions to mold men's minds. In this book he takes to its farthest point his support for the merging of the individual in the group. The individual counts for nothing by himself: without his fatherland he ceases to have a meaningful existence. The reader of *Emile* will note with irony or amazement the lengths to which Rousseau goes in arguing his case. No foreigners should be permitted to teach. Children should not be allowed to play alone. Only group activities should be permitted, with emulation and rivalry encouraged at every opportunity. Children should be accustomed from an early age to discipline and competition. Clearly, this is not the Rousseau who became the inspiration of the child-centered apostles of progressive education. However, we miss a crucial feature of Rousseau's thought if we ignore his belief that the natural man—the man who fulfills the vital parts of his nature—ultimately grows best in a social setting. We must look at *The Social Contract* and *Considerations on the Government of Poland* to see that Rousseau wanted his model to be set in a beneficent social context. But we must look at *Emile* to see that such a context can be created only by those who have enjoyed a natural development.

This selection is taken from *The Minor Educational Writings of Jean Jacques Rousseau,* edited by William Boyd, published in London by Blackie & Son, Ltd., in 1911.

CHAPTER IV   EDUCATION

This is the all-important article. It is education that must give the souls of the people a national form, and so shape their opinions and their tastes that they become patriots as much as inclination and passion as by necessity. A child ought to look upon his fatherland as soon as his eyes open to the light, and should continue to do so till the day of his death. Every true patriot sucks in the love of country with his mother's milk. This love is his whole existence. He thinks of nothing but his country. He lives only for his country. Take him by himself, and he counts for nothing. If his country ceases to exist, so also does he. If not dead, he is worse than dead.

National education is the privilege of free men. Only free men have common interests and are really united by law. The Frenchman, the Englishman, the Spaniard, the Italian, the Russian, are all much the same: when any one of them leaves college, he is already trained for licence,—which is only another name for servitude. At twenty years of age, a Pole ought to be a Pole and nothing but a Pole. When he is learning to read, I want him to read about his own country. At ten, he should be acquainted with all its productions; and at twelve, with all its provinces, highways, and towns. At fifteen, he should know all its history; at sixteen, all its laws. There should not have been a fine action or an illustrious man in all Poland, whose fame does not fill heart and memory, so that he can give instant account of them. From this it will be evident that it is not the ordinary studies, directed by foreigners and priests, that I want the children to pursue. The right ordering of the material, the sequence and the form of their studies, should be a matter for the law. Only Poles should be allowed to act as teachers; and these teachers should if possible all be married men, distinguished for character and probity as well as for good sense and intelligence, and destined at the end of a term of years for other occupations, not more important or more honourable (for that is not possible), but less arduous and of greater repute. Above all things, do not allow teaching to be made a profession. No public man in Poland should have any permanent position but that of a citizen. All the posts he fills, and especially important ones like this, should be considered simply as tests of fitness, stages by which he can mount higher after he has proved his worth. I would urge the Poles to pay special attention to this principle. I believe it to be the secret of a great strength in the state. . . .

In all the colleges there should be established a gymnasium or place of physical exercises for the children. The training of the body, though much neglected, is, in my opinion, the most important part of education, not only for making the children healthy and robust, but even more for the moral effect, which is generally neglected altogether, or sought by teaching the child a number of pedantic precepts that are only so many misspent words. I cannot repeat enough that a good education ought to be negative. If you keep the vices from springing up, you have done all that need be done for virtue. It is extremely easy to effect this in a good system of public education. The method is to keep the children always busy, not with troublesome lessons beyond their comprehension, which they hate, because (if for nothing else) they are compelled to remain in one place, but with exercises which give them pleasure by satisfying the needs of the growing body, and in other ways besides.

They should not be allowed to play separately at their own fancy, but made to play all together and in public, so that there may always be a common end to which they aspire, and by which they are moved to rivalry and emulation. Parents who prefer domestic education and want to have their children brought up under their own eyes, ought nevertheless to send them to these exercises. The instruction they get may be given at home and adapted to the individual, but their games should always be carried on in public and shared by all; for it is not simply a question of keeping the children busy, or of giving them a sturdy constitution and making them alert and graceful, but of accustoming them from an early age to discipline, to equality, to fraternity, to rivalry, to living under the eyes of their fellow-citizens and seeking public approbation. For this reason the prizes and rewards for the conquerors must not be distributed arbitrarily by the games masters or by the principals of the colleges, but be conferred with acclamation on the judgment of the spectators. These judgments, it may be reckoned, will always be just, especially if care is taken to render the games attractive to the public, by arranging them with a little ceremony and making a spectacle of them. If that is done, it may be assumed that all good people and all true patriots will make it a duty and a pleasure to lend assistance. . . .

It will be noted that I have only given general indications here, but they will be enough for those to whom I address myself. These imperfectly developed ideas of mine show in a dim way to the modern world the unknown roads by which the ancients brought men to a vigour of soul, a patriotic zeal, an esteem for the essentially personal qualities without regard to anything alien to humanity, which are no longer found among us, but which are fermenting in the hearts of all men, and only await suitable institutions to become active. If in this spirit you determine the education, the usages, the costumes, and the morals of the Poles, you will develop in them this ferment that as yet is kept inactive by corrupt maxims, by institutions that have outlived their day, and by a destructive egoistic philosophy. The nation will date its second birth from the terrible crisis out of which she is now emerging; and, seeing what it is that has made her members what they are, in spite of the lack of training, she will expect and get much more from a carefully thought-out system of education. She will cherish and respect the laws that flatter her noble pride, the laws that make and keep her free and happy. She will cast out of her heart the passions that set them at naught, and encourage those that cause them to be loved. In short, by renewing herself, she will acquire in this new age all the vigour of a young nation. But without these precautions expect nothing from your laws. However wise and foreseeing they may be, they will be evaded and prove of no effect. You will only have corrected some of the evils that do you harm, to introduce others you had not foreseen.

11   *The Scientific Humanist: Huxley*

Since the early nineteenth century, formulations of educational ideals and models have increasingly become responses to the growth and power of science and of its cousins, technology and industrialization. It was in England that the earliest scientific and industrial revolution occurred; hence it is appropriate that it is an Englishman, Thomas Henry Huxley (1825–1895), who is taken as the first spokesman of this scientific age.

The publication in 1859 of Darwin's *Origin of Species* was the beginning of a cultural revaluation that is still affecting us. It was also the beginning of a fierce battle between the partisans and antagonists of science, and Huxley was soon in the thick of it as "Darwin's Bulldog." He became the foremost exponent of the introduction of scientific thinking into wider aspects of life—not only into the study of nature but also into the study of society, of man, and of his education. At the same time Huxley was not a blind believer in science as a universal panacea. He foresaw the ignorant worship of pseudoscience that characterizes our own day and anticipated the abominable misteaching that makes much "scientific" instruction a wasteful error.

The model that Huxley holds up to us is not that of a person who has read many scientific books or memorized many formulas but one who has felt the inexorable pull of nature at first hand and has studied the laws of which that pull is an expression.

It was a broadly humanistic education—not a narrowly scientific one—that Huxley was advocating. He wanted educational opportunities for individuals, no matter to which group they belonged—workers, women, Negroes, down-trodden people. Industrial capitalism was distorting the face of England and there was growing support for education in order to supply better trained factory fodder. Huxley consistently fought this immoral cause and demanded an education for human beings because they were human beings and in order to make them better human beings. His writings constitute a most timely warning for the United States at the present time, when the concern of the industrial-military complex for trained manpower suffocates the concern of men and women for a liberating and humane education.

Emancipation—Black and White

In this selection, Huxley shows that he is a man who can transcend the assumptions of his own environment and era, and yet at the same time is deeply entrapped by them. His model of the educated person is broad enough to include two of the unemancipated groups of the nineteenth century—Negroes and women. With an effective blend of wit and irony, he argues strongly that human injustice should not add to the natural disadvantages that impede members of these groups. He celebrates the end of Negro slavery in America; and he goes far beyond most of his contemporaries in advocating a rigorous intellectual education for girls and in envisioning their entering business, law, and politics. But he has no doubt that, in fair and free competition, the "bigger-brained" and "smaller-jawed" white man will prevail over the Negro, and that the "big chests, the massive brains, the vigorous muscles and stout frames" of the men will defeat the child-bearing women. Such forms of blindness, such surrenders to conventional thinking, are particularly startling when they come from the most eminent biologist of the day. They should impell us to examine ourselves closely to see which contemporary assumptions we accept without criticism. And we should recognize in humility that we are still far from having solved the educational problems represented by differences of color and sex.

The article was first published in the *Reader*, May 20, 1865, and reprinted in Thomas Henry Huxley, *Lay Sermons, Addresses, and Reviews*, published by Appleton in New York in 1870.

Quashie's plaintive inquiry, "Am I not a man and a brother?" seems at last to have received its final reply—the recent decision of the fierce trial by battle on the other side of the Atlantic fully concurring with that long since delivered here in a more peaceful way.

The question is settled; but even those who are most thoroughly convinced that the doom is just, must see good grounds for repudiating half the arguments which have been employed by the winning side; and for doubting whether its ultimate results will embody the hopes of the victors, though they may more than realize the fears of the vanquished. It may be quite true that some negroes are better than some white men; but no rational man, cognizant of the facts, believes that the average negro is the equal, still less the superior, of the average white man. And, if this be true, it is simply incredible that, when all his disabilities are removed, and our prognathous relative has a fair field and no favour, as well as no oppressor, he will be able to compete successfully with his bigger-brained and smaller-jawed rival, in a contest which is to be carried on by thoughts and not by bites. The highest places in the hierarchy of civilization will assuredly not be within the reach of our dusky cousins, though it is by no means necessary that they should be restricted to the lowest. But whatever the position of stable equilibrium into which the laws of social gravitation may bring the negro, all responsibility for the result will henceforward lie between Nature and him. The white man may wash his hands of it, and the Caucasian conscience be void of reproach for evermore. And this, if we look to the bottom of the matter, is the real justification for the abolition policy.

The doctrine of equal natural rights may be an illogical delusion; emancipation may convert the slave from a well fed animal into a pauperised man; mankind may even have to do without cotton shirts; but all these evils must be faced, if the moral law, that no human being can arbitrarily dominate over another without grievous damage to his own nature, be, as many think, as readily demonstrable by experiment as any physical truth. If this be true, no slavery can be abolished without a double emancipation, and the master will benefit by freedom more than the freed-man.

The like considerations apply to all the other questions of emancipation which are at present stirring the world—the multifarious demands that classes of mankind shall be relieved from restrictions imposed by the artifice of man, and not by the necessities of Nature. One of the most important, if not the most important, of all these, is that which daily threatens to become the "irrepressible" woman question. What social and political rights have women? What ought they to be allowed, or not allowed to do, be and suffer? And, as involved in, and underlying all these questions, how ought they to be educated? . . .

Granting the alleged defects of women, is it not somewhat absurd to sanction and maintain a system of education which would seem to have been specially contrived to exaggerate all these defects?

Naturally not so firmly strung, nor so well balanced, as boys, girls are in great measure debarred from the sports and physical exercises which are justly thought absolutely necessary for the full development of the vigour of the more favoured sex. Women are, by nature, more excitable than men—prone to be swept by tides of emotion, proceeding from hidden and inward, as well as from obvious and external causes; and female education does its best to weaken every physical counterpoise to this nervous mobility—tends in all ways to stimulate the emotional part of the mind and stunt the rest. We find girls naturally timid, inclined to dependence, born conservatives; and we teach them that independence is unladylike; that blind faith is the right frame of mind; and that whatever we may be permitted, and indeed encouraged, to do to our brother, our sister is to be left to the tyranny of authority and tradition. With few insignificant exceptions, girls have been educated either to be drudges, or toys, beneath man; or a sort of angels above him; the highest ideal aimed at oscillating between Clärchen and Beatrice. The possibility that the ideal of womanhood lies neither in the fair saint, nor in the fair sinner; that the female type of character is neither better nor worse than the male, but only weaker; that women are meant neither to be men's guides nor their playthings, but their comrades, their fellows and their equals, so far as Nature puts no bar to that equality, does not seem to have entered into the minds of those who have had the conduct of the education of girls.

If the present system of female education stands self-condemned, as inherently absurd; and if that which we have just indicated is the true position of woman, what is the first step towards a better state of things? We reply, emancipate girls. Recognise the fact that they share the senses, perceptions, feelings, reasoning powers, emotions, of boys, and that the mind of the average girl is less different from that of the average boy, than the mind of one boy is from that of another; so that whatever argument justifies a given education for all boys, justifies its application to girls as well. So far from imposing artificial restrictions upon the acquirement of knowledge by women, throw every facility in their way. . . . Let us have "sweet girl graduates" by all means. They will be none the less sweet for a little wisdom; and the "golden hair" will not curl less gracefully outside the head by reason of there being brains within . . . Let them, if they so please, become merchants, barristers, politicians. Let them have a fair field, but let them understand, as the necessary correlative, that they are to have no favour. Let Nature alone sit high above the lists, "rain influence and judge the prize."

And the result? For our parts, though loth to prophesy, we believe it will be that of other emancipations. Women will find their place, and it will neither be that in which they have been held, nor that to which some of them aspire. Nature's old salique law will not be repealed, and no change of dynasty will be effected. The big chests, the massive brains, the vigorous muscles and stout frames, of the best men will carry the day, whenever it is worth their while to contest the prizes of life with the best women. And the hardship of it is, that the very improvement of the women will lessen their chances. Better mothers will bring forth better sons, and the impetus gained by the one sex will be transmitted, in the next generation, to the other. The most Darwinian of theorists will not venture to propound the doctrine, that the physical disabilities under which women have hitherto laboured, in the struggle for existence with men, are likely to be removed by even the most skilfully conducted process of education selection. . . .

In consequence of some domestic difficulties, Sydney Smith is said to have suggested that it would have been good for the human race had the model offered by the hive been followed, and had all the working part of the female community been neuters. Failing any thoroughgoing reform of this kind, we see nothing for it but the old division of humanity into men potentially, or actually, fathers, and women potentially, if not actually, mothers. And we fear that so long as this potential motherhood is her lot, woman will be found to be fearfully weighted in the race of life.

The duty of man is to see that not a grain is piled upon that load beyond what Nature imposes; that injustice is not added to inequality.

A Liberal Education: and Where to Find It

Huxley begins by analyzing mercilessly the ulterior motives of some of his contemporaries who were advocating education for the masses. He supports such education on the unfashionable grounds that the masses are human beings and that human beings flourish best with education and perish without it. There is no doubt that Huxley would question some of those who, in our own time, support education on the grounds that we need trained manpower if we are to compete successfully with other industrialized countries. He was concerned with men and women, not with manpower. The kind of education that he recommends is one that leads man to a knowledge of the laws of the natural world. Nature educates everyone from birth onwards, but her methods are harsh and wasteful. A deliberate and artificial education is needed to compensate for the defects in natural education. This, then, is a liberal education—one that enables man to live harmoniously with nature, escaping her punishments and benefitting from her rewards, through knowledge of and obedience to her laws of operation. Contemporary English education did not, in Huxley's eyes, begin to measure up to these requirements.

Originally given as an address to the South London Working Men's College, January 4, 1868, this lecture was subsequently published in *Macmillan's Magazine,* and reprinted in Thomas Henry Huxley, *Lay Sermons, Addresses, and Reviews,* published by Appleton in New York in 1870.

The business which the South London Working Men's College has undertaken is a great work; indeed, I might say, that Education, with which that college proposes to grapple, is the greatest work of all those which lie ready to a man's hand just at present.

And, at length, this fact is becoming generally recognised. . . . In fact, there is a chorus of voices, almost distressing in their harmony, raised in favour of the doctrine that education is the great panacea for human troubles, and that, if the country is not shortly to go to the dogs, everybody must be educated.

The politicians tell us, "you must educate the masses because they are going to be masters." The clergy join in the cry for education, for they affirm that the people are drifting away from church and chapel into the broadest infidelity. The manufacturers and the capitalists swell the chorus lustily. They declare that ignorance makes bad workmen; that England will soon be unable to turn out cotton goods, or steam engines, cheaper than other people; and then, Ichabod! Ichabod! the glory will be departed from us. And a few voices are lifted up in favour of the doctrine that the masses should be educated because they are men and women with unlimited capacities of being, doing, and suffering, and that it is as true now, as ever it was, that the people perish for lack of knowledge. . . .

These people inquire whether it is the masses alone who need a re-formed and improved education. They ask whether the richest of our public schools might not well be made to supply knowledge, as well as gentlemanly habits, a strong class feeling, and eminent proficiency in cricket. They seem to think that the noble foundations of our old universities are hardly fulfilling their functions in their present posture of half-clerical seminaries, half racecourses, where men are trained to win a senior wranglership, or a double-first, as horses are trained to win a cup, with as little reference to the needs of after-life in the case of the man as in that of the racer. And, while as zealous for education as the rest, they affirm that, if the education of the richer classes were such as to fit them to be the leaders and the governors of the poorer; and, if the education of the poorer classes were such as to enable them to appreciate really wise guidance and good governance; the politicians need not fear mob-law, nor the clergy lament their want of flocks, nor the capitalists prognosticate the annihilation of the prosperity of the country. . . .

Suppose it were perfectly certain that the life and fortune of every one of us would, one day or other, depend upon his winning or losing a game at chess. Don't you think that we should all consider it to be a primary duty to learn at least the names and the moves of the pieces; to have a notion of a gambit, and a keen eye for all the means of giving and getting out of check? Do you not think that we should look with a disapprobation amounting to scorn, upon the father who allowed his son, or the state which allowed its members, to grow up without knowing a pawn from a knight?

Yet it is a very plain and elementary truth, that the life, the fortune, and the happiness of every one of us, and, more or less, of those who are connected with us, do depend upon our knowing something of the rules of a game infinitely more difficult and complicated than chess. It is a game which has been played for untold ages, every man and woman of us being one of the two players in a game of his or her own. The chess-board is the world, the pieces are the phenomena of the universe, the rules of the game are what we call the laws of Nature. The player on the other side is hidden from us. We know that his play is always fair, just, and patient. But also we know, to our cost, that he never overlooks a mistake, or makes the smallest allowance for ignorance. To the man who plays well, the highest stakes are paid, with that sort of overflowing generosity with which the strong shows delight in strength. And one who plays ill is checkmated—without haste, but without remorse. . . .

Well, what I mean by Education is learning the rules of this mighty game. In other words, education is the instruction of the intellect in the laws of Nature, under which name I include not merely things and their forces, but men and their ways; and the fashioning of the affections and of the will into an earnest and loving desire to move in harmony with those laws. For me, education means neither more nor less than this. Anything which professes to call itself education must be tried by this standard, and if it fails to stand the test, I will not call it education, whatever may be the force of authority, or of numbers, upon the other side.

It is important to remember that, in strictness, there is no such thing as an uneducated man. Take an extreme case. Suppose that an adult man, in the full vigour of his faculties, could be suddenly placed in the world, as Adam is said to have been, and then left to do as he best might. How long would he be left uneducated? Not five minutes. Nature would begin to teach him, through the eye, the ear, the touch, the properties of objects. Pain and pleasure would be at his elbow telling him to do this and avoid that; and by slow degrees the man would receive an education, which, if narrow, would be thorough, real, and adequate to his circumstances, though there would be no extras and very few accomplishments. . . .

Thus the question of compulsory education is settled so far as Nature is concerned. Her bill on that question was framed and passed long ago. But, like all compulsory legislation, that of Nature is harsh and wasteful in its operation. Ignorance is visited as sharply as wilful disobedience—incapacity meets with the same punishment as crime. Nature's discipline is not even a word and a blow, and the blow first; but the blow without the word. It is left to you to find out why your ears are boxed.

The object of what we commonly call education—that education in which man intervenes and which I shall distinguish as artificial education—is to make good these defects in Nature's methods; to prepare the child to receive Nature's education, neither incapably nor ignorantly, nor with wilful disobedience; and to understand the preliminary symptoms of her displeasure, without waiting for the box on the ear. In short, all artificial education ought to be an anticipation of natural education. And a liberal education is an artificial education, which has not only prepared a man to escape the great evils of disobedience to natural laws, but has trained him to appreciate and to seize upon the rewards, which Nature scatters with as free a hand as her penalties.

That man, I think, has had a liberal education, who has been so trained in youth that his body is the ready servant of his will, and does with ease and pleasure all the work that, as a mechanism, it is capable of; whose intellect is a clear, cold, logic engine, with all its parts of equal strength, and in smooth working order; ready, like a steam engine, to be turned to any kind of work, and spin the gossamers as well as forge the anchors of the mind; whose mind is stored with a knowledge of the great and fundamental truths of Nature and of the laws of her operations; one who, no stunted ascetic, is full of life and fire, but whose passions are trained to come to heel by a vigorous will, the servant of a tender conscience who has learned to love all beauty, whether of Nature or of art, to hate all vileness, and to respect others as himself.

Such an one and no other, I conceive, has had a liberal education; for he is, as completely as a man can be, in harmony with Nature. He will make the best of her, and she of him. They will get on together rarely; she as his ever beneficent mother; he as her mouth-piece, her conscious self, her minister and interpreter.

Scientific Education

In Huxley's time, science was virtually ignored in English schools. The little "scientific" instruction that existed was a grotesque travesty of the term. No one was a more consistent or eloquent champion of *genuine* scientific education than Huxley. But he did not commit the opposite and equal error of many of his classical opponents by suggesting that a scientific education alone is enough to produce an educated person. He wanted science to take its place in a balanced program of literary, aesthetic, and scientific studies. Moreover, he was deeply concerned with the *way* in which a scientific education should be conducted. Even today it is doubtful whether most of the work that goes on in schools in the name of science would satisfy Huxley's stringent but sane requirements. It is not enough to read about scientific laws: one must "feel the pull" of them for oneself. And to those who claim that science is too difficult for the stupid masses, Huxley answers that such "stupidity" is not inborn but is created by the kind of educational crimes that we commit on children.

First delivered before the Liverpool Philomathic Society in April 1869, this lecture was subsequently published in *Macmillan's Magazine,* and reprinted in Thomas Henry Huxley, *Lay Sermons, Addresses, and Reviews,* published by Appleton in New York in 1870.

I hope you will consider that the arguments I have now stated, even if there were no better ones, constitute a sufficient apology for urging the introduction of science into schools. The next question to which I have to address myself is, What sciences ought to be thus taught? And this is one of the most important of questions, because my side (I am afraid I am a terribly candid friend) sometimes spoils its cause by going in for too much. There are other forms of culture beside physi-

293

cal science; and I should be profoundly sorry to see the fact forgotten, or even to observe a tendency to starve, or cripple, literary, or aesthetic, culture for the sake of science. Such a narrow view of the nature of education has nothing to do with my firm conviction that a complete and thorough scientific culture ought to be introduced into all schools. By this, however, I do not mean that every schoolboy should be taught everything in science. That would be a very absurd thing to conceive, and a very mischievous thing to attempt. What I mean is, that no boy nor girl should leave school without possessing a grasp of the general character of science, and without having been disciplined, more or less, in the methods of all sciences; so that, when turned into the world to make their own way, they shall be prepared to face scientific problems, not by knowing at once the conditions of every problem, or by being able at once to solve it; but by being familiar with the general current of scientific thought, and by being able to apply the methods of science in the proper way, when they have acquainted themselves with the conditions of the special problem. . . .

If the great benefits of scientific training are sought, it is essential that such training should be real: that is to say, that the mind of the scholar should be brought into direct relation with fact, that he should not merely be told a thing, but made to see by the use of his own intellect and ability that the thing is *so* and not otherwise. The great peculiarity of scientific training, that in virtue of which it cannot be replaced by any other discipline whatsoever, is this bringing of the mind directly into contact with fact, and practising the intellect in the completest form of induction; that is to say, in drawing conclusions from particular facts made known by immediate observation of Nature. . . .

But if scientific training is to yield its most eminent results, it must, I repeat, be made practical. That is to say, in explaining to a child the general phænomena of Nature, you must, as far as possible, give reality to your teaching by object-lessons; in teaching him botany, he must handle the plants and dissect the flowers for himself; in teaching him physics and chemistry, you must not be solicitous to fill him with information, but you must be careful that what he learns he knows of his own knowledge. Don't be satisfied with telling him that a magnet attracts iron. Let him see that it does; let him feel the pull of the one upon the other for himself. And, especially, tell him that it is his duty to doubt until he is compelled, by the absolute authority of Nature, to believe that which is written in books. Pursue this discipline carefully and conscientiously, and you may make sure that, however scanty may be the measure of information which you have poured into the boy's

mind, you have created an intellectual habit of priceless value in practical life. . . .

People talk of the difficulty of teaching young children such matters,
and in the same breath insist upon their learning their Catechism, which
contains propositions far harder to comprehend than anything in the
educational course I have proposed. Again: I am incessantly told that
we, who advocate the introduction of science into schools, make no
allowance for the stupidity of the average boy or girl; but, in my belief,
that stupidity, in nine cases out of ten, "*fit, non nascitur*," and is developed by a long process of parental and pedagogic repression of the
natural intellectual appetites, accompanied by a persistent attempt to
create artificial ones for food which is not only tasteless, but essentially
indigestible.

Universities: Actual and Ideal

In his recommendations for university education, Huxley reiterates many of his favorite themes. He shows his breadth of view by arguing that the university should take responsibility for the development of man's aesthetic faculty. In recommending Professors of Fine Arts in the university, Huxley was far in advance of his time. Again, he insists that the educated man is not one who satisfies certain rituals or appearances but one who *knows* through first-hand experience. He must have knowledge of science not just from books but through direct experience of the scientific method. In taking a cool look at examinations, Huxley anticipates our present sad domination by them; he regards them as necessary but evil. To be educated is to hold usable knowledge, not merely to have a facility for passing examinations. Huxley's model emerges as a human being who is at home in the natural world because of his intimate knowledge of its phenomena and its laws.

This essay was Huxley's Inaugural Address as Lord Rector of the University of Aberdeen, February 27, 1874. It was printed in the *Contemporary Review* in 1874, and reprinted in Thomas Henry Huxley, *Science and Culture, and Other Essays*, published by Appleton in New York in 1884.

In an ideal University, as I conceive it, a man should be able to obtain instruction in all forms of knowledge, and discipline in the use of all the methods by which knowledge is obtained. In such an University, the force of living example should fire the student with a noble ambition to emulate the learning of learned men, and to follow in the footsteps of the explorers of new fields of knowledge. And the very air he breathes should be charged with that enthusiasm for truth, that fanaticism of veracity, which is a greater possession than much learning; a nobler gift than the power of increasing knowledge; by so much greater and nobler than these, as the moral nature of man is greater than the intellectual; for veracity is the heart of morality.

But the man who is all morality and intellect, although he may be good and even great, is, after all, only half a man. There is beauty in the moral world and in the intellectual world; but there is also a beauty which is neither moral nor intellectual—the beauty of the world of Art. There are men who are devoid of the power of seeing it, as there are men who are born deaf and blind, and the loss of those, as of these, is simply infinite. There are others in whom it is an over-powering passion; happy men, born with the productive, or at lowest, the appreciative, genius of the Artist. But, in the mass of mankind, the Æsthetic faculty, like the reasoning power and the moral sense, needs to be roused, directed, and cultivated; and I know not why the development of that side of his nature, through which man has access to a perennial spring of ennobling pleasure, should be omitted from any comprehensive scheme of University education. . . .

It is only fair to the Scottish Universities to point out that they have long understood the value of Science as a branch of general education. I observe, with the greatest satisfaction, that candidates for the degree of Master of Arts in this University are required to have a knowledge, not only of Mental and Moral Philosophy, and of Mathematics and Natural Philosophy, but of Natural History, in addition to the ordinary Latin and Greek course; and that a candidate may take honours in these subjects and in Chemistry.

I do not know what the requirements of your examiners may be, but I sincerely trust they are not satisfied with a mere book knowledge of these matters. For my own part, I would not raise a finger, if I could thereby introduce mere book work in science into every Arts curriculum in the country. Let those who want to study books devote themselves to Literature, in which we have the perfection of books, both as to substance and as to form. If I may paraphrase Hobbes's well-known aphorism, I would say that "books are the money of Literature, but only the counters of Science," Science (in the sense in which I now use the term) being the knowledge of fact, of which every verbal description is but an incomplete and symbolic expression. And be assured that no teaching of science is worth anything, as a mental discipline, which is not based upon direct perception of the facts, and practical exercise of the observing and logical faculties upon them. Even in such a simple matter as the mere comprehension of form, ask the most practised and widely informed anatomist what is the difference between his knowledge of a structure which he has read about, and his knowledge of the same structure when he has seen it for himself; and he will tell you that the two things are not comparable—the difference is infinite. Thus I am very strongly inclined to agree with some learned schoolmasters who say that, in their experience, the teaching of science is all waste time. As they teach it, I have no doubt it is. But to teach it otherwise, requires an amount of personal labour and a development of means and appliances, which must strike horror and dismay into a man accustomed to mere book work; and who has been in the habit of teaching a class of fifty without much strain upon his energies. And this is one of the real difficulties in the way of the introduction of physical science into the ordinary University course, to which I have alluded. It is a difficulty which will not be overcome, until years of patient study have organised scientific teaching as well as, or I hope better than, classical teaching has been organised hitherto. . . .

Examination—thorough, searching examination—is an indispensable accompaniment of teaching; but I am almost inclined to commit myself to the very heterodox proposition that it is a necessary evil. I am a very old Examiner, having, for some twenty years past, been occupied with examinations on a considerable scale, of all sorts and conditions of men, and women too,—from the boys and girls of elementary schools to the candidates for Honours and Fellowships in the Universities. I will not say that, in this case as in so many others, the adage, that familiarity breeds contempt, holds good; but my admiration for the existing system of examination and its products, does not wax warmer as I see more of it. Examination, like fire, is a good servant, but a bad master; and there seems to me to be some danger of its becoming our master. I by no means stand alone in this opinion. Experienced friends of mine do not hesitate to say that students whose career they watch, appear to them to become deteriorated by the constant effort to pass this or that examination, just as we hear of men's brains becoming affected by the daily necessity of catching a train. They work to pass, not to know; and outraged science takes her revenge. They do pass, and they don't know. I have passed sundry examinations in my time, not without credit, and I confess I am ashamed to think how very little real knowledge underlay the torrent of stuff which I was able to pour out on paper. In fact, that which examination, as ordinarily conducted, tests, is simply a man's power of work under stimulus, and his capacity for rapidly and clearly producing that which, for the time, he has got into his mind. Now, these faculties are by no means to be despised. They are of great value in practical life, and are the making of many an advocate, and of many a so-called statesman. But in the pursuit of truth, scientific or other, they count for very little, unless they are supplemented by that long-continued, patient "intending of the mind," as Newton phrased it, which makes very little show in Examinations.

On the Study of Biology

In the course of defending the value of the study of biology, Huxley outlines a biological view of the nature of man and his place in the universe. The biologists place man squarely in nature as one of the higher animals. The only quality that they find in man that is not also present in other animals is the artistic faculty. Huxley goes on to argue for instruction in biology as part of the education of such a creature, and makes some practical suggestions for the treatment of biology in schools. He points out prophetically the danger that science will be taught as badly as classics—by starting with the "grammar" (definitions and classifications) instead of with first-hand experience of the subject matter. On this score he makes what was to become a famous suggestion—that the handiest subject for the study of biology is oneself. It is perhaps unnecessary to point out that Huxley's warning about science teaching has been, until very recently, largely unheeded in our schools.

This lecture was delivered on the occasion of an exhibition of scientific apparatus in the South Kensington Museum in London in 1876. It is reprinted here from Thomas H. Huxley, *Select Works*, published by John Alden in London in 1886.

I shall try to point out to you that you will feel the need of some knowledge of biology at a great many turns of this present nineteenth century life of ours. For example, most of us attach great importance to the conception which we entertain of the position of man in this universe, and his relation to the rest of nature. We have almost all been told, and most of us hold by the tradition, that man occupies an isolated and peculiar position in nature; that though he is in the world, he is not of the world; that his relations to things about him are of a remote character; that his origin is recent, his duration likely to be short, and that he is the great central figure round which other things in this world revolve. . . .

The biologists tell us that all this is an entire mistake. They turn to the physical organization of man. They examine his whole structure, his bony frame and all that clothes it. They resolve him into the finest particles into which the microscope will enable them to break it up. They consider the performance of his various functions and activities, and they look at the manner in which he occurs on the surface of the world. Then they turn to other animals, and taking the first handy domestic animal—say a dog—they profess to be able to demonstrate that the analysis of the dog leads them, in gross, to precisely the same results as the analysis of the man; that they find almost identically the same bones, having the same relations; that they can name the muscles of the dog by the names of the muscles of the man, and the nerves of the dog by those of the nerves of the man, and that such structures and organs of the sense as we find in the man such also we find in the dog; they analyze the brain and spinal cord, and they find that the nomenclature which fits the one answers for the other. They carry their microscopic inquiries in the case of the dog as far as they can, and they find that his body is resolvable into the same elements as those of the man. Moreover, they trace back the dog's and the man's development, and they find that, at a certain stage of their existence, the two creatures are not distinguishable the one from the other; they find that the dog and his kind have a certain distribution over the surface of the world, comparable in its way to the distribution of the human species. What is true of the dog they tell us is true of all the higher animals; and they assert that they can lay down a common plan for the whole of these creatures, and regard the man and the dog, the horse and the ox as minor modifications of one great fundamental unity. Moreover, the investigations of the last three-quarters of a century have proved, they tell us, that similar inquiries, carried out through all the different kinds of animals which are met with in nature, will lead us, not in one straight series, but by many roads, step by step, gradation by gradation, from man, at the summit, to specks of animated jelly at the bottom of the series. . . .

Thus, biologists have arrived at the conclusion that a fundamental uniformity of structure pervades the animal and vegetable worlds, and that plants and animals differ from one another simply as diverse modifications of the same great general plan.

Again, they tell us the same story in regard to the study of function. They admit the large and important interval which, at the present time, separates the manifestations of the mental faculties, observable in the higher forms of mankind, and even in the lower forms, such as we know them, from those exhibited by other animals; but, at the same time, they tell us that the foundations, or rudiments, of almost all the faculties of man are to be met with in the lower animals; that there is a unity of mental faculty as well as of bodily structure, and that, here also, the difference is a difference of degree and not of kind. I said "almost all," for a reason. Among the many distinctions which have been drawn between the lower creatures and ourselves, there is one which is hardly ever insisted on, but which may be very fitly spoken of in a place so largely devoted to Art as that in which we are assembled. It is this, that while, among various kinds of animals, it is possible to discover traces of all the other faculties of man, especially the faculty of mimicry, yet that particular form of mimicry which shows itself in the imitation of form, either by modelling or by drawing, is not to be met with. As far as I know, there is no sculpture or modelling, and decidedly no painting or drawing, of animal origin. I mention the fact, in order that such comfort may be derived therefrom as artists may feel inclined to take. . . .

Lastly comes the question as to when biological study may best be pursued. I do not see any valid reason why it should not be made, to a certain extent, a part of ordinary school training. I have long advocated this view, and I am perfectly certain that it can be carried out with ease, and not only with ease, but with very considerable profit to those who are taught; but then such instruction must be adapted to the minds and needs of the scholars. They used to have a very odd way of teaching the classical languages when I was a boy. The first task set you was to learn the rules of the Latin grammar in the Latin language—that being the language you were going to learn! I thought then that this was an odd way of learning a language, but did not venture to rebel against the judgment of my superiors. Now, perhaps, I am not so modest as I was then, and I allow myself to think that it was a very absurd fashion. But it would be no less absurd, if we were to set about teaching Biology by putting into the hands of boys a series of definitions of the classes and orders of the animal kingdom, and making them repeat them by heart. That is so very favorite a method of teaching, that I sometimes fancy the spirit of the old classical system has entered into the new scientific system, in which case I would much rather that any pretence at scientific teaching were abolished altogether. What really has to be done is to get into the young mind some notion of what animal and vegetable life is. In this matter, you have to consider practical convenience as well as other things. There are difficulties in the way of a lot of boys making messes with slugs and snails; it might not work in practice. But there is a very convenient and handy animal which everybody has at hand, and that is himself; and it is a very easy and simple matter to obtain common plants. Hence the general truths of anatomy and physiology can be taught to young people in a very real fashion by dealing with the broad facts of human structure. Such viscera as they cannot very well examine in themselves, such as hearts, lungs, and livers, may be obtained from the nearest butcher's shop. In respect to teaching something about the biology of plants, there is no practical difficulty, because almost any of the common plants will do, and plants do not make a mess—at least they do not make an unpleasant mess; so that, in my judgment, the best form of Biology for teaching to very young people is elementary human physiology on the one hand, and the elements of botany on the other; beyond that I do not think it will be feasible to advance for some time to come.

Science and Culture

Huxley gave this address at the opening of Sir Josiah Mason's Science College at Birmingham in 1880. Mason had left an explicit injunction that his college should make no provision for "mere literary instruction and education." Huxley takes this statement as the basis for an examination of the relationship between science and culture and of the place of science in the background of the educated person. At this time, advocates of scientific education were customarily attacked on two sides: by practical men of business, who believed in the rule of thumb and who saw no connection between theory and practice; and by classical scholars, who regarded themselves as the sole guardians of liberal culture. Huxley himself recognized the value of literary and classical studies, but was opposed to their monopolistic position in the curriculum at a time when scientific knowledge was expanding rapidly. His model of the educated man is not a "lop-sided" man with a purely literary of purely scientific background, but one who is equipped, through a well-balanced education, to deal effectively with the natural world.

The address is reprinted from Thomas Henry Huxley, *Science and Culture, and Other Essays,* published by Appleton in New York in 1884.

How often have we not been told that the study of physical science is incompetent to confer culture; that it touches none of the higher problems of life; and, what is worse, that the continual devotion to scientific studies tends to generate a narrow and bigoted belief in the applicability of scientific methods to the search after truth of all kinds. How frequently one has reason to observe that no reply to a troublesome argument tells so well as calling its author a "mere scientific specialist." And, as I am afraid it is not permissible to speak of this form of opposition to scientific education in the past tense; may we not expect to be told that this, not only omission, but prohibition, of "mere literary instruction and education" is a patent example of scientific narrow-mindedness? . . .

I hold very strongly by two convictions—The first is, that neither the discipline nor the subject-matter of classical education is of such direct value to the student of physical science as to justify the expenditure of valuable time upon either; and the second is, that for the purpose of attaining real culture, an exclusively scientific education is at least as effectual as an exclusively literary education.

I need hardly point out to you that these opinions, especially the latter, are diametrically opposed to those of the great majority of educated Englishmen, influenced as they are by school and university traditions. In their belief, culture is obtainable only by a liberal education; and a liberal education is synonymous, not merely with education and instruction in literature, but in one particular form of literature, namely, that of Greek and Roman antiquity. They hold that the man who has learned Latin and Greek, however little, is educated; while he who is versed in other branches of knowledge, however deeply, is a more or less respectable specialist, not admissible into the cultured caste. The stamp of the educated man, the University degree, is not for him. . . .

We have here to deal with two distinct propositions. The first, that a criticism of life is the essence of culture; the second, that literature contains the materials which suffice for the construction of such a criticism.

I think that we must all assent to the first proposition. For culture certainly means something quite different from learning or technical skill. It implies the possession of an ideal, and the habit of critically estimating the value of things by comparison with a theoretic standard. Perfect culture should supply a complete theory of life, based upon a clear knowledge alike of its possibilities and of its limitations.

But we may agree to all this, and yet strongly dissent from the assumption that literature alone is competent to supply this knowledge. After having learnt all that Greek, Roman, and Eastern antiquity have thought and said, and all that modern literatures have to tell us, it is not self-evident that we have laid a sufficiently broad and deep foundation for that criticism of life which constitutes culture.

Indeed, to any one acquainted with the scope of physical science, it is not at all evident. Considering progress only in the "intellectual and spiritual sphere," I find myself wholly unable to admit that either nations or individuals will really advance, if their common outfit draws nothing from the stores of physical science. I should say that an army, without weapons of precision, and with no particular base of operations, might more hopefully enter upon a campaign on the Rhine, than man, devoid of a knowledge of what physical science has done in the last century, upon a criticism of life. . . .

This distinctive character of our own times lies in the vast and constantly increasing part which is played by natural knowledge. Not only is our daily life shaped by it, not only does the prosperity of millions of men depend upon it, but our whole theory of life has long been influenced, consciously or unconsciously, by the general conceptions of the universe, which have been forced upon us by physical science.

In fact, the most elementary acquaintance with the results of scientific investigation shows us that they offer a broad and striking contradiction to the opinions so implicitly credited and taught in the middle ages.

The notions of the beginning and the end of the world entertained by our forefathers are no longer credible. It is very certain that the earth is not the chief body in the material universe, and that the world is not subordinated to man's use. It is even more certain that nature is the expression of a definite order with which nothing interferes, and that the chief business of mankind is to learn that order and govern themselves accordingly. Moreover this scientific "criticism of life" presents itself to us with different credentials from any other. If appeals not to authority, nor to what anybody may have thought or said, but to nature. It admits that all our interpretations of natural fact are more or less imperfect and symbolic, and bids the learner seek for truth not among words but among things. It warns us that the assertion which outstrips evidence is not only a blunder but a crime.

The purely classical education advocated by the representatives of the Humanists in our day, gives no inkling of all this. A man may be a better scholar than Erasmus, and know no more of the chief causes of the present intellectual fermentation than Erasmus did. Scholarly and pious persons, worthy of all respect, favour us with allocutions upon the sadness of the antagonism of science to their mediaeval way of thinking, which betray an ignorance of the first principles of scientific investigation, an incapacity for understanding what a man of science means by veracity, and an unconsciousness of the weight of established scientific truths, which is almost comical.

There is no great force in the *tu quoque* argument, or else the advocates of scientific education might fairly enough retort upon the modern Humanists that they may be learned specialists, but that they possess no such sound foundation for a criticism of life as deserves the name of culture. And, indeed, if we were disposed to be cruel, we might urge that the Humanists have brought this reproach upon themselves, not because they are too full of the spirit of the ancient Greek, but because they lack it. . . .

I am the last person to question the importance of genuine literary education, or to suppose that intellectual culture can be complete without it. An exclusively scientific training will bring about a mental twist as surely as an exclusively literary training. The value of the cargo does not compensate for a ship's being out of trim; and I should be very sorry to think that the Scientific College would turn out none but lop-sided men.

12 *The Communal Man: Marx*

The conditions that challenged Karl Marx (1818–1883) were the circumstances of life and work that nineteenth-century industrialism had brought upon the working class. Marx's response has altered the course of history in the past century and it continues to affect the lives of millions of people all over the world. His ideas were formed in reaction to the economic implications of capitalism and to the philosophical implications of Hegelianism. The latter was an important influence on him during his time at the University of Berlin in the 1830s. A crucial encounter for Marx was with Friedrich Engels (1820–1895), whom he met in Paris in 1844. Engels was manager of one of his father's factories near Manchester and hence was well acquainted with English industrial conditions. The two men discovered that they were in remarkable philosophical agreement, and hence began a life-long friendship and collaboration that resulted in some of the most influential works ever written. So close was their accordance that where one writes "Marx" it could almost always be substituted by "Marx and Engels."

A central concern of these men was to cure the alienation and dehumanization of man caused by the exploitative forces of capitalism. Under capitalism, Marx argued, men are regarded as things, as objects or functionaries more or less useful to the productive process. Because politics, law, and the forces of control are in the hands of the ruling class, who will not voluntarily surrender their power, Marx saw the need for a proletarian revolution in order to bring about communism. Only with the advent of communism, he argued, will the conditions of life improve, for then the State will represent the many rather than the few. It is necessary for the State to be actively involved in the regeneration and rehumanization of the people. The Soviet Union tried to bring about such a utopia through collectivist coercion and social manipulation. But this was a distortion of Marx's views and just as great an error as the liberal error of leaving men alone. There is a need for State intervention to remove gross inequalities and to expand opportunities, but ultimately human regeneration is a task for each individual.

Collectivism is as arid as *laissez-faire* individualism. What is needed for man's growth toward maturity is genuine community, that is, the voluntary drawing together of autonomous and socially responsible individuals. The human model that Marx offers for our examination is not the irresponsible individualist nor the torpid collectivist but the accountable communal man. In Marx's vision, the opposition between individual and group is healed. The communal man attains freedom not by fleeing from social relationships but precisely *through* social relationships. Individual freedom requires social authority.

Capital

Marx was appalled and angered by the conditions of life imposed on the English working class by the capitalist system. The principal work in which he documented and analyzed the exploitation and degradation of the worker was *Das Kapital,* the first volume of which appeared in 1867. The philosophical basis of Marx's analysis is to be found in his doctrine of historical materialism and in his use of the dialectical method, which he sharply distinguishes from the Hegelian dialectic. For Marx, the material dimension of history is primary. Economic production is the basis of life, and the prevailing ideas (religious, educational, and political) of a society are determined by its economic structure. The dialectical view of history led Marx to postulate a thesis of feudalism, dominated by the landowner; an antithesis of capitalism, dominated by the industrialist; and a resolution in the synthesis of communism, dominated by the proletariat. The phase of the capitalist bourgeoisie, he suggests, has now passed. There is no hope for the development of a self-fulfilled, socially realized individual under capitalism. In order to create the conditions under which this ideal man can flourish, there is need for proletarian revolt. Drawing heavily on the work of his friend Friedrich Engels and on the reports of Royal Commissions, Marx documents his claims with illustrations from nineteenth-century English industrialism. The introduction of machinery is used not to benefit the people who tend the machines but further to debase their lives. By using women and children in the factory, the capitalist employer reduces the independence and power of the man. Since the superior strength and experience of the man are made to count for less, his wages can be reduced. He is forced to sell the labor of his wife and children in order to survive. Although the Factory Acts enjoined that factory owners should provide education for their employees under fourteen years of age, the regulations were widely disregarded. And the measures taken to satisfy the terms of the Acts were often a mockery, as Marx attests.

These excerpts are taken from Karl Marx, *Capital: A Critique of Political Economy*, translated by Samuel Moore and Edward Aveling, edited by Frederick Engels, revised by Ernest Unterman, published by Random House, Inc., in New York in 1906.

PREFACE

To prevent possible misunderstanding, a word. I paint the capitalist and the landlord in no sense *couleur de rose*. But here individuals are dealt with only in so far as they are the personifications of economic categories, embodiments of particular class-relations and class-interests. My stand-point, from which the evolution of the economic formation of society is viewed as a process of natural history, can less than any other make the individual responsible for relations whose creature he socially remains, however much he may subjectively raise himself above them. . . .

My dialectic method is not only different from the Hegelian, but is its direct opposite. To Hegel, the life-process of the human brain, i.e., the process of thinking, which under the name of "the Idea," he even transforms into an independent subject, is the *demiurgos* of the real world, and the real world is only the external, phenomenal form of "the Idea." With me, on the contrary, the ideal is nothing else than the material world reflected by the human mind, and translated into forms of thought.

The mystifying side of Hegelian dialectic I criticised nearly thirty years ago, at a time when it was still the fashion. . . . The mystification which dialectic suffers in Hegel's hands, by no means prevents him from being the first to present its general form of working in a comprehensive and conscious manner. With him it is standing on its head. It must be turned right side up again, if you would discover the rational kernel within the mystical shell. . . .

PART IV

CHAPTER XV

SECTION 3. THE APPROXIMATE EFFECTS OF MACHINERY ON THE WORKMAN.

The starting point of Modern Industry is, as we have shown, the revolution in the instruments of labour, and this revolution attains its most highly developed form in the organised system of machinery in a factory. Before we inquire how human material is incorporated with this objective organism, let us consider some general effects of this revolution on the labourer himself.

a. Appropriation of Supplementary Labour-power by Capital. The Employment of Women and Children.

In so far as machinery dispenses with muscular power, it becomes a means of employing labourers of slight muscular strength, and those whose bodily development is incomplete, but whose limbs are all the more supple. The labour of women and children was, therefore, the first thing sought for by capitalists who used machinery. That mighty substitute for labour and labourers was forthwith changed into a means for increasing the number of wage-labourers by enrolling, under the direct sway of capital, every member of the workman's family, without distinction of age or sex. Compulsory work for the capitalist usurped the place, not only of the children's play, but also of free labour at home within moderate limits for the support of the family.*

The value of labour-power was determined, not only by the labour-time necessary to maintain the individual adult labourer, but also by

* Dr. Edward Smith, during the cotton crisis caused by the American Civil War, was sent by the English Government to Lancashire, Cheshire, and other places, to report on the sanitary condition of the cotton operatives. He reported, that from a hygienic point of view, and apart from the banishment of the operatives from the factory atmosphere, the crisis had several advantages. The women now had sufficient leisure to give their infants the breast, instead of poisoning them with "Godfrey's cordial." They had time to learn to cook. Unfortunately the acquisition of this art occurred at a time when they had nothing to cook. But from this we see how capital, for the purposes of its self-expansion, has usurped the labour necessary in the home of the family. This crisis was also utilised to teach sewing to the daughters of the workmen in sewing schools. An American revolution and a universal crisis in order that the working girls, who spin for the whole world, might learn to sew!

that necessary to maintain his family. Machinery, by throwing every member of that family on to the labour market, spreads the value of the man's labour-power over his whole family. It thus depreciates his labour-power. To purchase the labour-power of a family of four workers may, perhaps, cost more than it formerly did to purchase the labour-power of the head of the family, but, in return, four days' labour takes the place of one, and their price falls in proportion to the excess of the surplus-labour of four over the surplus-labour of one. In order that the family may live, four people must now, not only labour, but expend surplus-labour for the capitalist. Thus we see, that machinery, while augmenting the human material that forms the principal object of capital's exploiting power,* at the same time raises the degree of exploitation.

Machinery also revolutionises out and out the contract between the labourer and the capitalist, which formally fixes their mutual relations. Taking the exchange of commodities as our basis, our first assumption was that capitalist and labourer met as free persons, as independent owners of commodities; the one possessing money and means of production, the other labour-power. But now the capitalist buys children and young persons under age. Previously, the workman sold his own labour power, which he disposed of nominally as a free agent. Now he sells wife and child. He has become a slave dealer.† The demand for chil-

* "The numerical increase of labourers has been great, through the growing substitution of female for male, and above all, of childish for adult labour. Three girls of 13, at wages of from 6 shillings to 8 shillings a week, have replaced the one man of mature age, of wages varying from 18 shillings to 45 shillings." (Th. de Quincey: "The Logic of Political Econ., London, 1845." Note to p. 147.) Since certain family functions, such as nursing and suckling children, cannot be entirely suppressed, the mothers confiscated by capital, must try substitutes of some sort. Domestic work, such as sewing and mending, must be replaced by the purchase of ready-made articles. Hence, the diminished expenditure of labour in the house is accompanied by an increased expenditure of money. The cost of keeping the family increases, and balances the greater income. In addition to this, economy and judgment in the consumption and preparation of the means of subsistence becomes impossible. Abundant material relating to these facts, which are concealed by official political economy, is to be found in the Reports of the Inspectors of Factories, of the Children's Employment Commission, and more especially in the Reports on Public Health.

† In striking contrast with the great fact, that the shortening of the hours of labour of women and children in English factories was exacted from capital by the male operatives, we find in the latest reports of the Children's Employment Commission traits of the operative parents in relation to the traffic in children, that are truly revolting and thoroughly like slave-dealing. But the Pharisee of a capitalist, as may be seen from the same reports, denounces this brutality which he himself creates, perpetuates, and exploits, and which he moreover baptizes "Freedom of labour." "Infant labour has been called into aid . . . even to work for their

dren's labour often resembles in form the inquiries for negro slaves, such as were formerly to be read among the advertisements in American journals. . . .

The moral degradation caused by the capitalistic exploitation of women and children has been so exhaustively depicted by F. Engels in his "Lage der Arbeitenden Klasse Englands," and other writers, that I need only mention the subject in this place. But the intellectual desolation, artificially produced by converting immature human beings into mere machines for the fabrication of surplus-value, a state of mind clearly distinguishable from that natural ignorance which keeps the mind fallow without destroying its capacity for development, its natural fertility, this desolation finally compelled even the English Parliament to make elementary education a compulsory condition to the "productive" employment of children under 14 years, in every industry subject to the Factory Acts. The spirit of capitalist production stands out clearly in the ludicrous wording of the so-called education clauses in the Factory Acts, in the absence of an administrative machinery, an absence that again makes the compulsion illusory, in the opposition of the manufacturers themselves to these education clauses, and in the tricks and dodges they put in practice for evading them. "For this the legislature is alone to blame, by having passed a delusive law, which, while it would seem to provide that the children employed in factories shall be *educated*, contains no enactment by which that professed end can be secured. It provides nothing more than that the children shall on certain days of the week, and for a certain number of hours (three) in each day, be inclosed within the four walls of a place called a school, and that the employer of the child shall receive weekly a certificate to that effect signed by a person designated by the subscriber as a schoolmaster or schoolmistress."* Previous to the passing of the amended Factory Act, 1844, it happened, not unfrequently, that the certificates of attendance at school were signed by the schoolmaster or schoolmistress with a cross, as they themselves were unable to write. "On one occasion, on visiting a place called a school, from which certificates of school attendance had issued, I was so struck with the ignorance of the master, that I

---

own daily bread. Without strength to endure such disproportionate toil, without instruction to guide their future life, they have been thrown into a situation physically and morally polluted. The Jewish historian has remarked upon the overthrow of Jerusalem by Titus that it was no wonder it should have been destroyed, with such a signal destruction, when an inhuman mother sacrificed her own offspring to satisfy the cravings of absolute hunger." ("Public Economy Concentrated." Carlisle, 1833, p. 56.)

* Leonard Horner in "Reports of Insp. of Fact. for 30th June, 1857," p. 17.

said to him: "Pray, sir, can you read?" His reply was: "Aye, summat!" and as a justification of his right to grant certificates, he added: "At any rate, I am before my scholars." The inspectors, when the Bill of 1844 was in preparation, did not fail to represent the disgraceful state of the places called schools, certificates from which they were obliged to admit as a compliance with the laws, but they were successful only in obtaining thus much, that since the passing of the Act of 1844, the figures in the school certificate must be filled up in the handwriting of the schoolmaster, who must also sign his Christian and surname in full."* Sir John Kincaid, factory inspector for Scotland, relates experiences of the same kind. "The first school we visited was kept by a Mrs. Ann Killin. Upon asking her to spell her name, she straightway made a mistake, by beginning with the letter C, but correcting herself immediately, she said her name began with a K. On looking at her signature, however, in the school certificate books, I noticed that she spelt it in various ways, while her handwriting left no doubt as to her unfitness to teach. She herself also acknowledged that she could not keep the register. . . . In a second school I found the schoolroom 15 feet long, and 10 feet wide, and counted in this space 75 children, who were gabbling something unintelligible."† But it is not only in the miserable places above referred to that the children obtained certificates of school attendance without having received instruction of any value, for in many schools where there is a competent teacher, his efforts are of little avail from the distracting crowd of children of all ages, from infants of 3 years old and upwards; his livelihood, miserable at the best, depending on the pence received from the greatest number of children whom it is possible to cram into the space. To this is to be added scanty school furniture, deficiency of books, and other materials for teaching, and the depressing effect upon the poor children themselves of a close, noisome atmosphere. I have been in many schools, where I have seen rows of children doing absolutely nothing; and this is certified as school attendance, and, in statistical returns, such children are set down as being educated."‡ In Scotland the manufacturers try all they can to do without the children that are obliged to attend school. "It requires no further argument to prove that the educational clauses of the Factory Act, being held in such disfavour among mill owners tend in a great measure to exclude that class of children alike from the employment and the benefit of education contemplated by this Act."§

* L. Horner in "Rep. of Insp. of Fact. for 31st Oct., 1855," pp. 18, 19.
† Sir John Kincaid in "Rep. of Insp. of Fact. for 31st Oct., 1858," pp. 31, 32.
‡ L. Horner in "Reports, & c., for 31st Oct., 1857," pp. 17, 18.
§ Sir J. Kincaid in "Reports, & c., 31st Oct., 1856," p. 66.

Horribly grotesque does this appear in print works, which are regulated by a special Act. By that Act, "every child, before being employed in a print work must have attended school for at least 30 days, and not less than 150 hours, during the six months immediately preceding such first day of employment, and during the continuance of its employment in the print works, it must attend for a like period of 30 days, and 150 hours during every successive period of six months. . . . The attendance at school must be between 8 a.m. and 6 p.m. No attendance of less than 2½ hours, nor more than 5 hours on any one day, shall be reckoned as part of the 150 hours. Under ordinary circumstances the children attend school morning and afternoon for 30 days, for at least 5 hours each day, and upon the expiration of the 30 days, the statutory total of 150 hours having been attained, having, in their language, made up their book, they return to the print work, where they continue until the six months have expired, when another instalment of school attendance becomes due, and they again seek the school until the book is again made up. . . . Many boys having attended school for the required number of hours, when they return to school after the expiration of their six months' work in the print work, are in the same condition as when they first attended school as print-work boys, that they have lost all they gained by their previous school attendance. . . . In other print works the children's attendance at school is made to depend altogether upon the exigencies of the work in the establishment. The requisite number of hours is made up each six months, by instalments consisting of from 3 to five hours at a time, spreading over, perhaps, the whole six months. . . . For instance, the attendance on one day might be from 8 to 11 a.m., on another day from 1 p.m. to 4 p.m., and the child might not appear at school again for several days, when it would attend from 3 p.m. to 6 p.m.; then it might attend for 3 or 4 days consecutively, or for a week, then it would not appear in school for 3 weeks or a month, after that upon some odd days at some odd hours when the operative who employed it chose to spare it; and thus the child was, as it were, buffeted from school to work, from work to school, until the tale of 150 hours was told."*

---

* A. Redgrave in "Rep. of Insp. of Fact., 31st Oct., 1857," pp. 41–42. In those industries where the Factory Act proper (not the Print Works Act referred to in the text) has been in force for some time, the obstacles in the way of the education clauses have, in recent years, been overcome. In industries not under the Act, the views of Mr. J. Geddes, a glass manufacturer, still extensively prevail. He informed Mr. White, one of the Inquiry Commissioners: "As far as I can see, the greater amount of education which a part of the working class has enjoyed for some years past is an evil. It is dangerous, because it makes them independent." (Children's Empl. Comm., Fourth Report, Lond., 1865, p. 253.)

By the excessive addition of women and children to the ranks of the workers, machinery at last breaks down the resistance which the male operatives in the manufacturing period continued to oppose to the despotism of capital.* . . .

SECTION 9. THE FACTORY ACTS. SANITARY AND EDUCATION CLAUSES OF THE SAME. THEIR GENERAL EXTENSION IN ENGLAND.

. .. . Paltry as the education clauses of the Act appear on the whole, yet they proclaim elementary education to be an indispensable condition to the employment of children.† The success of those clauses proved for the first time the possibility of combining education and gymnastics‡ with manual labour, and, consequently, of combining manual labour with education and gymnastics. The factory inspectors soon found out by questioning the schoolmasters, that the factory children, although receiving only one half the education of the regular day scholars, yet learnt quite as much and often more. "This can be accounted for by the simple fact that, with only being at school for one half of the day, they are always fresh, and nearly always ready and willing to receive instruction. The system on which they work, half manual labour, and half school, renders each employment a rest, and a relief to the other; consequently, both are far more congenial to the child, than would be the case were he kept constantly at one. It is quite clear that a

* "Mr. E., a manufacturer . . . informed me that he employed females exclusively at his power-looms . . . gives a decided preference to married females, especially those who have families at home dependent on them for support; they are attentive, docile, more so than unmarried females, and are compelled to use their utmost exertions to procure the necessaries of life. Thus are the virtues, the peculiar virtues of the female character to be perverted to her injury—thus all that is most dutiful and tender in her nature is made a means of her bondage and suffering." (Ten Hours' Factory Bill. The Speech of Lord Ashley, March 15th, Lond., 1844, p. 20.)

† According to the English Factory Act, parents cannot send their children under 14 years of age into Factories under the control of the Act, unless at the same time they allow them to receive elementary education. The manufacturer is responsible for compliance with the Act. "Factory education is compulsory, and it is a condition of labour." (Rep. Insp. Fact. 31st Oct., 1863, p. 111.)

‡ On the very advantageous results of combining gymnastics (and drilling in the case of boys) with compulsory education for factory children and pauper scholars, see the speech of N. W. Senior at the seventh annual congress of "The National Association for the Promotion of Social Science," in "Report of Proceedings, & c., Lond. 1863," p. 63, 64, also the Rep. Insp. Fact., 31st Oct., 1865, p. 118, 119, 120, 126 sqq.

boy who has been at school all the morning, cannot (in hot weather particularly) cope with one who comes fresh and bright from his work."* Further information on this point will be found in Senior's speech at the Social Science Congress at Edinburgh in 1863. He there shows, amongst other things, how the monotonous and uselessly long school hours of the children of the upper and middle classes, uselessly add to the labour of the teacher, "while he not only fruitlessly, but absolutely injuriously, wastes the time, health, and energy of the children."† From the Factory system budded, as Robert Owen has shown us in detail, the germ of the education of the future, an education that will, in the case of every child over a given age, combine productive labour with instruction and gymnastics, not only as one of the methods of adding to the efficiency of production, but as the only method of producing fully developed human beings.

* Rep. Insp. Fact. 31st Oct. 1865, p. 118. A silk manufacturer naïvely states to the Children's Employment Commissioners: "I am quite sure that the true secret of producing efficient workpeople is to be found in uniting education and labour from a period of childhood. Of course the occupation must not be too severe, nor irksome, or unhealthy. But of the advantage of the union I have no doubt. I wish my own children could have some work as well as play to give variety to their schooling." (Ch. Empl. Comm. V. Rep. p. 82. n. 36.)

† Senior, l. c. p. 66. How Modern Industry, when it has attained to a certain pitch, is capable, by the revolution it effects in the mode of production and in the social conditions of production, of also revolutionizing people's minds, is strikingly shown by a comparison of Senior's speech in 1863, with his philippic against the Factory Act of 1833; or by a comparison, of the views of the congress above referred to, with the fact that in certain country districts of England poor parents are forbidden, on pain of death by starvation, to educate their children. Thus, e.g., Mr. Snell reports it to be a common occurrence in Somersetshire that, when a poor person claims parish relief, he is compelled to take his children from school. Mr. Wollarton, the clergyman at Feltham, also tells of cases where all relief was denied to certain families "because they were sending their children to school!"

The German Ideology

In 1844 Friedrich Engels visited Marx in Paris. Thus there began their long and close cooperation, which bore such momentous consequences. In 1845 Engels joined Marx in his exile in Brussels and the partnership entered its most fruitful stage, of which *The German Ideology,* completed in 1846, was a product. Only the last of three parts of the manuscript was published in the lifetime of the authors. The whole manuscript was first published in 1932 in Moscow. *The German Ideology* represents the earliest systematic statement of historical materialism. The first part, on Ludwig Feuerbach, contains the authors' views on the historical development of human society; on the relationship between economic forces and political, juridical, and intellectual activities; and on human relationships under communism. Marx and Engels contrast their own views with those of the German Hegelians, whose philosophy "descends from heaven to earth." Historical materialism ascends "from earth to heaven": it is based on the real lives of real men rather than on ideas and conceptions. Ideas are the products of the material conditions of society. The study of history must therefore begin with the study of the material dimensions of life. The dominant ideas of an epoch or society are the ideas of the ruling class, that is, the class that controls the means of material production. An ideology, in Marx's view, is a set of ideas that represents the interests of a special group or class, although claiming universal validity. In order to find the interest behind the ideology one must examine the social function of the ideas rather than their intellectual content. Philosophers have an exaggerated notion of their own autonomy and importance. They have studied the world: the task, however, is to change it. Marx and Engels were contemptuous of the philosophical purity and political ineffectiveness of Hegelian critics like Feuerbach, Bruno Bauer ("Saint Bruno"), and Max Stirner. The authors present their view of the ideal man by outlining the conditions of life in communist society. They contrast what they call a "natural" society, where men have no control over themselves or over social conditions and where there is a basic opposition between the individual and the group, with a communist society, where this split disappears and individual man becomes communal man. Under communism, each man's interests are identical with the interests of all: alienation is banished. Man no longer sees his fellows as hostile. Warfare between individuals and between groups comes to an end as we reach the classless society.

These passages are taken from Karl Marx and Friedrich Engels, *The German Ideology*, Parts I and III, edited by R. Pascal, published in New York, copyright 1939 by International Publishers, with whose permission they are reprinted.

The production of ideas, of conceptions, of consciousness, is at first directly interwoven with the material activity and the material intercourse of men, the language of real life. Conceiving, thinking, the mental intercourse of men, appear at this stage as the direct efflux of their material behaviour. The same applies to mental production as expressed in the language of the politics, laws, morality, religion, metaphysics of a people. Men are the producers of their conceptions, ideas, etc.—real, active men, as they are conditioned by a definite development of their productive forces and of the intercourse corresponding to these, up to its furthest forms. Consciousness can never be anything else than conscious existence, and the existence of men is their actual life-process. If in all ideology men and their circumstances appear upside down as in a *camera obscura*, this phenomenon arises just as much from their historical life-process as the inversion of objects on the retina does from their physical life-process.

In direct contrast to German philosophy which descends from heaven to earth, here we ascend from earth to heaven. That is to say, we do not set out from what men say, imagine, conceive, nor from men as narrated, thought of, imagined, conceived, in order to arrive at men in the flesh. We set out from real, active men, and on the basis of their real life-process we demonstrate the development of the ideological reflexes and echoes of this life-process. The phantoms formed in the human brain are also, necessarily, sublimates of their material life-process, which is empirically verifiable and bound to material premises. Morality, religion, metaphysics, all the rest of ideology and their corresponding forms of consciousness, thus no longer retain the semblance of independence. They have no history, no development; but men, developing their material production and their material intercourse, alter, along with this their real existence, their thinking and the products of their thinking. Life is not determined by consciousness, but consciousness by life. In the first method of approach the starting-point is consciousness taken as the living individual; in the second it is the real living individuals themselves, as they are in actual life, and consciousness is considered solely as *their* consciousness. . . .

Since we are dealing with the Germans, who do not postulate anything, we must begin by stating the first premise of all human existence, and therefore of all history, the premise namely that men must be in a position to live in order to be able to "make history." But life involves before everything else eating and drinking, a habitation, clothing and many other things. The first historical act is thus the production of the means to satisfy these needs, the production of material life itself. And indeed this is an historical act, a fundamental condition of all history, which to-day, as thousands of years ago, must daily and hourly be fulfilled merely in order to sustain human life. Even when the sensuous world is reduced to a minimum, to a stick as with Saint Bruno, it presupposes the action of producing the stick. The first necessity therefore in any theory of history is to observe this fundamental fact in all its significance and all its implications and to accord it its due importance. This, as is notorious, the Germans have never done, and they have never therefore had an earthly basis for history and consequently never a historian. The French and the English, even if they have conceived the relation of this fact with so-called history only in an extremely one-sided fashion, particularly as long as they remained in the toils of political ideology, have nevertheless made the first attempts to give the writing of history a materialistic basis by being the first to write histories of civil society, of commerce and industry. . . .

It is quite obvious from the start that there exists a materialistic connection of men with one another, which is determined by their needs and their mode of production, and which is as old as men themselves. This connection is ever taking on new forms, and thus presents a "history" independently of the existence of any political or religious nonsense which would hold men together on its own. . . .

With the division of labour, in which all these contradictions are implicit, and which in its turn is based on the natural division of labour in the family and the separation of society into individual families opposed to one another, is given simultaneously the distribution, and indeed the unequal distribution, (both quantitative and qualitative), of labour and its products, hence property: the nucleus, the first form, of which lies in the family, where wife and children are the slaves of the husband This latent slavery in the family, though still very crude, is the first property, but even at this early stage it corresponds perfectly to the definition of modern economists who call it the power of disposing of the labour-power of others. Division of labour and private property are, moreover, identical expressions: in the one the same thing is affirmed with reference to activity as is affirmed in the other with reference to the product of the activity.

Further, the division of labour implies the contradiction between the interest of the separate individual or the individual family and the communal interest of all individuals who have intercourse with one another. And indeed, this communal interest does not exist merely in the imagination, as "the general good," but first of all in reality, as the mutual interdependence of the individuals among whom the labour is divided. And finally, the division of labour offers us the first example of how, as long as man remains in natural society, that is as long as a cleavage exists between the particular and the common interest, as long therefore as activity is not voluntarily, but naturally, divided, man's own deed becomes an alien power opposed to him, which enslaves him instead of being controlled by him. For as soon as labour is distributed, each man has a particular, exclusive sphere of activity, which is forced upon him and from which he cannot escape. He is a hunter, a fisherman, a shepherd, or a critical critic, and must remain so if he does not want to lose his means of livelihood; while in communist society, where nobody has one exclusive sphere of activity but each can become accomplished in any branch he wishes, society regulates the general production and thus makes it possible for me to do one thing to-day and another to-morrow, to hunt in the morning, fish in the afternoon, rear cattle in the evening, criticize after dinner, just as I have a mind, without ever becoming hunter, fisherman, shepherd or critic. . . .

The ideas of the ruling class are in every epoch the ruling ideas: i.e., the class, which is the ruling material force of society, is at the same time its ruling intellectual force. The class which has the means of material production at its disposal, has control at the same time over the means of mental production, so that thereby, generally speaking, the ideas of those who lack the means of mental production are subject to it. The ruling ideas are nothing more than the ideal expression of the dominant material relationships, the dominant material relationships grasped as ideas; hence of the relationships which make the one class the ruling one, therefore the ideas of its dominance. The individuals composing the ruling class possess among other things consciousness, and therefore think. In so far, therefore, as they rule as a class and determine the extent and compass of an epoch, it is self-evident that they do this in their whole range, hence among other things rule also as thinkers, as producers of ideas, and regulate the production and distribution of the ideas of their age: thus their ideas are the ruling ideas of the epoch. . . .

The class making a revolution appears from the very start, merely because it is opposed to a *class,* not as a class but as the representative of the whole of society; it appears as the whole mass of society confronting the one ruling class. It can do this because, to start with, its interest really is more connected with the common interest of all other non-ruling classes, because under the pressure of conditions its interest has not yet been able to develop as the particular interest of a particular class. Its victory, therefore, benefits also many individuals of the other classes which are not winning a dominant position, but only in so far as it now puts these individuals in a position to raise themselves into the ruling class. When the French bourgeoisie overthrew the power of the aristocracy, it thereby made it possible for many proletarians to raise themselves above the proletariat, but only in so far as they became bourgeois. Every new class, therefore, achieves its hegemony only on a broader basis than that of the class ruling previously, in return for which the opposition of the non-ruling class against the new ruling class later develops all the more sharply and profoundly. Both these things determine the fact that the struggle to be waged against this new ruling class, in its turn, aims at a more decided and radical negation of the previous conditions of society than could all previous classes which sought to rule.

This whole semblance, that the rule of a certain class is only the rule of certain ideas, comes to a natural end, of course, as soon as society ceases at last to be organized in the form of class-rule, that is to say as soon as it is no longer necessary to represent a particular interest as general or "the general interest" as ruling. . . .

THESES ON FEUERBACH

XI

The philosophers have only *interpreted* the world differently, the point is, to *change* it.

Manifesto of the Communist Party

In Brussels in the 1840s Marx and Engels became deeply involved .
in the socialist working-class movement. They joined a German
workers' society, the "League of the Just." At first a secret society,
with branches in England, France, Belgium, and Switzerland, it
became the "League of the Communists," for which Marx and
Engels wrote the *Manifesto of the Communist Party* in 1847. In
this document, they reiterate their proposition that economic forces
govern political and intellectual developments. The history of man
under a system of private property has therefore been a struggle
between exploiting and exploited classes. The exploitation of the
many (the proletariat) by the few (the bourgeoisie) is made possible by the concentration of private property in the hands of the
few. Communism will therefore abolish private property. The proletariat will throw off the yoke of the exploiting bourgeois class and
establish itself as supreme. It will change the conditions of economic production and thus end the class warfare that mars capitalist society. Under communism, private education will be replaced
by State-provided education. This will bring about the development
of a new model of man: instead of being family-centered he will
be society-centered. His focus will be communal.

These passages are taken from Karl Marx and Friedrich Engels,
Manifesto of the Communist Party, translated by Samuel Moore,
edited by Friedrich Engels, published by Charles H. Kerr in Chicago in 1906.

PREFACE (BY FRIEDRICH ENGELS)

The *Manifesto* being our joint production, I consider myself bound
to state that the fundamental proposition which forms its nucleus, be-

longs to Marx. That proposition is: That in every historical epoch, the prevailing mode of economic production and exchange, and the social organisation necessarily following from it, form the basis upon which is built up, and from which alone can be explained, the political and intellectual history of that epoch; that consequently the whole history of mankind (since the dissolution of primitive tribal society, holding land in common ownership) has been a history of class struggles, contests between exploiting and exploited, ruling and oppressed classes; that the history of these class struggles form a series of evolutions in which, nowadays, a stage has been reached where the exploited and oppressed class—the proletariat—cannot attain its emancipation from the sway of the exploiting and ruling class—the bourgeoisie—without at the same time, and once and for all, emancipating society at large from all exploitation, oppression, class distinctions and class struggles.

II

PROLETARIANS AND COMMUNISTS

The distinguishing feature of Communism is not the abolition of property generally, but the abolition of bourgeois property. But modern bourgeois private property is the final and most complete expression of the system of producing and appropriating products that is based on class antagonisms, on the exploitation of the many by the few.

In this sense, the theory of the Communists may be summed up in the single sentence: Abolition of private property.

We Communists have been reproached with the desire of abolishing the right of personally acquiring property as the fruit of a man's own labour, which property is alleged to be the groundwork of all personal freedom, activity and independence.

Hard-won, self-acquired, self-earned property! Do you mean the property of the petty artisan and of the small peasant, a form of property that preceded the bourgeois form? There is no need to abolish that; the development of industry has to a great extent already destroyed it, and is still destroying it daily.

Or do you mean modern bourgeois private property?

But does wage-labour create any property for the labourer? Not a bit. It creates capital, i.e., that kind of property which exploits wage-labour, and which cannot increase except upon condition of getting a new supply of wage-labour for fresh exploitation. Property, in its present form, is based on the antagonism of capital and wage-labour. . . .

In bourgeois society, living labour is but a means to increase accumulated labour. In Communist society, accumulated labour is but a means to widen, to enrich, to promote the existence of the labourer.

In bourgeois society, therefore, the past dominates the present; in Communist society, the present dominates the past. In bourgeois society capital is independent and has individuality, while the living person is dependent and has no individuality.

And the abolition of this state of things is called by the bourgeois, abolition of individuality and freedom! And rightly so. The abolition of bourgeois individuality, bourgeois independence, and bourgeois freedom is undoubtedly aimed at.

By freedom is meant, under the present bourgeois conditions of production, free trade, free selling and buying.

But if selling and buying disappears, free selling and buying disappears also. This talk about free selling and buying, and all the other "brave words" of our bourgeoisie about freedom in general, have a meaning, if any, only in contrast with restricted selling and buying, with the fettered traders of the Middle Ages, but have no meaning when opposed to the Communist abolition of buying and selling, of the bourgeois conditions of production, and of the bourgeoisie itself.

You are horrified at our intending to do away with private property. But in your existing society, private property is already done away with for nine-tenths of the population; its existence for the few is solely due to its non-existence in the hands of those nine-tenths. You reproach us, therefore, with intending to do away with a form of property, the necessary condition for whose existence is the non-existence of any property for the immense majority of society.

In a word, you reproach us with intending to do away with your property. Precisely so; that is just what we intend.

From the moment when labour can no longer be converted into capital, money, or rent, into a social power capable of being monopolised, i.e., from the moment when individual property can no longer be transformed into bourgeois property, into capital, from that moment, you say, individuality vanishes.

You must, therefore, confess that by "individual" you mean no other person than the bourgeois, than the middle class owner of property. This person must, indeed, be swept out of the way, and made impossible. . . .

But don't wrangle with us so long as you apply, to our intended abolition of bourgeois property, the standard of your bourgeois notions of freedom, culture, law, etc. Your very ideas are but the outgrowth of the conditions of your bourgeois production and bourgeois property, just as your jurisprudence is but the will of your class made into a law for all, a will whose essential character and direction are determined by the economic conditions of existence of your class.

The selfish misconception that induces you to transform into eternal laws of nature and of reason, the social forms springing from your present mode of production and form of property—historical relations that rise and disappear in the progress of production—this misconception you share with every ruling class that has preceded you. What you see clearly in the case of ancient property, what you admit in the case of feudal property, you are of course forbidden to admit in the case of your own bourgeois form of property.

Abolition of the family! Even the most radical flare up at this infamous proposal of the Communists.

On what foundation is the present family, the bourgeois family, based? On capital, on private gain. In its completely developed form this family exists only among the bourgeoisie. But this state of things finds its complement in the practical absence of the family among the proletarians, and in public prostitution.

The bourgeois family will vanish as a matter of course when its complement vanishes, and both will vanish with the vanishing of capital.

Do you charge us with wanting to stop the exploitation of children by their parents? To this crime we plead guilty.

But, you will say, we destroy the most hallowed of relations, when we replace home education by social.

And your education! Is not that also social, and determined by the social conditions under which you educate, by the intervention of society, direct or indirect, by means of schools, etc.? The Communists have not invented the intervention of society in education; they do but seek to alter the character of that intervention, and to rescue education from the influence of the ruling class.

The bourgeois claptrap about the family and education, about the hallowed co-relation of parent and child, becomes all the more disgusting, the more, by the action of modern industry, all family ties among the proletarians are torn asunder, and their children transformed into simple articles of commerce and instruments of labour. . . .

Does it require deep intuition to comprehend that man's ideas, views, and conceptions, in one word, man's consciousness, changes with every change in the conditions of his material existence, in his social relations and in his social life?

What else does the history of ideas prove, than that intellectual production changes its character in proportion as material production is changed? The ruling ideas of each age have ever been the ideas of its ruling class. . . .

The history of all past society has consisted in the development of class antagonisms, antagonisms that assumed different forms at different epochs.

But whatever form they may have taken, one fact is common to all past ages, *viz.*, the exploitation of one part of society by the other. No wonder, then, that the social consciousness of past ages, despite all the mutiplicity and variety it displays, moves within certain common forms, or general ideas, which cannot completely vanish except with the total disappearance of class antagonisms. . . .

We have seen above, that the first step in the revolution by the working class, is to raise the proletariat to the position of ruling class, to win the battle of democracy.

The proletariat will use its political supremacy to wrest, by degrees, all capital from the bourgeoisie, to centralise all instruments of production in the hands of the state, i.e., of the proletariat organised as the ruling class; and to increase the total of productive forces as rapidly as possible.

Of course, in the beginning, this cannot be effected except by means of despotic inroads on the rights of property, and on the conditions of bourgeois production; by means of measures, therefore, which appear economically insufficient and untenable, but which, in the course of the movement, outstrip themselves, necessitate further inroads upon the old social order, and are unavoidable as a means of entirely revolutionising the mode of production.

These measures will of course be different in different countries.

Nevertheless in the most advanced countries, the following will be pretty generally applicable.

1. Abolition of property in land and application of all rents of land to public purposes.

2. A heavy progressive or graduated income tax.

3. Abolition of all right of inheritance.

4. Confiscation of the property of all emigrants and rebels.

5. Centralisation of credit in the hands of the state, by means of a national bank with state capital and an exclusive monopoly.

6. Centralisation of the means of communication and tranpsort in the hands of the state.

7. Extension of factories and instruments of production owned by the state; the bringing into cultivation of waste lands, and the improvement of the soil generally in accordance with a common plan.

8. Equal obligation of all to labour. Establishment of industrial armies, especially for agriculture.

9. Combination of agriculture with manufacturing industries; gradual abolition of the distinction between town and country, by a more equable distribution of the population over the country.

10. Free education for all children in public schools. Abolition of children's factory labour in its present form. Combination of education with industrial production, etc.

When, in the course of development, class distinctions have disappeared, and all production has been concentrated in the hands of a vast association of the whole nation, the public power will lose its political character. Political power, properly so called, is merely the organised power of one class for oppressing another. If the proletariat during its contest with the bourgeoisie is compelled, by the force of circumstances, to organise itself as a class; if, by means of a revolution, it makes itself the ruling class, and, as such sweeps away by force the old conditions of production, then it will, along with these conditions, have swept away the conditions for the existence of class antagonisms, and of classes generally, and will thereby have abolished its own supremacy as a class.

In place of the old bourgeois society, with its classes and class antagonisms, we shall have an association, in which the free development of each is the condition for the free development of all.

Economic and
Philosophical Manuscripts

Marx wrote these four manuscripts in 1844. Their first complete publication, however, did not take place until 1932. Hence they have not directly contributed to the development of the main stream of communist thinking. Nevertheless, they represent important aspects of Marx's humanism, which may be unwelcome to some critics both in the Soviet Union and in the West but which are needed to give a balanced picture of Marx's views. In the manuscripts Marx analyzes the dehumanization and alienation of man that occur under capitalism. Although he has in mind the consequences of Western industrialism, there is little doubt that he would have made much the same indictment of the results of State capitalism in the Soviet Union. Under capitalism, the demands of economic production come to dominate the requirements of human life. The type of values engendered by capitalism (productive efficiency, personal profit, impersonal control, amassing private property, avaricious competition) infuse all of life and characterize human relationships. Hence men become alienated from each other and ultimately from themselves. Production is more important than humanity: things dominate men. In our own day, Marx's view is symbolized in our domination by the Thing: the Bomb has become the psychological master of us all. Work in a capitalist system is not a fulfilling experience but enervative and degrading. Because of the meaninglessness of his work, man seeks to find himself only in his leisure time. Thus develops the pernicious split between work and play that so weakens both industrial life and education in our day. In education, we have largely lost the ability to play, and we are very far from being able to synthesize work and play. Similarly, the educational process is characterized by the separation of individual from individual and of group from group. Marx's solution is communism, which will abolish private property and remove alienation. Communism resolves human antagonisms and hence facilitates the rehumanization of man. The human model that Marx presents to us is a man who transcends the dichotomy between individual and species: he is both unique and universal; he is the individual, communal man. Marx resists the antithesis of man and society. His model is an unalienated, social individual, one who can identify with mankind as a whole and can affirm himself as a species-being.

These passages are taken from Karl Marx, *Early Writings*, translated and edited by T. B. Bottomore, published in London in 1963 by C. A. Watts and Co., Ltd., with whose permission they are reprinted.

ALIENATED LABOR

The worker is related to the *product of his labor* as to an *alien* object. For it is clear on this presupposition that the more the worker expends himself in work the more powerful becomes the world of objects which he creates in face of himself, the poorer he becomes in his inner life, and the less he belongs to himself. It is just the same as in religion. The more of himself man attributes to God the less he has left in himself. The worker puts his life into the object, and his life then belongs no longer to himself but to the object. The greater his activity, therefore, the less he possesses. What is embodied in the product of his labor is no longer his own. The greater this product is, therefore, the more he is diminished. The *alienation* of the worker in his product means not only that his labor becomes an object, assumes an *external* existence, but that it exists independently, *outside himself*, and alien to him, and that it stands opposed to him as an autonomous power. The life which he has given to the object sets itself against him as an alien and hostile force. . . .

What constitutes the alienation of labor? First, that the work is *external* to the worker, that it is not part of his nature; and that, consequently, he does not fulfill himself in his work but denies himself, has a feeling of misery rather than well being, does not develop freely his mental and physical energies but is physically exhausted and mentally debased. The worker therefore feels himself at home only during his leisure time, whereas at work he feels homeless. His work is not voluntary but imposed, *forced labor.* It is not the satisfaction of a need, but only a *means* for satisfying other needs. Its alien character is clearly shown by the fact that as soon as there is no physical or other compulsion it is avoided like the plague. External labor, labor in which man alienates himself, is a labor of self-sacrifice, of mortification. Finally, the external character of work for the workers is shown by the fact that it is not his own work but work for someone else, that in work he does not belong to himself but to another person. . . .

It is just in his work upon the objective world that man really proves himself as a *species-being.* This production is his active species life. By means of it nature appears as *his* work and his reality. The object of labor is therefore, the *objectification of man's species life;* for he no longer reproduces himself merely intellectually, as in consciousness, but actively and in a real sense, and he sees his own reflection in a world which he has constructed. While, therefore, alienated labor takes away the object of production from man, it also takes away his *species life,* his real objectivity as a species-being, and changes his advantage over animals into a disadvantage in so far as his inorganic body, nature, is taken from him.

Just as alienated labor transforms free and self-directed activity into a means, so it transforms the species life of man into a means of physical existence.

Consciousness, which man has from his species, is transformed through alienation so that species life becomes only a means for him.

Thus alienated labor turns the *species life of man,* and also nature as his mental species-property, into an *alien* being and into a *means* for his *individual existence.* It alienates from man his own body, external nature, his mental life and his *human* life.

A direct consequence of the alienation of man from the product of his labor, from his life activity and from his species life is that *man* is *alienated* from other *men.* When man confronts himself he also confronts *other* men. What is true of man's relationship to his work, to the product of his work and to himself, is also true of his relationship to other men, to their labor and to the objects of their labor.

In general, the statement that man is alienated from his species life means that each man is alienated from others, and that each of the others is likewise alienated from human life.

Human alienation, and above all the relation of man to himself, is first realized and expressed in the relationship between each man and other men. Thus in the relationship of alienated labor every man regards other men according to the standards and relationships in which he finds himself placed as a worker. . . .

PRIVATE PROPERTY AND COMMUNISM

Communism is the *positive* abolition of *private property,* of *human self-alienation,* and thus the real *appropriation* of *human* nature through and for man. It is, therefore, the return of man himself as a *social,* i.e., really human, being, a complete and conscious return which assimilates all the wealth of previous development. Communism as a fully-developed naturalism is humanism and as a fully-developed humanism is naturalism. It is the *definitive* resolution of the antagonism between man and nature, and between man and man. It is the true solution of the conflict between existence and essence, between objectification and self-affirmation, between freedom and necessity, between individual and species. It is the solution of the riddle of history and knows itself to be this solution. . . .

It is above all necessary to avoid postulating "society" once again as an abstraction confronting the individual. The individual *is* the *social being.* The manifestation of his life—even when it does not appear directly in the form of a communal manifestation, accomplished in association with other men—is therefore a manifestation and affirmation of *social life.* Individual human life and species-life are not *different things,* even though the mode of existence of individual life is necessarily either a more *specific* or a more *general* mode of species-life, or that of species-life a more *specific* or more *general* mode of individual life.

In his *species consciousness* man confirms his real *social life,* and reproduces his real existence in thought; while conversely, species-life confirms itself in species-consciousness and exists for itself in its universality as a thinking being. Though man is a unique individual—and it is just his particularity which make him an individual, a really *individual* communal being—he is equally the *whole,* the ideal whole, the subjective existence of society as thought and experienced. He exists in reality as the representation and the real mind of social existence, and as the sum of human manifestation of life.

13　The Psychological Man: Freud

Dominating the background of Sigmund Freud (1856–1939) was the fact that he was a Viennese Jew living in a prudish Roman Catholic society where anti-Semitism was epidemic. In his consulting room he heard stories that gave him an insight into the depths of repression compelled by Victorian, middle-class prudery and anachronistic, religious moralism. The prevailing anti-Semitism of his milieu drove him in upon his own cultural Judaism. His friends and patients were almost all Jews. Throughout his life he maintained a recognition of himself as an isolated figure, a member of a persecuted minority. His response to this situation was to transform his position of isolation into a pinnacle of independence from which he dared to look down with the unblinking vision of the scientist into the dark pit that his patients uncovered for him. From his Jewishness he claimed to have gained his moral courage and his intellectuality, which sustained his bold scrutiny and shaped its subsequent interpretation.

Freud perceived an essential conflict between the instinctual (especially sexual and aggressive) urges of man and the repressive demands of civilization, and he forged a model of the psychological man as one who has come to terms with this basic human dilemma. The psychological man must be able to live with contradictions: he has achieved an inner balance or equilibrium in the face of irreconcilable forces. The problem of instinct and civilization can never be fully resolved, in Freud's view. It is not merely a matter of reducing or removing social frustrations by, for example, allowing free sexual expression. The problem lies deeper in man's nature, which harbors a death instinct as well as a life instinct. A complete and harmonious integration of man's urges cannot be attained. The best to be hoped for is an ambivalent condition where the conflicting forces are contained in an endurable tension. Freud did not

333

advocate either moral asceticism or sensual permissiveness. Both err in breaking the tension that must continue to exist between sensuality and control, between id and ego, between love and death, between eros and thanatos, between the individual and society.

An important part of the delineation of the psychological man can be made in terms of his relationship to his society. Unlike Marx, Freud did not envisage man becoming free through his social relationships. For the psychological man, society represents a threat with which he must cope rather than a route to salvation. He has withdrawn from the more exigent of society's demands in an attempt to salvage his own private piece of the world as best he can. Self-salvation is his goal. He finds his ultimate authority in his own depths. He does not regard the traditional religious and political communities as models to which he should adjust, for he considers them diseased. Resigned to the costs of civilization, he measures his success by his ability to function in a sick society without being destroyed by it. In order to become at peace with society, he has reconciled himself to inexorable social authority without accepting conventional values. Freud's model is a man who has attained a degree of self-insight and self-awareness through putting a concern with the self above a concern with society. He is not markedly interested in public affairs, not heroic or self-sacrificial, not committed to risky ideals. His posture is somewhat Oriental in its self-absorption.

The psychological man regards civilization as hypocritical and is himself a skeptical realist. He is skeptical of the value of traditional and contemporary religious, moral, and political authority. Realistic enough to avoid being taken in by false illusions or vain hopes, he must be strong enough to live without the traditional consolations of religion and philosophy. His unsentimental view of himself and other men saves him from believing in a naïve theory of progress. Honesty and moral courage are essential qualities in facing all of life—himself as well as others, the unconscious as well as the conscious, feelings as well as thoughts. He does not deny reality (this is psychotic) nor does he lie down under its tyrannical demands (this is neurotic), but he struggles through to a level of honest self-expression despite the force of convention. Completely unromantic about sex, he can face its existence honestly. The goal of self-mastery is gained in part by talking about one's instincts and urges instead of repressing or ignoring them. For Freud, there are curative values in talk.

However, there is also an important rational, intellectual dimension to the psychological man. He gains mastery over himself not merely by expressing previously repressed emotions but by understanding those emotions through intellectual analysis. Reliable knowledge comes, in Freud's opinion, from scientific observation and intellectual reflection rather than from intuition and inspiration. Freud's model is a man of reason, although he does not regard reason in itself as his salvation. There is no certain salvation. Freud both affirmed the irrational and found a vital place for the rational.

Although the difference between health and sickness is, in Freud's view, one of degree rather than of kind, it is necessary to distinguish between the treatment of those considered sick, whom Freud tried to release from repression, and the general needs of society, where he defended a measure of repression. The price of civilization is the development of a sense of guilt in the individual. The psychological man can to some extent deal with his repressed emotions through dreams, play, humor, and art. He should be aesthetically expressive in the sense of learning to express previously repressed material in an aesthetically mastered way, just as children in play learn through active mastery to express and control experiences that they have previously absorbed passively.

Freud's superb and courageous realism somewhat disarms criticism of his views, but these are nevertheless not without ambiguities and frailties. When he talks disparagingly of "religion," for example, he often seems to mean "Roman Catholicism," a term that is far from exhausting the category of "religion." Some of his concepts have rigidities that are based on assumptions rather than proof, such as his view of human nature as essentially unchangeable. He sometimes glides too easily from the historical to the necessary: he assumes that a nonrepressive civilization is impossible by extrapolating from what *has* been to what is natural and necessary. If repression is closely linked with the fact of scarcity, as it seems to be, Freud's thesis may be decreasingly applicable in the era of abundance into which many industrialized nations appear to be passing. He is an acute analyst of the stifling demands of society, but he seems relatively unaware of the liberating potentialities of community, of the possibility of finding our freedom through others.

Freud is, of course, one of the great giants in the history of the West. We shall continue to explore the implications of his ideas for education, medicine, and virtually all aspects of life, into the foreseeable future. The neo-Freudians and other interpreters have tried hard to dissolve away by one means or another the tension that he postulated between instinct and civilization. But Freud insisted that it was irreducible, and we must consider carefully whether our attempts to deny it do not stem from the kind of wishful thinking that he so effectively exposed.

The Future of an Illusion

In this study, written and published in 1927, Freud turned to the examination of cultural problems, which was to be a major concern for the rest of his life. Much of the discussion in this work takes the form of a dialogue between Freud and an imaginary opponent. Freud makes clear that he considers religious doctrines to be illusions, that is, wish fulfillments that disregard reality and do not seek verification. His ideal person emerges as a man in whom intelligence is primary and who therefore opposes religion, which demands a deliberate stifling of intelligence. Freud suggests that religious education may be to blame for the intellectual atrophy that occurs between childhood and adulthood: intellectual emaciation necessarily follows from the attempt to achieve an uncritical acceptance of the beliefs that religion compels. The model of the psychological man is thus one who has the courage to grow out of his infantile dependence on the illusion of religion. He recognizes his cosmic insignificance, acknowledges that he is not the darling of a providential deity, but is not afraid to face life on these terms. The dictates of fate he accepts with resigned fortitude. In place of the illusory gods of traditional religion, the god whose authority he salutes is *logos* (reason). He uses reason and science as his guides for gaining knowledge of the world and power over his own life.

These selections are taken from *The Future of an Illusion*, in Volume XXI of *The Standard Edition of the Complete Psychological Works of Sigmund Freud*, translated and edited by James Strachey, in collaboration with Anna Freud, assisted by Alix Strachey and Alan Tyson, published in London in 1961 by The Hogarth Press and The Institute of Psycho-analysis. Reprinted by permission of Sigmund Freud Copyrights Ltd., Mr. James Strachey, The Hogarth Press Ltd., and Liveright Publishing Corporation.

Since men are so little accessible to reasonable arguments and are
so entirely governed by their instinctual wishes, why should one set
out to deprive them of an instinctual satisfaction and replace it by reasonable arguments? It is true that men are like this but have you asked
yourself whether they *must* be like this, whether their innermost nature
necessitates it? Can an anthropologist give the cranial index of a people
whose custom it is to deform their children's heads by bandaging them
round from their earliest years? Think of the depressing contrast between
the radiant intelligence of a healthy child and the feeble intellectual
powers of the average adult. Can we be quite certain that it is not
precisely religious education which bears a large share of the blame
for this relative atrophy? I think it would be a very long time before
a child who was not influenced began to trouble himself about God
and things in another world. Perhaps his thoughts on these matters
would then take the same paths as they did with his forefathers. But
we do not wait for such a development; we introduce him to the doctrines of religion at an age when he is neither interested in them nor
capable of grasping their import. Is it not true that the two main points
in the programme for the education of children to-day are retardation
of sexual development and premature religious influence? Thus by the
time the child's intellect awakens, the doctrines of religion have already
become unassailable. But are you of opinion that it is very conducive
to the strengthening of the intellectual function that so important a
field should be closed against it by the threat of Hell-fire? When a
man has once brought himself to accept uncritically all the absurdities
that religious doctrines put before him and even to overlook the contradictions between them, we need not be greatly surprised at the weakness
of his intellect. But we have no other means of controlling our instinctual
nature but our intelligence. How can we expect people who are under
the dominance of prohibitions of thought to attain the psychological
ideal, the primacy of the intelligence? You know, too, that women in
general are said to suffer from 'physiological feeble-mindedness'—that
is, from a lesser intelligence than men. The fact itself is disputable
and its interpretation doubtful, but one argument in favour of this intellectual atrophy being of a secondary nature is that women labour under
the harshness of an early prohibition against turning their thoughts to
what would most have interested them—namely, the problems of sexual
life. So long as a person's early years are influenced not only by a
sexual inhibition of thought but also by a religious inhibition and by
a loyal inhibition derived from this, we cannot really tell what in fact
he is like.

But I will moderate my zeal and admit the possibility that I, **too**, am chasing an illusion. Perhaps the effect of the religious prohibition of thought may not be so bad as I suppose; perhaps it will turn out that human nature remains the same even if education is not abused in order to subject people to religion. I do not know and you cannot know either. It is not only the great problems of this life that seem insoluble at the present time; many lesser questions are too difficult to answer. But you must admit that here we are justified in having a hope for the future—that perhaps there is a treasure to be dug up capable of enriching civilization and that it is worth making the experiment of an irreligious education. Should the experiment prove unsatisfactory I am ready to give up the reform and to return to my earlier, purely descriptive judgement that man is a creature of weak intelligence who is ruled by his instinctual wishes.

On another point I agree with you unreservedly. It is certainly senseless to begin by trying to do away with religion by force and at a single blow. Above all, because it would be hopeless. The believer will not let his belief be torn from him, either by arguments or by prohibitions. And even if this did succeed with some it would be cruelty. A man who has been taking sleeping draughts for tens of years is naturally unable to sleep if his sleeping draught is taken away from him. That the effect of religious consolations may be likened to that of a narcotic is well illustrated by what is happening in America. There they are now trying—obviously under the influence of petticoat government—to deprive people of all stimulants, intoxicants, and other pleasure-producing substances, and instead, by way of compensation, are surfeiting them with piety. This is another experiment as to whose outcome we need not feel curious.

Thus I must contradict you when you go on to argue that men are completely unable to do without the consolation of the religious illusion, that without it they could not bear the troubles of life and the cruelties of reality. That is true, certainly, of the men into whom you have instilled the sweet—or bitter-sweet—poison from childhood onwards. But what of the other men, who have been sensibly brought up? Perhaps those who do not suffer from the neurosis will need no intoxicant to deaden it. They will, it is true, find themselves in a difficult situation. They will have to admit to themselves the full extent of their helplessness and their insignificance in the machinery of the universe; they can no longer be the centre of creation, no longer the object of tender care on the part of a beneficent Providence. They will be in the same position as a child who has left the parental house where he was so warm and comfortable. But surely infantilism is destined to be surmounted. Men cannot remain children for ever; they must in the end go out into 'hostile

life.' We may call this *education to reality.* Need I confess to you
that the sole purpose of my book is to point out the necessity for this
forward step?

You are afraid, probably, that they will not stand up to the hard
test? Well, let us at least hope they will. It is something, at any rate,
to know that one is thrown upon one's own resources. One learns then
to make a proper use of them. And men are not entirely without assistance. Their scientific knowledge has taught them much since the days
of the Deluge, and it will increase their power still further. And, as
for the great necessities of Fate, against which there is no help, they
will learn to endure them with resignation. Of what use to them is
the mirage of wide acres in the moon, whose harvest no one has ever
yet seen? As honest smallholders on this earth they will know how
to cultivate their plot in such a way that it supports them. By withdrawing their expectations from the other world and concentrating all their
liberated energies into their life on earth, they will probably succeed
in achieving a state of things in which life will become tolerable for
everyone and civilization no longer oppressive to anyone. Then, with
one of our fellow-unbelievers, they will be able to say without regret:

> Den Himmel überlassen wir
> Den Engeln und den Spatzen.* . . .

Education freed from the burden of religious doctrines will not, it
may be, effect much change in men's psychological nature. Our god
Λόγος is perhaps not a very almighty one, and he may only be able
to fulfil a small part of what his predecessors have promised. If we
have to acknowledge this we shall accept it with resignation. We shall
not on that account lose our interest in the world and in life, for we
have one sure support which you lack. We believe that it is possible
for scientific work to gain some knowledge about the reality of the
world, by means of which we can increase our power and in accordance
with which we can arrange our life. If this belief is an illusion, then
we are in the same position as you. But science has given us evidence
by its numerous and important successes that it is no illusion. Science
has many open enemies, and many more secret ones, among those who
cannot forgive her for having weakened religious faith and for threatening to overthrow it. She is reproached for the smallness of the amount
she has taught us and for the incomparably greater field she has left
in obscurity. But, in this, people forget how young she is, how difficult

---

* ['We leave Heaven to the angels and the sparrows.' (Heine)]

her beginnings were and how infinitesimally small is the period of time since the human intellect has been strong enough for the tasks she sets. Are we not all at fault, in basing our judgements on periods of time that are too short? We should make the geologists our pattern. People complain of the unreliability of science—how she announces as a law to-day what the next generation recognizes as an error and replaces by a new law whose accepted validity lasts no longer. But this is unjust and in part untrue. The transformations of scientific opinion are developments, advances, not revolutions. A law which was held at first to be universally valid proves to be a special case of a more comprehensive uniformity, or is limited by another law, not discovered till later; a rough approximation to the truth is replaced by a more carefully adapted one, which in turn awaits further perfectioning. There are various fields where we have not yet surmounted a phase of research in which we make trial with hypotheses that soon have to be rejected as inadequate; but in other fields we already possess an assured and almost unalterable core of knowledge. Finally, an attempt has been made to discredit scientific endeavour in a radical way, on the ground that, being bound to the conditions of our own organization, it can yield nothing else than subjective results, whilst the real nature of things outside ourselves remains inaccessible. But this is to disregard several factors which are of decisive importance for the understanding of scientific work. In the first place, our organization—that is, our mental apparatus—has been developed precisely in the attempt to explore the external world, and it must therefore have realized in its structure some degree of expediency; in the second place, it is itself a constituent part of the world which we set out to investigate, and it readily admits of such an investigation; thirdly, the task of science is fully covered if we limit it to showing how the world must appear to us in consequence of the particular character of our organization; fourthly, the ultimate findings of science, precisely because of the way in which they are acquired, are determined not only by our organization but by the things which have affected that organization; finally, the problem of the nature of the world without regard to our percipient mental apparatus is an empty abstraction, devoid of practical interest.

No, our science is no illusion. But an illusion it would be to suppose that what science cannot give us we can get elsewhere.

Civilization and Its Discontents

In 1929 Freud produced his principal study of the irremovable conflict between man's instinctual drives and the restrictions imposed by civilization. The individual, in Freud's view, struggles between egoistic and altruistic urges, between the goal of personal happiness and that of community with others. Society, however, largely ignores the claim of individual happiness: it demands the renunciation or repression of egoistic urges—especially those of aggressiveness and sex—in the name of civilization. Freud argues that the demands of civilization are mercilessly inexorable and yet impossible for the individual to execute without harm. In the solution of this painful dilemma, Freud offers no comforting illusions or cheap consolations. The psychological man must be able to live without them.

This passage is taken from *Civilization and Its Contents*, in Volume XXI of *The Standard Edition of the Complete Psychological Works of Sigmund Freud*, translated and edited by James Strachey, in collaboration with Anna Freud, assisted by Alix Strachey and Alan Tyson, published in London in 1961 by The Hogarth Press and The Institute of Psycho-analysis. Reprinted by permission of Sigmund Freud Copyrights Ltd., Mr. James Strachey, The Hogarth Press Ltd., and W. W. Norton & Company.

In the developmental process of the individual, the programme of the pleasure principle, which consists in finding the satisfaction of happiness, is retained as the main aim. Integration in, or adaptation to, a human community appears as a scarcely avoidable condition which must be fulfilled before this aim of happiness can be achieved. If it could be done without that condition, it would perhaps be preferable. To put it in other words, the development of the individual seems to us to be a product of the interaction between two urges, the urge towards happiness, which we usually call 'egoistic,' and the urge towards union with others in the community, which we call 'altruistic.' Neither of these descriptions goes much below the surface. In the process of individual development, as we have said, the main accent falls mostly on the egoistic urge (or the urge towards happiness); while the other urge, which may be described as a 'cultural' one, is usually content with the role of imposing restrictions. But in the process of civilization things are different. Here by far the most important thing is the aim of creating a unity out of the individual human beings. It is true that the aim of happiness is still there, but it is pushed into the background. It almost seems as if the creation of a great human community would be most successful if no attention had to be paid to the happiness of the individual. The developmental process of the individual can thus be expected to have special features of its own which are not reproduced in the process of human civilization. It is only in so far as the first of these processes has union with the community as its aim that it need coincide with the second process.

Just as a planet revolves around a central body as well as rotating on its own axis, so the human individual takes part in the course of development of mankind at the same time as he pursues his own path in life. But to our dull eyes the play of forces in the heavens seems fixed in a never-changing order; in the field of organic life we can still see how the forces contend with one another, and how the effects of the conflict are continually changing. So, also, the two urges, the one towards personal happiness and the other towards union with other human beings must struggle with each other in every individual; and so, also, the two processes of individual and of cultural development must stand in hostile opposition to each other and mutually dispute the ground. But this struggle between the individual and society is not a derivative of the contradiction—probably an irreconcilable one—between the primal instincts of Eros and death. It is a dispute within the economics of the libido, comparable to the contest concerning the distribution of libido between ego and objects; and it does admit of an eventual accommodation in the individual, as, it may be hoped, it will also do in the future of civilization, however much that civilization may oppress the life of the individual to-day.

The analogy between the process of civilization and the path of individual development may be extended in an important respect. It can be asserted that the community, too, evolves a super-ego under whose influence cultural development proceeds. It would be a tempting task for anyone who has a knowledge of human civilizations to follow out this analogy in detail. I will confine myself to bringing forward a few striking points. The super-ego of an epoch of civilization has an origin similar to that of an individual. It is based on the impression left behind by the personalities of great leaders—men of overwhelming force of mind or men in whom one of the human impulsions has found its strongest and purest, and therefore often its most one-sided, expression. In many instances the analogy goes still further, in that during their lifetime these figures were—often enough, even if not always—mocked and maltreated by others and even despatched in a cruel fashion. In the same way, indeed, the primal father did not attain divinity until long after he had met his death by violence. The most arresting example of this fateful conjunction is to be seen in the figure of Jesus Christ—if, indeed, that figure is not a part of mythology, which called it into being from an obscure memory of that primal event. Another point of agreement between the cultural and the individual super-ego is that the former, just like the latter, sets up strict ideal demands, disobedience to which is visited with 'fear of conscience.' Here, indeed, we come across the remarkable circumstance that the mental processes concerned are actually more familiar to us and more accessible to consciousness as they are seen in the group than they can be in the individual man. In him, when tension arises, it is only the aggressiveness of the super-ego which, in the form of reproaches, makes itself noisily heard; its actual demands often remain unconscious in the background. If we bring them to conscious knowledge, we find that they coincide with the precepts of the prevailing cultural super-ego. At this point the two processes, that of the cultural development of the group and that of the cultural development of the individual, are, as it were, always interlocked. For that reason some of the manifestations and properties of the super-ego can be more easily detected in its behaviour in the cultural community than in the separate individual.

The cultural super-ego has developed its ideals and set up its demands. Among the latter, those which deal with the relations of human beings to one another are comprised under the heading of ethics. People have at all times set the greatest value on ethics, as though they expected that it in particular would produce especially important results. And it does in fact deal with a subject which can easily be recognized as the sorest spot in every civilization. Ethics is thus to be regarded as a therapeutic attempt—as an endeavour to achieve, by means of a command of the super-ego, something which has so far not been achieved by means of any other cultural activities. As we already know, the problem before us is how to get rid of the greatest hindrance to civilization—namely, the constitutional inclination of human beings to be aggressive towards one another; and for that very reason we are especially interested in what is probably the most recent of the cultural commands of the super-ego, the commandment to love one's neighbour as oneself. In our research into, and therapy of, a neurosis, we are led to make two reproaches against the super-ego of the individual. In the severity of its commands and prohibitions it troubles itself too little about the happiness of the ego, in that it takes insufficient account of the resistances against obeying them—of the instinctual strength of the id [in the first place], and of the difficulties presented by the real external environment [in the second]. Consequently we are very often obliged, for therapeutic purposes, to oppose the super-ego, and we endeavour to lower its demands. Exactly the same objections can be made against the ethical demands of the cultural super-ego. It, too, does not trouble itself enough about the facts of the mental constitution of human beings. It issues a command and does not ask whether it is possible for people to obey it. On the contrary, it assumes that a man's ego is psychologically capable of anything that is required of it, that his ego has unlimited mastery over his id. This is a mistake; and even in what are known as normal people the id cannot be controlled beyond certain limits. If more is demanded of a man, a revolt will be produced in him or a neurosis, or he will be made unhappy. The commandment, 'Love thy neighbour as thyself,' is the strongest defence against human aggressiveness and an excellent example of the unpsychological proceedings of the cultural super-ego. The commandment is impossible to fulfill; such an enormous inflation of love can only lower its value, not get rid of the difficulty. Civilization pays no attention to all this; it merely admonishes us that the harder it is to obey the precept the more meritorious it is to do so. But anyone who follows such a precept in present-day civilization only puts himself at a disadvantage *vis-à-vis* the person who disregards it. What a potent obstacle to civilization aggressiveness must be, if the defence against it can cause as much unhappiness as aggressiveness itself! 'Natural' ethics, as it is called, has nothing to offer here except the narcissistic satisfaction of being able to think oneself better than others. At this point the ethics based on religion introduces its promises of a better after-life. But so long as virtue is not rewarded here on earth, ethics will, I fancy, preach in vain. I too think it quite certain that a real change in the relations of human beings to possessions would be of more help in this direction than any ethical commands;

but the recognition of this fact among socialists has been obscured and made useless for practical purposes by a fresh idealistic misconception of human nature.

I believe the line of thought which seeks to trace in the phenomena of cultural development the part played by a super-ego promises still further discoveries. I hasten to come to a close. But there is one question which I can hardly evade. If the development of civilization has such a far-reaching similarity to the development of the individual and if it employs the same methods, may we not be justified in reaching the diagnosis that, under the influence of cultural urges, some civilizations, or some epochs of civilization—possibly the whole of mankind—have become 'neurotic?' An analytic dissection of such neuroses might lead to therapeutic recommendations which could lay claim to great practical interest. I would not say that an attempt of this kind to carry psycho-analysis over to the cultural community was absurd or doomed to be fruitless. But we should have to be very cautious and not forget that, after all, we are only dealing with analogies and that it is dangerous, not only with men but also with concepts, to tear them from the sphere in which they have originated and been evolved. Moreover, the diagnosis of communal neuroses is faced with a special difficulty. In an individual neurosis we take as our starting-point the contrast that distinguishes the patient from his environment, which is assumed to be 'normal.' For a group all of whose members are affected by one and the same disorder no such background could exist; it would have to be found elsewhere. And as regards the therapeutic application of our knowledge, what would be the use of the most correct analysis of social neuroses, since no one possesses authority to impose such a therapy upon the group? But in spite of all these difficulties, we may expect that one day someone will venture to embark upon a pathology of cultural communities.

For a wide variety of reasons, it is very far from my intention to express an opinion upon the value of human civilization. I have endeavoured to guard myself against the enthusiastic prejudice which holds that our civilization is the most precious thing that we possess or could acquire and that its path will necessarily lead to heights of unimagined perfection. I can at least listen without indignation to the critic who is of the opinion that when one surveys the aims of cultural endeavour and the means it employs, one is bound to come to the conclusion that the whole effort is not worth the trouble, and that the outcome of it can only be a state of affairs which the individual will be unable to tolerate. My impartiality is made all the easier to me by my knowing very little about all these things. One thing only do I know for certain and that is that man's judgements of value follow directly his wishes for happiness—that, accordingly, they are an attempt to support his illusions with arguments. I should find it very understandable if someone were to point out the obligatory nature of the course of human civilization and were to say, for instance, that the tendencies to a restriction of sexual life or to the institution of a humanitarian ideal at the expense of natural selection were developmental trends which cannot be averted or turned aside and to which it is best for us to yield as though they were necessities of nature. I know, too, the objection that can be made against this, to the effect that in the history of mankind, trends such as these, which were considered unsurmountable, have often been thrown aside and replaced by other trends. Thus I have not the courage to rise up before my fellow-men as a prophet, and I bow to their reproach that I can offer them no consolation: for at bottom that is what they are all demanding—the wildest revolutionaries no less passionately than the most virtuous believers.

The fateful question for the human species seems to me to be whether and to what extent their cultural development will succeed in mastering the disturbance of their communal life by the human instinct of aggression and self-destruction. It may be that in this respect precisely the present time deserves a special interest. Men have gained control over the forces of nature to such an extent that with their help they would have no difficulty in exterminating one another to the last man. They know this, and hence comes a large part of their current unrest, their unhappiness and their mood of anxiety. And now it is to be expected that the other of the two 'Heavenly Powers' eternal Eros, will make an effort to assert himself in the struggle with his equally immortal adversary. But who can foresee with what success and with what result?

Moses and Monotheism

Freud apparently completed this book in 1934 in Austria but did not publish it until he was in England in 1938, partly because of his fear of the reaction of the Roman Catholic hierarchy in Austria. In this passage he describes the development of the super-ego, a crucial mechanism in enabling the individual to abstain from satisfying instinctual urges and to come to terms with the demands of the outside world.

The passage is taken from *Moses and Monotheism*, in Volume XXIII of *The Standard Edition of the Complete Psychological Works of Sigmund Freud*, translated and edited by James Strachey, in collaboration with Anna Freud, assisted by Alix Strachey and Alan Tyson, published in London in 1964 by The Hogarth Press and The Institute of Psycho-analysis. Reprinted by permission of Sigmund Freud Copyrights Ltd., Mr. James Strachey, The Hogarth Press Ltd., and Alfred A. Knopf, Inc.

It is not obvious and not immediately understandable why an advance in intellectuality, a set-back to sensuality, should raise the self-regard both of an individual and of a people. It seems to presuppose the existence of a definite standard of value and of some other person or agency which maintains it. For an explanation let us turn to an analogous case in individual psychology which we have come to understand.

If the id in a human being gives rise to an instinctual demand of an erotic or aggressive nature, the simplest and most natural thing is that the ego, which has the apparatus of thought and the muscular apparatus at its disposal, should satisfy the demand by an action. This satisfaction of the instinct is felt by the ego as pleasure, just as its non-satisfaction would undoubtedly have become a source of unpleasure. Now a case may arise in which the ego abstains from satisfying the instinct in view of external obstacles—namely, if it perceives that the

action in question would provoke a serious danger to the ego. An absten-
tion from satisfaction of this kind, the renunciation of an instinct on
account of an external hindrance—or, as we say, in obedience to the
reality principle—is not pleasurable in any event. The renunciation of
the instinct would lead to a lasting tension owing to unpleasure, if it
were not possible to reduce the strength of the instinct itself by displace-
ments of energy. Instinctual renunciation can, however, also be imposed
for other reasons, which we correctly describe as *internal*. In the course
of an individual's development a portion of the inhibiting forces in the
external world are internalized and an agency is constructed in the
ego which confronts the rest of the ego in an observing, criticizing
and prohibiting sense. We call this new agency the *super-ego*. Thencefor-
ward the ego, before putting to work the instinctual satisfactions demanded by the id, has to take into account not merely the dangers
of the external world but also the objections of the super-ego, and it
will have all the more grounds for abstaining from satisfying the instinct.
But whereas instinctual renunciation, when it is for external reasons,
is *only* unpleasurable, when it is for internal reasons, in obedience to
the super-ego, it has a different economic effect. In addition to the
inevitable unpleasurable consequences it also brings the ego a yield
of pleasure—a substitutive satisfaction, as it were. The ego feels elevated; it is proud of the instinctual renunciation, as though it were
a valuable achievement. We believe we can understand the mechanism
of this yield of pleasure. The super-ego is the successor and representative of the individual's parents (and educators) who had supervised
his actions in the first period of his life; it carries on their functions
almost unchanged. It keeps the ego in a permanent state of dependence
and exercises a constant pressure on it. Just as in childhood, the ego
is apprehensive about risking the love of its supreme master; it feels
his approval as liberation and satisfaction and his reproaches as pangs
of conscience. When the ego has brought the super-ego the sacrifice
of an instinctual renunciation, it expects to be rewarded by receiving
more love from it. The consciousness of deserving this love is felt by
it as pride. At the time when the authority had not yet been internalized
as a super-ego, there could be the same relation between the threat
of loss of love and the claims of instinct: there was a feeling of security
and satisfaction when one had achieved an instinctual renunciation out
of love for one's parents. But this happy feeling could only assume
the peculiar narcissistic character of pride after the authority had itself
become a portion of the ego.

The Resistances to Psychoanalysis

Freud here defends psychoanalysis against accusations that it threatens culture and morality. It is true that psychoanalysis attempts to mitigate the strictness with which society compels the individual to renounce his instinctual drives. But Freud argues that such rigorous and uncompensated repression sometimes institutes such an overwhelming burden that it crushes the individual. We could profit from a more truthful discussion of our sexual instincts and of the ways in which society orders their renunciation.

The passage is taken from "The Resistances to Psychoanalysis," in Volume V of the *Collected Papers of Sigmund Freud,* edited by Ernest Jones, published in New York in 1959 by Basic Books, Inc., with whose permission it is reprinted.

Human civilization rests upon two pillars, of which one is the control of natural forces and the other the restriction of our instincts. The ruler's throne rests upon fettered slaves. Among the instinctual components which are thus brought into service, the sexual instincts, in the narrower sense of the word, are conspicuous for their strength and savagery. Woe, if they should be set loose! The throne would be overturned and the ruler trampled under foot. Society is aware of this—and will not allow the subject to be mentioned.

But why not? What harm could the discussion do? Psychoanalysis has never said a word in favour of unfettering instincts that would injure our community; on the contrary it has issued a warning and an exhortation to us to mend our ways. But society refuses to consent to the ventilation of the question because it has a bad conscience in more than one respect. In the first place it has set up a high ideal of morality—morality being restriction of the instincts—and insists that all its members shall fulfil that ideal without troubling itself with the possibility that obedience may bear heavily upon the individual. Nor is it sufficiently wealthy or well-organized to be able to compensate the individual for his expenditure in instinctual renunciation. It is consequently left to the individual to decide how he can obtain enough compensation for the sacrifice he has made to enable him to retain his mental balance. On the whole, however, he is obliged to live psychologically beyond his income, while the unsatisfied claims of his instincts make him feel the demands of civilization as a constant pressure upon him. Thus society maintains a condition of cultural hypocrisy, which is bound to be accompanied by a sense of insecurity and a necessity for guarding what is an undeniably precarious situation by forbidding criticism and discussion. This line of thought holds good for all the instinctual impulses, including, therefore, the egoistic ones. The question whether it applies to all possible forms of civilization, and not merely to those which have evolved hitherto, cannot be discussed here. As regards the sexual instincts in the narrower sense, there is the further point that in most people they are tamed insufficiently and in a manner which is psychologically wrong and are therefore readier than the rest to break loose.

Psychoanalysis has revealed the weaknesses of this system and has recommended that it should be altered. It proposes that there should be a reduction in the strictness with which instincts are repressed and that correspondingly more play should be given to truthfulness. Certain instinctual impulses, with whose suppression society has gone too far, should be permitted a greater amount of satisfaction; in the case of certain others the inefficient method of suppressing them by means of repression should be replaced by a better and securer procedure. As a result of these criticisms psychoanalysis is regarded as "inimical to culture" and has been put under a ban as a "social danger." This resistance cannot last for ever. No human institution can in the long run escape the influence of fair criticism; but men's attitude to psychoanalysis is still dominated by this fear, which gives rein to their passions and diminishes their power of logical argument.

Analysis Terminable
and Interminable

This paper, written in 1937, was among Freud's last psychoanalytic writings. In it he discusses the qualities of the psychoanalyst who, as a model of the psychological man, must be committed to the pursuit of truth and the discovery of reality. He must oppose all illusion and deception. The psychological man is not one who is devoid of all strong emotions and idiosyncracies. Nor will he have left all conflict behind. But he will be ready to face his conflicts and live with them.

The selection is taken from "Analysis Terminable and Interminable," in Volume XXIII of *The Standard Edition of the Complete Psychological Works of Sigmund Freud,* translated and edited by James Strachey, in collaboration with Anna Freud, assisted by Alix Strachey and Alan Tyson, published in London in 1964 by The Hogarth Press and The Institute of Psycho-analysis. Reprinted by permission of Sigmund Freud Copyrights Ltd., Mr. James Strachey, and The Hogarth Press Ltd. It also appeared in Volume V of the *Collected Papers of Sigmund Freud,* edited by Ernest Jones, published in New York in 1959 by Basic Books, Inc., with whose permission it is reprinted.

It cannot be disputed that analysts in their own personalities have not invariably come up to the standard of psychical normality to which they wish to educate their patients. Opponents of analysis often point to this fact with scorn and use it as an argument to show the uselessness of analytic exertions. We might reject this criticism as making unjustifiable demands. Analysts are people who have learned to practise a particular art; alongside of this, they may be allowed to be human beings like anyone else. After all, nobody maintains that a physician is incapable of treating internal diseases if his own internal organs are not sound; on the contrary, it may be argued that there are certain advantages in a man who is himself threatened with tuberculosis specializing in the treatment of persons suffering from that disease. But the cases are not on all fours. So long as he is capable of practising at all, a doctor suffering from disease of the lungs or heart is not handicapped either in diagnosing or treating internal complaints; whereas the special conditions of analytic work do actually cause the analyst's own defects to interfere with his making a correct assessment of the state of things in his patient and reacting to them in a useful way. It is therefore reasonable to expect of an analyst, as a part of his qualifications, a considerable degree of mental normality and correctness. In addition, he must possess some kind of superiority, so that in certain analytic situations he can act as a model for his patient and in others as a teacher. And finally we must not forget that the analytic relationship is based on a love of truth—that is, on a recognition of reality—and that it precludes any kind of sham or deceit.

Here let us pause for a moment to assure the analyst that he has our sincere sympathy in the very exacting demands he has to fulfil in carrying out his activities. It almost looks as if analysis were the third of those 'impossible' professions in which one can be sure beforehand of achieving unsatisfying results. The other two, which have been known much longer, are education and government. Obviously we cannot demand that the prospective analyst should be a perfect being before he takes up analysis, in other words that only persons of such high and rare perfection should enter the profession. But where and how is the poor wretch to acquire the ideal qualifications which he will need in his profession? The answer is, in an analysis of himself, with which his preparation for his future activity begins. For practical reasons this analysis can only be short and incomplete. Its main object is to enable his teacher to make a judgement as to whether the candidate can be accepted for further training. It has accomplished its purpose if it gives the learner a firm conviction of the existence of the unconscious, if it enables him, when repressed material emerges, to perceive in himself things which would otherwise be incredible to him, and if it shows him a first sample of the technique which has proved to be the only effective one in analytic work. This alone would not suffice for his instruction; but we reckon on the stimuli that he has received in his own analysis not ceasing when it ends and on the processes of remodelling the ego continuing spontaneously in the analysed subject and making use of all subsequent experiences in this newly-acquired sense. This does in fact happen, and in so far as it happens it makes the analysed subject qualified to be an analyst himself.

Unfortunately something else happens as well. In trying to describe this, one can only rely on impressions. Hostility on the one side and partisanship on the other create an atmosphere which is not favourable to objective investigation. It seems that a number of analysts learn to make use of defensive mechanisms which allow them to divert the implications and demands of analysis from themselves (probably by directing them on to other people), so that they themselves remain as they are and are able to withdraw from the critical and corrective influence of analysis. Such an event may justify the words of the writer who warns us that when a man is endowed with power it is hard for him not to misuse it. Sometimes, when we try to understand this, we are driven into drawing a disagreeable analogy with the effect of X-rays on people who handle them without taking special precautions. It would not be surprising if the effect of a constant preoccupation with all the repressed material which struggles for freedom in the human mind were to stir up in the analyst as well all the instinctual demands which he is otherwise able to keep under suppression. These, too, are 'dangers of analysis', though they threaten, not the passive but the active partner in the analytic situation; and we ought not to neglect to meet them. There can be no doubt how this is to be done. Every analyst should periodically—at intervals of five years or so—submit himself to analysis once more, without feeling ashamed of taking this step. This would mean, then, that not only the therapeutic analysis of patients but his own analysis would change from a terminable into an interminable task.

At this point, however, we must guard against a misconception. I am not intending to assert that analysis is altogether an endless business. Whatever one's theoretical attitude to the question may be, the termination of an analysis is, I think a practical matter. Every experienced analyst will be able to recall a number of cases in which he has bidden his patient a permanent farewell *rebus bene gestis*.* In cases of what is known as character-analysis there is a far smaller discrepancy between theory and practice. Here it is not easy to foresee a natural end, even if one avoids any exaggerated expectations and sets the analysis no excessive tasks. Our aim will not be to rub off every peculiarity of human character for the sake of a schematic 'normality,' nor yet to demand that the person who has been 'thoroughly analysed' shall feel no passions and develop no internal conflicts. The business of the analysis is to secure the best possible psychological conditions for the functions of the ego; with that it has discharged its task.

* ['Things having gone well.']

Why War?

In 1932 Albert Einstein and Freud engaged in an exchange of open letters under the auspices of the League of Nations. Their subject concerned ways to avoid war. Freud, as always, is the complete realist, with no illusions about the "goodness" of human nature or about the "equality" of all men. The dependence and submissiveness of most men engenders the need for leaders who are intellectually independent, not cowed by the authority of church or state, committed to the search for truth, and habitually governed by reason.

The passage is taken from "Why War?" in Volume V of the *Collected Papers of Sigmund Freud*, edited by Ernest Jones, published in New York in 1959 by Basic Books Inc., with whose permission it is reprinted.

Our mythological theory of instincts makes it easy for us to find a formula for *indirect* methods of combating war. If willingness to engage in war is an effect of the destructive instinct, the most obvious plan will be to bring Eros, its antagonist, into play against it. Anything that encourages the growth of emotional ties between men must operate against war. These ties may be of two kinds. In the first place they may be relations resembling those towards a loved object, though without having a sexual aim. There is no need for psychoanalysis to be ashamed to speak of love in this connection, for religion itself uses the same words: "Thou shalt love thy neighbour as thyself." This, however, is more easily said than done. The second kind of emotional tie is by means of identification. Whatever leads men to share important interests produces this community of feeling, these identifications. And the structure of human society is to a large extent based on them.

A complaint which you make about the abuse of authority brings me to another suggestion for the indirect combating of the propensity to war. One instance of the innate and ineradicable inequality of men is their tendency to fall into the two classes of leaders and followers. The latter constitute the vast majority; they stand in need of an authority which will make decisions for them and to which they for the most part offer an unqualified submission. This suggests that more care should be taken than hitherto to educate an upper stratum of men with independent minds, not open to intimidation and eager in the pursuit of truth, whose business it would be to give direction to the dependent masses. It goes without saying that the encroachments made by the executive power of the State and the prohibition laid by the Church upon freedom of thought are far from propitious for the production of a class of this kind. The ideal condition of things would of course be a community of men who had subordinated their instinctual life to the dictatorship of reason. Nothing else could unite men so completely and so tenaciously, even if there were no emotional ties between them. But in all probability that is a Utopian expectation. No doubt the other indirect methods of preventing war are more practicable, though they promise no rapid success. An unpleasant picture comes to one's mind of mills that grind so slowly that people may starve before they get their flour.

14 *The Reflective Man: Dewey*

The unprecendentedly rapid change in the social and economic conditions of American life was the first challenge that stimulated the thinking of John Dewey (1859–1952), growing up in the second half of the nineteenth century. Immigration, urbanization, and industrialization were creating a new America, but the schools seemed largely oblivious of the fact. Acute dissatisfaction with the lack of connection between the child's classroom activities and his life outside the school led Dewey to his pedagogical experiments in the Laboratory School at the University of Chicago and to the early formulation of his educational principles in *My Pedagogic Creed*. His responses to the arid formalism of traditional education became a stream of philosophical and pedagogical writings that made him the leader of the progressive education movement. Although he had many disagreements with aspects of progressive education as they were practiced, his formulations provided the movement with a rigorous intellectual core.

It is interesting that Dewey was born in the year of the publication of Darwin's *Origin of Species,* for the challenge of Darwinism was a second major stimulus to the shaping of Dewey's ideas. Darwin's and Huxley's picture of the human organism was influential in persuading Dewey to see man not as an isolated figure but as one in interaction with his environment. The educated man is always viewed by Dewey in a social context.

A third force operating on Dewey's intellectual development was the pragmatism of C. S. Peirce and William James. Under the influence of these men, Dewey created a model of the educated man as the reflective man, one who is critical of the authority of custom and tradition as the determinant of belief and action and prefers the method of science, of "organized intelligence," as the best way to solve his problems. Science, Dewey believed, is the appropriate method of inquiry for a democracy, which calls especially for its values of objectivity, free inquiry, and cooperation. Democracy and science became the twin pillars of Dewey's own commitment.

A fourth influence that must be mentioned for its impact on Dewey's thought was the philosophy of Hegel. Both in discipleship and in reaction, Dewey's response to Hegel's ideas formed a permanent deposit in his thinking. A major part of Dewey's philosophical endeavor was a sustained attempt to synthesize many of the dualisms of traditional philosophy. The reflective behavior that he judged to be the mark of the educated man is characterized by a synthesis of the dualisms of science and morals, ends and means, thought and action. There should be no dualism between moral and intellectual education. Thus the intellectual habits of open-minded inquiry and responsible, experimental action, which are characteristic of the reflective man's behavior, are moral attributes.

Foolish and uninformed criticism of Dewey, for faults of "progressive education" that he himself struggled to correct, has tended to distract attention from some of the genuine weaknesses in his thinking. The exclusive power he accorded to science depreciates the importance of other methods of gaining knowledge, such as the contemplative, the intuitive, and the emotional. Democracy and science were close to absolutes in Dewey's thought, especially up to 1930. But many evils have been committed in the name of these values; they need to be examined critically, like other values; and ultimately they are not self-evidently good. Dewey's attempt to base morals on science was not markedly successful. From a fact nothing of value necessarily follows. Science still is not answering our "why" questions. Dewey's pragmatic viewpoint, moreover, prevented him from envisioning the educated person as one who can enjoy the world without wishing to change or redeem it. Above all, Dewey was insufficiently moved by the Freudian revolution. The greatest defect in his philosophy was his failure to recognize the extent to which irrational forces govern men's beliefs and conduct.

My Pedagogic Creed

This early statement of his educational viewpoint, first published in 1897, shows Dewey at his most confident and enthusiastic. Since 1894 he had been at the University of Chicago, where he set up the Laboratory School to test some of his ideas in practice. It was a period of revolutionary vision and optimistic zeal. Many of the undocumented claims put forward in this creed were subsequently elaborated, analyzed, and justified in Dewey's later writings. He shows us the model of a child growing not in isolation but in essential interaction with his social environment. Dewey's program is child-centered in the sense that the child's powers and purposes form the *starting point* for the educational process, but they do not define the *end* of that process. In order to avoid a one-sided distortion, there is a need to hold both the psychological and the sociological dimensions simultaneously in perspective. The child's interests are important: they should be neither humored nor repressed. To repress them is to commit the fault of much traditional education by ignoring the child's unique bent. To humor them is to commit the fault of some progressive education by failing to discover the underlying power below the passing whim. These transient interests should be duly recognized, but the goal should be to transform them into lasting powers and long-term concerns. The teacher's role is not to impose his values or ideas but to select and order the experiences the child encounters and to help him to respond reflectively to those experiences. Subject matter should consist of activities that enable the child to reflect upon his social experiences. When subject matter precedes or is unrelated to the child's experiences it is largely meaningless. It gains meaning through being made the medium for continued reflection upon and reconstruction of experience.

"My Pedagogic Creed" was published in *The School Journal*, Volume LIV, Number 3 (January 16, 1897), pages 77–80.

ARTICLE I. WHAT EDUCATION IS.

I believe that all education proceeds by the participation of the individual in the social consciousness of the race. This process begins unconsciously almost at birth, and is continually shaping the individual's powers, saturating his consciousness, forming his habits, training his ideas, and arousing his feelings and emotions. Through this unconscious education the individual gradually comes to share in the intellectual and moral resources which humanity has succeeded in getting together. He becomes an inheritor of the funded capital of civilization. The most formal and technical education in the world cannot safely depart from this general process. It can only organize it; or differentiate it in some particular direction.

I believe that the only true education comes through the stimulation of the child's powers by the demands of the social situations in which he finds himself. Through these demands he is stimulated to act as a member of a unity, to emerge from his original narrowness of action and feeling and to conceive of himself from the standpoint of the welfare of the group to which he belongs. Through the responses which others make to his own activities he comes to know what these mean in social terms. The value which they have is reflected back into them. For instance, through the response which is made to the child's instinctive babblings the child comes to know what those babblings mean; they are transformed into articulate language and thus the child is introduced into the consolidated wealth of ideas and emotions which are now summed up in language.

I believe that this educational process has two sides—one psychological and one sociological; and that neither can be subordinated to the other or neglected without evil results following. Of these two sides, the psychological is the basis. The child's own instincts and powers furnish the material and give the starting point for all education. Save as the efforts of the educator connect with some activity which the child is carrying on of his own initiative independent of the educator, education becomes reduced to a pressure from without. It may, indeed, give certain external results but cannot truly be called educative. Without insight into the psychological structure and activities of the individual, the educative process will, therefore, be haphazard and arbitrary. If it chances to coincide with the child's activity it will get a leverage; if it does not, it will result in friction, or disintegration, or arrest of the child nature.

I believe that knowledge of social conditions, of the present state of civilization, is necessary in order properly to interpret the child's powers. The child has his own instincts and tendencies, but we do not know what these mean until we can translate them into their social equivalents. We must be able to carry them back into a social past and see them as the inheritance of previous race activities. We must also be able to project them into the future to see what their outcome and end will be. In the illustration just used, it is the ability to see in the child's babblings the promise and potency of a future social intercourse and conversation which enables one to deal in the proper way with that instinct.

I believe that the psychological and social sides are organically related and that education cannot be regarded as a compromise between the two, or a superimposition of one upon the other. We are told that the psychological definition of education is barren and formal—that it gives us only the idea of a development of all the mental powers without giving us any idea of the use to which these powers are put. On the other hand, it is urged that the social definition of education, as getting adjusted to civilization, makes of it a forced and external process, and results in subordinating the freedom of the individual to a preconceived social and political status.

I believe each of these objections is true when urged against one side isolated from the other. In order to know what a power really is we must know what its end, use, or function is; and this we cannot know save as we conceive of the individual as active in social relationships. But, on the other hand, the only possible adjustment which we can give to the child under existing conditions, is that which arises through putting him in complete possession of all his powers. With the advent of democracy and modern industrial conditions, it is impossible to foretell definitely just what civilization will be twenty years from now. Hence it is impossible to prepare the child for any precise set of conditions. To prepare him for the future life means to give him command of himself; it means so to train him that he will have the full and ready use of all his capacities; that his eye and ear and hand may be tools ready to command, that his judgment may be capable of grasping the conditions under which it has to work, and the executive forces be trained to act economically and efficiently. It is impossible to reach this sort of adjustment save as constant regard is had to the individuals' own powers tastes, and interests—says, that is, as education is continually converted into psychological terms.

In sum, I believe that the individual who is to be educated is a social individual and that society is an organic union of individuals. If we eliminate the social factor from the child we are left only with an abstraction; if we eliminate the individual factor from society, we are left only with an inert and lifeless mass. Education, therefore, must begin with a psychological insight into the child's capacities, interests, and habits. It must be controlled at every point by reference to these same considerations. These powers, interests, and habits must be continually interpreted—we must know what they mean. They must be translated into terms of their social equivalents—into terms of what they are capable of in the way of social service.

ARTICLE II. WHAT THE SCHOOL IS.

I believe that the school is primarily a social institution. Education being a social process, the school is simply that form of community life in which all those agencies are concentrated that will be most effective in bringing the child to share in the inherited resources of the race, and to use his own powers for social ends.

I believe that education, therefore, is a process of living and not a preparation for future living.

I believe that the school must represent present life—life as real and vital to the child as that which he carries on in the home, in the neighborhood, or on the play-ground.

I believe that education which does not occur through forms of life, or that are worth living for their own sake, is always a poor substitute for the genuine reality and tends to cramp and to deaden.

I believe that the school, as an institution, should simplify existing social life; should reduce it, as it were, to an embryonic form. Existing life is so complex that the child cannot be brought into contact with it without either confusion or distraction; he is either overwhelmed by the multiplicity of activities which are going on, so that he loses his own power of orderly reaction, or he is so stimulated by these various activities that his powers are prematurely called into play and he becomes either unduly specialized or else disintegrated.

I believe that, as such simplified social life, the school life should grow gradually out of the home life; that it should take up and continue the activities with which the child is already familiar in the home.

I believe that it should exhibit these activities to the child, and reproduce them in such ways that the child will gradually learn the meaning of them, and be capable of playing his own part in relation to them.

I believe that this is a psychological necessity, because it is the only way of securing continuity in the child's growth, the only way of giving a background of past experience to the new ideas given in school.

I believe it is also a social necessity because the home is the form of social life in which the child has been nurtured and in connection with which he has had his moral training. It is the business of the school to deepen and extend his sense of the values bound up in his home life.

I believe that much of present education fails because it neglects this fundamental principle of the school as a form of community life. It conceives the school as a place where certain information is to be given, where certain lessons are to be learned, or where certain habits are to be formed. The value of these is conceived as lying largely in the remote future; the child must do these things for the sake of something else he is to do; they are mere preparation. As a result they do not become a part of the life experience of the child and so are not truly educative.

I believe that the moral education centers about this conception of the school as a mode of social life, that the best and deepest moral training is precisely that which one gets through having to enter into proper relations with others in a unity of work and thought. The present educational systems, so far as they destroy or neglect this unity, render it difficult or impossible to get any genuine, regular moral training.

I believe that the child should be stimulated and controlled in his work through the life of the community.

I believe that under existing conditions far too much of the stimulus and control proceeds from the teacher, because of neglect of the idea of the school as a form of social life.

I believe that the teacher's place and work in the school is to be interpreted from this same basis. The teacher is not in the school to impose certain ideas or to form certain habits in the child, but is there as a member of the community to select the influences which shall affect the child and to assist him in properly responding to these influences.

I believe that the discipline of the school should proceed from the life of the school as a whole and not directly from the teacher.

I believe that the teacher's business is simply to determine on the basis of larger experience and riper wisdom, how the discipline of life shall come to the child.

I believe that all questions of the grading of the child and his promotion should be determined by reference to the same standard. Examinations are of use only so far as they test the child's fitness for social life and reveal the place in which he can be of the most service and where he can receive the most help.

ARTICLE III.   THE SUBJECT-MATTER OF EDUCATION.

I believe that the social life of the child is the basis of concentration, or correlation, in all his training or growth. The social life gives the unconscious unity and the background of all his efforts and of all his attainments.

I believe that the subject-matter of the school curriculum should mark a gradual differentiation out of the primitive unconscious unity of social life.

I believe that we violate the child's nature and render difficult the best ethical results, by introducing the child too abruptly to a number of special studies, of reading, writing, geography, etc., out of relation to this social life.

I believe, therefore, that the true center of correlation on the school subjects is not science, nor literature, nor history, nor geography, but the child's own social activities.

I believe that education cannot be unified in the study of science, or so called nature study, because apart from human activity, nature itself is not a unity; nature in itself is a number of diverse objects in space and time, and to attempt to make it the center of work by itself, is to introduce a principle of radiation rather than one of concentration.

I believe that literature is the reflex expression and interpretation of social experience; that hence it must follow upon and not precede such experience. It, therefore, cannot be made the basis, although it may be made the summary of unification.

I believe once more that history is of educative value in so far as it presents phases of social life and growth. It must be controlled by reference to social life. When taken simply as history it is thrown into the distant past and becomes dead and inert. Taken as the record of man's social life and progress it becomes full of meaning. I believe, however, that it cannot be so taken excepting as the child is also introduced directly into social life.

I believe accordingly that the primary basis of education is in the child's powers at work along the same general constructive lines as those which have brought civilization into being.

I believe that the only way to make the child conscious of his social heritage is to enable him to perform those fundamental types of activity which make civilization what it is.

I believe, therefore, in the so-called expressive or constructive activities as the center of correlation.

I believe that this gives the standard for the place of cooking, sewing, manual training, etc., in the school.

I believe that they are not special studies which are to be introduced over and above a lot of others in the way of relaxation or relief, or as additional accomplishments. I believe rather that they represent, as types, fundamental forms of social activity; and that it is possible and desirable that the child's introduction into the more formal subjects of the curriculum be through the medium of these activities.

I believe that the study of science is educational in so far as it brings out the materials and processes which make social life what it is.

I believe that one of the greatest difficulties in the present teaching of science is that the material is presented in purely objective form, or is treated as a new peculiar kind of experience which the child can add to that which he has already had. In reality, science is of value because it gives the ability to interpret and control the experience already had. It should be introduced, not as so much new subject-matter, but as showing the factors already involved in previous experience and as furnishing tools by which that experience can be more easily and effectively regulated.

I believe that at present we lose much of the value of literature and language studies because of our elimination of the social element. Language is almost always treated in the books of pedagogy simply as the expression of thought. It is true that language is a logical instrument, but it is fundamentally and primarily a social instrument. Language is the device for communication; it is the tool through which one individual comes to share the ideas and feelings of others. When treated simply as a way of getting individual information, or as a means of showing off what one has learned, it loses its social motive and end.

I believe that there is, therefore, no succession of studies in the ideal school curriculum. If education is life, all life has, from the outset, a scientific aspect; an aspect of art and culture and an aspect of communication. It cannot, therefore, be true that the proper studies for one grade are mere reading and writing, and that at a later grade, reading, or literature, or science, may be introduced. The progress is not in the succession of studies but in the development of new attitudes towards, and new interests in, experience.

I believe finally, that education must be conceived as a continuing reconstruction of experience; that the process and the goal of education are one and the same thing.

I believe that to set up any end outside of education, as furnishing its goal and standard, is to deprive the educational process of much of its meaning and tends to make us rely upon false and external stimuli in dealing with the child.

ARTICLE IV.   THE NATURE OF METHOD.

I believe that the question of method is ultimately reducible to the question of the order of development of the child's powers and interests. The law for presenting and treating material is the law implicit within the child's own nature. Because this is so I believe the following statements are of supreme importance as determining the spirit in which education is carried on:

1. I believe that the active side precedes the passive in the development of the child nature; that expression comes before conscious impression; that the muscular development precedes the sensory; that movements come before conscious sensations. I believe that consciousness is essentially motor or impulsive; that conscious states tend to project themselves in action.

I believe that the neglect of this principle is the cause of a large part of the waste of time and strength in school work. The child is thrown into a passive, receptive or absorbing attitude. The conditions are such that he is not permitted to follow the law of his nature; the result is friction and waste.

I believe that ideas (intellectual and rational processes) also result from action and devolve for the sake of the better control of action. What we term reason is primarily the law of orderly or effective action. To attempt to develop the reasoning powers, the powers of judgment, without reference to the selection and arrangement of means in action, is the fundamental fallacy in our present methods of dealing with this matter. As a result we present the child with arbitrary symbols. Symbols are a necessity in mental development, but they have their place as tools for economizing effort; presented by themselves they are a mass of meaningless and arbitrary ideas imposed from without.

2. I believe that the image is the great instrument of instruction. What a child gets out of any subject presented to him is simply the images which he himself forms with regard to it.

I believe that if nine tenths of the energy at present directed towards making the child learn certain things, were spent in seeing to it that the child was forming proper images, the work of instruction would be indefinitely facilitated.

I believe that much of the time and attention now given to the preparation and presentation of lessons might be more wisely and profitably expended in training the child's power of imagery and in seeing to it that he was continually forming definite, vivid, and growing images of the various subjects with which he comes in contact in his experience.

3. I believe that interests are the signs and symptoms of growing power. I believe that they represent dawning capacities. Accordingly the constant and careful observation of interests is of the utmost importance for the educator.

I believe that these interests are to be observed as showing the state of development which the child has reached.

I believe that they prophesy the stage upon which he is about to enter.

I believe that only through the continual and sympathetic observation of childhood's interests can the adult enter into the child's life and see what it is ready for, and upon what material it could work most readily and fruitfully.

I believe that these interests are neither to be humored nor repressed. To repress interest is to substitute the adult for the child, and so to weaken intellectual curiosity and alertness, to suppress initiative, and to deaden interest. To humor the interests is to substitute the transient for the permanent. The interest is always the sign of some power below; the important thing is to discover this power. To humor the interest is to fail to penetrate below the surface and its sure result is to substitute caprice and whim for genuine interest.

4. I believe that the emotions are the reflex of actions.

I believe that to endeavor to stimulate or arouse the emotions apart from their corresponding activities, is to introduce an unhealthy and morbid state of mind.

I believe that if we can only secure right habits of action and thought, with reference to the good, the true, and the beautiful, the emotions will for the most part take care of themselves.

I believe that next to deadness and dullness, formalism and routine, our education is threatened with no greater evil than sentimentalism.

I believe that this sentimentalism is the necessary result of the attempt to divorce feeling from action.

ARTICLE V.   THE SCHOOL AND SOCIAL PROGRESS.

I believe that education is the fundamental method of social progress and reform.

I believe that all reforms which rest simply upon the enactment of law, or the threatening of certain penalties, or upon changes in mechanical or outward arrangements, are transitory and futile.

I believe that education is a regulation of the process of coming to share in the social consciousness; and that the adjustment of individual activity on the basis of this social consciousness is the only sure method of social reconstruction.

I believe that this conception has due regard for both the individualistic and socialistic ideals. It is duly individual because it recognizes the formation of a certain character as the only genuine basis of right living. It is socialistic because it recognizes that this right character is not to be formed by merely individual precept, example, or exhortation, but rather by the influence of a certain form of institutional or community life upon the individual, and that the social organism through the school, as its organ, may determine ethical results.

I believe that in the ideal school we have the reconciliation of the individualistic and the institutional ideals.

I believe that the community's duty to education is, therefore, its paramount moral duty. By law and punishment, by social agitation and discussion, society can regulate and form itself in a more or less haphazard and chance way. But through education society can formulate its own purposes, can organize its own means and resources, and thus shape itself with definiteness and economy in the direction in which it wishes to move.

I believe that when society once recognizes the possibilities in this direction, and the obligations which these possibilities impose, it is impossible to conceive of the resources of time, attention, and money which will be put at the disposal of the educator.

I believe it is the business of every one interested in education to insist upon the school as the primary and most effective interest of social progress and reform in order that society may be awakened to realize what the school stands for, and aroused to the necessity of endowing the educator with sufficient equipment properly to perform his task.

I believe that education thus conceived marks the most perfect and intimate union of science and art conceivable in human experience.

I believe that the art of thus giving shape to human powers and adapting them to social service, is the supreme art; one calling into its service the best of artists; that no insight, sympathy, tact, executive power is too great for such service.

I believe that with the growth of psychological service, giving added insight into individual structure and laws of growth; and with growth of social science, adding to our knowledge of the right organization of individuals, all scientific resources can be utilized for the purposes of education.

I believe that when science and art thus join hands the most commanding motive for human action will be reached; the most genuine springs of human conduct aroused and the best service that human nature is capable of guaranteed.

I believe, finally, that the teacher is engaged, not simply in the training of individuals, but in the formation of the proper social life.

I believe that every teacher should realize the dignity of his calling; that he is a social servant set apart for the maintenance of proper social order and the securing of the right social growth.

I believe that in this way the teacher always is the prophet of the true God and the usherer in of the true kingdom of God.

Toward a New Individualism

In 1930 Dewey wrote a series of articles for *The New Republic* under the general title, *Individualism, Old and New*. The final article in this series, "Toward a New Individualism," from which the following passages are taken, summarizes his views on the changes in the concept of the individual that are demanded by new social and economic conditions. Dewey makes clear his opposition to *laissez-faire* liberalism. The rugged, self-interested individualism of the pioneer era may have been appropriate and useful when man's relationship to physical nature was the paramount consideration. But this traditional American individualism has become merely a seeking for private profit and is pernicious and anachronistic in an urban, industrial society where large groups must work together in complex situations and where man's crucial relationship is to his fellowman. Now that the wilderness is tamed, our problems are basically social, and a new type of individual is needed for these tasks. It should be the goal of education to prepare such people. Dewey does not see the educated man apart from his environment. For Dewey, neither the individual nor society has any meaning without the other. The educated man must have a knowledge of the social forces operating on him in order to avoid being helplessly molded by them. Modern society engenders a need for corporate action and concern, but this must issue in the rediscovery of the individual in a new social context. Man needs to feel himself united with a social whole. If he does not experience this unity he will seek superficial sociability or merely conform to conventional thinking.

These excerpts are from John Dewey, "Toward a New Individualism," *The New Republic*, Volume LXII, Number 794 (February 19, 1930).

Just as the new individualism cannot be achieved by extending the benefits of the older economic individualism to more persons, so it cannot be obtained by a further development of generosity, good will and altruism. Such traits are desirable, but at the same time they are more or less constant expressions of human nature. There is much in the present situation that stimulates them to active operation. They are probably more marked features of American life than of any other civilization at any time. Our charity and philanthropy are partly the manifestation of an uneasy conscience. Partly, however, they are prophetic of a type of mind already in process of formation, but still lacking the organic character that will enable it to manifest itself in ordinary human relationships outside of relief and assistance.

The chief obstacle to the creation of a type of individual whose pattern of thought and desire is enduringly marked by consensus with others, and in whom sociability is one with cooperation in all regular human associations, is the persistence of that feature of the earlier individualism which defines industry and commerce by ideas of private pecuniary profit. Why, for example, is there such zeal for standardized likeness? It is not, I imagine, because conformity for its own sake appears to be a great boon. It is rather because a certain kind of conformity gives defense and protection to the pecuniary features of our present regime. The foreground may be filled with depiction of the horror of change, and with the clamor for law and order and the support of the Constitution. But behind there is desire for perpetuation of that regime which defines individual initiative and ability by success in conducting business so as to make money.

It is not too much to say that the whole significance of the older individualism has now shrunk to a pecuniary scale and measure. The virtues that are supposed to attend rugged individualism may be vocally proclaimed, but it takes no great insight to see that what is cherished is measured by its connection with those activities that make for success in business conducted for personal gain. Hence, the irony of the gospel of "individualism" in business conjoined with suppression of individuality in thought and speech. One cannot imagine a bitterer comment on any professed individualism than that it subordinates the only creative individuality—that of mind—to the maintenance of a regime which gives a few an opportunity for being shrewd in the management of monetary business.

It is claimed, of course, that the individualism of economic self-seeking, even if it has not produced the adjustment of ability and reward and the harmony of interests earlier predicted, has given us the advantage of material prosperity. It is not needful to raise here the question of how far that material prosperity extends. For it is not true that its moving cause is pecuniary individualism. That has been the cause of some great fortunes, but not of national wealth; it counts in the process of distribution, but not in ultimate creation. Scientific insight taking effect in machine technology has been the great productive force. For the most part, economic individualism interpreted as energy and enterprise devoted to private profit, has been an adjunct, often a parasitical one, to the movement of technical and scientific forces.

The scene in which individuality is now to be created has been transformed. The pioneer . . . had no great need for any ideas beyond those that sprang up in the immediate tasks in which he was engaged. His intellectual problems grew out of struggle with the forces of physical nature. The wilderness was a reality and it had to be subdued. The type of character that evolved was strong and hardy, often picturesque, and sometimes heroic. Individuality was a reality because it corresponded to conditions. Irrelevant traditional ideas in religion and morals were carried along, but they were reduced to a size where they did no harm; indeed, they could easily be interpreted in such a way as to be a reinforcement to the sturdy and a consolation to the weak and failing.

But it is no longer a physical wilderness that has to be wrestled with. Our problems grow out of social conditions: they concern human relations rather than man's direct relationship to physical nature. The adventure of the individual, if there is to be any venturing of individuality and not a relapse into the deadness of complacency or of despairing discontent, is henceforth an unsubdued social frontier. The issues cannot be met with ideas improvised for the occasion. The problems to be solved are general, not local. They concern complex forces that are at work throughout the whole country, not those limited to an immediate and almost face-to-face environment. Traditional ideas are more than irrelevant. They are an encumbrance; they are the chief obstacle to the formation of a new individuality integrated within itself and with a liberated function in the society wherein it exists. A new individualism has to be achieved which uses all the resources of the science and technology that have mastered physical forces as means to attain truly human ends. As long as we retain the older individualistic philosophy, our purposes will not be framed out of the positive consequences of even our industrial activity; nor will our means be based upon acknowledged possession of the techniques by which a meed of success has been attained in the material field. Only when we begin to use the vast resources of technology at our command as methods to achieve purposes that are avowedly social, will there be an approach to a new individual, an individual as much related and unified as the present individual is divided and distracted.

The nature of a newly emerging individualism cannot be described until progress has been made in its actual creation; but neither shall we make a start in this creation until we surrender the habit of opposing the corporate and social to the individual, and until we realize that the utmost in socialism will effect only a restandardization of an almost exclusively material culture, unless it be accompanied by the instituting of a new type of individual mind. Technology, taken in its broadest sense, offers an answer to our problem. It furnishes us with means that may be utilized in transforming the forces of our industrialized society into factors in producing individuals who are not only possessed of material goods, but also equipped with a high quality of desire and thought.

Democracy and Education

In 1916 appeared the volume *Democracy and Education,* which came to be regarded as Dewey's major statement of his philosophy of education. Central in his philosophy are the concepts of democracy and growth. Education, in Dewey's view, is not to be seen as having some absolute or external end: it is an end in itself. The process of education consists of arranging the environment so as to foster the growth of the student. And this growth is not toward some fixed goal: growth carries its own justification. Certainly, the adult environment should not be regarded as the goal toward which we educate the child. To do this would be to ignore the uniqueness of each child and to impose undesirable adult patterns like the aversion to novelty, to unpredictability, and to uncertainty. Both child and adult are capable of growth, but children possess some special strengths, like curiosity, responsiveness, and openness. Childhood must be lived fully, not regarded as a disease that time alone will cure. The child's behavior is not to be indulged or worshipped, nor is it to be impatiently suppressed, but it is to be studied as a sign of some underlying capacity that needs to be developed. Hence Dewey's model can manifest himself at any age: he is the child or adult who is still growing. The educated person, therefore, is the self-educating person. The concept of an educated person as a final product gives way to a concept of continual process. We can measure the value of an education by the degree to which it stimulates a desire in the individual for more education. There is no final victory for growth and education. Growth takes place where there is freedom to associate and cooperate with others and to exchange ideas with them. Hence Dewey was a proponent of democracy as the facilitator of these conditions. But "democracy" is a term that has been much abused. It is too vague and ambiguous a concept to be accepted uncritically. However, if we follow the general spirit of Dewey's philosophy, we will be prompted to believe that "democracy," like other concepts, should be carefully examined rather than viewed as sacrosanct.

This passage is taken from John Dewey, *Democracy and Education: An Introduction to the Philosophy of Education,* published in New York, copyright 1916 by the Macmillan Company, with whose permission it is reprinted.

CHAPTER IV

EDUCATION AS GROWTH

. . . When it is said that education is development, everything depends upon *how* development is conceived. Our net conclusion is that life is development, and that developing, growing, is life. Translated into its educational equivalents, this means (*i*) that the educational process has no end beyond itself; it is its own end; and that (*ii*) the educational process is one of continual reorganizing, reconstructing, transforming.

1. Development when it is interpreted in *comparative* terms, that is, with respect to the special traits of child and adult life, means the direction of power into special channels: the formation of habits involving executive skill, definiteness of interest, and specific objects of observation and thought. But the comparative view is not final. The child has specific powers; to ignore that fact is to stunt or distort the organs upon which his growth depends. The adult uses his powers to transform his environment, thereby occasioning new stimuli which redirect his powers and keep them developing. Ignoring this fact means arrested development, a passive accommodation. Normal child and normal adult alike, in other words, are engaged in growing. The difference between them is not the difference between growth and no growth, but between the modes of growth appropriate to different conditions. With respect to the development of powers devoted to coping with specific scientific and economic problems we may say the child should be growing in manhood. With respect to sympathetic curiosity, unbiased responsiveness, and openness of mind, we may say that the adult should be growing in childlikeness. One statement is as true as the other.

Three ideas which have been criticized, namely, the merely privative nature of immaturity, static adjustment to a fixed environment, and rigidity of habit, are all connected with a false idea of growth or development,—that it is a movement toward a fixed goal. Growth is regarded as *having* an end, instead of *being* an end. The educational counterparts of the three fallacious ideas are first, failure to take account of the instinctive or native powers of the young; secondly, failure to develop initiative in coping with novel situations; thirdly, an undue emphasis upon drill and other devices which secure automatic skill at the expense of personal perception. In all cases, the adult environment is accepted as a standard for the child. He is to be brought up *to* it.

Natural instincts are either disregarded or treated as nuisances as obnoxious traits to be suppressed, or at all events to be brought into conformity with external standards. Since conformity is the aim, what is distinctively individual in a young person is brushed aside, or regarded as a source of mischief or anarchy. Conformity is made equivalent to uniformity. Consequently, there are induced lack of interest in the novel, aversion to progress, and dread of the uncertain and the unknown. Since the end of growth is outside of and beyond the process of growing, external agents have to be resorted to to induce movement towards it. Whenever a method of education is stigmatized as mechanical we may be sure that external pressure is brought to bear to reach an external end.

2. Since in reality there is nothing to which growth is relative save more growth, there is nothing to which education is subordinate save more education. It is a commonplace to say that education should not cease when one leaves school. The point of this commonplace is that the purpose of school education is to insure the continuance of education by organizing the powers that insure growth. The inclination to learn from life itself and to make the conditions of life such that all will learn in the process of living is the finest product of schooling.

When we abandon the attempt to define immaturity by means of fixed comparison with adult accomplishments, we are compelled to give up thinking of it as denoting lack of desired traits. Abandoning this notion, we are also forced to surrender our habit of thinking of instruction as a method of supplying this lack by pouring knowledge into a mental and moral hole which awaits filling. Since life means growth, a living creature lives as truly and positively at one stage as at another, with the same intrinsic fullness and the same absolute claims. Hence education means the enterprise of supplying the conditions which insure growth, or adequacy of life, irrespective of age. We first look with impatience upon immaturity, regarding it as something to be got over as rapidly as possible. Then the adult formed by such educative methods looks back with impatient regret upon childhood and youth as a scene of lost opportunities and wasted powers. This ironical situation will endure till it is recognized that living has its own intrinsic quality and that the business of education is with that quality.

Realization that life is growth protects us from that so-called idealizing of childhood which in effect is nothing but lazy indulgence. Life is not to be identified with every superficial act and interest. Even though it is not always easy to tell whether what appears to be mere surface fooling is a sign of some nascent as yet untrained power, we must remember that manifestations are not to be accepted as ends in themselves. They are signs of possible growth. They are to be turned into means of development, of carrying power forward, not indulged or cultivated for their own sake. Excessive attention to surface phenomena (even in the way of rebuke as well as of encouragement) may lead to their fixation and thus to arrested development. What impulses are moving toward, not what they have been, is the important thing for parent and teacher.

Human Nature and Conduct

A central feature of Dewey's philosophy was the attempt to synthe-size many of the dualisms of traditional philosophy. Mind and body, work and play, child and curriculum, the individual and society, were dualisms that Dewey rejected in their either-or form. His study of *Human Nature and Conduct* epitomizes this synthetic ap-proach in its treatment of the relationship between man and society, as is shown by the book's subtitle: *An Introduction to Social Psy-chology*. The model that Dewey would persuade us to accept is not the man who lives an exclusively interior life, who concentrates on self-purification on the assumption that, if individual men are saved, the salvation of society will follow automatically. Nor is he the man who regards all significant change as occurring in the external world and men as merely reflections of their environment. The educated man is rather one who recognizes that man's freedom lies in his *interaction* with the natural and social environment. He strives to influence the quality of his life and his society through the exercise of his intelligence, applying it to the study of social problems and acting in accordance with his conclusions. Freedom is achieved through reflective thinking and action. The educated man is not one who submissively accepts his moral standards from external authority but one who works them out through intelligent reflection upon the probable consequences of various possible courses of action.

This passage is from John Dewey *Human Nature and Conduct: An Introduction to Social Psychology,* published in New York, copy-right 1922 by Henry Holt & Company. Reprinted by permission of Holt, Rinehart and Winston, Inc.

If we turn from concrete effects upon character to theoretical issues, we single out the discussion regarding freedom of will as typical of the consequences that come from separating morals from human nature. Men are wearied with bootless discussion, and anxious to dismiss it as a metaphysical subtlety. But nevertheless it contains within itself the most practical of all moral questions, the nature of freedom and the means of its achieving. The separation of morals from human nature leads to a separation of human nature in its moral aspects from the rest of nature, and from ordinary social habits and endeavors which are found in business, civic life, the run of companionships and recreations. These things are thought of at most as places where moral notions need to be applied, not as places where moral ideas are to be studied and moral energies generated. In short, the severance of morals from human nature ends by driving morals inwards from the public open out-of-doors air and light of day into the obscurities and privacies of an inner life. The significance of the traditional discussion of free will is that it reflects precisely a separation of moral activity from nature and the public life of men.

One has to turn from moral theories to the general human struggle for political, economic and religious liberty, for freedom of thought, speech, assemblage and creed, to find significant reality in the conception of freedom of will. Then one finds himself out of the stiflingly close atmosphere of an inner consciousness and in the open-air world. The cost of confining moral freedom to an inner region is the almost complete severance of ethics from politics and economics. The former is regarded as summed up in edifying exhortations, and the latter as connected with arts of expediency separated from larger issues of good.

In short, there are two schools of social reform. One bases itself upon the notion of a morality which springs from an inner freedom, something mysteriously cooped up within personality. It asserts that the only way to change institutions is for men to purify their own hearts, and that when this has been accomplished, change of institutions will follow of itself. The other school denies the existence of any such inner power, and in so doing conceives that it has denied all moral freedom. It says that men are made what they are by the forces of the environment, that human nature is purely malleable, and that till institutions are changed, nothing can be done. Clearly this leaves the outcome as hopeless as does an appeal to an inner rectitude and benevolence. For it provides no leverage for change of environment. It throws us back upon accident, usually disguised as a necessary law of history or evolution, and trusts to some violent change, symbolized by civil war, to usher in an abrupt millennium. There is an alternative to being penned in between these two theories. We can recognize that all conduct is *interaction* between elements of human nature and the environment, natural and social. Then we shall see that progress proceeds in two ways, and that freedom is found in that kind of interaction which maintains an environment in which human desire and choice count for something. There are in truth forces in man as well as without him. While they are infinitely frail in comparison with exterior forces, yet they may have the support of a foreseeing and contriving intelligence. When we look at the problem as one of an adjustment to be intelligently attained, the issues shifts from within personality to an engineering issue, the establishment of arts of education and social guidance.

How We Think

Dewey's clearest analysis of reflective thinking as the characteristic mark of the educated person is to be found in *How We Think*. To this book has been attributed a major responsibility for the development of the problem approach and the project method in American pedagogy. The reflective man, Dewey makes clear, is one who uses the pragmatic method of attacking problems. The steps in this method are systematically outlined. Thinking begins not spontaneously but with a doubt, perplexity, or problem. Once the inquiry is under way, the reflective person does not seek early closure: he is patient in the search and is ready to look for the best solution rather than the first one. He is willing to postpone judgment until he can justify his conclusion. It does no good to have students amass knowledge and develop skill unless they are able to use these accomplishments in making sound judgments about vital issues. For Dewey, the educated model is not a person of any particular academic qualifications, but rather one who makes good, relevant, and discriminating judgments and who acts intelligently in the light of them.

These excerpts are taken from John Dewey, *How We Think: A Restatement of the Relation of Reflective Thinking to the Educational Process*, published in Boston in 1933 by D. C. Heath and Company, with whose permission they are reprinted.

The origin of thinking is some perplexity, confusion, or doubt. Thinking is not a case of spontaneous combustion; it does not occur just on 'general principles.' There is something that occasions and evokes it. General appeals to a child (or to a grown-up) to think, irrespective of the existence in his own experience of some difficulty that troubles him and disturbs his equilibrium, are as futile as advice to lift himself by his boot-straps.

Given a difficulty, the next step is suggestion of some way out—the formation of some tentative plan or project, the entertaining of some theory that will account for the peculiarities in question, the consideration of some solution for the problem. The data at hand cannot supply the solution; they can only suggest it. What, then, are the sources of the suggestion? Clearly, past experience and a fund of relevant knowledge at one's command. If the person has had some acquaintance with similar situations, if he has dealt with material of the same sort before, suggestions more or less apt and helpful will arise. But unless there has been some analogous experience, confusion remains mere confusion. Even when a child (or a grown-up) has a problem, it is wholly futile to urge him to think when he has no prior experiences that involve some of the same conditions.

There may, however, be a state of perplexity and also previous experience out of which suggestions emerge, and yet thinking need not be reflective. For the person may not be sufficiently *critical* about the ideas that occur to him. He may jump at a conclusion without weighing the grounds on which it rests; he may forego or unduly shorten the act of hunting, inquiring; he may take the first 'answer,' or solution, that comes to him because of mental sloth, torpor, impatience to get something settled. One can think reflectively only when one is willing to endure suspense and to undergo the trouble of searching. To many persons both suspense of judgment and intellectual search are disagreeable; they want to get them ended as soon as possible. They cultivate an over-positive and dogmatic habit of mind, or feel perhaps that a condition of doubt will be regarded as evidence of mental inferiority. It is at the point where examination and test enter into investigation that the difference between reflective thought and bad thinking comes in. To be genuinely thoughtful, we must be willing to sustain and protract that state of doubt which is the stimulus to thorough inquiry, so as not to accept an idea or make positive assertion of a belief until justifying reasons have been found. . . .

The function of reflective thought is, therefore, to transform a situation in which there is experienced obscurity, doubt, conflct, disturbance of some sort, into a situation that is clear, coherent, settled, harmonious. . . .

There is no better way to decide whether genuine inference has taken place than to ask whether it terminated in the substitution of a clear, orderly, and satisfactory situation for a perplexed, confused, and discordant one. Partial and ineffectual thinking ends in conclusions that are formally correct but that make no difference in what is personally and immediately experienced. Vital inference always leaves one who thinks with a world that is experienced as different in some respect, for some object in it has gained in clarity and orderly arrangement. Genuine thinking winds up, in short, with an appreciation of new values. . . .

THE ESSENTIAL FUNCTIONS OF REFLECTIVE ACTIVITY

We now have before us the material for the analysis of a complete act of reflective activity. In the preceding chapter we saw that the two limits of every unit of thinking are a perplexed, troubled, or confused situation at the beginning and a cleared-up, unified, resolved situation at the close. The first of these situations may be called *pre*-reflective. It sets the problem to be solved, out of it grows the question that reflection has to answer. In the final situation the doubt has been dispelled; the situation is *post*-reflective; there results a direct experience of mastery, satisfaction, enjoyment. Here, then, are the limits within which reflection falls.

Five Phases, or Aspects, of Reflective Thought

In between, as states of thinking, are (1) *suggestions*, in which the mind leaps forward to a possible solution; (2) an intellectualization of the difficulty or perplexity that has been *felt* (directly experienced) into a *problem* to be solved, a question for which the answer must be sought; (3) the use of one suggestion after another as a leading idea, or *hypothesis*, to initiate and guide observation and other operations in collection of factual material; (4) the mental elaboration of the idea or supposition as an idea or supposition (*reasoning*, in the sense in which reasoning is a part, not the whole, of inference); and (5) testing the hypothesis by overt or imaginative action. . . .

From one point of view the whole process of thinking consists of making a series of judgments that are so related as to support one another in leading to a final judgment—the conclusion. In spite of this fact, we have treated reflective activity as a whole, first, because judgments do not occur in isolation but in connection with the solution of a problem, the clearing away of something obscure and perplexing, the solution of a difficulty; in short, as units in reflective activity. The purpose of solving a problem determines what kind of judgments should be made. If I were suddenly to announce that it would take twenty-two and a half yards of carpet to cover a certain floor, it might be a perfectly correct statement, but as a *judgment* it would be senseless if it did not bear upon some question that had come up. Judgments need to be *relevant* to an issue as well as correct. Judging is the act of selecting and weighing the bearing of facts and suggestions as they present themselves, as well as of deciding whether the alleged facts are really facts and whether the idea used is a sound idea or merely a fancy. We may say, for short, that a person of sound judgment is one who, in the idiomatic phrase, has 'horse sense'; he is a good judge of *relative values;* he can estimate, appraise, evaluate, with tact and discernment.

It follows that the heart of a good habit of thought lies in the power to pass judgments *pertinently* and *discriminatingly.* We sometimes meet men with little schooling whose advice is greatly relied upon and who are spontaneously looked to when an emergency arises, men who are conspicuously successful in conducting vital affairs. They are the persons of sound judgment. A man of sound judgment in any set of affairs is an *educated* man as respects those affairs, whatever his schooling or academic standing. And if our schools turn out their pupils in that attitude of mind which is conducive to good judgment in any department of affairs in which the pupils are placed, they have done more than if they sent out their pupils possessed *merely* of vasts stores of information or high degrees of skill in specialized branches.

15 *The Cultured Man: Eliot*

T. S. Eliot (1888–1965) was born in St. Louis, Missouri, but he spent the greater part of his adult life in England, eventually becoming a British subject and a member of the Church of England. He found in the greater stability and richer tradition of European culture the authority he sought as an antidote to the self-centered license that he judged to be characteristic of modern—especially American—society. The conditions that elicited his celebrated response were the cultural decline and prevalent vulgarity he preceived around him. He was contemptuous of many features of contemporary life, especially the emphasis on technical efficiency, gross materialism, and social striving. Like a latter-day Plato, he had a marked fear of social chaos and cultural disintegration, which led him to seek permanent principles of education and permanent standards of excellence. Like a latter-day St. Augustine, he saw Christian civilization threatened by a deluge of barbarism, which prompted him to advocate a classical education that had Christianity at its center.

Eliot was typical of many converts in that he was a stricter and more rigorous defender of his adopted culture, tradition, and religion than most of those who were born into them. He believed that tradition is not something that can be created deliberately. Hence the cultured man is not a person who can be consciously planned for or produced at will. He emerges out of a particular cultural context, with the family playing a crucial part. Formal schooling, for Eliot, is a less important influence.

This model of the cultured man is an aristocratic figure. Culture and equality are incompatible concepts in Eliot's view. Not all people have an equal right to education; a different type of education is appropriate for different kinds of people; and clear distinctions should be made between the educated and the uneducated. It is most important to provide an excellent education for the minority who are to be the guardians of the culture. The lower classes should be educated largely through the training of habits and should be protected in a somewhat Platonic manner by the upper classes. Eliot's paternalistic and aristocratic views were firmly bolstered by his strong belief in the doctrines of original sin and divine grace. Hence he tended to be pessimistic about man in this world, although more optimistic about him in the next.

In evaluating Eliot's ideas, it is tempting to apply a Marxian analysis to the social and economic bases of his formulations. For example, Eliot is contemptuous of the person who wants to use education in order to "get ahead"; but he made his criticisms from a position of firm personal and financial security. He was contemptuous of ambitious social classes; but he was an accepted member of the upper stratum of English society. He was contemptuous of nations that saw education as a means to economic prosperity; but he enjoyed the benefits of living in one of the most affluent nations in the world.

One of Eliot's greatest values is that he prompts us to look more closely at some of our conventional assumptions. But some of his own assumptions are also worthy of scrutiny. For example, he eloquently attacks provincialism. But is he himself not provincial in his inability to envision a cultural transformation stemming from anywhere but Europe? And although we should study carefully his views on the importance of a cultural tradition as a source of freedom and creativity, we should also note his apparent failure to acknowledge that a tradition can be a stifling rather than a liberating form of authority.

After Strange Gods

Eliot delivered the Page-Barbour Lectures at the University of Virginia in 1933. Subsequently published under the title, *After Strange Gods,* they contain an attempt to formulate a theory of literary criticism. Eliot firmly opposes the cult of personality in literature. Being oneself is an inadequate goal; we must judge whether that self is good or bad. And these judgments must not be merely personal views, which are limited by self-deception, prejudice, and original sin, but they must be corrected by tradition, under the supervision of religious orthodoxy. Similarly, moral values are not to be determined by each man for himself: his duty is to follow traditional and orthodox formulations. This is necessary because most men are unfit to make such decisions for themselves. The majority of people are incapable either of strong emotion or of controlling those emotions they experience. Nor are they capable of distinguishing between good and bad. Eliot subscribes explicitly to the Puritan idea of life as a moral struggle: man is most real when he is in moral travail. Unrestrained passion is not a mark of the cultured man. Those who abandon themselves to feeling become reduced in their humanity. Thus the model that Eliot's view implies is one created out of conflict and struggle, one whose naturally evil propensities are controlled and corrected by the guiding hand of tradition.

These passages are taken from T. S. Eliot, *After Strange Gods: A Primer of Modern Heresy,* published in New York in 1934 by Harcourt, Brace and World, Inc., with whose permission they are reprinted.

With the disappearance of the idea of Original Sin, with the disappearance of the idea of intense moral struggle, the human beings presented to us both in poetry and in prose fiction today, and more patently among the serious writers than in the underworld of letters, tend to become less and less real. It is in fact in moments of moral and spiritual struggle depending upon spiritual sanctions, rather than in those "bewildering minutes" in which we are all very much alike, that men and women come nearest to being real. If you do away with this struggle, and maintain that by tolerance, benevolence, inoffensiveness and a redistribution or increase of purchasing power, combined with a devotion, on the part of an élite, to Art, the world will be as good as anyone could require, then you must expect human beings to become more and more vaporous. . . .

What I have wished to illustrate, by reference to the authors whom I have mentioned in this lecture, has been the crippling effect upon men of letters, of not having been born and brought up in the environment of a living and central tradition. . . .

When morals cease to be a matter of tradition and orthodoxy—that is, of the habits of the community formulated, corrected, and elevated by the continuous thought and direction of the Church—and when each man is to elaborate his own, then *personality* becomes a thing of alarming importance. . . .

Extreme emotionalism seems to be a symptom of decadence; it is a cardinal point of faith in a romantic age, to believe that there is something admirable in violent emotion for its own sake, whatever the emotion or whatever its object. But it is by no means self-evident that human beings are most real when most violently excited; violent physical passions do not in themselves differentiate men from each other, but rather tend to reduce them to the same state; and the passion has significance only in relation to the character and behaviour of the man at other moments of his life and in other contexts. Furthermore, strong passion is only interesting or significant in strong men, those who abandon themselves without resistance to excitements which tend to deprive them of reason, become merely instruments of feeling and lose their humanity; and unless there is moral resistance and conflict there is no meaning. But as the majority is capable neither of strong emotion nor of strong resistance, it always inclines to admire passion for its own sake, unless instructed to the contrary; and, if somewhat deficient in vitality, people imagine passion to be the surest evidence of vitality. . . .

The number of people in possession of any criteria for discriminating between good and evil is very small; the number of the half-alive hungry for any form of spiritual experience, or what offers itself as spiritual experience, high or low, good or bad, is considerable. My own generation has not served them very well. Never has the printing-press been so busy, and never have such varieties of buncombe and false doctrine come from it. . . .

In an age of unsettled beliefs and enfeebled tradition the man of letters, the poet, and the novelist, are in a situation dangerous for themselves and for their readers. I tried to safeguard myself, in my first lecture, from being taken to be merely a sentimental admirer of some real or imaginary past, and from being taken as a faker of traditions. Tradition by itself is not enough; it must be perpetually criticised and brought up to date under the supervision of what I call orthodoxy; and for the lack of this supervision it is now the sentimental tenuity that we find it. Most "defenders of tradition" are mere conservatives, unable to distinguish between the permanent and the temporary, the essential and the accidental. But I left this theory as a bare outline, to serve as a background for my illustration of the dangers of authorship today. Where there is no external test of the validity of a writer's work, we fail to distinguish between the truth of his view of life and the personality which makes it plausible; so that in our reading, we may be simply yielding ourselves to one seductive personality after another. The first requisite usually held up by the promoters of personality is that a man should "be himself"; and this "sincerity" is considered more important than that the self in question should, socially and spiritually, be a good or a bad one. This view of personality is merely an assumption on the part of the modern world, and is no more tenable than several other views which have been held at various times and in several places. The personality thus expressed, the personality which fascinates us in the work of philosophy or art, tends naturally to be the *unregenerate* personality, partly self-deceived and partly irresponsible, and because of its freedom, terribly *limited* by prejudice and self-conceit, capable of much good or great mischief according to the natural goodness or impurity of the man: and we are all, naturally, impure. All that I have been able to do here is to suggest that there are standards of criticism, not ordinarily in use, which we may apply to whatever is offered too us as works of philosophy or of art, which might help to render them safer and more profitable for us.

Modern Education
and the Classics

This is Eliot's attempt to convince the English (America he has already written off as a lost cause) of the virtues of classical studies. His defense of the classics is based upon his assumption of the need to preserve and foster Christian civilization. This can be done only through a Christian education, based upon classical studies. All education should be directed by a Christian hierarchy, with revived monastic teaching orders playing a crucial role. The characteristic note of Puritan authority is again evident in Eliot's injunctions. That a student may not want to study the classics or may show no aptitude in their study should not exempt him. Even at the university the student should not be trusted to follow the bent of his own talents or interests. He must be compelled to study that in which he has no interest. The educated person is one who, whatever his personal inclinations, has become acquainted with a broad classical culture. He pursues education in order to acquire wisdom, rather than for economic or social advantage.

The selections are taken from T. S. Eliot, "Modern Education and the Classics," in *Essays Ancient and Modern,* published in London by Faber and Faber in 1936, reprinted in *Selected Essays,* published in New York in 1950 by Harcourt, Brace and World, Inc., with whose permission they are reprinted.

One might almost speak of a *crisis* of education. There are particular problems for each country, for each civilization, just as there are particular problems for each parent; but there is also a general problem for the whole civilized world, and for the uncivilized so far as it is being taught by its civilized superiors, a problem which may be as acute in Japan, in China or in India as in Britain or Europe or America. The progress (I do not mean the extension) of education for several centuries has been from one aspect a drift, from another aspect a push; for it has tended to be dominated by the idea of *getting on*. The individual wants more education, not as an aid to the acquisition of wisdom but in order to get on; the nation wants more in order to get the better of other nations, the class wants it to get the better of other classes, or at least to hold its own against them. Education is associated therefore with technical efficiency on the one hand, and with rising in society on the other. Education becomes something to which everybody has a 'right', even irrespective of his capacity; and when everyone gets it—by that time, of course, in a diluted and adulterated form—then we naturally discover that education is no longer an infallible means of getting on, and people turn to another fallacy: that of 'education for leisure'— without having revised their notions of 'leisure'. As soon as this precious motive of snobbery evaporates, the zest has gone out of education; if it is not going to mean more money, or more power over others, or a better social position, or at least a steady and respectable job, few people are going to take the trouble to acquire education. For deteriorate it as you may, education is still going to demand a good deal of drudgery. And the majority of people are incapable of enjoying leisure—that is, unemployment *plus* an income and a status of respectability—in any but pretty simple forms—such as balls propelled by hand, by foot, and by engines or tools of various types; in playing cards; or in watching dogs, horses or other men engage in feats of speed or skill. The uneducated man with an empty mind, if he be free from financial anxiety or narrow limitation, and can obtain access to golf-clubs, dance halls, etc., is, for all I can see, as well equipped to fill his leisure contentedly as is the educated man. . . .

Another fallacy of liberal education is that the student who advances to the university should take up the study that interests him most. For a small number of students this is in the main right. Even at a very early stage of school life, we can identify a few individuals with a definite inclination towards one group of studies or another. The danger for these fortunate ones is that if left to themselves they will overspecialize, they will be wholly ignorant of the general interests of human beings. We are all in one way or another naturally lazy, and it is much easier to confine ourselves to the study of subjects in which we excel. But the great majority of the people who are to be educated have no very strong inclination to specialize, because they have no definite gifts or tastes. Those who have more lively and curious minds will tend to smatter. No one can become really educated without having pursued some study in which he took no interest—for it is a part of education to *learn to interest ourselves* in subjects for which we have no aptitude. . . .

The longer the better schools and the older universities in this country [England] (for they have pretty well given up the struggle in America) can maintain some standard of classical education, the better for those who look to the future with an active desire for reform and an intelligent acceptance of change. But to expect from our educational institutions any more positive contribution to the future would be vain. As only the Catholic and the communist know, *all* education must be ultimately religious education. I do not mean that education should be confined to postulants for the priesthood or for the higher ranks of Soviet bureaucracy; I mean that the hierarchy of education should be a religious hierarchy. The universities are too far gone in secularization, they have too long lost any common fundamental assumption as to what education is *for*, and they are too big. It might be hoped that they would eventually follow, or else be relegated to preservation as curious architectural remains; but they cannot be expected to lead.

It is quite possible, of course, that the future may bring neither a Christian nor a materialistic civilization. It is quite possible that the future may bring nothing but chaos or torpor. In that event, I am not interested in the future; I am only interested in the two alternatives which seem to me worthy of interest. I am only here concerned with readers who are prepared to prefer a Christian civilization, if a choice is forced upon them; and it is only upon readers who wish to see a Christian civilization survive and develop that I am urging the importance of the study of Latin and Greek. If Christianity is not to survive, I shall not mind if the texts of the Latin and Greek languages became more obscure and forgotten than those of the language of the Etruscans. And the only hope that I can see for the study of Latin and Greek, in their proper place and for the right reasons, lies in the revival and expansion of monastic teaching orders. There are other reasons, and of the greatest weight, for desiring to see a revival of the monastic life in its variety, but the maintenance of Christian education is not the least. The first educational task of the communities should be the *preservation* of education within the cloister, uncontaminated by the deluge of barbarism outside; their second, the provision of education for the laity, which should be something more than education for a place in the Civil Service, or for technical efficiency, or for social or public success. It would not be that tawdry adornment, 'education for leisure'. As the world at large becomes more completely secularized, the need becomes more urgent that professedly Christian people should have a Christian education, which should be an education both for this world and for the life of prayer in this world.

The Idea of a Christian Society

In 1939, some six months before the outbreak of World War II, Eliot delivered three lectures at the invitation of the Master and Fellows of Corpus Christi College of Cambridge University. Subsequently published as *The Idea of a Christian Society*, the lectures provided the substance for considerable debate on both sides of the Atlantic. Eliot argues stringently for a Christian organization of society, which he sees as the only alternative to a pagan, materialistic, totalitarian society. The idea of "democracy" is inadequate, he argues, as a defense against these threats, for democracy as a political philosophy is derived from particular ethical assumptions, which in turn are derived from particular religious assumptions. In Eliot's model society, therefore, all education will be Christian education, that is, it will be directed by Christian philosophy and Christian purposes. But this education is not something to which everyone has an equal right: it is more appropriate for some than for others. Those who receive it should be clearly distinguished from those who do not. The educated person can be identified by the knowledge and culture he has acquired. This requirement will be the same for all educated people, for there must be a uniformity of culture and an agreement upon what every cultured person should know.

These selections are from T. S. Eliot, *The Idea of a Christian Society*, published in New York in 1940 by Harcourt, Brace and World, Inc., with whose permission they are reprinted.

My thesis has been, simply, that a liberalised or negative condition of society must either proceed into a gradual decline of which we can see no end, or (whether as a result of catastrophe or not) reform itself into a positive shape which is likely to be effectively secular. We need not assume that this secularism will approximate closely to any system in the past or to any that can now be observed in order to be apprehensive about it: the Anglo-Saxons display a capacity for *diluting* their religion, probably in excess of that of any other race. But unless we are content with the prospect of one or the other of these issues, the only possibility left is that of a positive Christian society. The third will only commend itself to those who agree in their view of the present situation, and who can see that a thoroughgoing secularism would be objectionable, in its consequences, even to those who attach no positive importance to the survival of Christianity for its own sake. . . .

The rulers and would-be rulers of modern states may be divided into three kinds, in a classification which cuts across the division of fascism, communism and democracy. There are such as have taken over or adapted some philosophy, as of Marx or Aquinas. There are those who, combining invention with eclecticism have devised their own philosophy—not usually distinguished by either the profundity or the consistency one expects of a philosophy of life—and there are those who pursue their tasks without appearing to have any philosophy at all. I should not expect the rulers of a Christian State to be philosophers, or to be able to keep before their minds at every moment of decision the maxim that the life of virtue is the purpose of human society— *virtuosa. . . . vita est congregationis humanae finis;* but they would neither be self-educated, nor have been submitted in their youth merely to that system of miscellaneous or specialised instruction which passes for education: they would have received a Christian education. The purpose of a Christian education would not be merely to make men and women pious Christians: a system which aimed too rigidly at this end alone would become only obscurantist. A Christian education would primarily train people to be able to think in Christian categories, though it could not compel belief and would not impose the necessity for insincere profession of belief. What the rulers believed, would be less important than the beliefs to which they would be obliged to conform. And a skeptical or indifferent statesman, working within a Christian frame, might be more effective than a devout Christian statesman obliged to conform to a secular frame. For he would be required to design his policy for the government of a Christian Society. . . .

For the great majority of the people—and I am not here thinking of social classes, but of intellectual strata—religion must be primarily a matter of behaviour and habit, must be integrated with its social life, with its business and its pleasures; and the specifically religious emotions must be a kind of extension and sanctification of the domestic and social emotions. Even for the most highly developed and conscious individual, living in the world, a consciously Christian direction of thought and feeling can only occur at particular moments during the day and during the week, and these moments themselves recur in consequence of formed habits; to be conscious, without remission, of a Christian and a non-Christian alternative at moments of choice, imposes a very great strain. The mass of the population, in a Christian society, should not be exposed to a way of life in which there is too sharp and frequent a conflict between what is easy for them or what their circumstances dictate and what is Christian. The compulsion to live in such a way that Christian behaviour is only possible in a restricted number of situations, is a very powerful force against Christianity; for behaviour is as potent to affect belief, as belief to affect behaviour. . . .

However bigoted the announcement may sound, the Christian can be satisfied with nothing less than a Christian organisation of society—which is not the same thing as a society consisting exclusively of devout Christians. It would be a society in which the natural end of man—virtue and well-being in community—is acknowledged for all, and the supernatural end—beatitude—for those who have the eyes to see it. . . .

In the field of education it is obvious that the conformity to Christian belief and the possession of Christian knowledge, can no longer be taken for granted; nor can the supremacy of the theologian be either expected or imposed in the same way. In any future Christian society that I can conceive, the educational system will be formed according to Christian presuppositions of what education—as distinct from mere instruction—is for; but the personnel will inevitably be mixed: one may even hope that the mixture may be a benefit to its intellectual vitality. The mixture will include persons of exceptional ability who may be indifferent or disbelieving; there will be room for a proportion of other persons professing other faiths than Christianity. The limitations imposed upon such persons would be similar to those imposed by social necessity upon the politician who, without being able to believe the Christian faith, yet has abilities to offer in the public service, with which his country could ill dispense. . . .

In a Christian Society education must be religious, not in the sense that it will be administered by ecclesiastics, still less in the sense that it will exercise pressure, or attempt to instruct everyone in theology, but in the sense that its aims will be directed by a Christian philosophy of life. It will no longer be merely a term comprehending a variety of unrelated subjects undertaken for special purposes or for none at all. . . .

You cannot expect continuity and coherence in politics, you cannot expect reliable behaviour on fixed principles persisting through changed situations, unless there is an underlying political philosophy: not of a party, but of the nation. You cannot expect continuity and coherence in literature and the arts, unless you have a certain uniformity of culture, expressed in education by a settled, though not rigid agreement as to what everyone should know to some degree, and a positive distinction— however undemocratic it may sound—between the educated and the uneducated. I observed in America, that with a very high level of intelligence among undergraduates, progress was impeded by the fact that one could never assume that any two, unless they had been at the same school under the influence of the same masters at the same moment, had studied the same subjects or read the same books, though the number of subjects in which they had been instructed was surprising. Even with a smaller amount of total information, it might have been better if they had read fewer, but the same books. In a negative liberal society you have no agreement as to there being any body of knowledge which any educated person should have acquired at any particular stage: the idea of wisdom disappears, and you get sporadic and unrelated experimentation. A nation's system of education is much more important than its system of government; only a proper system of education can unify the active and the contemplative life, action and speculation, politics and the arts. . . .

So long as we consider "education" as a good in itself of which everyone has a right to the utmost, without any ideal of the good life for society or for the individual, we shall move from one uneasy compromise to another. To the quick and simple organization of society for ends which, being only material and worldly, must be as ephemeral as worldly success, there is only one alternative. As political philosophy derives its sanction from ethics, and ethics from the truth of religion, it is only by returning to the eternal source of truth that we can hope for any social organisation which will not, to its ultimate destruction, ignore some essential aspect of reality. The term "democracy," as I have said again and again, does not contain enough positive content to stand alone against the forces that you dislike—it can easily be transformed by them. If you will not have God (and He is a jealous God) you should pay your respects to Hitler or Stalin.

What is a Classic?

In 1944 Eliot gave the Presidential Address to the Virgil Society. In it, he predictably defends Virgil as a unique classic, enthroning him as "the consciousness of Rome" and Latin's "supreme voice." Since Latin is the essential bloodstream of European literature and since it is only from Europe that any future world harmony will come, the study of the classics must be a central part of the cultured person's education. The educated person is one who has cast off his temporal provincialism by transcending the intellectual boundaries of his own era.

The passage is taken from T. S. Eliot, "What is a Classic?" in *On Poetry and Poets,* published in London by Faber and Faber in 1957; reprinted with permission of Faber & Faber Ltd., and Farrar, Straus and Giroux, Inc.

By 'provincial' I mean . . . a distortion of values, the exclusion of some, the exaggeration of others, which springs, not from lack of wide geographical perambulation, but from applying standards acquired within a limited area, to the whole of human experience; which confounds the contingent with the essential, the ephemeral with the permanent. In our age, when men seem more than ever prone to confuse wisdom with knowledge, and knowledge with information, and to try to solve problems of life in terms of engineering, there is coming into existence a new kind of provincialism which perhaps deserves a new name. It is a provincialism, not of space, but of time; one for which history is merely the chronicle of human devices which have served their turn and been scrapped, one for which the world is the property solely of the living, a property in which the dead hold no shares. The menace of this kind of provincialism is, that we can all, all the peoples on the globe, be provincials together; and those who are not content to be provincials, can only become hermits. If this kind of provincialism led to greater tolerance, in the sense of forbearance, there might be more to be said for it; but it seems more likely to lead to our becoming indifferent, in matters where we ought to maintain a distinctive dogma or standard, and to our becoming intolerant, in matters which might be left to local or personal preference. We may have as many varieties of religion as we like, provided we all send our children to the same schools. But my concern here is only with the corrective to provincialism in literature. We need to remind ourselves that, as Europe is a whole (and still, in its progressive mutilation and disfigurement, the organism out of which any greater world harmony must develop), so European literature is a whole, the several members of which cannot flourish, if the same blood-stream does not circulate throughout the whole body. The blood-stream of European literature is Latin and Greek—not as two systems of circulation, but one, for it is through Rome that our parentage in Greece must be traced. What common measure of excellence have we in literature, among our several languages, which is not the classical measure? What mutual intelligibility can we hope to preserve, except in our common heritage of thought and feeling in those two languages, for the understanding of which, no European people is in any position of advantage over any other? No modern language could aspire to the universality of Latin, even though it came to be spoken by millions more than ever spoke Latin, and even though it came to be the universal means of communication between peoples of all tongues and cultures. No modern language can hope to produce a classic, in the sense in which I have called Virgil a classic. Our classic, the classic of all Europe, is Virgil.

Notes Towards the
Definition of Culture

This book is centrally important to Eliot's attempt to define the cultured person and the cultured society. His concept of culture includes refinement of manners, sensibility to the arts, intellectual ability, and knowledge of the accumulated wisdom of the past. None of these accomplishments in itself is sufficient to mark a person as cultured: all are required. Hence only a minority of people are capable of becoming cultured, and the perfectly cultured person is not to be found. For the preservation and transmission of culture, it is necessary for society to have a clear class structure, with an aristocracy that possesses a more conscious culture than the masses. The principle agency for the transmission of culture is the family. Power and responsibility should be largely hereditary. It is a serious error, in Eliot's judgment, to use the educational system as a means to equalize opportunities or to produce intellectual *élites*. Such meritocracies will be connected only by their professional and intellectual interests: they will lack essential social and cultural unity. When all who are capable of profiting from higher education can obtain it, we are in danger of carrying education too far. Education for all is a dangerous practice: it causes unhappiness, lowers standards, and adulterates and degrades culture.

These passages are from T. S. Eliot, *Notes Towards the Definition of Culture*, published in New York in 1949 by Harcourt, Brace and World, Inc., with whose permission they are reprinted.

We know that good manners, without education, intellect or sensibility to the arts, tends towards mere automatism; that learning without good manners or sensibility is pedantry; that intellectual ability without the more human attributes is admirable only in the same way as the brilliance of a child chess prodigy; and that the arts without intellectual context are vanity. And if we do not find culture in any one of these perfections alone, so we must not expect any one person to be accomplished in all of them; we shall come to infer that the wholly cultured individual is a phantasm; and we shall look for culture, not in any individual or in any one group of individuals, but more and more widely; and we are driven in the end to find it in the pattern of the society as a whole. This seems to me a very obvious reflection: but it is frequently overlooked. People are always ready to consider themselves persons of culture, on the strength of one proficiency, when they are not only lacking in others, but blind to those they lack. An artist of any kind, even a very great artist, is not for this reason alone a man of culture: artists are not only often insensitive to other arts than those which they practice, but sometimes have very bad manners or meagre intellectual gifts. The person who contributes to culture, however important his contribution may be, is not always a "cultured person."

It does not follow from this that there is no meaning in speaking of the culture of an individual, or of a group or class. We only mean that the culture of the individual cannot be isolated from that of the group, and that the culture of the group cannot be abstracted from that of the whole society; and that our notion of "perfection" must take all three senses of "culture" into account at once. Nor does it follow that in a society, of whatever grade of culture, the groups concerned with each activity of culture will be distinct and exclusive: on the contrary, it is only by an overlapping and sharing of interests, by participation and mutual appreciation, that the cohesion necessary for culture can obtain. A religion requires not only a body of priests who know what they are doing, but a body of worshippers who know what is being done. . . .

All that concerns me at the moment is the question whether, by education alone, we can ensure the transmission of culture in a society in which some educationists appear indifferent to class distinctions, and from which some other educationists appear to want to remove class distinctions altogether. There is, in any case, a danger of interpreting "education" to cover both too much and too little: too little, when it implies that education is limited to what can be taught; too much, when it implies that everything worth preserving can be transmitted by teaching. In the society desired by some reformers, what the family can transmit will be limited to the minimum, especially if the child is to be . . . manipulated by a unified educational system "from the cradle to the grave." And unless the child is classified, by the officials who will have the task of sorting him out, as being just like his father, he will be brought up in a different—not necessarily a better, because all will be equally good, but a different—school environment, and trained on what the official opinion of the moment considers to be "the genuinely democratic lines." The élites, in consequence, will consist solely of individuals whose only common bond will be their professional interest: with no social cohesion, with no social continuity. They will be united only by a part, and that the most conscious part, of their personalities; they will meet like committees. The greater part of their "culture" will be only what they share with all the other individuals composing their nation.

The case for a society with a class structure, the affirmation that it is, in some sense, the "natural" society, is prejudiced if we allow ourselves to be hypnotised by the two contrasted terms *aristocracy* and *democracy*. The whole problem is falsified if we use these terms antithetically. What I have advanced is not a "defence of aristocracy"—an emphasis upon the importance of one organ of society. Rather it is a plea on behalf of a form of society in which an aristocracy should have a peculiar and essential function, as peculiar and essential as the function of any other part of society. What is important is a structure of society in which there will be, from "top" to "bottom," a continuous gradation of cultural levels: it is important to remember that we should not consider the upper levels as possessing *more* culture than the lower, but as representing a more conscious culture and a greater specialisation of culture. I incline to believe that no true democracy can maintain itself unless it contains these different levels of culture. The levels of culture may also be seen as levels of power, to the extent that a smaller group at a higher level will have equal power with a larger group at a lower level; for it may be argued that complete equality means universal irresponsibility; and in such a society as I envisage, each individual would inherit greater or less responsibility towards the commonwealth, according to the position in society which he inherited—each class would have somewhat different responsibilities. A democracy in which everybody had an equal responsibility in everything would be oppressive for the conscientious and licentious for the rest. . . .

It is always desirable that a part of the education of those persons who are either born into, or qualified by their abilities to enter, the superior political grades of society, should be instruction in history, and that a part of the study of history should be the history of political theory. The advantage of the study of Greek history and Greek political theory, as a preliminary to the study of other history and other theory, is its *manageability*: it has to do with a small area, with men rather

than masses, and with the human passions of individuals rather than
with those vast impersonal forces which in our modern society are a
necessary convenience of thought, and the study of which tends to obscure the study of human beings. The reader of Greek philosophy, moreover, is unlikely to be over-sanguine about the effects of political theory;
for he will observe that the study of political forms appears to have
arisen out of the failure of political systems; and that neither Plato
nor Aristotle was much concerned with prediction, or very optimistic
about the future. . . .

We have already found that the purpose of education has been defined
as the making people happier. The assumption that it *does* make people
happier needs to be considered separately. That the educated person
is happier than the uneducated is by no means self-evident. Those who
are conscious of their lack of education are discontented, if they cherish
ambitions to excel in occupations for which they are not qualified; they
are sometimes discontented, simply because they have been given to
understand that more education would have made them happier. Many
of us feel some grievance against our elders, our schools or our universities for not having done better by us: this can be a way of extenuating
our own shortcomings and excusing our failures. On the other hand,
to be educated above the level of those whose social habits and tastes
one has inherited, may cause a division within a man which interferes
with happiness; even though, when the individual is of superior intellect,
it may bring him a fuller and more useful life. And to be trained, taught
or instructed above the level of one's abilities and strength may be
disastrous; for education is a strain, and can impose greater burdens
upon a mind than that mind can bear. Too much education, like too
little education, can produce unhappiness. . . .

It follows from what has been said in an earlier chapter about classes
and élites, that education should help to preserve the class and to select
the élite. It is right that the exceptional individual should have the
opportunity to elevate himself in the social scale and attain a position
in which he can exercise his talents to the greatest benefit of himself
and of society. But the ideal of an educational system which would
automatically sort out everyone according to his native capacities is
unattainable in practice; and if we made it our chief aim, would disorganise society and debase education. It would disorganise society, by
substituting for classes, élites of brains, or perhaps only of sharp wits.
Any educational system aiming at a complete adjustment between education and society will tend both to restrict education to what will lead
to success in the world, and to restrict success in the world to those
persons who have been good pupils of the system. The prospect of

a society ruled and directed only by those who have passed certain examinations or satisfied tests devised by psychologists is not reassuring: while it might give scope to talents hitherto obscured, it would probably obscure others, and reduce to impotence some who should have rendered high service. Furthermore, the ideal of a uniform system such that no one capable of receiving higher education could fail to get it, leads imperceptibly to the education of too many people, and consequently to the lowering of standards to whatever this swollen number of candidates is able to reach. . . .

Besides the motive of giving everyone as much education as possible, because education is in itself desirable, there are other motives affecting educational legislation: motives which may be praiseworthy, or which simply recognise the inevitable, and which we need mention here only as a reminder of the complexity of the legislative problem. One motive, for instance, for raising the age-limit of compulsory schooling is the laudable desire to protect the adolescent, and fortify him against the more degrading influences to which he is exposed on entering the ranks of industry. We should be candid about such a motive; and instead of affirming what is to be doubted, that everyone will profit by as many years of tuition as we can give him, admit that the conditions of life in modern industrial society are so deplorable, and the moral restraints so weak, that we must prolong the schooling of young people simply because we are at our wits' end to know what to do to save them. Instead of congratulating ourselves on our progress, whenever the school assumes another responsibility hitherto left to parents, we might do better to admit that we have arrived at a stage of civilisation at which the family is irresponsible, or incompetent, or helpless; at which parents cannot be expected to train their children properly; at which many parents cannot afford to feed them properly, and would not know how, even if they had the means; and that Education must step in and make the best of a bad job. . . .

The culture of Europe has deteriorated visibly within the memory of many who are by no means the oldest among us. And we know, that whether education can foster and improve culture or not, it can surely adulterate and degrade it. For there is no doubt that in our headlong rush to educate everybody, we are lowering our standards, and more and more abandoning the study of those subjects by which the essentials of our culture—of that part of it which is transmissible by education—are transmitted; destroying our ancient edifices to make ready the ground upon which the barbarian nomads of the future will encamp in their merchandised caravans.

The Aims of Education

Eliot gave four lectures on "The Aims of Education" in the fall of 1950 at the University of Chicago, under the auspices of the Committee on Social Thought. They contain some of his clearest and most focused thinking on the subject of education. Eliot makes clear his view that education is broader than the kind of activities that go on in schools and universities. The educated man is part of a whole cultural tradition rather than merely the product of a particular school. Moreover, he is active in the personal assimilation of this tradition, rather than passively receptive of a particular training. Eliot's model is not a man trained for adjustment to his society: he must develop standards that go beyond his own time and place.

The excerpts are taken from T. S. Eliot, "The Aims of Education," first published in *Measure*, Volume II, Number 1 (December 1950), and reprinted in *To Criticize the Critic, and Other Writings*, copyright 1965 by Valerie Eliot, published in New York by Farrar, Straus and Giroux, Inc., with whose permission they are reprinted.

The highest type of educated man is not simply a man who has been through the best educational institutions; he is, to begin with, more educable than most, and is one who has done much to educate himself since he ceased to be a pupil. . . . When we think of the individual, we are apt, I believe, and rightly, to be stressing what the man does for himself, rather than what is done to him. And the perfectly educated man, like the perfectly cultured man, does not exist; and the kind of perfection in question differs according to the environment. It is easier to think in terms of the group. In earlier times, of which there remain vestiges, it was the *social* group; in our time it is more importantly the technical group. So long as you are concerned merely with a small group of the same social rank, the question of the purpose or meaning of education hardly arises. For the fact that all of the pupils have much the same background, have nominally the same religious allegiance, and will proceed to later activities within the same group, means that a great deal of "education" in the widest sense can be taken for granted or ignored. And where a technical education is concerned, its aim is clear, its success or failure can be measured; the only question is at what age to begin. The students will, no doubt, come from very different backgrounds, and will eventually scatter, to lead, apart from their professional activities, very different lives; but the question of what they should be taught, and in what order, is a manageable one. The real difficulty arises when the word *education* is taken in its most recent meaning, "culture, or development of powers, formation of character." For the meaning in relation to a social or professional group is distinguished by all the things that it is not; whereas in the widest sense, education covers the whole of life for the whole of society. . . .

No one is educated to play his part in a democracy, if he has merely been adapted to the particular routine of democracy in which he finds himself; he must be educated to criticize his own democracy, to measure it against what democracy should be, and to recognize the differences between what is proper and workable in one democracy and what is proper and workable in another. He must be adapted to it, certainly: for without being adapted to it, he cannot play a part in it, he can hardly survive in it. But he must not be completely adapted to it in the form in which he finds it around him; for that would be to train a generation to be completely incapable of any change or improvement, unable to make discoveries or experiments, or to adapt itself to those changes which go on perpetually without anyone's having deliberately intended to bring them about.

16 *The Planned Man: Skinner*

B. F. Skinner (born 1904) is unique in the radical vision with which he has explored the implications of science for the creation of a new model of the educated person. In responding to the unprecedented possibilities for the control of human behavior that lie in recently developed scientific techniques, Skinner has challenged a traditional model of man, in which many people have a considerable intellectual and emotional investment. Hence he has stimulated controversy and incurred wrath. The conventional model that he questions is that of man as a free agent, who acts in accordance with the decisions of an inner self that is neither fully explicable nor fully controllable by scientific means. In this traditional view, man achieves intellectual and moral autonomy only as the result of a long struggle; he is responsible for his victories, for which he therefore deserves praise, and for his failures, for which he deserves blame.

Skinner's scientific research and its technological outcomes (the most famous example of which is programmed instruction, or the so-called "teaching machine") have led him to postulate a different human model. He sees man operating within a wholly determined, orderly universe. All human behavior is externally caused and controlled. There are no arbitrary, uncaused, ultimately mysterious, or inherently inexplicable, human acts. What we at present categorize in this way are merely acts that an embryonic science of human behavior has not yet explained. The explanations will come in good time. Meanwhile, we are failing to use the scientific knowledge we possess to improve the human lot. One of Skinner's strongest points is the claim that it is not a question of freedom or control, but of who is to control us. Since our actions are externally caused, we are controlled anyway. Should we use science to control men's behavior rationally and for good ends or should we leave control to those parties (business, politics, organized religion, the mass media of communication) that have special interests of their own to nurture?

Scientific experimentation is the criterion to which Skinner would have us give our loyalty. It is the only means to gain reliable knowledge. Discussion about the nature of man, for example, should be settled by experimentation rather than by revelation or traditional authority. Experimentation would be the basis of life in Skinner's projected model society, as described in his novel, *Walden Two*. Values must be scientifically tested and based, not merely the products of conventional thinking. Science will, if we permit it, produce a society in which men are effortlessly good and happy. Instead of struggle, competition, and punishment, we shall have secure contentment, painless virtue, and cheerful efficiency. All this can be achieved through positive reinforcement, that is, rewarding people for behaving in ways that lead to the good life in the good society.

In such a society there will emerge a new model of the educated person. Although Skinner's plan allows for great diversity of types of educated people, they will possess certain common characteristics. Scientific knowledge of the control of human behavior will be used to create a planned man, one who will behave in the way best calculated to achieve society's goals. For Skinner, the ultimate value is the survival of mankind. Hence the educated man will be capable of cooperation with his fellows, since it is this, rather than aggressive competitiveness, that will lead to survival. He will be not a fanatical zealot but a rational, critical, and creative thinker. Behavioral engineering will have removed his antisocial tendencies and he will want only what is good for himself and his society.

Predictably, Skinner's ideas have been roundly attacked. Many of the criticisms leveled at him have been marked by ignorance, fear, misinterpretation, or simple malevolence. At times, the shrill hysteria of his attackers reveals that he is touching a sensitive wound. Nevertheless, there are important questions that need to be asked about some of Skinner's proposals. It would appear that his model of society is a loftier vision than his model of man. One can be more optimistic about the social efficiency of his utopia than about the individual growth of the members of it. Although his people would probably be happy in the sense of being certainly content, they might lack the kind of happiness that comes from experiential intensity and unpredictability.

Moreover, one must question some of the assumptions of Skinner's plan for moral education. Can virtue be made as completely a matter of habit as he implies? In Walden Two, ethical training will be completed by early childhood. Is there no place, then, for adult moral growth? Skinner's proposals fail to recognize that morality and maturity are involved with participation in making choices and decisions. Since such participation would be slight for his planned man, the chances for adult growth in morality and maturity would also be slight.

Finally, and most important, there are major difficulties in finding justifications for Skinner's plans. He claims to base his values on science, but ultimately science cannot justify any value claim. His ultimate goal of the survival of mankind, for example, does not receive its justifying support from science but from some deeper assumption that is not amenable to scientific proof. It is not enough to say, as Skinner does, that values must be scientifically tested and based. This decision to use science is itself a choice based on values that cannot ultimately be scientifically justified.

Walden Two

The publication in 1948 of Skinner's utopian novel, *Walden Two,* initiated a controversy that still continues. Critics of Skinner's ideas are apt to be opposed to his deterministic assumptions, contemptuous of his confidence in behavioral engineering, or appalled by his proposals for a completely planned society. In Walden Two, education is not a separate function but an integral part of the total culture. Hence children do not study school subjects in order to "discipline" the mind: they learn whatever is functionally relevant. For example, a student does not study a foreign language unless it is personally valuable for him. Educational experiences are planned not in accordance with traditional modes but in the light of the contemporary demands of life in Walden Two. There is therefore no communal religious training for children: the need for religion has disappeared as the traditional "religious" hopes and fears have been respectively satisfied and removed. Through behavioral engineering, desirable qualities are trained into, and undesirable qualities trained out of, all members of the community. Artificial adversities are created for children to teach them self-control and tolerance of frustration. Emotions are carefully controlled. People in Walden Two are trained to feel only useful emotions, like joy and love. Harmful emotions like sorrow, hate, anger, fear, and rage are conditioned out. Some emotions, like jealousy, which may play a useful role in competitive societies, are no longer needed in the cooperative atmosphere of Walden Two and are also removed. Feelings of contempt and superiority are systematically expunged: people in Walden Two take no joy in personal triumph or in domination over others. Competition is discouraged. Special approbation for individuals, personal favoritism, and expressions of gratitude are all absent as a result of deliberate conditioning. No distinction of seniority or superordination are observed; there is no strong leadership; all personal contributions to the community are anonymous.

411

The following statements are made in the novel by Frazier, the fictional founder of Walden Two, whose views represent the closest approximation to those of Skinner. The excerpts are from B. F. Skinner, *Walden Two*, published in New York in 1948 by The Macmillan Company, with whose permission they are reprinted.

"We . . . don't require all our children to develop the same abilities or skills. We don't insist upon a certain set of courses. I don't suppose we have a single child who has had a 'secondary school education,' whatever that means. But they've all developed as rapidly as advisable, and they're well educated in many useful respects. By the same token we don't waste time in teaching the unteachable. The fixed education represented by a diploma is a bit of conspicuous waste which has no place in Walden Two. We don't attach an economic or honorific value to education. It has its own value or none at all.

"Since our children remain happy, energetic, and curious, we don't need to teach 'subjects' at all. We teach only the techniques of learning and thinking. As for geography, literature, the sciences—we give our children opportunity and guidance, and they learn them for themselves. In that way we dispense with half the teachers required under the old system, and the education is incomparably better. Our children aren't neglected, but they're seldom, if ever, *taught* anything.

"Fame is . . . won at the expense of others. Even the well-deserved honors of the scientist or man of learning are unfair to many persons of equal achievement who get none. When one man gets a place in the sun, others are put in a denser shade. From the point of view of the whole group there's no gain whatsoever, and perhaps a loss.

"We are opposed to personal competition. We don't encourage competitive games, for example, with the exception of tennis or chess, where the exercise of skill is as important as the outcome of the game; and we never have tournaments, even so. We never mark any member for special approbation. There must be some other source of satisfaction in one's work or play, or we regard an achievement as quite trivial. A triumph over another man is never a laudable act. Our decision to eliminate personal aggrandizement arose quite naturally from the fact that we were thinking about the whole group. We could not see how the group could gain from individual glory.

"Walden Two isn't a religious community. It differs in that respect from all other reasonably permanent communities of the past. We don't give our children any religious training, though parents are free to do so if they wish. Our conception of man is not taken from theology but from a scientific examination of man himself. And we recognize no revealed truths about good or evil or the laws or codes of a successful society.

"The simple fact is, the religious practices which our members brought to Walden Two have fallen away little by little, like drinking and smoking. It would take me a long time to describe, and I'm not sure I could explain, how religious faith becomes irrelevant when the fears which nourish it are allayed and the hopes fulfilled—here on earth. We have no need for formal religion, either as ritual or philosophy. But I think we're a devout people in the best sense of that word, and we're far better behaved than any thousand church members taken at random."

Freedom and the Control
of Men

In this important essay Skinner elaborates and defends some of
the controversial claims put forward in *Walden Two*. Democracy,
he suggests, has produced science, but now science must question
some of the assumptions of democracy, such as the idea of man's
personal responsibility for his behavior and its origins. Science sees
the causes of human behavior as lying outside of man. Therefore,
instead of waiting for man to exercise his supposed freedom in
order to improve himself, or waiting for the vagaries of chance
to create the ideal society, we should utilize science to bring about
human and social progress. Skinner wants to use scientific control
in order to build a society where it will be easy to be good, and
an educational process where it will be easy to be excellent. Scorn-
ful of our Puritan culture, where hard work and diligent effort
are admired and where life is made unnecessarily difficult, he wants
to replace it with a culture that admires play and rewards effortless
achievement. Skinner asks some searching questions about our
present educational assumptions. Do we produce human diversity
through education merely because of our inefficiency, that is, because we fail with some students? Would we want an educational
process that made all students identically excellent? If not, are
we sincere in the goals we ostensibly pursue? Skinner's own model
of the educated person is one who is happy, informed, skillful,
well behaved, and productive. We are now at the stage, he claims,
where we can proceed to plan scientifically for such a model.

These passages are taken from B. F. Skinner, "Freedom and
the Control of Men," published in *The American Scholar*, Volume
25, Number 1 (Winter 1955–1956); reprinted with permission of
B. F. Skinner.

The second half of the twentieth century may be remembered for its solution of a curious problem. Although Western democracy created the conditions responsible for the rise of modern science, it is now evident that it may never fully profit from that achievement. The so-called "democratic philosophy" of human behavior to which it also gave rise is increasingly in conflict with the application of the methods of science to human affairs. Unless this conflict is somehow resolved, the ultimate goals of democracy may be long deferred.

I

Just as biographers and critics look for external influences to account for the traits and achievements of the men they study, so science ultimately explains behavior in terms of "causes" or conditions which lie beyond the individual himself. As more and more causal relations are demonstrated, a practical corollary becomes difficult to resist: it should be possible to *produce* behavior according to plan simply by arranging the proper conditions. Now, among the specifications which might reasonably be submitted to a behavior technology are these: Let men be happy, informed, skillful, well behaved and productive. . . .

III

. . . With a world of their own making almost within reach, men of good will have been seized with distaste for their achievement. They have uneasily rejected opportunities to apply the techniques and findings of science in the service of men, and as the import of effective cultural design has come to be understood, many of them have voiced an outright refusal to have any part in it. Science has been challenged before when it has encroached upon institutions already engaged in the control of human behavior; but what are we to make of benevolent men, with no special interests of their own to defend, who nevertheless turn against the very means of reaching long-dreamed-of goals?

What is being rejected, of course, is the scientific conception of man and his place in nature. So long as the findings and methods of science are applied to human affairs only in a sort of remedial patchwork, we may continue to hold any view of human nature we like. But as the use of science increases, we are forced to accept the theoretical structure with which science represents its facts. The difficulty is that this structure is clearly at odds with the traditional democratic conception of man. Every discovery of an event which has a part in shaping a man's behavior seems to leave so much the less to be credited to the man himself;

and as such explanations become more and more comprehensive, the contribution which may be claimed by the individual himself appears to approach zero. Man's vaunted creative powers, his original accomplishments in art, science and morals, his capacity to choose and our right to hold him responsible for the consequences of his choice—none of these is conspicuous in this new self-portrait. Man, we once believed, was free to express himself in art, music and literature, to inquire into nature, to seek salvation in his own way. He could initiate action and make spontaneous and capricious changes of course. Under the most extreme duress some sort of choice remained to him. He could resist any effort to control him, though it might cost him his life. But science insists that action is initiated by forces impinging upon the individual, and that caprice is only another name for behavior for which we have not yet found a cause.

In attempting to reconcile these views it is important to note that the traditional democratic conception was not designed as a description in the scientific sense but as a philosophy to be used in setting up and maintaining a governmental process. It arose under historical circumstances and served political purposes apart from which it cannot be properly understood. In rallying men against tyranny it was necessary that the individual be strengthened, that he be taught that he had rights and could govern himself. To give the common man a new conception of his worth, his dignity, and his power to save himself, both here and hereafter, was often the only resource of the revolutionist. When democratic principles were put into practice, the same doctrines were used as a working formula. This is exemplified by the notion of personal responsibility in Anglo-American law. All governments make certain forms of punishment contingent upon certain kinds of acts. In democratic countries these contingencies are expressed by the notion of responsible choice. But the notion may have no meaning under governmental practices formulated in other ways and would certainly have no place in systems which did not use punishment.

The democratic philosophy of human nature is determined by certain political exigencies and techniques, not by the goals of democracy. But exigencies and techniques change; and a conception which is not supported for its accuracy as a likeness—is not, indeed, rooted in fact at all—may be expected to change too. No matter how effective we judge current democratic practices to be, how highly we value them or how long we expect them to survive, they are almost certainly not the *final* form of government. The philosophy of human nature which has been useful in implementing them is also almost certainly not the last word.

The ultimate achievement of democracy may be long deferred unless we emphasize the real aims rather than the verbal devices of democratic thinking. A philosophy which has been appropriate to one set of political exigencies will defeat its purpose if, under other circumstances it prevents us from applying to human affairs the science of man which probably nothing but democracy itself could have produced. . . .

V

Those who reject the scientific conception of man must, to be logical oppose the methods of science as well. The position is often supported by predicting a series of dire consequences which are to follow if science is not checked. A recent book by Joseph Wood Krutch, *The Measure of Man*, is in this vein. Mr. Krutch sees in the growing science of man the threat of an unexampled tyranny over men's minds. If science is permitted to have its way, he insists, "we may never be able really to think again." A controlled culture will, for example, lack some virtue inherent in disorder. We have emerged from chaos through a series of happy accidents, but in an engineered culture it will be "impossible for the unplanned to erupt again." But there is no virtue in the accidental character of an accident, and the diversity which arises from disorder can not only be duplicated by design but vastly extended. The experimental method is superior to simple observation just because it multiplies "accidents" in a systematic coverage of the possibilities. Technology offers many familiar examples. We no longer wait for immunity to disease to develop from a series of accidental exposures, nor do we wait for natural mutations in sheep and cotton to produce better fibers; but we continue to make use of such accidents when they occur, and we certainly do not prevent them. Many of the things we value have emerged from the clash of ignorant armies on darkling plains, but it is not therefore wise to encourage ignorance and darkness.

It is not always disorder itself which we are told we shall miss but certain admirable qualities in men which flourish only in the presence of disorder. A man rises above an unpropitious childhood to a position of eminence, and since we cannot give a plausible account of the action of so complex an environment, we attribute the achievement to some admirable faculty in the man himself. But such "faculties" are suspiciously like the explanatory fictions against which the history of science warns us. We admire Lincoln for rising above a deficient school system, but it was not necessarily something *in him* which permitted him to become an educated man in spite of it. His educational environment was certainly unplanned, but it could nevertheless have made a full contribution to his mature behavior. He was a rare man, but the circumstances of his childhood were rare too. We do not give Franklin Delano Roosevelt the same credit for becoming an educated man with the help of Groton and Harvard, although the same behavior processes may have been involved. The founding of Groton and Harvard somewhat reduced the possibility that fortuitous combinations of circumstances would erupt to produce other Lincolns. Yet the founders can hardly be condemned for attacking an admirable human quality.

Another predicted consequence of a science of man is an excessive uniformity. We are told that effective control—whether governmental, religious, educational, economic or social—will produce a race of men who differ from each other only through relatively refractory genetic differences. That would probably be bad design, but we must admit that we are not now pursuing another course from choice. In a modern school, for example, there is usually a syllabus which specifies what every student is to learn by the end of each year. This would be flagrant regimentation if anyone expected every student to comply. But some will be poor in particular subjects, others will not study, others will not remember what they have been taught, and diversity is assured. Suppose, however, that we someday possess such effective educational techniques that every student will in fact be put in possession of all the behavior specified in a syllabus. At the end of the year, all students will correctly answer all questions on the final examination and "must all have prizes." Should we reject such a system on the grounds that in making all students excellent it has made them all alike? Advocates of the theory of a special faculty might contend that an important advantage of the present system is that the good student learns *in spite of* a system which is so defective that it is currently producing bad students as well. But if really effective techniques are available, we cannot avoid the problem of design simply by preferring the status quo. At what point should education be deliberately inefficient?

Such predictions of the havoc to be wreaked by the application of science to human affairs are usually made with surprising confidence. They not only show a faith in the orderliness of human behavior; they presuppose an established body of knowledge with the help of which it can be positively asserted that the changes which scientists propose to make will have quite specific results—albeit not the results they foresee. But the predictions made by the critics of science must be held to be equally fallible and subject also to empirical test. We may be sure that many steps in the scientific design of cultural patterns will produce unforeseen consequences. But there is only one way to find out. And the test must be made, for if we cannot advance in the design of cultural patterns with absolute certainty, neither can we rest completely confident of the superiority of the status quo.

VI

Apart from their possibly objectionable consequences, scientific methods seem to make no provision for certain admirable qualities and faculties which seem to have flourished in less explicitly planned cultures; hence they are called "degrading" or "lacking in dignity." (Mr. Krutch has called the author's *Walden Two* an "ignoble Utopia.") The conditioned reflex is the current whipping boy. Because conditioned reflexes may be demonstrated in animals, they are spoken of as though they were exclusively subhuman. It is implied, as we have seen, that no behavioral processes are involved in education and moral discourse or, at least, that the processes are exclusively human. But men do show conditioned reflexes (for example, when they are frightened by all instances of the control of human behavior because some instances engender fear), and animals do show processes similar to the human behavior involved in instruction and moral discourse. When Mr. Krutch asserts that " 'Conditioning' is achieved by methods which by-pass or, as it were, short-circuit those very reasoning faculties which education proposes to cultivate and exercise," he is making a technical statement which needs a definition of terms and a great deal of supporting evidence.

If such methods are called "ignoble" simply because they leave no room for certain admirable attributes, then perhaps the practice of admiration needs to be examined. We might say that the child whose education has been skillfully planned has been deprived of the right to intellectual heroism. Nothing has been left to be admired in the way he acquires an education. Similarly, we can conceive of moral training which is so adequate to the demands of the culture that men will be good practically automatically, but to that extent they will be deprived of the right to moral heroism, since we seldom admire automatic goodness. Yet if we consider the end of morals rather than certain virtuous means, is not "automatic goodness" a desirable state of affairs? Is it not, for example, the avowed goal of religious education? T. H. Huxley answered the question unambiguously: "If some great power would agree to make me always think what is true and do what is right, on condition of being a sort of clock and wound up every morning before I got out of bed, I should close instantly with the offer." Yet Mr. Krutch quotes this as the scarcely credible point of view of a "proto-modern"

and seems himself to share T. S. Eliot's contempt for ". . . systems
so perfect / That no one will need to be good."

"Having to be good" is an excellent example of an expendable honorific. It is inseparable from a particular form of ethical and moral control.
We distinguish between the things we *have* to do to avoid punishment
and those we *want* to do for rewarding consequences. In a culture
which did not resort to punishment we should never "have" to do anything except with respect to the punishing contingencies which arise
directly in the physical environment. And we are moving toward such
a culture, because the neurotic, not to say psychotic, by-products of
control through punishment have long since led compassionate men to
seek alternative techniques. Recent research has explained some of the
objectionable results of punishment and has revealed resources of at
least equal power in "positive reinforcement." It is reasonable to look
forward to a time when man will seldom "have" to do anything, although
he may show interest, energy, imagination and productivity far beyond
the level seen under the present system (except for rare eruptions of
the unplanned).

What we have to do we do with *effort*. We call it "work." There
is no other way to distinguish between exhausting labor and the possibly
equally energetic but rewarding activity of play. It is presumably good
cultural design to replace the former with the latter. But an adjustment
in attitudes is needed. We are much more practiced in admiring the
heroic labor of a Hercules than the activity of one who works without
having to. In a truly effective educational system the student might
not "have to work" at all, but that possibility is likely to be received
by the contemporary teacher with an emotion little short of rage.

We cannot reconcile traditional and scientific views by agreeing upon
what is to be admired or condemned. The question is whether anything
is to be so treated. Praise and blame are cultural practices which have
been adjuncts of the prevailing system of control in Western democracy.
All peoples do not engage in them for the same purposes or to the
same extent, nor, of course, are the same behaviors always classified
in the same way as subject to praise or blame. In admiring intellectual
and moral heroism and unrewarding labor, and in rejecting a world
in which these would be uncommon, we are simply demonstrating our
own cultural conditioning. By promoting certain tendencies to admire
and censure, the group of which we are a part has arranged for the
social reinforcement and punishment needed to assure a high level of
intellectual and moral industry. Under other and possibly better controlling systems, the behavior which we now admire would occur, but not
under those conditions which make it admirable, and we should have

no reason to admire it because the culture would have arranged for its maintenance in other ways.

To those who are stimulated by the glamorous heroism of the battle-field, a peaceful world may not be a better world. Others may reject a world without sorrow, longing or a sense of guilt because the relevance of deeply moving works of art would be lost. To many who have devoted their lives to the struggle to be wise and good, a world without confusion and evil might be an empty thing. A nostalgic concern for the decline of moral heroism has been a dominating theme in the work of Aldous Huxley. In *Brave New World* he could see in the application of science to human affairs only a travesty on the notion of the Good (just as George Orwell, in *1984*, could foresee nothing but horror). In a recent issue of *Esquire*, Huxley has expressed the point this way: "We have had religious revolutions, we have had political, industrial, economic and nationalistic revolutions. All of them, as our descendants will dis-cover, were but ripples in an ocean of conservatism—trivial by compari-son with the psychological revolution toward which we are so rapidly moving. *That* will really be a revolution. When it is over, the human race will give no further trouble." (Footnote for the reader of the future: This was not meant as a happy ending. Up to 1956 men had been admired, if at all, either for causing trouble or alleviating it. Therefore—)

It will be a long time before the world can dispense with heroes and hence with the cultural practice of admiring heroism, but we move in that direction whenever we act to prevent war, famine, pestilence and disaster. It will be a long time before man will never need to submit to punishing environments or engage in exhausting labor, but we move in that direction whenever we make food, shelter, clothing and labor-sav-ing devices more readily available. We may mourn the passing of heroes but not the conditions which make for heroism. We can spare the self-made saint or sage as we spare the laundress on the river's bank strug-gling against fearful odds to achieve cleanliness.

The Control of
Human Behavior

One of Skinner's more thoughful critics has been Carl Rogers. At the 1956 meeting of the American Psychological Association the two men participated in a symposium, where they engaged in a sharp exchange of views. Part of their discussion was subsequently published in the journal, *Science*. From this publication, some of Skinner's remarks have been selected. He reiterates his goal of an ideal society where virtue and wisdom can be acquired without a difficult moral struggle or hard work. Our Puritan admiration for the student who learns without external aids or as a result of strenuous effort impedes our educational progress, in Skinner's opinion. We err in laying responsibility for learning failure on some internal processes in the student rather than on poor pedagogy or ineffective control of the environment. There is no alternative to control: it is simply a matter of *who* is to control. I do not grant the child "freedom" merely by leaving him alone. If I do not exercise control, I leave him to be manipulated by other forces in his environment—past, present, or future. To refuse to use scientific control in order to shape human behavior is a failure in responsibility. If we ask to what end this control must be exerted, Skinner responds with his model of the healthy, happy, secure, productive, and creative person, which his ideal society will produce. The ultimate value is the survival of mankind, although Skinner acknowledges that he cannot scientifically justify this value.

These remarks by Skinner appear in Carl R. Rogers and B. F. Skinner, "Some Issues Concerning the Control of Human Behavior," *Science*, Volume 124, Number 3231 (November 30, 1956), pages 1057–1066, and are reprinted with permission of B. F. Skinner and the American Association for the Advancement of Science.

The techniques of education were once frankly aversive. The teacher was usually older and stronger than his pupils and was able to "make them learn." This meant that they were not actually taught but were surrounded by a threatening world from which they could escape only by learning. Usually they were left to their own resources in discovering how to do so. Claude Coleman has published a grimly amusing reminder of these older practices. He tells of a schoolteacher who published a careful account of his services during 51 years of teaching, during which he administered: ". . . 911,527 blows with a cane; 124,010 with a rod; 20,989 with a ruler; 136,715 with the hand; 10,295 over the mouth; 7,905 boxes on the ear; [and] 1,115,800 slaps on the head. . . ."

Progressive education was a humanitarian effort to substitute positive reinforcement for such aversive measures, but in the search for useful human values in the classroom it has never fully replaced the variables it abandoned. Viewed as a branch of behavioral technology, education remains relatively inefficient. We supplement it, and rationalize it, by admiring the pupil who learns *for himself;* and we often attribute the learning process, or knowledge itself, to something *inside* the individual. We admire behavior which seems to have inner sources. Thus we admire one who *recites* a poem more than one who simply *reads* it. We admire one who *knows* the answer more than one who *knows where to look it up.* We admire the *writer* rather than the *reader.* We admire the arithmetician who can do a problem in his head rather than with a slide rule or calculating machine, or in "original" ways rather than by a strict application of rules. In general we feel that any aid or "crutch"— except those aids to which we are now thoroughly accustomed—reduces the credit due. In Plato's *Phaedrus,* Thamus, the king, attacks the invention of the alphabet on similar grounds! He is afraid "it will produce forgetfulness in the minds of those who learn to use it, because they will not practice their memories. . . ." In other words, he holds it more admirable to remember than to use a memorandum. He also objects that pupils "will read many things without instruction . . . [and] will therefore seem to know many things when they are for the most part ignorant." In the same vein we are today sometimes contemptuous of book learning, but, as educators, we can scarcely afford to adopt this view without reservation.

By admiring the student for knowledge and blaming him for ignorance, we escape some of the responsibility of teaching him. We resist any analysis of the educational process which threatens the notion of inner wisdom or questions the contention that the fault of ignorance lies with the student. More powerful techniques which bring about the same changes in behavior by manipulating *external* variables are decried as brainwashing or thought control. We are quite unprepared to judge *effective* educational measures. As long as only a few pupils learn much of what is taught, we do not worry about uniformity or regimentation. We do not fear the feeble technique; but we should view with dismay a system under which every student learned everything listed in a syllabus—although such a condition is far from unthinkable. Similarly, we do not fear a system which is so defective that the student must *work* for an education; but we are loath to give credit for anything learned without effort—although this could well be taken as an ideal result—and we flatly refuse to give credit if the student already knows what a school teaches.

A world in which people are wise and good without trying, without "having to be," without "choosing to be," could conceivably be a far better world for everyone. In such a world we should not have to "give anyone credit"—we should not need to admire anyone—for being wise and good. From our present point of view we cannot believe that such a world would be admirable. We do not even permit ourselves to imagine what it would be like. . . .

People behave in ways which, as we say, conform to ethical, governmental, or religious patterns because they are reinforced for doing so. The resulting behavior may have far-reaching consequences for the survival of the pattern to which it conforms. And whether we like it or not, survival is the ultimate criterion. This is where, it seems to me, science can help—not in choosing a goal, but in enabling us to predict the survival value of cultural practices. Man has too long tried to get the kind of world he wants by glorifying some brand of immediate reinforcement. As science points up more and more of the remoter consequences, he may begin to work to strengthen behavior, not in a slavish devotion to a chosen value, but with respect to the ultimate survival of mankind. Do not ask me why I want mankind to survive. I can tell you why only in the sense in which the physiologist can tell you why I want to breathe. Once the relation between a given step and the survival of my group has been pointed out, I will take that step. And it is the business of science to point out just such relations.

The values I have occasionally recommended (and Rogers has not led me to recant) are transitional. Other things being equal, I am betting on the group whose practices make for healthy, happy, secure, productive, and creative people. And I insist that the values recommended by Rogers are transitional, too, for I can ask him the same kind of question. Man as a process of becoming—*what?* Self-actualization—for what? Inner control is no more a goal than external.

What Rogers seems to me to be proposing, both here and elsewhere, is this: Let us use our increasing power of control to create individuals who will not need and perhaps will no longer respond to control. Let us solve the problem of our power by renouncing it. At first blush this seems as implausible as a benevolent despot. Yet power has occasionally been foresworn. A nation has burned its Reichstag, rich men have given away their wealth, beautiful women have become ugly hermits in the desert, and psychotherapists have become nondirective. When this happens, I look to other possible reinforcements for a plausible explanation. A people relinquish democratic power when a tyrant promises them the earth. Rich men give away wealth to escape the accusing finger of their fellowmen. A woman destroys her beauty in the hope of salvation. And a psychotherapist relinquishes control because he can thus help his client more effectively.

The solution that Rogers is suggesting is thus understandable. But is he correctly interpreting the result? What evidence is there that a client ever becomes truly *self*-directing? What evidence is there that he ever makes a truly *inner* choice of ideal or goal? Even though the therapist does not do the choosing, even though he encourages "self-actualization"—he is not out of control as long as he holds himself ready to step in when occasion demands—when, for example, the client chooses the goal of becoming a more accomplished liar or murdering his boss. But supposing the therapist does withdraw completely or is no longer necessary—what about all the other forces acting upon the client? Is the self-chosen goal independent of his early ethical and religious training? or the folk-wisdom of his group? of the opinions and attitudes of others who are important to him? Surely not. The therapeutic situation is only a small part of the world of the client. From the therapist's point of view it may appear to be possible to relinquish control. But the control passes, not to a "self," but to forces in other parts of the client's world. The solution of the therapist's problem of power cannot be *our* solution, for we must consider *all* the forces acting upon the individual. The child who must be prodded and nagged is something less than a fully developed human being. We want to see him hurrying to his appointment, not because each step is taken in response to verbal reminders from his mother, but because certain temporal contingencies, in which dawdling has been punished and hurrying reinforced, have worked a change in his behavior. Call this a state of better organization, a greater sensitivity to reality, or what you will. The plain fact is that the child passes from a temporary verbal control exercised by his parents to control by certain inexorable features of the environment. I should suppose that something of the same sort happens in successful psychotherapy. Rogers seems to me to be saying this: Let us put an end, as quickly as possible, to any pattern of master-and-slave, to any direct obedience to command, to the submissive following of suggestions. Let the individual be free to adjust himself to more rewarding features of the world about him. In the end, let his teachers and counselors "wither away," like the Marxist state. I not only agree with this as a useful ideal, I have constructed a fanciful world to demonstrate its advantages. It saddens me to hear Rogers say that "at a deep philosophic level" *Walden Two* and George Orwell's *1984* "seem indistinguishable." They could scarcely be more unlike—at any level. The book *1984* is a picture of immediate aversive control for vicious selfish purposes. The founder of *Walden Two*, on the other hand, has built a community in which neither he nor any other person exerts any *current* control. His achievement lay in his original *plan*, and when he boasts of this ("It is enough to satisfy the thirstiest tyrant") we do not fear him but only pity him for his weakness.

Another critic of *Walden Two*, Andrew Hacker, has discussed this point in considering the bearing of mass conditioning upon the liberal notion of autonomous man. In drawing certain parallels between the Grand Inquisition passage in Dostoevsky's *Brothers Karamazov*, Huxley's *Brave New World*, and *Walden Two*, he attempts to set up a distinction to be drawn in any society between conditioners and conditioned. He assumes that "the conditioner can be said to be autonomous in the traditional liberal sense." But then he notes: "Of course the conditioner has been conditioned. But he has not been conditioned by the conscious manipulation of another *person*." But how does this affect the resulting behavior? Can we not soon forget the origins of the "artificial" diamond which is identical with the real thing? Whether it is an "accidental" cultural pattern, such as is said to have produced the founder of *Walden Two*, or the engineered environment which is about to produce his successors, we are dealing with sets of conditions generating human behavior which will ultimately be measured by their contribution to the strength of the group. We look to the future, not the past, for the test of "goodness" or acceptability.

If we are worthy of our democratic heritage we shall, of course, be ready to resist any tyrannical use of science for immediate or selfish purposes. But if we value the achievements and goals of democracy we must not refuse to apply science to the design and construction of cultural patterns, even though we may then find ourselves in some sense in the position of controllers. Fear of control, generalized beyond any warrant, has led to a misinterpretation of valid practices and the blind rejection of intelligent planning for a better way of life. In terms which I trust Rogers will approve, in conquering this fear we shall become more mature and better organized and shall, thus, more fully actualize ourselves as human beings.

Man

In this paper, read before a meeting of the American Philosophical Society in 1964, Skinner gives a behavioristic view of man. It should be possible eventually, Skinner argues, to explain man completely through the external influences operating on him. If we cannot yet do this, it is because science is not effective enough, rather than because there is an inaccessible, residual "self" inside man that really makes his choices and determines his behavior. Skinner envisages scientific and technological developments that will lead us to abandon traditional notions like justice and a sense of freedom. There will eventually be no need for currently admired virtues like self-control and personal responsibility. Admiration is itself a form of social control: it induces people to do hard, dangerous, or painful things. Behavioral technology will render this form of control unnecessary. In education, there will be no need to admire the hard-working student when the same results can be achieved through enjoyable play. Skinner is urging us to abandon our Puritan model of the educated person and substitute for it a model of the effective, productive, virtuous person who is made thus by intelligent, scientific, behavioral control. There will then be no need for moral or intellectual struggle. Human excellence will be achieved without difficulty and without reducing the range of human diversity.

The passage is taken from B. F. Skinner, "Man," *Proceedings of the American Philosophical Society*, Volume 108, Number 6 (December 1964), pages 482–485; reprinted with permission of B. F. Skinner and the American Philosophical Society.

Man has long sought to explain his behavior by searching for its causes. Historians and biographers have traced human achievements to conditions of birth, climate, culture, and personal contacts, and some of them have joined philosophers and essayists in more sweeping generalizations. Science has naturally worked in the same direction. The social sciences specialize in statistical demonstrations, but psychology and physiology are closer to history and biography in concentrating on the individual. In any case, more and more of the behavior of organisms, including man, is being plausibly related to events in their genetic and environmental histories. If other sciences are any guide, human behavior may ultimately be accounted for entirely in such terms.

The traditional conception, of course, is very different. It holds that a man behaves as he does because of his wishes, impulses, emotions, attitude, and so on. His behavior is important only as the expression of an inner life. Many psychologists still subscribe to this view. The good Freudian attributes observable behavior to a drama played in non-physical space by an immanent triumvirate scarcely to be distinguished from the spirits and demons of early animism. Other psychologists merely divide the inner personae into parts, each of which still carries on its little share of mental life. Thus, where a scientific analysis relates behavior to the physical environment, the mentalist may insist that the mind observes only a none-too-reliable copy of the environment called subjective experience. Where a scientific analysis shows that we react in a given way because similar actions in our past have had particular consequences, the mentalist may insist that we act because we have stored memories of past actions and of their consequences, which we now scan in order to reach certain expectations leading to an act of will which initiates behavior. Where a scientific analysis traces certain disturbing patterns of behavior to a history of punishment, the mentalist may argue that the disturbance is in the personality and that it is the effect of anxiety, just possibly generated by punishment. The traditional conception of man is an example of an explanatory strategy which was once common in other sciences. It has survived in psychology, possibly because of the extraordinary complexity of the subject matter. As plausible connections with external variables are demonstrated in spite of that complexity, however, the need for inner explanations is reduced. An effective scientific analysis would presumably dispense with them altogether.

That such an analysis will be simpler, more expedient, and more useful will not necessarily mean its adoption, because the older view served other than scientific functions. A behavioristic reinterpretation of mental life is not a fundamental issue for many people, but everyone has a stake in human behavior, and there are other reasons why the scientific picture may not seem to be a picture of man at all. Certain long-admired characteristics of human behavior seem to be neglected, and their absence is more threatening than any implication about the nature of consciousness or the existence of free will.

C. S. Lewis, for example, has gone so far as to argue that science is embarked upon "the abolition of man."° He is concerned with the neglect of a familiar feature of the traditional picture—an indwelling sense of justice, a felt standard of rightness, an inner source of values. To the traditionalist a human act is not simply a physical movement, it is a judgment, or the expression of a judgment, reached only by applying certain standards of conduct. It is not the act which is essentially human (morally acceptable though it may be), but the application of the standard. We may condition a man to behave in virtuous ways as we condition animals to behave according to any set of specifications, but such a man will not *be* virtuous. According to this view he can be virtuous only if he has not been conditioned to behave well automatically but has arrived at given forms of virtuous conduct by consulting his sense of rightness. (The argument is reminiscent of the complaint that a rational religion destroys piety, that proof of the existence of God deprives men of the opportunity to demonstrate their faith.)

If this traditional conception of man is to continue to challenge the scientific view, however, some thorny questions need to be answered. What *is* happening when a man refers to a standard of rightness? Can this form of behavior be analyzed? Where do standards come from? If the answer is that they come from the genetic or environmental history, then the scientific view is not in danger. And this appears to be the case. Lewis, for example, acknowledges that the sentiments he so highly values must be learned. "The little human animal," he says, "would not at first have the right responses"—indeed, in that sense would not yet be human. And he quotes Plato with approval to the effect that such things as taste and compassion must be taught before a child is "of an age to reason." These are the contentions of an environmentalist. The values to which a man must be able to appeal in order to be human are not originally his, and something beyond him is therefore ultimately responsible for his action. (The same unhappy story can be told of all inner explanations of human conduct, for the explanations must themselves be explained—possibly in terms of other inner events but eventually, and necessarily, in terms of forces acting upon a man from without.)

A small issue survives at a technical level. How are we to teach a child to behave well? We can begin by conditioning him to make so

° C. S. Lewis, *The Abolition of Man* (New York, 1947).

many purely automatic, right responses, but we shall find that the number which must thus be taught is distressingly large. It is more efficient if not actually necessary, to teach him to examine each new occasion as it arises and, by applying certain rules, to arrive at an appropriate response. Such is our practice in teaching multiplication. Up to twelve-times-twelve we condition specific responses, each of which can be quite automatic, implying no understanding of multiplication. Beyond that, we find it expedient to condition certain procedures which permit the child to arrive at a vast number of specific products which it would not be efficient to condition separately.

It is sometimes argued that there is an element of freedom in the application of standards which is lacking in the automatic execution of right responses. But a sense of freedom is another of those inner attributes which lose their force as we more clearly understand man's relation to his environment. Freedom—or, rather, behavior which "feels free"—is also the product of a history of conditioning. In that remark-abe book, *Émile,* Jean Jacques Rousseau tried to find replacements for the punitive methods of the schools of his time. He insisted that students should behave as they want, rather than as they are forced to behave through physical coercion. He showed an extraordinary ingenuity in substituting positive inducements for punishment. But he was not turning education over to the pupil himself.

"Let [the child] believe that he is always in control, though it is always you [the teacher] who really controls. There is no subjugation so perfect as that which keeps the appearance of freedom, for in that way one captures volition itself. The poor baby, knowing nothing, able to do nothing, having learned nothing, is he not at your mercy? Can you not arrange everything in the world which surrounds him? Can you not influence him as you wish? His work, his play, his pleasures, his pains, are not all these in your hands and without his knowing it? Doubtless he ought to do only what he wants; but he ought to want to do only what you want him to do; he ought not to take a step which you have not foreseen; he ought not to open his mouth without your knowing what he will say.*"

Thus spoke a great champion of human freedom! Like a sense of rightness or justice, the dispositions which make a given act feel free come from the environment. The surviving question is again technical. What is the best way to bring about those changes which are the object

* Jean Jacques Rousseau, *Émile ou de L'Éducation* (Amsterdam et Francfort, 1762), p. 121 in the Classiques Garnier Édition.

of education? There are many advantages in arranging matters so that the pupil does what he wants to do, but he must be carefully prepared to want to do those things which are required for effective instruction.

Another human attribute which seems to be missing from the scientific picture concerns what one does *not* want to do. In the traditional view a man has duties as well as rights: there are things he must do or suffer the consequences. He is responsible for his conduct in the sense that, if he does not behave in a given way, it is only fair that he be punished. To escape punishment—either the natural punishments of the physical environment or the social punishments of society—he engages in an activity called self-control.* When the same ultimate "good" behavior is achieved without using punishment, self-control in this sense is unnecessary.

The omission of personal responsibility from the scientific conception of man has been particularly deplored by Joseph Wood Krutch.† When we regard a criminal as in need of treatment rather than punishment, for example, we deprive him of "the human attribute of responsibility." Treatment is only one way of generating good behavior without punishment. Preventive steps are likely to be more valuable. For example, we might control stealing by creating a world free of inciting circumstances (for example, a world in which there is nothing one does not already have or where nothing is within reach to be stolen) or by conditioning behavior which is incompatible with stealing or displaces it (for example, we might strongly reinforce "respecting the property of others" or teach easier, legal ways of getting things). When we solve the problem in any of these ways, we leave no room for personal responsibility or self-control. We leave no room for moral struggle; and if to struggle is human, we have indeed destroyed something of man.

The same argument holds for nongovernmental punishments. Smoking cigarettes is "naturally" punished by lung cancer or the threat of lung cancer, as overeating is punished by obesity, illness, and the threat of an early death. Aggressive action is punished by retaliative measures. All these aversive consequences normally lead to some measure of self-control. But we can reduce the inclination to smoke, eat, or act aggressively in the other ways—and with it the need to control oneself. Appropriate drugs have this effect. A tranquilizer reduces the need to control aggression, an appetite-suppressant reduces the need to control eating, and a drug which would reduce the tendency to smoke cigarettes would reduce the need to control one's smoking habits. Another form of control would be to build a world in which the positive reinforcements now

* B. F. Skinner, *Science and Human Behavior* (New York, 1953).
† Joseph Wood Krutch, *The Measure of Man* (Indianapolis and New York, 1954).

accorded these behaviors are carefully managed. In such a world a man would be either naturally wise and good or at least easily taught to be wise and good. There would be no place for intellectual and moral struggle.*

Any technology, physical or social, which reduces punishing consequences reduces the need for self-control and personal responsibility. If the same acceptable conduct is achieved, it is difficult to see why anyone should object. The trouble is that the characteristics which are thus dismissed have long been admired. We admire people who apply ethical and moral standards, who accept responsibility, and who control themselves. We admire them in part because the results are reinforcing to us, for the individual is thus induced to conform to the interests of others. We also admire such behavior just in order to support it. Admiration is a social practice used to eke out a defective control. There are certain kinds of heroism, for example, which society can engender only by effusively admiring them. We induce men to die for their country by convincing them that it is sweet and decorous to do so. Students work hard to be admired by their teachers. Men undergo exhausting labor and suffer pain with patience because they are admired for doing so. Yet technological progress is directed toward making all this unnecessary. In a world at peace there will be no military heroism to admire. We shall no longer admire patient suffering when men seldom need to suffer. We do not even now give men credit for exhausting labor if the labor can be "saved," and we shall not admire students who work hard when there are techniques of education in which they need not "work" at all. We shall no longer admire wrestling with the devil, if it turns out that the devil is simply a slight disturbance in the hypothalamus which can be allayed by a suitable drug.

In turning to external and manipulable variables, a scientific analysis moves away from supposed inner activities which we have tried to reach through admiration. The inner activity, needing to be admired, naturally seems admirable. Thus we admire a man who can multiply by applying rules more than one who merely recites the multiplication table in an automatic fashion, but we admire the latter far beyond one who simply uses a calculating machine. The calculating machine has been designed to reduce the behavior required in multiplication to external, sharply defined, relatively infallible, and almost effortless responses. It improves multiplication, but makes the multiplier less admirable. Plato records an objection to the invention of the alphabet on similar grounds: if

* Carl R. Rogers and B. F. Skinner, "Some Issues Concerning the Control of Human Behavior," *Science* 124 (1956): pp. 1057–1066.

texts were generally available, a man would seem to know things which he had merely read.* But the alphabet was invented precisely to enable one man to profit from the direct knowledge of another. Must we destroy all physical and social inventions in order to recapture a man we can wholeheartedly admire?

Two important features often said to be missing from the scientific picture of man are actually emphasized in it. If man has no freedom of choice, if he can initiate no action which alters the causal stream of his behavior, then he may seem to have no control over his own destiny. The scientific view of man according to Krutch is a "dead end."† The fact is, however, that men control both their genetic and environmental histories, and in *that* sense they do, indeed, control themselves. Science and technology are concerned with changing the world in which men live, and changes are made precisely because of their effects on human behavior. We have reached the stage, far from a dead end, in which man can determine his future with an entirely new order of effectiveness. C. S. Lewis would still protest; in *The Abolition of Man* he wrote, " . . the power of man to make himself what he pleases means . . . the power of some men to make other men what *they* please." But it has always been thus. Men control themselves by controlling the world in which they live. They do this as much when they exercise self-control, as when they make changes in their culture which alter the conduct of others.

Another feature of the traditional concept which is emphasized rather than abolished is individuality. Some practices derived from a scientific knowledge of human behavior could no doubt lead to regimentation, as practices consonant with traditional conceptions have often done, but there is nothing in the scientific position which makes this inevitable. On the contrary, as the product of a set of genetic and environmental variables man is most reassuringly unique. The uniqueness of the human fingerprint once came as a surprise and, because of its practical usefulness, is still a familiar symbol of individuality. But the body which each man derives from his genetic history is a vast system of unique structures of which the whorls on the ball of the thumb are a ridiculously trivial example. Equally idiosyncratic are all those characteristics which a man derives from his environment. It is true that certain scientific practices are simplified when these sources of individuality are minimized, but there is nothing in scientific practice or theory which threat-

* Plato, *Phaedrus*. Jowett Translation, II: 274e–275b.

† Joseph Wood Krutch, "What I Learned about Existentialism," *Saturday Review* 45 (April 21, 1962).

ens individuality or questions the possibility that some collocations of variables arising from these sources will have the outstanding results we attribute to talent or genius.

It is not easy to abandon notions like a sense of justice, a sense of freedom, and personal responsibility or to accept a new interpretation of man's individuality and his power to control his own destiny. Yet it would be remarkable if any conception of man did not occasionally need revision. Human behavior is extraordinarily complex, and it is unlikely that a true definitive account has been reached so soon. The traditional conception has certainly not made us conspicuously successful in dealing with human affairs. The alternative picture which a science of behavior asks us to accept is not really frightening. Man survives unchanged. Physics does not change the nature of the world it studies, and no science of behavior can change the essential nature of man, even though both sciences yield technologies with a vast power to manipulate their subject matters. Science leads us to see man in a different light, but he is nevertheless the same man we once saw in another light. If we must have something to admire, let it be man's willingness to discard a flattering portrait of himself in favor of a more accurate and hence more useful picture. Even here admiration is superfluous. The hard fact is that the culture which most readily acknowledges the validity of a scientific analysis is most likely to be successful in that competition between cultures which, whether we like it or not, will decide all such issues with finality.

17 The Existential Man: Buber

The twentieth century has witnessed the extension of the scientific method to more and more aspects of the study of man. This has been particularly true in America, where pragmatism and behaviorism have exerted strong influence. There is no doubt that science brings power and precision to the study of many human problems, as it does to the study of natural phenomena. But many observers have become concerned about some of the more dubious consequences of the applications of science. In particular, there has been a reaction against the scientific view of man as an object to be categorized, studied "objectively," or subsumed under a generalization. The power of science derives largely from this capacity to categorize, objectify, and generalize. But such procedures may militate against understanding a man as a whole, unique being. Some of those philosophers who can loosely be termed existentialists have been prominent in this reaction. Martin Buber (1878–1865) has played an outstanding role in deepening our understanding of man through an existentialist discernment.

Out of his creative response to the challenge of scientific thinking, Buber has drawn a model of the educated person as one whose life is characterized by existential decision making. Such a person does not use an abstract moral code or set of principles to determine choices in advance of existential situations. Principles and traditions are useful, but only as checks or reminders, not as infallible guides. Values are viewed in the concrete, as lived by a man in relating to another man. Thus man is seen not as a member of a category but as a unique person.

Vital to Buber's ethics is the concept of responsibility, viewed in terms of one's response to another. Thus the dialogue or the sphere of the interhuman becomes a central focus of concern. Several things follow from this. The educated person must know how to listen as well as how to talk. He must have ears as well as a

435

mouth. Moreover, since genuine dialogue depends upon authenticity, upon *being* rather than *seeming*, one needs the courage to be oneself in relationships. Courage thus becomes a cardinal quality of Buber's model. Freedom is regarded by Buber as necessary but not sufficient for genuine education. There must be freedom for the student to explore, but there must also be an encounter with the authority of the teacher's values.

I and Thou

The publication of Buber's *Ich und Du* in 1923 was a major event in the intellectual history of the West. Published in English in 1937, it has become widely recognized as a classic. Although the meaning may be difficult to comprehend at first reading, the book amply repays repeated study. Buber reveals here a constant underlying assumption of his philosophy—that all life must be hallowed, that any worldly experience can be a gateway to the eternal Thou. Hence he inquires how we can understand our relationship with God in the light of our experience with the concrete world of man. This inquiry leads him to an analysis of the distinctions between the categories of I-Thou and I-It, the world to be met and the world to be used. In the I-Thou relationship, I relate to the other as a unique person rather than as a member of a category. In the I-It relationship, I observe or use or classify the other person or thing. I-It relationships have an appropriate place—for example, in scientific observation—but they are not sufficient for full human existence. Hence the existential man becomes aware of freedom by going out to seek an authentic encounter with the other. Deeply concerned with human relationships, he does not exploit the world or others. He does not attempt to force destiny but accepts its power on himself. His life is unified by a unique and transcending purpose, to which he gives himself completely.

This passage is taken from Martin Buber, *I and Thou,* translated by Ronald Gregor Smith, published in New York in 1958 by Charles Scribner's Sons. It is reprinted with permission of Charles Scribner's Sons and T. & T. Clark, Ltd.

As freedom and destiny, so arbitrary self-will and fate belong together. But freedom and destiny are solemnly promised to one another and linked together in meaning; while arbitrary self-will and fate, soul's spectre and world's nightmare, endure one another, living side by side and avoiding one another, without connexion or conflict, in meaninglessness—till in an instant there is confused shock of glance on glance, and confession of their non-redemption breaks from them. How much eloquent and ingenious spirituality is expended to-day in the effort to avert, or at least to veil, this event!

The free man is he who wills without arbitrary self-will. He believes in reality, that is, he believes in the real solidarity of the real twofold entity *I* and *Thou*. He believes in destiny, and believes that it stands in need of him. It does not keep him in leading-strings, it awaits him, he must go to it, yet does not know where it is to be found. But he knows that he must go out with his whole being. The matter will not turn out according to his decision; but what is to come will come only when he decides on what he is able to will. He must sacrifice his puny, unfree will, that is controlled by things and instincts, to his grand will, which quits defined for destined being. Then he intervenes no more, but at the same time he does not let things merely happen. He listens to what is emerging from himself, to the course of being in the world; not in order to be supported by it, but in order to bring it to reality as it desires, in its need of him, to be brought—with human spirit and deed, human life and death. I said *he believes*, but that really means *he meets*.

The self-willed man does not believe and does not meet. He does not know solidarity of connexion, but only the feverish world outside and his feverish desire to use it. Use needs only to be given an ancient name, and it companies with the gods. When this man says *Thou*, he means "O my ability to use," and what he terms his destiny is only the equipping and sanctioning of his ability to use. He has in truth no destiny, but only a being that is defined by things and instincts, which he fulfils with the feeling of sovereignty—that is, in the arbitrariness of self-will. He has no grand will, only self-will, which he passes off as real will. He is wholly incapable of sacrifice, even though he may have the word on his lips; you know him by the fact that the word never becomes concrete. He intervenes continually, and that for the purpose of "letting things happen." Why should destiny, he says to you, not be given a helping hand? Why should the attainable means required by such a purpose not be utilised? He sees the free man, too, in this way; he can see him in no other. But the free man has no purpose here and means there, which he fetches for his purpose: he has only the one thing, his repeated decision to approach his destiny. He has made this decision, and from time to time, at every parting of ways, he will renew it. But he could sooner believe he was not alive than that the decision of his grand will was inadequate and needed to be supported by a means. He believes; he meets. But the unbelieving core in the self-willed man can perceive nothing but unbelief and self-will, establishing of a purpose and devising of a means. Without sacrifice and without grace, without meeting and without presentness, he has as his world a mediated world cluttered with purposes. His world cannot be anything else, and its name is fate. Thus with all his sovereignty he is wholly and inextricably entangled in the unreal. He knows this whenever he turns his thoughts to himself; that is why he directs the best part of his spirituality to averting or at least to veiling his thoughts.

Elements of the Interhuman

In the spring of 1957 the Washington, D.C., School of Psychiatry brought Buber from Jerusalem to give the William Alanson White Memorial Lectures. In one of these lectures, "Elements of the Interhuman," Buber elaborated on the life of dialogue, which was a perennial focus of his philosophy. It is in his human relationships, Buber argues, that man reaches his heights and lives most fully. Genuine relationship and dialogue require a full acceptance of the other person: this means "making him present" in a concrete way, entering imaginatively and intuitively into his life. It is radically different from the reductive method, which reduces man to a category, a formula, or a generalization. Genuine dialogue is based on the unreserved recognition of the other's uniqueness, of his difference from myself. I may disagree with his views but must do so without rejecting him as a person. Relating to our fellows is often intractably difficult. Usually we speak not *to* each other but *past* each other. The dialogue demands authenticity and honesty in our responses: it is destroyed by deception and pretense. Hence courage is a centrally important quality in the model that Buber portrays. The essential courage is to live authentically with the reality of one's being, rather than in accordance with the impression one makes on others.

These selections are from Martin Buber, "Elements of the Interhuman," translated by Ronald Gregor Smith, in *The Knowledge of Man*, edited by Maurice Friedman, published in New York in 1965 by Harper & Row, Inc., with whose permission they are reprinted.

The widespread tendency to live from the recurrent impression one makes instead of from the steadiness of one's being is not a 'nature.'

It originates, in fact, on the other side of interhuman life itself, in men's dependence upon one another. It is no light thing to be confirmed in one's being by others, and seeming deceptively offers itself as a help in this. To yield to seeming is man's essential cowardice, to resist it is his essential courage. But this is not an inexorable state of affairs which is as it is and must so remain. One can struggle to come to oneself—that is, to come to confidence in being. One struggles, now more successfully, now less, but never in vain, even when one thinks he is defeated. One must at times pay dearly for life lived from the being; but it is never too dear. Yet is there not bad being, do weeds not grow everywhere? I have never known a young person who seemed to me irretrievably bad. Later indeed it becomes more and more difficult to penetrate the increasingly tough layer which has settled down on a man's being. Thus there arises the false perspective of the seemingly fixed 'nature' which cannot be overcome. It is false; the foreground is deceitful; man as man can be redeemed. . . .

By far the greater part of what is today called conversation among men would be more properly and precisely described as speechifying. In general, people do not really speak to one another, but each, although turned to the other, really speaks to a fictitious court of appeal whose life consists of nothing but listening to him. Chekhov has given poetic expression to this state of affairs in *The Cherry Orchard,* where the only use the members of a family make of their being together is to talk past one another. But it is Sartre who has raised to a principle of existence what in Chekhov still appears as the deficiency of a person who is shut up in himself. Sartre regards the walls between the partners in a conservation as simply impassable. For him it is inevitable human destiny that a man has directly to do only with himself and his own affairs. The inner existence of the other is his own concern, not mine; there is no direct relation with the other, nor can there be. This is perhaps the clearest expression of the wretched fatalism of modern man, which regards degeneration as the unchangeable nature of *Homo sapiens* and the misfortune of having run into a blind alley as his primal fate, and which brands every thought of a breakthrough as reactionary romanticism. He who really knows how far our generation has lost the way of true freedom, of free giving between I and Thou, must himself, by virtue of the demand implicit in every great knowledge of this kind, practise directness—even if he were the only man on earth who did it—and not depart from it until scoffers are struck with fear, and hear in his voice the voice of their own suppressed longing.

The chief presupposition for the rise of genuine dialogue is that each

should regard his partner as the very one he is. I become aware of
him, aware that he is different, essentially different from myself, in the
definite, unique way which is peculiar to him, and I accept whom I
thus see, so that in full earnestness I can direct what I say to him
as the person he is. Perhaps from time to time I must offer strict opposition to his view about the subject of our conversation. But I accept
this person, the personal bearer of a conviction, in his definite being
out of which his conviction has grown—even though I must try to show,
bit by bit, the wrongness of this very conviction. I affirm the person
I struggle with: I struggle with him as his partner, I confirm him as
creature and as creation, I confirm him who is opposed to me as him
who is over against me. It is true that it now depends on the other
whether genuine dialogue, mutuality in speech arises between us. But
if I thus give to the other who confronts me his legitimate standing
as a man with whom I am ready to enter into dialogue, then I may
trust him and suppose him to be also ready to deal with me as
partner.

But what does it mean to be 'aware' of a man in the exact sense
in which I use the word? To be aware of a thing or a being means,
in quite general terms, to experience it as a whole and yet at the same
time without reduction or abstraction, in all its concreteness. But a man,
although he exists as a living being among living beings and even as
a thing among things, is nevertheless something categorically different
from all things and all beings. A man cannot really be grasped except
on the basis of the gift of the spirit which belongs to man alone among
all things, the spirit as sharing decisively in the personal life of the
living man, that is, the spirit which determines the person. To be aware
of a man, therefore, means in particular to perceive his wholeness as
a person determined by the spirit; it means to perceive the dynamic
centre which stamps his every utterance, action, and attitude with the
recognizable sign of uniqueness. Such an awareness is impossible, however, if and so long as the other is the separated object of my contemplation or even observation, for this wholeness and its centre do not let
themselves be known to contemplation or observation. It is only possible
when I step into an elemental relation with the other, that is, when
he becomes present to me. Hence I designate awareness in this special
sense as 'personal making present.'

The perception of one's fellow man as a whole, as a unity, and as
unique—even if his wholeness, unity, and uniqueness are only partly
developed, as is usually the case—is opposed in our time by almost
everything that is commonly understood as specifically modern. In our
time there predominates an analytical, reductive, and deriving look be-

tween man and man. This book is analytical, or rather pseudo analytical, since it treats the whole being as put together and therefore able to be taken apart—not only the so-called unconscious which is accessible to relative objectification, but also the psychic stream itself, which can never, in fact, be grasped as an object. This look is a reductive one because it tries to contract the manifold person, who is nourished by the microcosmic richness of the possible, to some schematically survey-able and recurrent structures. And this look is a deriving one because it supposes it can grasp what a man has become, or even is becoming, in genetic formulae, and it thinks that even the dynamic central principle of the individual in this becoming can be represented by a general concept. An effort is being made today radically to destroy the mystery between man and man. The personal life, the ever near mystery, once the source of the stillest enthusiasms, is levelled down.

What I have just said is not an attack on the analytical method of the human sciences, a method which is indispensable wherever it fur-thers knowledge of a phenomenon without impairing the essentially different knowledge of its uniqueness that transcends the valid circle of the method. The science of man that makes use of the analytical method must accordingly always keep in view the boundary of such a contemplation, which stretches like a horizon around it. This duty makes the transposition of the method into life dubious; for it is exces-sively difficult to see where the boundary is in life.

If we want to do today's work and prepare tomorrow's with clear sight, then we must develop in ourselves and in the next generation a gift which lives in man's inwardness as a Cinderella, one day to be a princess. Some call it intuition, but that is not a wholly unambiguous concept. I prefer the name 'imagining the real,' for in its essential being this gift is not a looking at the other, but a bold swinging—demanding the most intensive stirring of one's being—into the life of the other. This is the nature of all genuine imagining, only that here the realm of my action is not the all-possible, but the particular real person who confronts me, whom I can attempt to make present to myself just in this way, and not otherwise, in his wholeness, unity, and uniqueness, and with his dynamic centre which realizes all these things ever anew. . . .

In the moral realm Kant expressed the essential principle that one's fellow man must never be thought of and treated merely as a means, but always at the same time as an independent end. The principle is expressed as an 'ought' which is sustained by the idea of human dignity. My point of view, which is near to Kant's in its essential features, has another source and goal. It is concerned with the presuppositions of the interhuman. Man exists anthropologically not in his isolation, but in the completeness of the relation between man and man; what humanity is can be properly grasped only in vital reciprocity. For the proper existence of the interhuman it is necessary, as I have shown, that the semblance not intervene to spoil the relation of personal being to personal being. It is further necessary, as I have also shown, that each one means and makes present the other in his personal being. That neither should wish to impose himself on the other is the third basic presupposition of the interhuman. These presuppositions do not include the demand that one should influence the other in his unfolding; this is, however, an element that is suited to lead to a higher stage of the interhuman.

That there resides in every man the possibility of attaining authentic human existence in the special way peculiar to him can be grasped in the Aristotelian image of entelechy, innate self-realization; but one must note that it is an entelechy of the work of creation. It would be mistaken to speak here of individuation alone. Individuation is only the indispensable personal stamp of all realization of human existence. The self as such is not ultimately the essential, but the meaning of human existence given in creation again and again fulfils itself as self. The help that men give each other in becoming a self leads the life between men to its height. The dynamic glory of the being of man is first bodily present in the relation between two men each of whom in meaning the other also means the highest to which this person is called, and serves the self-realization of this human life as one true to creation without wishing to impose on the other anything of his own realization. . . .

In genuine dialogue the turning to the partner takes place in all truth, that is, it is a turning of the being. Every speaker 'means' the partner or partners to whom he turns as this personal existence. To 'mean' someone in this connection is at the same time to exercise that degree of making present which is possible to the speaker at that moment. The experiencing senses and the imagining of the real which completes the findings of the senses work together to make the other present as a whole and as a unique being, as the person that he is. But the speaker does not merely perceive the one who is present to him in this way; he receives him as his partner, and that means that he confirms this other being, so far as it is for him to confirm. The true turning of his person to the other includes this confirmation, this acceptance. Of course, such a confirmation does not mean approval; but no matter in what I am against the other, by accepting him as my partner in genuine dialogue I have affirmed him as a person.

Further, if genuine dialogue is to arise, everyone who takes part in it must bring himself into it. And that also means that he must be willing on each occasion to say what is really in his mind about the subject of the conversation. And that means further that on each occasion he makes the contribution of his spirit without reduction and without shifting his ground. Even men of great integrity are under the illusion that they are not bound to say everything 'they have to say.' But in the great faithfulness which is the climate of genuine dialogue, what I have to say at any one time already has in me the character of something that wishes to be uttered, and I must not keep it back, keep it in myself. It bears for me the unmistakable sign which indicates that it belongs to the common life of the word. Where the dialogical word genuinely exists, it must be given its right by keeping nothing back. To keep nothing back is the exact opposite of unreserved speech. Everything depends on the legitimacy of 'what I have to say.' And of course I must also be intent to raise into an inner word and then into a spoken word what I have to say at this moment but do not yet possess as speech. To speak is both nature and work, something that grows and something that is made, and where it appears dialogically, in the climate of great faithfulness, it has to fulfill ever anew the unity of the two.

Associated with this is that overcoming of semblance to which I have referred. In the atmosphere of genuine dialogue, he who is ruled by the thought of his own effect as the speaker of what he has to speak, has a destructive effect. If instead of what has to be said, I try to bring attention to my *I*, I have irrevocably miscarried what I had to say; it enters the dialogue as a failure, and the dialogue is a failure. Because genuine dialogue is an ontological sphere which is constituted by the authenticity of being, every invasion of semblance must damage it.

But where the dialogue is fulfilled in its being, between partners who have turned to one another in truth, who express themselves without reserve and are free of the desire for semblance, there is brought into being a memorable common fruitfulness which is to be found nowhere else. At such times, at each such time, the word arises in a substantial way between men who have been seized in their depths and opened out by the dynamic of an elemental togetherness. The interhuman opens out what otherwise remains unopened. . . .

Of course it is not necessary for all who are joined in a genuine dialogue actually to speak; those who keep silent can on occasion be especially important. But each must be determined not to withdraw when the course of the conversation makes it proper for him to say what he has to say. No one, of course, can know in advance what

Models of Man

it is that he has to say; genuine dialogue cannot be arranged beforehand. It has indeed its basic order in itself from the beginning, but nothing can be determined, the course is of the spirit, and some discover what they have to say only when they catch the call of the spirit.

But it is also a matter of course that all the participants, without exception, must be of such nature that they are capable of satisfying the presuppositions of genuine dialogue and are ready to do so. The genuineness of the dialogue is called in question as soon as even a small number of those present are felt by themselves and by the others as not being expected to take any active part.

Education

In 1925 Buber gave an address in Heidelberg to the Third International Educational Conference, whose subject was "The Development of the Creative Powers in the Child." The following excerpts from that address concern his idea of the educated person. A vital aspect of Buber's view is that such a person is *responsible*. This concept of responsibility is essentially involved with a creative *response* to existential life situations. Growth in freedom thus implies a growth in personal responsibility for our actions. Buber considers our culture too diverse and complex to permit a single educational model to dominate. In such a time the only general direction that remains is a response to the divine, creative Spirit of the cosmos.

These selections are from Martin Buber, "Education," in *Between Man and Man*, translated by Ronald Gregor Smith, published in London in 1947 by Routledge & Kegan Paul, Ltd., and in New York in 1965 by The Macmillan Company, with whose permission they are reprinted.

This fragile life between birth and death can . . . be a fulfilment—if it is a dialogue. In our life and experience we are addressed; by thought and speech and action, by producing and by influencing we are able to answer. For the most part we do not listen to the address, or we break into it with chatter. But if the word comes to us and the answer proceeds from us then human life exists, though brokenly, in the world. The kindling of the response in that "spark" of the soul, the blazing up of the response, which occurs time and again, to the unexpectedly approaching speech, we term responsibility. We practise responsibility for that realm of life allotted and entrusted to us for which we are able to respond, that is, for which we have a relation of deeds which may count—in all our inadequacy—as a proper response. The extent to which a man, in the strength of the reality of the spark, can keep a traditional bond, a law, a direction, is the extent to which he is permitted to lean his responsibility on something (more than this is not vouchsafed to us, responsibility is not taken off our shoulders). As we "become free" this leaning on something is more and more denied to us, and our responsibility must become personal and solitary.

From this point of view education and its transformation in the hour of the crumbling of bonds are to be understood. . . .

The question which is always being brought forward—"To where, to what, must we educate?"—misunderstands the situation. Only times which know a figure of general validity—the Christian, the gentleman, the citizen—know an answer to that question, not necessarily in words, but by pointing with the finger to the figure which rises clear in the air, out-topping all. The forming of this figure in all individuals, out of all materials, is the formation of a "culture." But when all figures are shattered, when no figure is able any more to dominate and shape the present human material, what is there left to form?

Nothing but the image of God.

That is the indefinable, only factual, direction of the responsible modern educator. This cannot be a theoretical answer to the question "To what?," but only, if at all, an answer carried out in deeds; an answer carried out by non-doing.

The educator is set now in the midst of the need which he experiences in inclusion, but only a bit deeper in it. He is set in the midst of the service, only a bit higher up, which he invokes without words; he is set in the *imitatio Dei absconditi sed non ignoti*.

When all "directions" fail there arises in the darkness over the abyss the one true direction of man, towards the creative Spirit, towards the Spirit of God brooding on the face of the waters, towards Him of whom we know not whence He comes and whither He goes.

That is man's true autonomy which no longer betrays, but responds.

Man, the creature, who forms and transforms the creation, cannot create. But he, each man, can expose himself and others to the creative Spirit. And he can call upon the Creator to save and perfect His image.

Community

The goal of community constantly infuses Buber's philosophy. The educated man does not develop in isolation: he emerges in community. There is a vast difference between a community and a collective. The two are, in fact, often alternatives. Collectives happen when man flees from the personal responsibility for another that is involved in community. A collective merely brings men together and, metaphorically speaking, places them side by side. Uniformity is its characteristic. In a community, by contrast, members voluntarily draw toward each other and there is, metaphorically speaking, a facing or meeting, an I-Thou relationship. Diversity and uniqueness are its characteristics.

The passage is taken from Martin Buber, "Dialogue," in *Between Man and Man*, translated by Ronald Gregor Smith, published in London in 1947 by Routledge & Kegan Paul, Ltd., and in New York in 1965 by The Macmillan Company, with whose permission it is reprinted.

The feeling of community does not reign where the desired change of institutions is wrested in common, but without community, from a resisting world. It reigns where the fight that is fought takes place from the position of a community struggling for its own reality as a community. But the future too is decided here at the same time; all political "achievements" are at best auxiliary troops to the effect which changes the very core, and which is wrought on the unsurveyable ways of secret history by the moment of realization. No way leads to any other goal but to that which is like it.

But who in all these massed, mingled, marching collectivities still perceives what that is for which he supposes he is striving—what community is? They have all surrendered to its counterpart. Collectivity is not a binding but a bundling together; individuals packed together, armed and equipped in common, with only as much life from man to man as will inflame the marching step. But community, growing community (which is all we have known so far) is the being no longer side by side but *with* one another of a multitude of persons. And this multitude, though it also moves towards one goal, yet experiences everywhere a turning to, a dynamic facing of, the other, a flowing from *I* to *Thou*. Community is where community happens. Collectivity is based on an organized atrophy of personal existence, community on its increase and confirmation in life lived towards one other. The modern zeal for collectivity is a flight from community's testing and consecration of the person, a flight from the vital dialogic, demanding the staking of the self, which is in the heart of the world.

What Is Common to All

The highest model that Buber offers us is the free man who voluntarily comes together with others in community, who attains the level of being able to speak as an authentic We. Buber finds inadequate both collectivism, which values the collective above the self, and individualism, which glorifies individual existence and regards the self as sufficient and absolute. We need to recognize what is common to all without sacrificing human uniqueness. For this we must be able to listen to each other and thus come to know a Thou. Then, and only then, is it possible for us to know a We. Genuine community requires genuine dialogue.

The passage is from Martin Buber, "What Is Common to All," translated by Maurice Friedman. It appeared in the *Review of Metaphysics*, Volume XI, Number 3 (March 1958), and in *The Knowledge of Man*, published in New York in 1965 by Harper & Row, Inc., with whose permission it is reprinted.

For the typical man of today the flight from responsible personal existence has singularly polarized. Since he is not willing to answer for the genuineness of his existence, he flees either into the general collective which takes from him his responsibility or into the attitude of a self who has to account to no one but himself and finds the great general indulgence in the security of being identical with the Self of being. Even if this attitude is turned into a deepened contemplation of existing being, it remains a flight from the leaping fire.

The clearest mark of this kind of man is that he cannot really listen to the voice of another; in all his hearing, as in all his seeing, he mixes observation. The other is not the man over against him whose claim stands over against his own in equal right; the other is only his object. But he who existentially knows no Thou will never succeed in knowing a We.

In our age, in which the true meaning of every word is encompassed by delusion and falsehood, and the original intention of the human glance is stifled by tenacious mistrust, it is of decisive importance to find again the genuineness of speech and existence as We. This is no longer a matter which concerns the small circles that have been so important in the essential history of man; this is a matter of leavening the human race in all places with genuine We-ness. Man will not persist in existence if he does not learn anew to persist in it as a genuine We.

We had to confront the degenerate Western spirit with its origin and have therefore summoned the help of Heracleitus. But now he parts from us in our need or we part from him. For what he designates as the common has nothing that is over against it as such: logos and cosmos are, to him, self-contained; there is nothing that transcends them. And even when Heracleitus bears witness to the divine as at once bearing a name and being nameless, even then there is no real transcendence. No salvation is in sight for us, however, if we are not able again 'to stand before the face of God' in all reality as a We—as it is written in that faithful speech that once from Israel, the southern pillar of the bridge between the East and the West, started on its way.

In our age this We standing before the divine countenance has attained its highest expression through a poet, through Friedrich Hölderlin (1770–1843). He says of the authentic past of man as man, 'since we have been a dialogue and have been able to hear from one another.' And after that comes the words, 'But we are soon song'. The self-contained communality of Heracleitus that overspans the opposites has here become the choral antiphony which, as we know from Hölderlin, is directed upward.

The Education of Character

Buber addressed the National Conference of Jewish Teachers of Palestine at Tel Aviv in 1939 on the subject, "The Education of Character." His major themes of dialogue, relationship, and community are reiterated and developed. The model appears here as the "great character," one who acts authentically and with integrity of person. He behaves existentially, that is, in accordance with the unique demands of each situation. Although he does not ignore traditional norms, he does not follow them unreflectively or from slavish habit. The educated person accepts responsibility for his actions and for himself. He is concerned with the achievement of unity in his person and with the development of genuine community with other persons.

The selections are from Martin Buber, "The Education of Character," in *Between Man and Man*, translated by Ronald Gregor Smith, published in London in 1947 by Routledge & Kegan Paul, Ltd., and in New York in 1965 by The Macmillan Company, with whose permission they are reprinted.

The great character can be conceived neither as a system of maxims nor as a system of habits. It is peculiar to him to act from the whole of his substance. That is, it is peculiar to him to react in accordance with the uniqueness of every situation which challenges him as an active person. Of course there are all sorts of similarities in different situations; one can construct types of situations, one can always find to what section the particular situation belongs, and draw what is appropriate from the hoard of established maxims and habits, apply the appropriate maxim, bring into operation the appropriate habit. But what is untypical in the particular situation remains unnoticed and unanswered. To me that seems the same as if, having ascertained the sex of a new-born child, one were immediately to establish its type as well, and put all the children of one type into a common cradle on which not the individual name but the name of the type was inscribed. In spite of all similarities every living situation has, like a newborn child, a new face, that has never been before and will never come again. It demands of you a reaction which cannot be prepared beforehand. It demands nothing of what is past. It demands presence, responsibility; it demands you. I call a great character one who by his actions and attitudes satisfies the claim of situations out of deep readiness to respond with his whole life, and in such a way that the sum of his actions and attitudes expresses at the same time the unity of his being in its willingness to accept responsibility. As his being is unity, the unity of accepted responsibility, his active life, too, coheres into unity. And one might perhaps say that for him there rises a unity out of the situations he has responded to in responsibility, the indefinable unit of a moral destiny.

All this does not mean that the great character is beyond the acceptance of norms. No responsible person remains a stranger to norms. But the command inherent in a genuine norm never becomes a maxim and the fulfilment of it never a habit. Any command that a great character takes to himself in the course of his development does not act in him as part of his consciousness or as material for building up his exercises, but remains latent in a basic layer of his substance until it reveals itself to him in a concrete way. What it has to tell him is revealed whenever a situation arises which demands of him a solution of which till then he had perhaps no idea. . . .

A section of the young is beginning to feel today that, because of their absorption by the collective, something important and irreplaceable is lost to them—personal responsibility for life and the world. These young people, it is true, do not yet realize that their blind devotion to the collective, e.g. to a party, was not a genuine act of their personal life; they do not realize that it sprang, rather, from the fear of being left, in this age of confusion, to rely on themselves, on a self which no longer receives its direction from eternal values. Thus they do not yet realize that their devotion was fed on the unconscious desire to have responsibility removed from them by an authority in which they believe or want to believe. They do not yet realize that this devotion was an escape. I repeat, the young people I am speaking of do not yet realize this. But they are beginning to notice that he who no longer, with his whole being, decides what he does or does not, and assumes responsibility for it, becomes sterile in soul. And a sterile soul soon ceases to be a soul.

This is where the educator can begin and should begin. He can help the feeling that something is lacking to grow into the clarity of consciousness and into the force of desire. He can awaken in young people the courage to shoulder life again. He can bring before his pupils the image of a great character who denies no answer to life and the world, but accepts responsibility for everything essential that he meets. He can show his pupils this image without the fear that those among them who most of all need discipline and order will drift into a craving for aimless freedom: on the contrary, he can teach them in this way to recognize that discipline and order too are starting-points on the way towards self-responsibility. He can show that even the great character is not born perfect, that the unity of his being has first to mature before expressing itself in the sequence of his actions and attitudes. But unity itself, unity of the person, unity of the lived life, has to be emphasized again and again. The confusing contradictions cannot be remedied by the collectives, not one of which knows the taste of genuine unity and which if left to themselves would end up like the scorpions imprisoned in a box, in the witty fable, by devouring one another. This mass of contradictions can be met and conquered only by the rebirth of personal unity, unity of being, unity of life, unity of action—unity of being, life and action together. This does not mean a static unity of the uniform, but the great dynamic unity of the multiform in which multiformity is formed into unity of character. Today the great characters are still "enemies of the people", they who love their society, yet wish not only to preserve it but to raise it to a higher level. To-morrow they will be the architects of a new unity of mankind. It is the longing for personal unity, from which must be born a unity of mankind, which the educator should lay hold of and strengthen in his pupils. Faith in this unity and the will to achieve it is not a "return" to individualism, but a step beyond all the dividedness of individualism and collectivism. A great and full relation between man and man can only exist between unified and responsible persons. That is why it is much more rarely found in the totalitarian collective than in any historically earlier form of society: much more rarely also in the authoritarian party than in any earlier form of free association. Genuine education of character is genuine education for community.

Teaching and Deed

In line with his concern for the hallowing of all life, for infusing the profane with a spiritual dimension, Buber strove to emphasize the continuity between many other supposed dualisms. In this address, delivered at the *Lehrhaus* in Frankfort-am-Main in 1934, he questions the validity of a dualistic conception of teaching and deed. He urges the recognition of a continuity between learning and life, rather than the encouragement of knowledge for its own sake. In opposition to an "ivory tower" attitude, he insists that learning must be related to consequent action. Thus, in order to be considered an educated person, it is not enough to have one's cognitive faculties trained: one's inmost spirit must be infused by what he has learned. Buber's model is a person who can transform his knowledge and belief into consistent action.

The passage is taken from Martin Buber, "Teaching and Deed," translated by O. Marx, in *Israel and the World,* published in New York in 1963, copyright 1948, 1963 by Schocken Books, Inc., with whose permission it is reprinted.

We have already indicated that in our case teaching is inseparably bound up with doing. Here, if anywhere, it is impossible to teach or to learn without living. The teachings must not be treated as a collection of knowable material; they resist such treatment. Either the teachings live in the life of a responsible human being, or they are not alive at all. The teachings do not center in themselves; they do not exist for their own sake. They refer to, they are directed toward the deed. In this connection the concept of "deed" does not, of course, connote "activism," but life that realizes the teachings in the changing potentialities of every hour.

Among all the peoples in the world, Israel is probably the only one in which wisdom that does not lead directly to the unity of knowledge and deed is meaningless. This becomes most evident when we compare the biblical concept of *hokhmah* with the Greek concept of *sophia*. The latter specifies a closed realm of thought, knowledge for its own sake. It is totally alien to the *hokhmah*, which regards such a delimitation of an independent spiritual sphere, governed by its own laws, as the misconstruction of meaning, the violation of continuity, the severance of thought from reality.

The supreme command of *hokhmah* is the unity of teaching and life, for only through this unity can we recognize and avow the all-embracing unity of God. In the light of our doctrine, He who gives life and gives that life meaning is wronged by a teaching which is satisfied with and delights in itself, which rears structures however monumental above life, and yet does not succeed in wresting even a shred of realization out of all the outer and inner obstacles we must struggle with in every precarious hour of our lives. For our God makes only one demand upon us. He does not expect a humanly unattainable completness and perfection, but only the willingness to do as much as we possibly can at every single instant.

Man is a creature able to make spirit independent of physical life, and his great danger is that he may tolerate and even sanction existence on two different levels: one, up above and fervently adored, the habitation of the spirit; and one down below, the dwelling of urges and petty concerns, equipped with a fairly good conscience acquired in hours of meditation in the upper story.

The teachings do not rely on the hope that he who knows them will also observe them. Socratic man believes that all virtue is cognition, and that all that is needed to do what is right is to know what is right. This does not hold for Mosaic man who is informed with the profound experience that cognition is never enough, that the deepest part of him must be seized by the teachings, that for realization to take place his elemental totality must submit to the spirit as clay to the potter.

Here dualism is fought with the utmost vigor. "One who studies with a different intent than to act," says the Talmud, "it would have been more fitting for him never to have been created." It is bad to have teaching without the deed, worse when the teaching is one of action. Living in the detached spirit is evil, and worse when the spirit is one of ethos. Again and again, from the Sayings of the Fathers down to the definitive formulation of hasidism, the simple man who acts is given preference over the scholar whose knowledge is not expressed in deeds. "He whose deeds exceed his wisdom, his wisdom shall endure; but he whose wisdom exceeds his deeds, his wisdom shall not endure." And in the same vein: "He whose wisdom exceeds his deeds—what does he resemble? A tree with many boughs and few roots. A wind, springing up, uproots it, and overturns it. But he whose deeds exceed his wisdom—what does he resemble? A tree with few boughs but many roots. Though all the winds in the world come and blow at it, it cannot be budged." What counts is not the extent of spiritual possessions, not the thoroughness of knowledge, nor the keenness of thought, but to know what one knows and to believe what one believes so directly that it can be translated into the life one lives.

Education and World-View

In this address, given in Frankfort-am-Main in 1935, Buber again attempts to establish unity out of dualism. The model he proposes is the man of existential responsibility. His *Weltanschauung*, or world-view, is not merely an intellectual appendage: it is something that represents him wholly and that governs his behavior. There should be no dichotomy between belief and action, or between ends and means. We cannot reach an end whose nature is different from the nature of the means by which we try to reach it. Buber is speaking here to those who would use war as a means to peace, censorship as a means to freedom, autocracy as a means to democracy. Consistency between ends and means is a mark of the man of authentic commitment. It matters less what his world-view is than the genuineness with which he holds it.

The selection is taken from Martin Buber, "Education and World-View," in *Pointing the Way*, edited and translated by Maurice Friedman, published in New York in 1957 by Harper & Row, Inc., with whose permission it is reprinted.

In the uniform marching line of the group today there is no distinguishing any more between one person's step which is the expression of his direction-moved existence and another person's step which is nothing else than an eloquent gesture. And yet this distinction, which cuts straight across each group, is more important than that between groups and groups. For only those who realize with their life-substance will establish new, viable reality. Success may depend upon the impetus of the troop, but upon the genuineness of the individuals depends what this success will announce in the depths of the future: genuine victory or its counterfeit. The work of education has a twofold influence upon the adherents of the world-views: a founding one and a postulating one. First, it helps each to take its root in the soil of its world through

459

enabling him to experience this world widely and densely. It provides him access to it, exposes him to the action of its working forces. And, secondly, it educates in each his 'world-view-conscience' that examines ever anew his authentication of his world-view and opposes to the absence of any obligation to put his world-view into effect the obligation of the thousand small realizations of it.

Certainly what one believes is important, but still more important is how one believes it. This 'how' is no æsthetic nor even an ethical category. It is a question of reality in the most exact sense, of the whole reality, in relation to which the categories of the æsthetic and the ethical are only abstractions. Does a world-view dwell in the head or in the whole man? Does it live only in the hours of proclamation or also in the silent private periods of his life? Does he use it or does he give himself to it? That is the distinction between men of genuine conviction and the men of fictitious conviction—between the conviction that is so fully realized that it enters entirely into reality and the conviction that is facilely effectuated and effectuated until nothing is left of it. It is a question of the existential responsibility of the person for having a world-view; this my group cannot take from me, it may not.

Let no one call this 'individualism!' It does, indeed, concern persons, but not for the sake of the persons; it concerns them for the sake of the future. Whether in the realm of any particular world-view the men of genuine conviction or the men of fictitious conviction will be dominant, whether the decisions that are to be made are made from the standpoint of the existential responsibility or not, what takes place in the internal front dividing truth and falsehood that extends straight across all world-views—upon these questions still more depends than upon whether any particular world-view is 'victorious' or not. Upon such questions depends whether the historically recorded victory is a genuine victory and not perhaps a catastrophe. How far the future community will correspond to the desired image depends essentially upon the life-attitude of present-day persons—not only of those who lead but of each individual in the ranks. The goal does not stand fast and wait. He who takes a road that in its nature does not already represent the nature of the goal will miss the goal, no matter how fixedly he holds it in sight. The goal that he reaches will resemble the road he has reached it by.

We live—one must say it ever again—in a time in which the great dreams, the great hopes of mankind, have one after another been fulfilled as the caricature of themselves. What is the cause of this massive experience? I know of none save the power of fictitious conviction. This power I call the uneducated quality of the man of this age. Opposed to it stands the education that is true to its age and adjusts to it, the education that leads man to a lived connection with his world and enables him to ascend from there to faithfulness, to standing the test, to authenticating, to responsibility, to decision, to realization.

The education I mean is a guiding towards reality and realization. That man alone is qualified to teach who knows how to distinguish between appearance and reality, between seeming realization and genuine realization, who rejects appearance and chooses and grasps reality, no matter what world-view he chooses. This education educates the adherents of all world-views to genuineness and to truth. It educates each of them to take his world-view seriously: to start from the genuineness of its ground and to move towards the truth of its goal.

Philosophical Interrogations

In one of his last statements on education, part of a series of interrogations of prominent contemporary philosophers, Buber demonstrates again the remarkable unity that has bound his ideas. The rehallowing of all existence is vital. There must be no schism between the sacred and profane: the holy must infuse all of human life. For the existential man, the realization of such unity comes through ever deeper involvement of the whole self in life. Then his actions will become characterized by unified consistency and genuine directness.

The selection is an exchange between Robert Assagioli and Martin Buber on "Education." It appears in "Interrogation of Martin Buber," conducted by Maurice S. Friedman, in *Philosophical Interrogations*, edited by Sydney and Beatrice Rome, published in New York, copyright 1964 by Holt, Rinehart and Winston, Inc., with whose permission it is reprinted.

Robert Assagioli: Your essay on "Hasidism and Modern Man" contains in my opinion an important and most timely message. How can present-day humanity, and particularly modern youth, be induced or helped to the rediscovery and the recognition of the "Sacred"? In what ways and by what means—expressed in terms understandable and acceptable by modern man—do you think that (also apart from the message of Hasidism) the *totalité lésée de l'homme* (the injured wholeness of man) can be re-established?

Buber: This question is especially important, but in this general form hardly adequate to be answered. I know no generally applicable methods that merely need to be set forth in order to effect a transformation. I do not believe that a How, formulable as a principle, exists here. Only the personal involvement of the educating man can help, the man who himself knows the holy and who knows how; in this our time, persons of the most varied kinds suffer the often unavowed, indeed, on occasion, vigorously denied, pain over the unholiness of their lives. I say personal involvement; therefore, not an already existing teaching that lies to hand and needs only to be transmitted to those who suffer in this manner in order that they may learn that the holy exists and what the holy is; furthermore, that it is just this which the sufferer misses, and finally what he has to do to attain it. No, what can help is the simple personal life, the educator's own life, in which the everyday and its actions are hallowed, a life that is so lived that he who suffers from the unholiness can, and finally even will, participate in it. I have known no one whom I might call a saint, but many whose everyday performances, without being meant to be holy actions, work exactly such.

But what is meant here by holy? Now, quite simply this, that the one who lives in contact with this man feels against his will, against his *Weltanschauung:* That is genuine to the roots; that is not a shoot from an alien stem; its roots reach into that sphere from whose inaccessibility I suffer in the overlucid hours of midnight. And at first unwillingly, then also willingly, the man thus affected in contact is himself drawn into connection with that sphere. It is indeed a matter of "hallowing"; it is a matter, hence, of the *humanly* holy; and what is to be understood by that, in my view, does not admit of any definition and any method that can be taught; one learns to know it in doing something spontaneously, otherwise than one is accustomed to do, at first only "more really," that is, "putting more of oneself into it," then with more intention, more meaning, finally opening oneself to the sphere from which the meaning of our existence comes to us.

The crisis that has come over the human world has its origin in the dehallowing of existence. It appears, at times, as if the crisis would assume the sinister tempo of "world history." Is there not reason to despair that education could overtake it, or at all obviate it? True education is never in vain, even if the hour makes it appear so. Whether it manifests itself before or in or after the threatening catastrophe—the fate of man will depend on whether the rehallowing of existence takes place.

INDEX